FINANCIAL PLANNING: THE CPAs' PRACTICE GUIDE

JIM H. AINSWORTH, CPA, CFA, CLU

JOHN WILEY & SONS, INC.

New York   Chichester   Brisbane   Toronto   Singapore

This text is printed on acid-free paper.

This publication is designed to provide accurate and
authoritative information in regard to the subject
matter covered. It is sold with the understanding that
the publisher is not engaged in rendering legal, accounting,
or other professional services. If legal advice or other
expert assistance is required, the services of a competent
professional person should be sought.

Library of Congress Cataloging in Publication Data:
Ainsworth, Jim H.
　　Financial Planning: The CPAs' Practice Guide
　Jim H. Ainsworth.
　　　p. cm.
　　Includes index.
　　ISBN 0-471-07428-4 (paper)
　　1. Financial planners—United States.　2. Financial planners—
United States—Marketing.　3. Financial services industry—United
States.　I. Title.
　HG179.5.A37　1994
　332.6′2—dc20　　　　　　　　　　　　　94-10355
　　　　　　　　　　　　　　　　　　　　　　CIP

Printed in the United States of America

10 9 8 7 6 5 4 3 2 1

Subscription Notice

Acknowledgments

My sincere appreciation to the staff at Ainsworth Money Management, Inc. for pulling together information accumulated over an eight-year period. To the staff at 1st Global Partners, Inc. for filling in for me while I worked on this project and for assistance in formatting, printing, etc.

Thanks also to Jan, my partner in life, and to my children, Damon and Tia, Shelly and Kevin, Justin, and my grandson Caden for supporting me on such a crazy endeavor.

Foreword—What's Happening To Our Profession?

I was disenchanted with my career after holding various jobs in industry for eight years. I kept getting bosses who could not do things as well as I thought they could be done. I decided that the only true job security and satisfaction came from being your own boss. For many months, I took stock of my talents and abilities to see what business I should try. It seemed that my CPA certificate was the best ticket to the entrepeneurial world.

I scouted various locations and found a community that had no CPA firm that was also close to where I grew up. Upon visiting the local bank, I discovered that my certificate would not count for much when used as collateral for a loan. Disappointed but determined, I began investigating other alternatives for financing my new venture. I found the Small Business Administration also unsympathetic to my intangible collateral. I decided to open my CPA firm in conjunction with another business that had more tangible collateral—something the people at SBA would be more likely to understand. I opted for a western-wear store. I would have the proverbial "store-front-CPA-back-type of business. Using this plan, I was able to secure adequate financing to put food on the table while I built my business.

In blissful ignorance of the rigors of opening a CPA firm from scratch, I moved my family (including two preschoolers) from Dallas to the small northeast Texas community of Commerce. According to signposts at the city limits, the population at that time was 10,800. With no clients, no employees, and no funds, I opened a CPA practice and the retail store simultaneously, in 1973. Even though another CPA who had grown up in Commerce had beat me to the punch by about a month, I knew that there was no turning back. My regular salary had been given up, the house sold.

I started to feel as if someone or something was sending me a message when I discovered that the name I had chosen for my store had been taken by a "greasy spoon" local cafe. To add insult to injury, I learned that the proprietor had the same last name as mine. Now, what are the odds of that happening in a town of 10,800?

In spite of these setbacks, I continued; I had no other choice. The CPA rules at the time did not allow me to market my services other than showing my face in the community whenever possible. I had no clients four months after opening my doors. In January of 1974, I picked up my first $25 fee on a nonrecurring engagement. My landlord took pity on me and hired me to do an analysis on some equipment he was considering purchasing. If I had not had the retail business, I would have probably given up. Although too small to be very profitable, it provided enough to keep me solvent. More important, it provided an outlet for my energies that were not being used by the CPA practice.

During the 1974 tax season, I prepared approximately 20 returns. I didn't have a copy machine, so I had to go down the street and pay 10 cents per copy. Still, it was encouraging to actually have some revenue to put on my financial statements. As you can imagine, my 20 clients got exemplary service. Word of mouth spread, friends were made in the community, and my business began to grow. I still have clients who remember my office in back of the store. They remember when I had a tray for every accounting client and there were only three trays. In 1977, business was good enough to take on a partner. Mary Lambert, also blissfully ignorant of what she was in for, joined me.

I could recount many stories of how those 20 tax clients and three write-up clients grew to over 100 small business clients and over 600 individuals. However, that is not what this book is about. It is about financial and investment planning in CPA practices in the 1990s, and beyond.

Unwittingly, I had entered the public accounting profession on its way to a peak. I enjoyed growth rates of 20, 30, 50, and even 100 percent. However, in 1983, I began to notice a decline in my rate of growth. A move was afoot to make the tax laws much simpler, personal computers were being talked about as being available to everyone in future years, competition was heating up, employees were demanding more, and fee resistance was more intense. I began to feel a little less secure. I tried everything to keep my growth levels.

I opened branch offices in neighboring towns, trying to attract young professionals as eager as I was to build a large firm. Some of my efforts were successful, others were not. Although I was increasing the revenues, profits were actually decreasing. At its peak, the firm had grown to 18 people, but I was working harder and making less.

In 1976, I began marketing financial planning services to my clients. My tax planning clients were receptive, but they were only about 2 percent of my overall client base. Others liked the idea, but didn't quite understand how the road to *their* financial security began with writing *me* a check for the road map. Undeterred, I charged on. Everything I read lead me to believe that financial planning was the service that would set me apart from my competitors like tax planning and expertly prepared returns had done before. In addition, everything I saw on my clients' tax returns told me that they needed a financial road map. Their investments were too concentrated; many were paying too much in taxes despite my advice to take tax-saving measures; many were going to be unprepared for retirement; many family businesses would be lost in the event of death of a family member; there were no education funds set aside, and many did not have emergency funds.

I prepared many financial plans for clients that I now call "coffee table decorations." The futility of preparing financial plans without the ability to implement them started coming to me when I was visiting a client's home and saw one of my beautifully bound, properly thick financial plans gathering dust in a prominent position on the client's coffee table. The client was proud of having had the plan done and somehow felt better for the effort, but I knew that not one of the steps I had recommended had ever been done. I never turned a profit in my financial planning efforts until I began implementing them myself.

THE TEAM APPROACH

I did implement some plans using the team approach but I became completely frustrated when my clients failed to implement the plans I had so carefully prepared using my expensive software. When I calculated the amount I was earning per hour on financial plans, it *paled* in comparison to what I could earn on a tax return. Adding a team approach to implementation would only make matters worse, but I felt the obligation to bring value to the plans I was preparing. Thus, I sought closer associations with brokers, insurance agents, and attorneys. I spent a great deal of time and effort getting the team together to implement a plan. Only a few were ever completely implemented. Clients grew tired of my fees, the attorney's fees, and the whole process before we could get it completed.

By the time the "team" was assembled, I had already charged my client for more hours than he would allow. I was into the "free zone." Yet, time demands for implementation continued to mount as I met with the client, the attorney, the stockbroker, and the insurance agent. When the team finally assembled in a room, egos were so huge and tensions so high that you could hear the walls expanding. I was off the billable clock, the attorney was on, and the broker and insurance agent were happy as "two pigs in the sunshine." My client was uncertain at best. By the time a plan was implemented, my rate per hour had dropped below minimum wage. My incentive for implementing became "professional responsibility" in the purest sense since I had negative economic incentive. As usually happens, the lack of economic incentive began to work on my high ideals and fewer plans were implemented.

Besides economic incentives, other factors were at work. I did not feel comfortable in the implementation process. I especially did not feel good about evaluating the products recommended by the insurance agent and broker. They did whatever I said to do. Deep down inside, I knew that I was not qualified to hold that much power over product selection. I became extremely conservative in my product evaluation, even when my client felt comfortable with more risk. Also, I found that my two pig friends kept "coming back to the trough" even after the plan was implemented.

At tax time, I often found my clients holding limited parternships and other investment products I had not recommended and which were not part of my plan. My client invariably thought that I had recommended the products through my two associates. Frustration set in.

Finally, the largest plan I had ever prepared proved pivotal for me to make a change. The grossly unfair method of compensation for members of the "team" finally got to me. In this particular engagement, I provided the client, the plan, the solution, and the product evaluation. Team members, however, earned these approximate amounts of compensation:

Attorney	$5,000	$150 per hour
Stockbroker	$38,000	$4000 per hour
Insurance Agent	$42,000	$3500 per hour
Team Captain (me)	$1,800	$20 per hour

Something was definitely wrong with the system. I had to find a way to fix it or stop doing financial plans.

This was about 1985. I had been doing fee-only planning for over nine years without a significant increase in business. We had automated our accounting practice in 1981. With the purchase of an IBM System 23, one of the first PCs ever built, we did our returns using purchased software. It was a nightmare, but challenging. We were the only business in town with a PC. Once again, we had been able to distinguish ourselves from our competition. Tax revenues were continuing to climb.

I began to see signs of trouble on the horizon again by the tax season of 1985. Although tax software was too expensive for my clients to purchase then, I could see that it would soon be within their reach. I realized that a lot of the work that made me feel truly professional before was now being done by computers. The fellow down the street who sold used cars and gave haircuts during the off season now prepared tax returns that looked exactly like mine. What a deal! Get a haircut, trade in your car, and get your tax return done all in the same place! Over a period of time, I lost three employees who went into competition with me. Education and years of experience were being usurped by the ability to purchase good software.

Again, a pivotal event pushed me in a new direction. A good client and friend brought me his tax data. Somewhat shyly, he presented me with his return already prepared by his 16-year-old daughter on her home computer with software purchased for less than $70. He asked me to evaluate her work because she had always "looked up to me." "Of course," he said, "I want you to prepare my return like you always have; just look hers over and give her some pointers." You already know the rest. Her return was absolutely perfect. If she had owned a laser printer, it would have looked just like the one I prepared. How can you charge a client a professional fee for something a junior in high school can do?

Desperate to keep our competitive edge, I listed the things that were happening to the profession and my business.

1. My accounting clients were buying or considering buying PCs to bring their accounting "inside."
2. My tax clients were beginning to purchase home software for doing returns.
3. My competitors were doing the job a lot better with software than they ever could without it. Even with limited knowledge, menu-driven tax software would take them through an average tax return. Their overhead was lower because they usually only worked during tax season and did not maintain a staff, so their prices were lower than mine.
4. Audit liability insurance was getting higher as fee pressure and competition mounted for audit work.
5. Public sentiment was growing against tax law complexity and "accountants and lawyers."
6. Rumblings about the 1986 tax law were starting to mount.

Another blow was struck when the 1986 tax law was passed. New tax legislation did not usually concern me, since some had been passed virtually every year I had been in public accounting. Originally frustrated about having to discard facts that I had learned the previous year, I soon learned how to adapt. If you have the "basics" of how the system works, changes are not as hard to learn. The 1986 Act was different, however. I found it to be one of the most inane, damaging pieces of legislation ever passed. I spoke against it wherever I could find an audience. In a midnight session, Congress slammed through a piece of legislation that led the way into a recession, an uncontrollable deficit, destruction of the real estate market, and the failure of many banks and S & Ls. As a footnote, it also destroyed the tax planning part of my practice and did more damage to my already wounded tax practice.

I do not want to mislead you, despite all my worry about the "incremental value and professional nature" of my services declining, our tax revenue continued to increase every year. The rate of increase, however, was less than we had enjoyed in the past and we had to work doubly hard to maintain it. Revenue in the other parts of our practice had virtually stopped growing. Our town had shrunk from 10,800 to 6,700. I had always believed that if you are not growing, you are going to shrink. It's just impossible to stand still.

The 1986 Tax Act Reform pushed my clients' tax returns into two primary categories:

1. So easy that anyone could do them (difficult to justify the fee).
2. So complex that clients could not understand or appreciate how complex their returns had become with this legislation (difficult to justify the fee).

Neither my clients nor myself understood the justification or rationalization for the law. It was almost impossible for anyone to plan because we had a completely new tax code and no regulations. Planning was "anybody's guess." Even today, people are still wondering how to correctly prepare tax returns under this horrific piece of legislation. *Money* magazine has great fun each year having 250 or so naive tax preparers take its annual "test" and getting 249 different answers. It then holds forth with the "correct" tax return and pokes fun at the hapless tax pros who fell for the trap. My question is, who made the *Money* pros "king of the tax code." Their answer could be just as incorrect as the other 250. It's all a matter of interpretation.

Just as I was recovering from these onslaughts to my profession, along comes *electronic filing* and *instant refunds*. Yes, we even hung out the obligatory "Fast Refund" and "Refund Anticipation" signs. We did not want to be in this business, but we had to answer the demands of the marketplace. The lot was cast. The final blow had been struck.

We were no longer a professional firm, we were a tax-return factory. I had to make a living, but I could no longer hold my head high. I turned once again to financial planning. Everything I saw and read continued to tell me that this was the service clients wanted and needed most. If that was so, why did my clients reject my efforts to provide them with the service? Why couldn't I make money at doing something really professional that helped my clients—something that only a few could do as well as I? The answer came when I attended a motivational seminar. The message was:

1. Decide what you want to do (set goals).
2. Do what you love.
3. Love what you do.
4. If you are helping others while accomplishing your own goals, money will take care of itself.

I knew I wanted to do financial planning. I knew I needed to know more about products and the implementation phase to do it well. I knew that I had to control the entire process in order to get the best deal for my client and for myself. I had to offer my clients an alternative way to pay.

The answer for all of these needs seemed to lie in becoming a registered representative and offering commission-based products. I had explored this option as early as 1979, but found that barriers in the CPA profession kept me from accepting commissions. I even pursued leaving the profession and affiliating with a broker–dealer. However, the broker-dealers I approached did not appear interested in a person who had just done fee-only planning. In 1985, I took the Series 7 and 63 tests and became a registered representative. The remainder of this book is the story of the mistakes I made, the successes I achieved in adding this new angle to my existing CPA practice, and the "recipe" I developed during the ensuing seven years for doing this thing right. I will tell you how I went from being a good producer to a top producer in one year (a 300 percent increase), and how you can achieve the same or higher levels of production in your own practice.

In 1992, I joined with Tony Batman in forming 1st Global Partners, Inc. in order to bring these principles, practices, and rules to you. They are not just my ideas. I carefully documented my successes and failures for over seven years. The other teachings included here are not new. They are proven principles. If you apply them, make a commitment, and be persistent, you will succeed.

In the following pages, you will learn about TOPS, the acronym for *Trust, Opportunity, Pain,* and *Solution.* I used this method of selling to increase my production by 300 percent. My close rate increased to 90 percent. All of this was done without using the usual, traditional hard-sale techniques you and I do not like. You will also learn about TAPS, the acronym for *Technical, Attitude, Products,* and *Selling.* It describes the four major parts of the curriculum followed in the RePP training program. It is presented in the following pages in order of importance, not in the TAPS order. If you participate in the RePP training program, the various courses will not be presented in sequential order. It is proper and preferable to learn them simultaneously. Follow these guidelines, and you will be immensely successful in this field. It will change your life like it did mine.

10 REASONS FOR PROVIDING FINANCIAL PLANNING TO YOUR CLIENTS

Before we embark on our journey to success, let us review the 10 most important reasons why you should be involved in financial planning:

1. Your clients want and need the service—dozens of surveys confirm this fact.
2. The other profit centers in public accounting are subject to possible shrinkage and higher costs. They are beleaguered by competition, automation, fee resistance, Congress, the President, and the media.
3. Normal services offered by CPA firms no longer enjoy the level of prestige and professionalism they once did. The personal computer has brought tax-return capability to your lesser competition and your clients. Audit failures have pointed out the weaknesses of financial statements according to GAAP and the audit process itself. Bookkeeping clients are taking their accounting inside using their own PC.
4. Your current services coupled with financial planning and investment planning complement each other and allow you to once again distinguish yourself from your competitors.
5. Traditional CPA services are negative in nature. Clients compare going to your firm with going to the dentist. But helping people reach their financial goals should be a positive experience.
6. Financial planning will bring a host of new contacts and services to your firm.

7. You need the training to become a well-rounded financial professional. Otherwise, you will always be inferior to the polished product salesman when evaluating financial products.

8. Often, you are your client's only financial advisor. You may be their only protection from an impoverished retirement or having their estates destroyed by taxes.

9. You could provide the only chance your clients' children have for a quality education.

10. Financial and investment planning are financially rewarding.

The savings rate in America is abysmal. Congress and the current administration are hell-bent on making it worse. Millions of Americans need financial advice but do not have a broker or an advisor because they feel they do not "qualify" or that the services will be too expensive. If you can make just one person's life better by learning this technique, wouldn't it be worth it?

Contents

Chapter 11   Other Marketing Tips   113

PART 3   TECHNICAL—THE TOOLS OF FINANCIAL PLANNING   117

Chapter 12   Retirement Plans   119

Chapter 13   Education Funding   155

Chapter 14   Insurance—Do CPAs Really Need to Sell Any?   163

Chapter 15   Taxes for NonTax Pros   181

Chapter 16   Estate Planning   189

Chapter 17   Asset Protection   215

Chapter 18   Asset Allocation   221

Chapter 19   Charitable Giving   235

Chapter 20   Planning for the Elderly   241

PART I

Attitude—You Must Be Positive About Yourself, Your Career, and Your Staff

1

Determine Your Lifestyle Attitude

"You must have clear goals, and you must be able to articulate them clearly."

Norman Schwarzkopf

Why am I talking about attitude in a book about CPAs and financial planning? Because I have found that CPAs only become successful in financial planning *after* they have *decided* to become successful. They know why they want to be successful and they know just how successful they want to be in terms of written goals. Some CPAs that I interviewed or trained could not identify the reason for their success, but further questioning invariably led to their decision to become successful and to formulate written goals.

If you think that the attitudinal skills you will learn in this book and in the RePP are going to be more of the "rah-rah," feel-good type of training you may have had before, you are only partially right. Take it from a born pessimist and skeptic—properly applied using our unique system, this stuff even works for CPAs. I do not want to stereotype the profession—that has already been done. As a group, however, we continue to earn the stereotype that others have placed upon us. We are no longer seen as bookkeepers with granny glasses and eye shades, but we continue to be seen as stodgy and conservative. We want to retain the conservative image that contributes to our clients' trust, but we must also cultivate the image of professionals who are capable of making creative and bold decisions that have major impact on our clients' lives.

Before you can change some of your behavior patterns in order to enhance your success, *you* must decide to change. In order to make that decision, you must be aware of the reasons for the change and believe in the reasons for making the changes. Attitudinal training delivers that awareness.

I became interested in this type of training because I felt a strong need to bring balance to my life. I could not seem to focus on what was the right balance. I found that if I spent too much time at work, I resented it and was unhappy at home and work. If I took time off for family and leisure, then I could not be happy because I felt as if my business and my clients were suffering. My creativity and productivity seemed to run in high peaks and low valleys. I wanted to be happier and more productive without damaging my family, my health, my business or my clients. I began reading books on positive thinking and attending a few seminars. I also began buying tapes and listening to them on occasion. The books left me feeling better for short periods of time. The seminars left me feeling great until I got back to the office and looked at the phone messages and my in box. Then everything I learned or felt seemed to disappear in the face of the "real world." I was soon back in the same old rut. Tapes that I could listen to in my car or at home seemed to be the most effective because I could rewind them and listen again, but they also failed to last as long as I thought they should.

I almost resigned myself to the fact that I was not meant to be influenced by all this "feel-good" stuff. Maybe the people talking about it were just selling tapes or fees. Even more comforting was the rationale that maybe I was just too "intelligent" or perceptive to be deceived by anyone or to trick myself into being happy when things were not really all that good.

After several years of haphazardly dabbling in motivational training, the reason for my failure dawned on me. *I was not doing what all the books, tapes, and speakers said to do.* To this day, I cannot explain why a person with normal intelligence would pay good money for a book, seminar, training school, or tape and fail to use the information provided. I *thought* I believed in the information I was absorbing. I could even point to some success in the half-hearted attempts I had made to apply the principles I had learned. However, I did not believe strongly enough to make the sacrifices necessary to truly apply the principles that later changed my career and my life. I was too caught up in the day-to-day activities of running a business, community activities, and learned habits that I could not stop to actually determine where I was going. In other words, I had been in my comfort zone so long that it had become a deep rut that I could not seem to get out of.

I wish I could point to a momentous event or action that caused me to get out of the rut and start to apply the principles in this book. There was none. At least, not that I can remember. Instead of an event or action, it was a process. One of the key points that I can give you is that it is a *process*. In order to begin the process, you must learn to take advantage of your most creative and energetic periods. During one of these periods, you must stop the tax return, audit, or other work you are doing, find a quiet place, and write down your goals and ideas for accomplishing them. You must learn that *one hour of planning your work and your life is worth eight hours doing productive work*. Planning saves time, it doesn't cost time. As a CPA used to billable time, remember who your most important client is—you. Do not worry if the ideas and plans do not flow instantly. You are not wasting time; you are thinking and you should allow yourself time to think.

Will reading this entire book be an instant panacea of happiness and success? No. Remember, it is a process. I routinely expected a book, seminar, or tape to be the key that I had been searching for—the one that would give me the secret to eternal happiness and success in business. I heard lots of stories about people who had found this proverbial key to happiness or success in a single sentence, phrase, or spiritual experience. That probably will not happen to you. Instead, there will be a series of events, knowledge, and practice that will keep you on the road to the achievement of your goals. Earl Nightingale said that "Success is the progressive achievement of a worthy goal." Note the word "progressive." This is a journey. Do not expect to arrive at blissful happiness and prosperity overnight. Getting on the right road will make you happy.

I also expected not to lapse. I used to think that I was subject to bouts of depression. When I read more about depression, I learned that it was not my problem. I now call my prior condition "recession." I would often experience periods when I had self-doubt, that no matter how hard I tried, I could not reach the pinnacle for which I had been striving. I could simply not balance all areas of my life. One was always found wanting. I still have periods of "recession," however, they are fewer now and I do not ever take them very seriously. I know they are temporary and will pass. I know where I am going and I know that circumstances, people, and events will help me to get there. The road may be circuitous, but I will get there, nonetheless.

THE IMPORTANCE OF SETTING GOALS

Remember the old saying, "People do not plan to fail; they just fail to plan." If you do not know where you are going, how can you possibly expect to get there? Setting goals, committing them to memory, and making plans for steps you must take to achieve them, brings to your aid the people, circumstances, and events that lead to their achievement. This is not to say that there are mysterious forces that will start working to help you achieve your goals—they come about as a result of your belief in your goals. I have read and heard hundreds of accounts from individuals who have had their goals realized by a chain of circumstances, events, and individuals that came about as a result of concentration on their goals.

It is important that you start your plan by setting goals because:

1. Goals bring purpose to your life.
2. Goals bring focus and vision and clarity to your plans.
3. Goals provide a course correction to bring you back when you stray off course.
4. Goals help you in your decision-making process. You can make many decisions by asking yourself the simple question, "will it help me in achieving my goals?"
5. Goals save time. If you know where you are going, you can often find the shortest and fastest route to get there.
6. Goals reduce stress and save energy. With goals, you are not stressed out over decisions that conflict with your goals, your mind is less cluttered, and you spend less time chasing projects that are not leading you toward your goals.
7. Goals contribute toward happiness and inner peace. You have a vision of where you are going, what you want to accomplish, and how others will be helped through the achievement of your goals.
8. Goals help avoid procrastination. One of the reasons for procrastination is indecision and failure to see value in what we are about to do. If the task involves your goals, the goal system will motivate you to get it done.
9. Setting goals and "massaging" them into your changing needs and circumstances opens your mind to new ideas and possibilities.
10. Goals help you become a better thinker.

HOW TO SET GOALS

If goals are so important, why do most people not set them? In a study done at Harvard University in 1953, a survey of the graduating seniors found that only 3 percent had set goals. In a follow up done some 20 years later, that 3 percent of the class was worth more than the entire other 97 percent combined. Why didn't the other 97 percent do something that seems so simple?

1. They did not realize the importance of goals.
2. They did not know how to set goals.
3. They were reluctant to write down their goals because of the fear of failure. If they had no goals, then they did not have to face the prospect of not meeting them.
4. Fear of ridicule (rejection) for not meeting them if others found out about their goals.

Now that you are convinced of the need to set goals, we will talk about how to set them and overcome these obstacles. During the years when I attended seminars, read books, and listened to tapes about self-improvement and motivation, I began to notice a common theme. It was always the same—set goals. I did not disagree with that, I just did not understand the importance. I thought I knew what my goals were and it was unnecessary to write them down. I hope you will not be as stubborn.

When I finally decided to follow the advice I was paying for, I sat down to write out my goals. After all, how difficult could it be? I found it to be somewhat intimidating. I thought it would be easy, but found it was not. Even though I was doing it in private, I also found it to be embarrassing. After all, I was in my late thirties and a man that age should know where he wants to go. I did not. I am still perfecting the art of goal setting. I am still learning. These are the steps that have worked for me. You will probably develop your own style after a period of time.

Instead of just thinking of goals, try thinking of your hopes, dreams, desires, and aspirations. That is what we are talking about. Not just plain old goals.

1. Find a quiet place where you feel comfortable and can relax without interruption. Try to choose a time when you are in a good mood. Go through some relaxation techniques so that your mind can flow easily. Try to clear your mind of all conscious thoughts. Stay in the relaxed mode for approximately 15 minutes.
2. Use your computer or a note pad, whichever you prefer, and set up five sheets:
   (a) Family
   (b) Emotional and spiritual
   (c) Career and financial
   (d) Physical
   (e) Major definitive purpose
3. Write the acronym SMART on the bottom line of each sheet.
   S = Specific
   M = Measurable
   A = Achievable
   R = Realistic
   T = Traceable

   After you have written down all your goals, make sure that each one meets the SMART test. If it does not, it should be reworded until it does. For example, under ''emotional'' many people write ''I want to be happy.'' A great goal that everyone shares, but it fails the test. It is easy to get goals to meet the SMART test in the Career, Financial, and Physical categories, but more difficult for the Family, Emotional, Spiritual, and Purposes categories. Allow yourself some leeway on the SMART test for these categories, especially on the Purpose category. That is hard to measure at first.

4. Start the thought process by thinking about what you want out of life for each of the areas listed. Goals should be something you really want for yourself.

5. Start writing the goals randomly on the sheets as they come to you. I usually concentrate on one type of goal at a time, but invariably I wind up going from sheet to sheet as ideas start to flow. Remember, do not try to write as if your goals are going to be published in the local newspaper. These are for you and you will always control who sees them. Do not put them to the SMART test until you are finished. Just let your thoughts flow freely.

6. As you write, *visualize* what it will look and feel like to actually accomplish your goals. What would you do, where would you go, how would you feel, what would you say, what would you buy, what would your friends and family say? For example, if your goal is to be the top producer for next year, visualize yourself accepting the award and making a speech with your family watching.

7. When you have finished writing down all the goals that come to mind, give them the SMART test and restate as needed.

8. Now subject each goal to another test. For each goal, repeat these questions:
    (a) Do I really want this? (The Want Test)
    (b) Do I need it? If you want it so bad that the want will not go away, then you need it. (The Need Test)
    (c) Am I willing to do what it takes to get it? Am I willing to spend time, money, and experience personal growth pain in order to reach it? (The Sacrifice Test)
    (d) Do I have what it takes to reach it? This refers to the realistic and achievable part of the SMART test. This step requires you to take stock of your mental and physical resources to see if your goal is really attainable. That does not mean to discard goals that require you to stretch. This is a test to see if you are committed enough to use what you have, and go out and get more of what is needed to achieve your goal. If you truly do not believe in the goal, then maybe it is not a goal after all. (The Resource Test)

    If your goals do not meet these tests, then move them to a sixth page labelled ''Dreams.'' You may want to change these dreams to goals later. I have done it many times.

9. Restate the goals into present tense as if they were already accomplished. This was difficult for me to do. It somehow seemed to be misleading or deceptive. I was always taught to never pretend to be something you are not. Never fake it. I now believe it is OK and productive to ''Fake it 'til you make it.''

10. Set target dates on the financial and career goals and other goals that seem suited to a target date.

11. Reread your goals and start another free thinking session about what should be your *major definite purpose* in life. This goal should encompass

the "theme" set by the goals you have listed, taking into account your profession, talents, abilities, and resources. Think about what you can do to help others while achieving your own goals. Why were you put here?

After you have completed the goals and stated your major definitive purpose, you should have a list that only needs a little cleaning up to get started toward accomplishment. It is a list that will change frequently as you hone your goal-setting skills. If you have a long list of goals as I do, you may want to break them down even further and prioritize them as to importance. For example, I have a list of things I want to own that I consider by-products of my goals list. If your list is overly long, then do prioritize it by importance and by target dates. *Make a summary list of your most important goals.* This is the list that you will refer to daily.

ESTABLISHING A BELIEF SYSTEM

Establishing a belief system or determining exactly what your belief system is can be more difficult than setting goals. Many trainers start with a basic belief system before they set goals. Either method is acceptable. Almost everyone has a belief system; some just have difficulty in expressing what it is. What does a belief system have to do with setting goals? Research has shown that if your goals are not congruent with your belief system, you will either fail to achieve your goals or goal achievement will leave you asking "Is that all there is?" For example, if one of your goals is to own a Corvette convertible, but your belief system says that indulging in such extravagance is wrong and selfish, then you will either fail to reach your goal of having a Corvette or you will feel guilty all the time you own it.
So how do you find out what your beliefs are?

1. Go back to your goal setting procedure. Find a quiet place to let your mind wander.
2. Review your goals to see what beliefs about life in general, yourself, and your career that they conjure up.
3. Start writing your beliefs as they come to you. Do not try to make them perfect or grammatically correct—just write. You can polish them later.
4. It occasionally helps to segregate your beliefs into the same categories as your goals (i.e., career and financial, family, etc.).

2

Conserving Your Most Valuable Resource—Time

"Do ye value life? Then waste not time, for that is the stuff of which life is made."

Benjamin Franklin

All of us have the same amount of time—some just squeeze more productivity and enjoyment out of every hour. This chapter is devoted to helping you better use this unique resource. Time is a unique resource because everyone has the same amount of it. It cannot be stockpiled or accumulated, we all spend it at the same rate, and it cannot be turned off.

CPAs, like a lot of other professionals, sell time. When you sell time, its value as a commodity becomes real. Our natural inclination is to think in terms of rates per hour. We set up time-keeping systems to insure that our clients will be billed properly. In spite of time systems, I continually found that I was short on billable vs. nonbillable time. I worked on getting more billable time. I segregated all activities into billable vs. nonbillable. That kind of attitude tends to get your life out of balance. Try telling a wife or husband that you cannot spend time with them because that is nonbillable time.

One day, I made the mistake of calculating what I would make if 100 percent of my working hours were billable. It was not enough. That is when I decided I had to find a way to get more out of time. Since most of us do keep time records out of necessity, I will not touch on that aspect of time management. Keeping those records has probably alerted you to the difficulty of managing time. Most CPAs stop there. They accept this as part of the price of the profession and continue to let time control their lives. Many adopt a negative mental attitude. They see injustice in becoming slaves to their clients, monitor their lives and memories from one tax season to the next, and succumb to guilt every time they take time off. If you read and practice the ideas discussed in this chapter, you will be able to control time and your life. You will start to feel better about yourself, your profession, and life in general.

WHY WE MUST LEARN TO MANAGE TIME

Time is profitable. Time is life, but it is also money. Managing it is financially rewarding. Managing time can reduce stress. If you have that "out of control" feeling a lot, then you are leading a life that is too stressful. Time management is essential to high self-esteem and a balanced, happy life.

There are two misconceptions that work against us in learning to become excellent time managers.

1. *Organized people are boring.* We have all heard such phrases as ''Time management stifles my creativity,'' ''I just want to go with the flow,'' or ''Don't take away my spontaneity.'' That is the backwards way to look at time management. Taking control of time actually stimulates creativity and allows your spirit and thoughts to soar. Managing time allows us to be more productive while still having time for family and leisure activities. It also allows us time to think. It is the people who do not manage time who suffer. They lead unbalanced, nonproductive lives. They may be free spirits, but they are usually plagued by self-doubt, low productivity, and low self-esteem. Their lives are a series of extreme highs and lows or one continuous low. A person who controls his time and his life smooths out most of the rough edges of life and stays on a high plateau.

2. *Rushing, always talking on the phone, being late to appointments, or being unable to attend meetings due to ''time constraints'' are often seen as signs of a prosperous, busy, productive person.* Just the opposite is true. These are signs of a person who is not in control of time. Time is controlling him. Time managers are calm, relaxed, able to focus on the task at hand without taking phone calls or interruptions, show up at meetings on time, and attend educational seminars from start to finish.

HOW TO GET CONTROL OF TIME

Decide to Take Control

Time management is important to your health, well-being, and prosperity. This concept is essential to the implementation of the recommended steps in the remainder of this program. You must learn to manage your time before you can make any further progress.

Set Goals

Yes, we are back to goal setting again. Why is setting goals so important to time management? If you do not have goals, you are going nowhere and you will probably reach your destination. If you do not know where you are going, then inevitably you will take a circuitous path and that path will take longer.

Make and Keep Lists

Set up the following lists:

Daily ''To Do'' Lists.   If you do not keep daily ''to do'' lists, you do not like prosperity and serenity. You like havoc, chaos, long hours, and low productivity per hour. You may be doing all right without the lists, but I guarantee that you will do 50 percent better with them. These lists should be considered ''conditions of employment.'' It does not matter whether you use a computer or handwritten list. Keeping the lists is the important thing.

You say that you do not have time to make lists? You do not have time *not* to make lists! Lists do not cost time; they provide you with direction for daily activities.

Why should you make "to do" lists every day and when should you do them? Preferably, you should make them before you go home the night before. Some people like to wake early in the morning and do the list. Either is effective. Doing them the last part of the day will activate your subconscious to work on the next day's activities during the night. Making them in the middle of the day is the worst time, but it is still better than nothing—at least the last half of the day will be productive.

"To do" lists take the clutter out of your mind. Without lists, you will constantly be putting out fires or doing nothing because you cannot think of what it was you were supposed to do. You will not forget as many things. You will be able to *prioritize* your tasks and focus better on what is important. Prioritize based on two factors:

1. Value in terms of dollars.
2. Urgency (the degree of pain that will occur if the job is not done today).

Adding to the lists on a daily basis when a new task comes up keeps you focused on the task at hand rather than letting your mind wander to the project that can wait. Crossing things off the list gives you a great feeling of accomplishment.

What about tasks that arise that you cannot possibly do today or tomorrow? Keep a page for each day for at least 30 days. When a new task comes up just select a day when you think you can tackle it and write it down on that day's list. See Figure 2-1 for a sample "to do" list.

Project and Long-term Lists.   Keeping long-term and project lists separate from daily "to do" lists can be confusing. There is bound to be a point when the two overlap. Most computer programs allow specific project lists to "merge" into your daily to do lists. This is ideal. If you are keeping the lists by hand or your software does not do the merging, then you have to look at your project lists often or manually list the tasks on your project list onto your daily "to do" list.

What are project lists or long-term lists? You may say why bother to have them if you are going to merge with the daily "to do" lists anyway? *Project lists* are specific larger projects that require the completion of several tasks. Often, these tasks must be completed in sequential order. Each task on the list must be assigned a due date. Also, the project may involve several people and separate meetings. If the tasks are commingled with your daily tasks, then it is hard to determine the total status of the project. For example, I keep a project list on each National Conference. The list contains all the tasks that have to be done in sequential order and to whom the tasks are assigned. The tasks assigned to me are on my daily "to do" lists. The tasks assigned to others had better be on *their* daily "to do" lists.

How does a project list differ from a long-term list? *Long-term lists* usually contain projects as well as tasks that have not been assigned due dates as yet. They are things you want to do, possibly need to do, but resources have not been committed to yet. You may not have the resources to do them or the timing may not be right to do them now. So why keep a long-term list? Because that is part of planning. The long-term list is part of your overall plan and contains projects and tasks that you do not want to forget. That is what lists are all about— *not forgetting*. See Figure 2-2 for an example of a project list.

Figure 2-1.   Sample "To Do" List.

Date: _____   Name: _____

To Do List For:

Today _____ Tomorrow _____ Short Term _____ Long Term _____

Item #	Project	*	$	Total Pts.	Priorities	Complete
1	REVIEW GOALS	***				
2	PREPARE TO DO LIST	***				
3						
4						
5						
6						
7						
8						
9						
10						
11						
12						

OUR CREED: Think—Follow Through—Finish

*—Urgency Rating one to three stars—10 points each
$—Value Rating one to three dollar signs—20 points each

Figure 2-2   Sample Project List

Priority #	Project

You only have to make one list each day—*the daily "to do" list*. You look at your goal list every day, but it is only redone when you feel the need (usually about every 60 days). You will probably need to review your project list at least twice a week depending on the urgency and importance of the project and the people who are assisting you. Also, remember the alternative—chaos and stress.

Let us summarize what we have learned so far about lists.

1. Keep a daily "to do" list. Prioritize each project according to dollar value and urgency.
2. Keep separate sheets set up for 30 days if you are using a manual system.
3. Keep project lists for major projects. List the tasks to be done on the project in priority order (may have to be sequential).
4. Be sure that the tasks on your project lists are always included on your daily "to do" lists as they come due.
5. Keep long-term lists to keep from forgetting projects or tasks that do not have due dates yet.
6. Review your goals daily.
7. Review your dreams, want, and to do lists as the thoughts enter your mind to add to them.
8. Revise your goals list about every 60 days. (You may want to do it sooner or wait until 90 days.)
9. As you revise your goal list, add to your Victory list.

Does that make it simpler? Memorize these nine steps and practice the procedure for at least 21 days. By that time, it will become a habit.

MANAGING TIME AND PEOPLE

Managing your own projects and the projects you are given by clients is tough enough. Most people totally lose control when other people are involved. Many CPAs are partners in a small firm or are sole proprietors. Not only must they manage their own time, but they must also manage others as well. Often, employees are concerned about time only in the context of what they will be paid per hour, time off, and quitting time. It is up to you to set a good example and be sure that they follow it. In this section, we will show you how to do that. First a word of caution: Don't expect perfection in getting other people to be as concerned as you are about making your business profitable. I admit to suffering a good deal of frustration in this area because I expected too much too soon. Building a good team is essential to your success, but it is a long process that requires commitment. Your goals should be to:

1. Set a good example.
2. Provide the tools and skills necessary for your employees to be efficient.
3. Monitor their progress.
4. Provide guidance, direction, and motivation.
5. Delegate to your staff and give them responsibility.

Your Staff Should Maintain Daily "To Do" Lists

They should use them for *personal* as well as *work* tasks. Personal? Yes. They can even write down things like run before breakfast, attend Rotary Club, and the like. Writing these things down and marking them off as accomplishments keeps the juices flowing. You must make the lists a condition of employment.

Purchase a Task or Project Management Software System

The one we use is over six-years old and was purchased for less than $100. I am sure they are cheaper and better now. This system should be operated by someone other than yourself. Otherwise, you will be relegated to the role of monitor and bookkeeper and will probably be rolled over by your own system.

Task Lists for Every Staff Member Must Be Input into a Central System

Personal tasks are an exception. We use a small form called a *task assignment sheet* that is routed to the central person. Tax returns, for example, are assigned a task. If you are assigning a task to someone, the form makes you route the task form to the assignee after it is entered into the system. Networks can make this system more efficient, although we do not use a network yet. Again, whether or not you use a manual system or software, it should be "automatic" that tasks are fed into a central system at the same time that they are added to individual "to do" lists. All tasks must be given a due date. Most systems allow you to enter the assignee and the supervisor. Each week, the employee in charge of the central monitoring system will print:

1. A consolidated list of everything that was due the prior week and what is coming due the next week.
2. A list of each employee's tasks in due date order.
3. A list of all projects with tasks.

Weekly Staff Meetings Must Be Held to Report on All Tasks and Projects

Lists should be printed and distributed at least 24 hours prior to the scheduled weekly staff meeting. Everyone should compare the central list to their own to make sure they are ready to report during the meeting. At the meeting, each project for the past week and the next week is read by the responsible party and reported on. It must be announced as complete, changed, eliminated for a reason, or moved to a new date with reason given. *Read aloud?* Yes. You will be surprised how motivating it is to complete projects when you know that you will read them aloud weekly.

Let us backtrack now and talk more about the meeting itself. We hold our meetings weekly. We have tried many different times. I recommend early morning or late afternoon. Late afternoon is probably preferable because employees will speed up in order to get home on time. Each meeting should have an agenda. A typical agenda would include discussions on:

1. Read aloud projects and reports;
2. Special reports by each attendee;

3. New products;
4. Problems incurred with clients, software, or new tax laws; and
5. New employees, announcements about existing ones, and so forth.

The meeting should last no longer than an hour and many will be over in less than half that time.

Meetings are notorious time-wasters. However, a regularly scheduled meeting like this will keep communication flowing throughout the firm, motivate the completion of projects, monitor progress on special projects, and *eliminate the necessity of so many special meetings that interrupt everyone's schedule.* They also provide a forum for you to give instructions without embarrassment to specific individuals, and for employees to offer recommendations and show their value. We also found that tax season meetings were especially valuable. We knew what returns had problems so that everyone knew what was going on when a client called in about his return (all tax returns are assigned a project automatically when the client's file is pulled).

What about recurring tasks? We keep a list called the *end-of-month list*. It is a check-off sheet that must be completed by month-end. If any projects remain incomplete at month-end, they are added to the master task list. The end-of-month list is a list of all reports that must be done during the month, regularly scheduled payments that must be made, and so on. If you have a software system, I suggest that you use the recurring task feature to add these to your system like any other task. A good system will feed your recurring task into the system and pop up remainders for you when the task is due.

In the sales and marketing portion of this book, we will discuss how to develop a marketing plan. The marketing plan should be handled as a combination recurring task list (because a lot of the tasks are recurring) and a major project list (because a lot of the tasks for each marketing category must be performed in a sequential manner).

LEARN TO DELEGATE TO YOUR STAFF

Many sole proprietors do not have any employees or are limited to only one. That is the way I started out. However, as soon as I got enough billings to keep myself busy, I added staff as quickly as I could. You should always pay someone at a lower rate while you do something at a higher rate.

Why have a staff if you do not delegate to them? Like a lot of entrepreneurs, I was a "control freak" for many years. Nobody could do the job as well as I could. I soon realized that with that attitude, my staff became a liability rather than an asset. Most people who know me will describe me as a "hard-nosed entrepreneur." I have little patience with people who do not give 100 percent and who will not take responsibility for their own lives. I am always on guard for those who are perennial "victims" of circumstances or of others. I believe that the source of most people's problems can be found by looking in the mirror. I say this to let you know that even a hard case like me can learn to delegate and bring out the best in people.

Numerous studies have shown that the primary source of motivation for most people is a sense of accomplishment, importance, and recognition for a job well done. The only way to get a sense of importance and accomplishment is to have responsibility. Many of our businesses are too small to offer vertical growth for our employees. In order to keep a good employee, you must offer growth through expansion of responsibilities which leads to new opportunities. Here are some ideas for delegating:

1. Carefully screen people before you hire them. You will still make a few mistakes, but not as many as when you hire in a panic.
2. Do not concentrate so heavily on particular skills (although they are important). Instead, concentrate on attitude, enthusiasm, and general intelligence.
3. Give your employees slightly more responsibility than they think they can handle.
4. Try to stay out of the details while they are doing the job.
5. Input the job into your monitoring system and require reports during staff meetings.
6. Do not let them reverse delegate the job back to you little by little. *Reverse delegation* is a serious problem. It is human nature for people to take the path of least resistance and to avoid getting out of their comfort zone. You should always keep your staff slightly out of their comfort zone.

To keep employees from giving a project back to you piece by piece, just refuse to accept it. Use watch words *think, follow through, and finish.* Most employees will not use their minds, fail to follow through, and leave projects unfinished.

Think.   Ask employees to think about what they just did or asked you about. The correct way to do it or the answer to the question is clearly within their abilities. It also means that you want them to give you a recommended solution as if they were the owners of the business.

Follow Through.   This means just what it says. Do not let a project just hang there. This is usually the case for a project that has no specific deadline for completion because a series of sequential events have to occur before the project is brought to a conclusion. Such projects tend to get stopped in the middle because the staff gets a sense of completion from doing several steps. They also can have a problem with time sequence. If a project does not have a deadline for completion, the employees tend to drop the ball in the middle. There is a natural resistance to such projects because of the knowledge that one event must end before the next one begins. Sales or marketing projects that require the customer to take some form of action before the next step can occur are typical of this type of resistance. In order to avoid this, you must handle these as projects with tasks in your system. Assign deadlines to each task even though they are sequential. Keep a stamp in your office that says ''Follow Through!''

Finish.   Sometimes employees will take a project to the edge of their comfort zone only to give it back to you to finish. In many cases, your time would be less if you had started the project and carried it through to completion rather than picking it up in the middle. You must demand that your employees finish the projects that you assign them.

People need help to get out of their comfort zones. By definition, that means that they must suffer a little pain. If not, they will wind up in a rut. Many of the steps we have discussed will not work the first or even second time. You must be persistent and continuous in your efforts if you are going to build a great team.

Let us summarize the tasks for managing time when other people are involved:

1. Employees must maintain daily "to do" lists as a condition of employment.
2. Enter all tasks of all employees into a central system maintained by someone other than yourself.
3. Print a consolidated list and separate lists for each employee prior to your weekly staff meeting. Also, separate lists of tasks by major project.
4. Report on all projects during weekly meeting.
5. Follow a stated agenda for the remainder of reports for staff meeting.
6. Be sure that all recurring tasks are also included in your central system.
7. Delegate, learn, and use the terms Think, Follow through, and Finish.

You now have a system for monitoring your own projects as well as those of your staff. Nothing should "drop through the cracks" in this system. Clients should get their projects done on time, billable time should all be captured, and your stress should be reduced.

THE THIEVES OF TIME

Thief #1—Procrastination

Most of us are natural procrastinators. We have a natural tendency to take the path of least resistance and that leads downhill. Let us talk about ways to get this most terrible of thieves out of your life.

1. *Get rid of all the myths about procrastination.* Like time management, people love to brag about being procrastinators. It is socially acceptable. We believe that it makes us more loved and accepted by our friends and peers. To say in a group that you never procrastinate is like saying "I am smarter than everyone here." You do not have to boast of being self-disciplined, but you will be admired for it, even if people do not want to admit it. Procrastination is like a cancer in your personal and professional life. It affects you and everyone around you negatively. It is not easy to get rid of, but it is very possible if you decide that is what you really want to do.
2. *Decide that you want to stop being a procrastinator.*
3. *Start keeping track of your procrastination instances.* List what negative effect procrastination had in each case. List what positive effects may have occurred if you had not procrastinated.
4. *Stop rationalizing and making excuses for putting things off.* Call yourself all the names you deserve, forgive yourself, and "get on with it."
5. *Use the time management techniques outlined in the rest of this book.* They will cure you of procrastination. However, this is like the chicken or egg. Which comes first curing procrastination or good time management skills? I do not know. I think it depends on the intensity of your procrastination problem. If it is bad, then you may need to tackle procrastination first.

Practice Identifying Saddle Burrs.   Learn to distinguish between what is *significant* and what is urgent. This is the most important step in overcoming procrastination. However, it is also one of those things that is profoundly simple in concept but exceedingly difficult to explain or implement.

Most time management courses and books concentrate on the priority approach and the a, b, c rating of projects. This is valid, but they also usually tell you to rate projects in terms of their *positive* benefits. Many go a step further and tell you to rate projects as to the *negative* things that will happen if they are not done. In practice, however, most of us still have difficulty in properly prioritizing projects because we overlook the projects that seem *insignificant* in nature. Many of these projects are mundane, routine tasks that have little or no positive benefit. We just naturally move them down the priority scale. *That is the most common mistake in time management.*

These little projects are called *saddle burrs*. Think of a burr under the saddle of a horse; the horse is your business or a client. It is a small inconvenience at first, but it gradually grows into a major pain for the horse and he will throw you from the saddle because of it. Think of the pain from being thrown and how you could have avoided it by simply looking under the saddle and removing the burr.

Saddle burrs must be removed instantly. They are urgent tasks that will cause you much grief if they are not done right away. You can spot saddle burrs by evaluating the negative consequences of not doing unimportant tasks. Here are some example of saddle burrs:

1. Invoices are due for payment. What happens if you do not pay bills right away?
   (a) You think you have more spendable cash than you really do.
   (b) Either your monthly financials are off, or you have to spend a lot of time accruing unpaid invoices. Accruing them usually adds 400 percent to their handling time. Remember, you have to reverse the accrual or make sure that all invoices are coded against accounts payable. Do not bother with accruing? OK—then your cash and your financials are wrong.
   (c) Your suppliers think you are a poor manager of time and business and spread the word among your clients.
   (d) You ''forget'' why you bought the service or product or what you did with it when you got it. This adds 200 percent to handling time.
   (e) It is much harder to challenge a questionable invoice after you have let the invoice become delinquent or waited until the last minute to pay.
   (f) You miss discounts.
2. Not preparing financial statements monthly. If you do not give this a priority rule:
   (a) You cannot effectively manage a business without having current financial statements.
   (b) Sooner or later, you will be embarrassed by a client, a banker or creditor when you, a CPA, cannot produce current financial statements on your own business on a moment's notice.
   (c) It takes approximately twice as long to produce financial statements after the information has gone stale, than it does when the information is current.
3. Not returning telephone calls within 24 hours. We will talk about the telephone as another thief of time later, but this concerns returning telephone calls only. There are some exceptions to this rule, but they are few.

(a) If you do not return calls within 24 hours, you make your caller's life miserable and he will return the favor.

(b) You do not come off as the busy executive, but as a harried unorganized person who your caller would not recommend to others because you cannot manage your own affairs.

(c) You will miss opportunities.

(d) If urgent action is required as a result of the phone call, you may miss the deadline.

(e) Your caller may be only available for a short period of time.

Are you starting to get the similarity of the saddle burrs? They usually involve these common traits:

1. They can be done quickly, but if not done, no immediate pain results.
2. Their negative effects can be long term and severe.
3. They usually involve poor habit patterns.
4. They involve the path of least resistance type thinking. That is, not doing them now will not hurt me this instant, and they will not have an immediate positive impact either.
5. Taking care of saddle burrs indicates habit patterns rather than short-term conscious action.
6. Long-term effects of not doing them are severe.
7. Doing them later rather than now increases the time required exponentially—usually 500 percent!

Learn the Elephant and Pie Approach.   How do you eat an elephant? One bite at a time. That is how you tackle big or unpleasant projects. Since you would rather eat pies than elephants, visualize each major project as a big pie with several slices. Some slices are invariably easier to "eat" than others. Start with one of those. The key is to *get started!*

Remember the 500 Percent Rule.   When you throw a project into a corner, the time required to complete it starts growing exponentially, usually expanding to 500 percent of what it would have taken to do it when the project was fresh. This is because of a phenomenon of the mind that I cannot explain. I have tested it, however, and the 500 percent rule almost always works. I really started to believe it when I noticed it was true for easy projects as well as long and difficult ones. Somehow, the project loses its appeal and values as it gets older. It starts to grow in your mind and makes you feel guilty. The solution—do it on time and save the 500 percent!

Develop a Speed Mentality.   This is something that came natural to me, and I always thought of it as a negative until I saw an expert recommend this in print. The speed mentality simply recognizes that tasks must be performed as rapidly as possible to promote efficiency and profitability. It does not mean that your heart rate is pumping to maximum capacity. Once you recognize that speed is important, you can relax and operate with speed and efficiency. If you do not have a speed mentality, you will endure more stress when a job must be done quickly because you must change your normal work habits to get it done.

Visualize Completing the Project.   Instead of seeing yourself going through the drudgery of doing the project and encountering all the difficulties, visualize yourself reaping the rewards of a completed job.

Plan Rewards for Yourself.   As each slice of the pie is eaten, give yourself small rewards. Rewards can range from something as simple as having a coke break, playing a round of golf, or taking a cruise. The only rules are that the reward should be decided in advance and it should reflect the value of the completed task or portion thereof. Have you ever noticed how much more productive you are just before a vacation? The concept works!

Use Motivational Phrases to Inspire Yourself.   W. Clement Stone had his sales force repeat the phrase ''Do it Now'' every day.

Be Decisive.   Analyze your actions to see if you are allowing many projects to be delayed because you cannot make a decision. If you are waiting until this or that takes place, or this particular project is complete, or your child gets out of school, or tax season is over, or this audit is completed, ask yourself these questions: Does the project involve something that leads me toward my goals? It is going to make me feel good when it is finished? If the answers are yes, stop being a wimp. Do it now!

Learn to Focus.   Many very intelligent, competent people are unable to focus on a particular project and carry it through to completion. They are continually distracted by other projects, people, mail, etc. They have a speed mentality, work fast, and generally get a lot of small things done, but are unable to get the big projects done. They also have difficulty with the urgent tasks that may appear insignificant (saddle burrs). Thus, they live their lives ''behind the eight ball.'' The eight ball often becomes a giant bowling ball because of all the bad things that happen when big important projects are not completed. They are excellent candidates for all the health and mental problems that come with un-controlled stress. How do you learn to focus, follow through, and finish?

1. Set goals and read them daily.
2. Admit your problem. (Denial of the existence of this problem is prevalent because the individuals see themselves as high achievers, intelligent, etc. That is often true, but it does not mean that they do not have this problem.)
3. Follow the rules of good time management. For this type of individual, this is doubly important. If you have this problem, you must organize each day around your task list.
4. Designate blocked off portions of time on your calendar to work on big projects. Keep the appointment with yourself and the project.
5. Think time and creative time alone is essential to this type of individual. Treat it as an appointment with yourself.
6. Use positive affirmations (talk to yourself). I say things like, ''This is what I am doing right now. It deserves all the attention I can give it. I know that there are other things that demand my attention, but this has got to be finished.''

Thief #2—People

People take a lot of your time without giving any value for your most precious resource. Here are some suggestions to minimize time stolen by people.

Keep a Time Log.   Most CPAs are already doing this. But you may want to keep a separate log of the number of times you are interrupted by *people* during the day. This will tell you how much time is being stolen from you. After you are convinced, you can drop the time log except as you need it for billing purposes.

Schedule Your Day Using Your Calendar.   Compare your ''to do'' list with your calendar. Block off times when you will work on the tasks on your list.

Close Your Office Door.   Forget the myths about open door policy. You will not appear as unfriendly or aloof, just efficient. You work on intricate complicated projects that are time sensitive. Each of your clients deserves your undivided attention. You can open your door when you are working on less complicated projects and interruptions will not disturb you. You can also have a regularly scheduled ''open door'' time for staff to come in with questions. Just tell your employees that clients are paying for your time; they deserve all of it. A 30-second interruption during the preparation of a complicated tax return can cause a 20-minute delay in recapturing your train of thought. In addition to delays, it causes errors and omissions.

Bring all Visits to Conclusion as Soon as Possible.   Stand up. Stare at your work. Use phrases such as ''Thanks for bringing that to my attention'' or ''Glad I could help you; now what else can I do for you?''

Client Interruptions.   Clients, of course, deserve your service and attention. But that pertains to all clients, not just those who drop by to see you without an appointment. In dealing with these types of interruptions, you must:

1. Use your staff effectively. They must have a list of VIP clients who will not interrupt you unless it is important. They must also have a list of nuisance clients who you want to avoid because you know they steal a lot of your time.
2. Use your invisible client. The invisible client is the one whose project you are working on but who is not there. You are charging him for your time, so he deserves your complete attention. It is perfectly OK to have your staff say, ''Jim is with a client right now. I am sure he would want to see you, though. If it is urgent, then I can interrupt him. If not, can I give you an appointment as soon as possible? Or can someone else help you?'' Those questions will teach your nuisance clients to appreciate your time and will satisfy your good clients. If the client says it is urgent, go out of your office, close the door (leaving the invisible client inside), and converse with your VIP client in any available space other than your own office. This will guarantee to cut the visit short.

Is this being deceptive to your clients? I think not. How about the invisible client? He brings in his tax return faithfully every year, let's you handle all of his investments, and seldom drops by except to pay his bill. Should his work be delayed or his bill increase because you were interrupted?

Thief #3—The Telephone

The telephone is essential to your business just as people are. Here is how to make the telephone a tool rather than a thief.

1. *Screen your calls.* There are many top level executives who pick up their own phones. Many believe that this adds a personal touch. I like to call someone who does this. However, people who can afford this luxury are usually not doers, they are strictly managers. They also do not work directly on highly creative, complex tasks. They *manage* the people who work on these tasks. That allows them freedoms you and I may not enjoy. We have to be managers *and* doers. Therefore, I believe in screening calls. There are right ways and wrong ways to do this, however.

   CALLER: "Is Jim there?"

   Wrong? "May I say who is calling?"

   Right! "Yes he is here; he is with a client/on the other line right now." Always answer the question *before* you screen the call. Otherwise, it appears that whether or not you're in is determined by the degree of the caller's importance. After answering the question, then say, "I'm sure he will want to speak to you, I don't know how long he will be tied up. Shall I interrupt him or can I take a message and have him get back to you? How long are you going to be at this number?"

   CALLER: "No, don't interrupt him; just have him give me a call. How long do you think he will be tied up?"

   Right! Your receptionist should know from your calendar or instructions how long you will be tied up. "His calendar says that he has appointments back to back until noon. Will that be soon enough for a call back?"

   CALLER: "Yes, I need to speak to him for just a minute. Please interrupt him."

   This is OK. Your caller knows that you are either on the phone or with another client. He will respect your time and keep the call short. You have been interrupted, but your client knows he is important and the interruption is minimal. This also saves a lot of telephone tag.

   CALLER: "Have Jim call me as soon as he can."

   Wrong! "May I tell him what this is concerning?" If the caller wanted to tell his business to the receptionist, he would have asked for the receptionist, not you.

   Right! "Is there a file or other information I can pull for Jim so that he can be better prepared for your call?" This is about as far as you can go to get information about the call. Often, this one question will take care of the call. It will alert the receptionist to the nature of the call and may allow her to handle the call herself or give it to a staff member. Ever have a client leave an urgent message to later find out that all he wanted was to make an appointment to bring in his tax return—a task you will have to delegate to the person he talked to in the first place? This one question solves many of those problems.

2. *Use telephone message pads.* Fill them out completely. Always have your receptionist get a return number and put it on the message form. If the client says, "He has it," she should look it up and put it on the message, anyway. You may indeed have the number, but it may require looking through files or Rolodexes for a minute or so. Every minute counts.

3. *Avoid telephone tag.* Your receptionist should be alerted when you are continually missing another party. It is up to you to stop the tag by taking the call.

4. *Keep your calls short and productive.* Try talking standing up. Use ending phrases, like, "Thanks for the call; anything else I can help you with?" or "I know you are busy, so I won't keep you."

5. *Put a smile on your face; it shows in your voice.*

6. *Have the receptionist pull the file and as much information as possible before returning the call.* Especially during tax season, you should know the status of the return in-house or the amount of refund before you make the call. This saves a lot of time and possibly a return call.

7. *Have a list of items you wish to cover with someone before you make a call.* Check them off as you go. The caller will appreciate your brevity and efficiency.

8. *Provide your receptionist with a VIP list of people whose calls get priority.*

9. *Have regular times during each day when you will take all calls so that screening is not 100 percent.* Your clients will learn when is the best time to reach you. By the same token, have times when you will take only urgent calls.

10. *Have a designated place where phone messages will be placed.* This should not be your in-box. It should not be on your desk. If your receptionist is constantly interrupting you giving you messages, you may as well be taking calls. I keep one spindle beside my in-box outside my office for incoming calls. A second spindle is on my desk for calls I have returned but have not been resolved.

Thief #4—Your In-Box

Most of us have problems with in-boxes. We cannot resist getting into them and scattering their contents on our desks and in various other locations inside our offices. We are constantly emptying them before preparing to do anything with the contents. Here are some ways to improve on these time wasting habits.

1. *Locate your in-box outside your office and out of your sight if possible.* If you do not, you will constantly be glancing up when someone puts something in it. In my prior office arrangement, the box was just outside my door. I could see it when my door was open. I could even hear it when someone put something in it when my door was closed. I could not resist the temptation to see what it was. Result? Interruptions, lack of focus, and wasted time. I moved it to an adjoining room. I only go to it when I am prepared to work on its contents.

2. *Have an urgent in-box on top of your regular in-box.* This allows your staff to tell you what must be acted upon ASAP.

3. *Keep a mail-out tray, a filing tray, and a work-out tray.* This keeps your staff from confusing the categories.

4. *Dump it, delegate it, do it, or delay it.* When you do schedule time for emptying your file tray, follow the four Ds:

(a) *Dump it*–If it is junk mail, do not read it, no matter what tantalizing phrases are on the outside of the envelope. If you cannot bring yourself to throw it out, then keep a basket beside your desk for those things you may want to look at later but your are not sure if they have any value now. For those items you definitely want to keep for future reference but require no action now, put in your "to be filed" tray.

(b) *Delegate it*—If it is something that staff can handle, write a short note of instruction and put it in your out tray—*now*!

(c) *Do it*—If is something that you can do in a few minutes, treat it like saddle burr and do it *now*. Try to handle these types of things only once.

(d) *Delay it*—Delay is not a good word; it refers to items that come to your in-box that cannot be handled now, cannot be delegated, and cannot be thrown away. But delay does not mean to put it on a pile on your desk or in the corner of your office.

What about the mounds of reading material that come across your desk? How can you possibly absorb it all? Unfortunately, you cannot. You need to focus on a few product groups and only glance at the others. You must speed read a large portion of the material, however. Do not spend an hour reading *The Wall Street Journal* or the daily paper every morning. Above all, do not use these as excuses for not going to work. They can be great thieves of time.

I try to catch the news on morning TV while I do preliminary exercises or on my radio on the way to work. There is not enough time to read the daily papers from cover to cover. You are better off devoting an hour a day to reading time early in the morning or late at night. You should concentrate on periodicals or books on the profession. This book has listed many periodicals and books to read.

Thief #5—Lost Files

Looking for files is the purest form of wasting time. Here are some of the ways that you can use to keep this problem under control:

1. *Keep your filing current*. I know this seems obvious, but most of us have trouble with it. Tax season is the worst. The staff wants to put off filing because of the work load. You can file 50 files in a lot less time than you can search for one lost one.

2. *Color code your files*. If you have separate colors for various categories of files, you are much less likely to misfile. Even the least experienced file clerks will notice a green folder should not be filed in a drawer filled with red ones.

3. *Maintain a file directory*. The directory should show the categories of files with appropriate colors and locations.

4. *Label the outside of your file drawers and color code the labels to match the contents.* This is obvious, but often overlooked.

5. *Do not allow yourself or others to keep files in their offices for prolonged periods of time.*

6. *When a file is removed, have cardboard replacements ready to identify where the file is being kept.* The cardboard sheet should have a column for file name and a column for who is checking it out with the date.

7. *For items that have not had files set up yet because you have not had time to look at them, use vertical, open, file holders to hold red (high priority), green (next priority), and yellow (low priority) see-through plastic folders.* Use these for files that you do not want to get "out of sight, out of mind."

Thief #6—The TV

Television is the leader in pure time wasters. Most of what we watch on television is drivel. It cannot even be classified as escapism, which we all need now and then. Most weekly programs are 30 percent commercials. Eliminate your habit of flopping on the couch after the evening meal and watching three hours of cotton candy for the mind. You will gain your largest block of time for improvement. The habit may be hard to break. After all, we all need a little bit of relaxation after a hard day's work. If hooked on a few favorite programs, use the VCR as salvation. With the VCR you can tape only a couple of your favorite shows.

Thief #7—Meetings Without Agendas

Need I say more?

Thief #8—Reinventing the wheel

When you do something that is a little different, complex, or better, *document it*. The next time it comes up, you will not have to go through the grueling process again. This is especially important on particular knowledge or skills gained by your staff. If one of them leaves, be sure there is a "trail" for the successor.

THE TOOLS OF TIME MANAGEMENT

We have now covered the essentials of managing time. We have talked about: the importance of setting goals; making and keeping lists and the various types of lists to keep; managing other people's time as well as your own; and the thieves of time and how to keep them away from your precious resource. Here are some of the tools of time management along with tips on their uses.

Tool #1—Calendars

You should have at least two calendars. One is for your appointments and the other to hold the physical stuff such as invitations to seminars and the like. Many people use time management calendars such as Day-Timers. A third appointment calendar should be kept with your receptionist to make your appointments. The receptionist should make the appointment on his/her calendar and then give you an appointment note to post to yours. Compare and update both calendars daily; a good reason for a network.

You can use a computer calendar and a desk calendar as well. The computer calendar can be used for all appointments and reminders while the desk calendar can hold physical reminders for events and seminars.

Tool #2—Lists

I hope that the use of lists was adequately covered under earlier sections on lists. Refer back to the discussion on the eight basic lists.

Tool #3—Color Coded Files

This is covered in a prior section. Refer to pages 25–26.

Tool #4—The In-Box

Yes, this is a thief of time as well as a great tool. See the thief of time discussion on pages 24–25.

Tool #5—The Mini Recorder

Use a small tape recorder for several purposes:

1. Dictate messages to your assistant or to yourself.
2. Dictate letters and memos to be transcribed.
3. Have your goals taped and listen to them on the way to work.
4. Use it as a second memory when you travel. It is easier to enter something into a recorder than to try to decipher a hastily handwritten note on the back of a business card. Also, most of us can talk a lot faster than we can write. This allows you to enter a lot more information than you would if you were writing.
5. You can use the recorder to dictate specific notes about tax returns that were prepared. In the heat of preparing a return, the recorder can help you to just talk about what you need to remember about how to prepare the return and what you need to know for next year. These tapes can be later transcribed and added to the top of the client's file.

Tool #6—Capture the Moment During Tax Season

Nobody will argue that tax season is very busy for tax professionals. Most CPA firms operate like a "well-oiled machine" during February, March, and April. Most are at least three times as productive as they are during the remainder of the year. You do not want to work that hard all year, but you should be able to reproduce some of that efficiency and enthusiasm that comes with tax season. I usually came up with my best ideas and plans during tax season. Since there was no time to implement them, they very often made a passing trip through my mind and never came to reality. When I needed to recall them in the off season, I could only remember a few. Very frustrating!

Here are some tools to use to capture those ideas without taking excessive time. I emphasize, however, that the time savings techniques shared in this book should allow you the ability to act on many of the ideas *during tax season*.

1. *The big sheet/idea folder*. Keep a big stack of 8-1/2″ by 11″ paper within reach of where you work. When an idea comes to you that you cannot implement right away, write that idea down in a few key words or phrases and place the sheet in a tax season follow-up folder. Around April 20, start reviewing this file and prioritize. Add them to your task list.

Why big sheets? Because the business cards, paper napkins, and scraps of small paper tend to get lost. Also, your notes are hard to read when they are written on small sheets.

2. *The Investment Prospect Report.* When selling financial products. You will see many opportunities for financial planning as you prepare tax returns and visit with clients. Try to act on these items during tax season. When that is not possible, complete an Investment Prospect Report. The IPR is routed and placed in the client's investment file. Check off points on the IPR provide for the task to be added to the central task system. When the task comes due, pull the file and review your notes on the IPR to refresh your memory of ideas and what you discussed with the client. This keeps good leads from being missed and makes you look a lot smarter in front of the client.

Tool #7—Taped Audio Cassettes

This is a great way to learn while you are driving your car. This makes maximum use of time that is otherwise unproductive.

Tool #8—Condensed Book Services

There are services that review books in your field, write short reviews, and condense versions of the key points in the books. For example, ''Global Gambits'' is a clipping service provided by our firm that has copies of the best articles in our field taken from several periodicals.

Tool #9—The Binder for Business Cards

A binder with alphabet tabs for holding business cards is a very valuable information source that saves time in searching for addresses and information.

Tool #10—Marketing and Technical Information Binders

Set up binders in your office for the various categories of the technical aspects of financial planning as well as the marketing aspects. As you come across articles or information you think is relevant, copy it for these centralized binders.

OTHER HELPFUL HINTS TO CONSERVE TIME

1. Do not write your own checks. Sign them but do not write them. Bills with prepared checks should be presented to you ready for your signature.
2. Take reading material with you at all times. Read on airplanes, in waiting rooms, etc.
3. Do your toughest work during the best part of your day.
4. Know when to quit. If you are getting fuzzy or overtired, hang it up and get some rest. Sleeping will usually not only leave you refreshed, but it will provide ideas and new perspective.
5. Know when to work more. If you are consistently overwhelmed even though you are using good time management, you may need to come in a little early or stay a little late to work uninterrupted. Time spent in un-

interrupted work is worth four to five times the time spent during regular working hours.

6. Read only the articles that interest you in periodicals. Copy them or cut them out and file in the marketing and publications binders if you think you will want to refer to them again.

CONCLUSION

You now have a basic understanding of time management; you know why you must manage time. Hopefully, we have destroyed the myths about good time management. You should know the basic steps to getting control of this valuable resource including deciding to do it, setting goals, and making lists. You know how to make lists and how to use them as well as how to manage the time of people on your staff. I have shared tips on delegating and how to attack the "thieves of time." I gave you several tools and hints to how to apply them. So how much are you going to save and what are you going to do with it? Typical savings include:

Setting goals, making, and keeping lists	15 hrs per wk.
Stopping the thieves of time (TV etc.)	15–20 hrs per wk.
Other hints and tools	5

You can save 40 hours per week! I am only half kidding when I say that. Assuming that you were already using half of the ideas, then I saved you 20. What are you going to do with it? Here are my suggestions:

1. If you are doing financial planning as a sideline to your core business, then use this time to move it up to at least an equal footing with your other business. Done correctly, it will make you more total money for less effort than your current practice does.

2. Read books and periodicals on financial planning! If you read only one hour per day for one year you will be good in this profession. Do it for two years, you will be above your peer group. Three years and you will be an expert, four years and you will be a nationally known authority. Why not start today? Read one book per month and you will rank in the top 1 percent of your profession.

3. Set aside blocks of time on your calendar for thinking, creating, and planning. Keep a folder of notes for these times to spark the creative process. Find a quiet secluded spot where you can be totally alone. Sit down, go through relaxation techniques, and just clear your mind. Try not to think about anything for half an hour. That is very difficult. Do not worry about the ideas. They will come. You will get better at this every time you do it.

4. Attend more seminars and workshops in the financial planning profession.

5. Join professional associations and attend meetings and conventions.

6. Take more leisure time. Yes, I said leisure time. Pleasure and productivity are not mutually exclusive when it comes to the use of our time. The twenty-four hours each of us get each day comes around only once. Squeeze every drop of pleasure, knowledge, and productivity you can get from it.

Can we do it all? When I first started studying self-improvement and time management, I thought that the instructors were asking the impossible. As I am writing this book, I am serving as President of a start-up financial services firm that includes a broker–dealer and as President of my own financial planning firm with over 350 clients; commuting three hours per day; assisting in the care of my mother who is in a nursing home with a debilitating illness; spending quality time with my wife who has recently returned to college to get a degree in art; enjoying our two grown children and their spouses, a new grandson, and a son in high school. I also enjoy a good deal of leisure time, exercise at least five times per week, and read seven hours per week. Time management works.

Read one hour on professional subjects per day, read your goals, spend a half hour thinking, make lists, exercise, leisure, family time, religion, community service, and work? When we consider all these things, there is certainly a tendency to freeze and do nothing. This is one of the times when something sounds more difficult than it is. Practicing time management just becomes a good habit after a short period of time. Look at the alternatives and the benefits. It is worth it!

3

Increasing Your Profits By Adding Financial Planning Services and Products

"You become what you think about"—to achieve success in any area, you must have a mental picture of your idea of success."

We discussed good time management practices in Chapter 2. This chapter will deal more specifically with how you can add financial planning and products to what appears to be an already crowded schedule. Most CPAs are jealous entrepreneurs. They built their practices based on personal service to their clients and are understandably reluctant to do anything that might jeopardize that personal service relationship. Unfortunately, most CPAs also are notoriously poor managers of time. Only attorneys, who also sell time, are worse.

We have already covered in some detail why most CPA firms must add time management in order to remain competitive and *retain* their current clients. After accepting this fact, there are two more questions to be answered:

1. Am I in danger of damaging client relationships?
2. How do I find time when I am overworked now?

DELEGATING RESPONSIBILITIES

We have covered this subject in Chapter 2, but it deserves an even closer look before instituting financial planning. CPAs are notoriously poor delegators for many reasons. Let us discuss just a few of the most common excuses:

1. *Clients want me to do it!* You are absolutely right. You would love for the top lawyer in the firm you have hired to work on finding your lost birth certificate. You would like for the top surgeon in the hospital to work on your hangnail. You want the best mechanic in the dealership to change your spark plugs. However, if that happens, I will show you an inefficient legal or health practice and a poorly run auto dealership. Your clients will understand when you do not perform every little detail for them on every-

thing. In fact, I found that my clients respected my time more after I started delegating some client contact to staff.

2. *The work I do is too complex to trust to subordinates.* Admit it! About 50 percent of what you are doing could be done by someone with less than two years of experience in the business. I think you know that many of the types of returns you do are currently being prepared by a "chain" tax preparation service by clerks with only six weeks training. Also, software is now good enough to rely on in most cases. Will they do it as well or as fast as you? Probably not, at least in the beginning. But if you have procedures in place for proof and control and have conveyed to them your commitment to quality, then they will do it to the customer's satisfaction.

3. *I do not have any subordinates.* Calculate the maximum amount you can earn if you are able to bill 60 percent of your total time. If that is enough for you, you are doomed to stay in your comfort zone. If you want to earn more, then hire someone.

4. *It takes too long to train staff.* It does take a long time and sometimes it is very frustrating. However, if you want to grow and want to know that your practice could go on at least for a period of time if you were ill, then you must have trained staff. Also, almost all of us will someday tire of dealing with minutiae.

5. *My clients will be hurt when I tell them.* "I cannot face my clients and tell them that someone else will be dealing with them. It is like saying I have outgrown them. Their feelings will be hurt." This is difficult but find a way to personally inform your clients of the change. Use these reasons:

   (a) Computers have changed the way we do business. The *very expensive* software we purchase is so good that calculation errors are almost non-existent. That allows you to use staff for some of the things you used to do.

   (b) The organizer provided has a list of almost fool-proof questions that your highly trained staff can go through and be sure that nothing is left to chance.

   (c) Your staff is highly trained and are anxious to accept more responsibility and client contact. If you do not give it to them, they will seek it elsewhere. Besides, they are ready.

   (d) You have to do everything possible to slow the increase in fees. Notice I did not say no increase, or decrease. Since your clients are aware that your time is the most expensive in the place, they will get the picture.

   (e) Tax laws have changed, making it necessary to change your method of operation. (Do not tell them that their tax return has become so simple that anyone could do it.)

   (f) Ask the client, "Would you rather the highest paid person in the place [I know, that is not always true] look at your return to be sure that it is correct *after* it has been input and go over it in detail with you or would you rather that person spend billable time going through supporting data *before* it is prepared?"

   (g) If I can delegate staff to the pre-interview and input on the computer, I can devote more time to making sure the return was done correctly and go over it in detail with you when it is finished.

   (h) At the request of my clients and in response to very evident needs in the marketplace, I have expanded my services to include a more thorough analysis of your tax return to give you advice on what actions you should take to reduce your taxes and reach your financial goals in coming years. In the past, I have been a *reporter* of past events; now, I will not only advise you about your current return, I will be able to assist you in taking steps toward your goal of reduced taxes and increased financial security in future years.

(i) Finally, what is all the big fuss about, anyway? If the client insists on doing business the same old way in spite of reasons (a) through (h), then assure him he can. Most will cooperate. For those who do not, see the section on rating clients.

6. *I can't find good employees.* I admit that this is a tough one. Finding people who can survive in the world of small business is tough, much less finding those who will prosper. In interviewing employees, I use the acronym EARRS to remember the primary traits I am looking for.

(a) *E is for Enthusiasm.* Prospective employees must have enthusiasm. It must be evident in their smile, walk, and talk.

(b) *A is for Attitude.* Applicants must answer questions with the right attitude. The attitude must be one of willingness to learn and to cooperate. They must understand the necessity to sacrifice in order to gain. They should have goals that they can recite back to you. They should know that a price may have to be paid in terms of hard work and some personal sacrifice in order to attain those goals. Are they willing to pay the price to get what they want? They should know that forty hours per week is for sustenance; over forty is for success.

(c) *R is for Resourcefulness.* I find this quality lacking in a lot of good candidates. It is the ability to reach out of their comfort zone and to gather together all the resources at their disposal to finish a project, even if it is unfamiliar to them. I like associates who are not afraid to ask dumb questions of anyone who might have information available needed to get the project finished. They will look in files, search through computer information, make phone calls, etc. to learn everything there is to know about the project and how to complete it. The next time it is assigned, they will know how to do it better than you do. Employees who rely on you for specific instructions as to where to find all the information they need, who to call, and what to say, will not remember as well the next time the project comes up. Clear instructions are very good, but small businesses often cannot function the way large businesses can. Entrepreneurs often are not prone to give detailed instructions; they expect employees to be resourceful. That may be wrong, but that is the way the world really is.

(d) *R is for Responsibility.* Most employees are taught in college, high school, and in seminars to avoid accepting responsibility for what happens to them. They are taught to place blame on other people and events. Not enough training, unclear instructions, long hours, etc. are the reasons for poor performance. Find employees who take responsibility for everything that happens to them. They cannot control all events, but they can control their reactions to them. Most can find the source of their problems by looking in the mirror. The same goes for us entrepreneurs.

(e) *S is for Skills.* Even if the EARR is present, you may not be able to hire an applicant if they need specialized training to handle the job that you have open. If computer skills are not there and are required, then keep interviewing until you get them.

RATING CLIENTS

Rating clients becomes important if you are going to add both new products and services. Many CPAs talk about "firing" their clients, but that is not necessary. Set up a rating system and then follow a set procedure such as the following:

1. *Clients who are slow to pay.* Follow a simple rule. Do not get in any deeper. Before you do any more work, require a reduction of the prior balance and payment in advance for the work you are about to perform. Estimate the fee on the high side. Delegate all work done for this client to staff. You cannot afford to work for this client.

2. *Clients who do not pay at all.* They *usually* will not be back. If they come back, require payment in advance and a full payment of old balances. Delegate future work.

3. *Clients who complain about fees regularly.* This is a perfect reason to delegate their work. The only alternatives are to raise their fees until they leave.

4. *Clients who do not follow rules, observe appointments, procrastinate, and do not follow your advice.* Raise their fees. Delegate their work.

A, B, C Client Ratings

After you have identified all of the above client types and acted accordingly, go through your entire client list and rate your clients as A, B, or C in overall importance to your firm. You need to do whatever it takes to please your A clients as long as you can ethically do it and it is profitable. B clients should be delegated to your highest level staff. You should seldom, if ever, see C clients other than to say hello.

1, 2, 3 Client Ratings

Go through your clients and rate them again as to their viability as financial planning prospects. *Caution*—most CPAs do this and identify only about 5 percent of their clients as financial planning prospects. 85 percent should be a more realistic number of prospects—expect approximately 30 percent to be 1s, 40 percent to be 2s, and 15 percent to be 3s. Since you have a close relationship with your clients, you should be able to go through the entire rating process in only about 30 minutes for each 100 clients. A lot of CPAs complain that their clients have no money. If that is true, which it is not, then you have been doing a poor job of advising them. Is this a temporary condition or a permanent one? If they do not want it to be a permanent one, then they need your help. Many CPAs also complain that they ask their clients if they need financial planning assistance only to be turned down. Do not give up. Approach your inquiry into financial planning matters with the same professionalism that you do in gathering tax data.

After you have finished rating your clients, complete a cover sheet for their tax file. Alert your staff that you want to:

1. Do post-tax interviews with all of the As and 1s. You may have to do pre-interviews with the As also.

2. From the B list, delegate tax return preparation including the pre-inter-

view on at least 80 percent. Try to post-interview at least 80 percent. This may not be the same 80 percent, though. You should interview all the 1s, 80 percent of 2s, and 35 percent of the 3s.

3. Neither interview nor prepare any returns from the C list. Post-interview 100 percent of the 1s, at least 50 percent of the 2s, and 20 percent of the 3s.

I caution you again to be careful when discounting someone as not being a financial planning prospect. Almost everyone is, should be, someday will be, or has a friend or relative who they can refer. How many people do you know who:

1. Could not reduce taxes by making some move or another with investments?
2. Do not need to retire earlier or wealthier than they would without your help?
3. Could not use assistance in setting up an education fund for a grandchild or child?
4. Do not have an estate tax problem?
5. Have the wrong kind or amount of insurance?
6. Have all their investments in too few or too many places?
7. Do not have or need an emergency fund?
8. Own a business but do not need help in setting up a retirement plan or transferring to heirs, or selling?
9. Have their wills, powers of attorney, and estate plans completely in order?

If you have more than 5 percent of your clients who meet all of these criteria, then you may be able to assist those 5 percent with investing one day. It is worth it to let them know you are in the business if they ever need you. Compliment them on a job well done, and ask for referrals of folks not as fortunate or astute as they are.

Remember: Every one of your clients is a prospect for business or a referral. Let them all know that you are in the business.

USING ASSISTANTS IN YOUR PRACTICE TO HELP SELL SERVICES

Involve your assistants and staff in all phases of your financial planning practice from the first day. If it is too late for you to follow that advice, start involving them tomorrow. Except for the most efficient in time management, staff involvement is critical to the enjoyment of the profession as well as its success. The following tasks can be delegated to your assistants thereby freeing up your time.

Greeting Clients and Answering Calls.   Get your clients involved with your staff from the first day. Introduce them and teach both the client and your staff what type of problems they can handle without bothering you.

Setting Appointments.   I hate setting appointments, therefore, I am not very good at it. So why should I do it? The nice thing about having a CPA practice is that you are not cold calling. Your receptionist can set all appointments with your clients.

Handling Introductory Interviews.   An introductory interview is the interview that takes place when a new client walks in off the street or a client comes in with his data but does not need to see a tax preparer. It consists of checking to see if he brought the prior year's returns, filled out his organizer, has all W-2s, etc. If the client is missing material, a lot of time can be saved by rescheduling the appointment once he retrieves all the necessary paperwork. It is better to have the receptionist's time wasted. (Of course, try to bill for it if you can.)

Asking a Few Key Questions About Financial Planning.   When a client comes in with her tax return data, have someone hand her a sheet containing questions about her financial goals. The staff member should tell her about your full service financial planning available at no cost. Do not ask for an appointment, just present it as a service that will be provided. After all, who would turn down a half hour of free time with a CPA? If a client does proactively say she does not want the service, then do not waste your time. For the wise clients who do not turn down the freebie, you will gain key information about her goals to discuss when you do the post-interview. At worst, the client will not be able to give your staff the information and does not bring it back. At least, she will have had the chance to look at it and think about it. She will not be surprised when you hit her with the question about her goals again.

Gathering Data.   Gathering data in order to do a small or large financial plan can be excruciating for a CPA who is used to having his clients trained to bring in data in a certain way. It can also be excruciating for the client. He is embarrassed when he does not know what his goals are, what his risk tolerance is, and where his assets are located. He would rather be embarrassed in front of a nice staff person than you.

Preparing Applications.   Get your assistant licensed or at least fingerprinted so that she can work on applications. After you have mastered the art of application completion, delegate it. Your assistant should have them ready when the client comes in. You can review them before or after the client signs, or both. You can then move on to the next sale. Remember, you are best at making the sale. Spend your time doing just that.

Taking the Money.   Separate yourself from the money. Let an assistant take it. Do not get involved in the questions of ''who should I make this check to'' or writing the check yourself. It is too easy to sign your client's only check by mistake, delay, and possibly kill the sale. Other reasons for not handling money include:

1. When you remove the client to another part of the office from where the sale is completed and go on to another client, the client considers the transaction completed. It is much less likely that he/she will back out before you get the paperwork done.
2. Your client will vent all his anxieties with your assistant. After the emotion of making a buying decision with you, he will have plenty of time to justify it with logic with a well-trained assistant to assure him. This also saves a lot of buyers' remorse calls after you get home at night.

3. Risks can be explained again to your client in a nonthreatening environment. Your assistant should be provided with a standard form to complete for each transaction to ensure that the client clearly understands the risks you explained to her during the sales process. If the investment is going to make the client uncomfortable, it is better to find it out now than later. Also, your client will appreciate your openness and frankness in discussing these issues to insure that she is fully informed.

4. A relationship is established between your assistant and your client on this transaction. Guess who will get the call when the client's name is spelled wrong or a social security number is input incorrectly? You do not want or need those types of calls.

5. Your assistant will establish an all-important network of people in back offices that can get your clients' problems solved quickly in your absence.

Affording Opportunities for Growth.   One of the primary reasons for turnover in small CPA firms is the lack of opportunity for growth. Using an assistant for these duties will offer that opportunity.

Training.   Assistants should be offered training from yourself and outside sources as well. Take them with you to conferences. Send them to seminars and workshops.

PART **II**

Selling—Marketing Financial Planning Services and Products

4

Generating Sales Using TOPS

"Act boldly, and unseen forces will come to your aid"

The acronym TOPS stands for Trust, Opportunity, Pain, and Solution. These make up the sequential steps that can make CPAs successful in providing positive financial services to their clients. The methods we will discuss in the following pages are similar to a lot of sales training programs, but they are also different. CPAs are not considered great salesmen. Therefore, any marketing plan must begin with an examination of the reasons behind this problem.

WHY CPAs DO NOT SELL FINANCIAL PLANNING SERVICES

Most of the articles written today about CPAs entering financial planning say that we will never be a force in this field because we cannot sell. They say that we cannot develop the kind of relationships required to get a client to do something he does not have to do due to some law or regulation.

There is a lot of support for this argument. Only a small percentage of the CPAs who belong to the AICPA's PFP division actually *practice* personal financial planning. CPAs are showing a definite desire to become more professional and knowledgeable, though. Large numbers are going after the designations offered through the AICPA and the College for Financial Planning. If so many are getting the credentials, why are so few actually practicing? We can throw in the usual excuses of time constraints, liability, etc. but those just do not wash. The CPAs knew about those when they started getting the additional education. They clearly have seen the need to add financial planning to their practices because of their own needs of professional growth and because their clients are asking for it. Why then, do they not *do it*?

Much as I hate to agree with the "experts" on this issue, I think that sales reluctance is the primary culprit. That is the limit to my agreement with these pundits, however. They think that we can never overcome our natural tendency away from sales. I disagree.

In most cases, we do not like to be sold. We are uncomfortable in a sales situation when we are the buyer. We detest high pressure sales, in particular. We bristle when we are asked redundant questions like "If I could show you a way to double your income in 30 days with no effort or expense on your part, would you be interested?" Our left brains start churning and we think, "Of course, anyone would be interested. But if that were possible, you would be doing it yourself instead of selling to me; or whatever you are doing is probably illegal or unethical; or you are lying.'' We do not like to be asked what color we want or how we want to take delivery *before* we have decided to buy. Our images of salesmen are tainted by memories of such experiences.

CPAs have had to sell their services from a completely different perspective. The standard response should be ''CPAs can sell—they have been selling themselves for years.'' That's true, but the perspective from which we sold seems different than selling financial services and products. Why?

1. Our clients had to have our standard services. There was not a question as to whether or not they would buy, just from whom they were going to buy. They do not need financial planning and investment products.

2. The services we sold were largely ''negative.'' We found comfort in the ''us against them'' position as defenders of our clients from the IRS or other regulatory authorities. Investments and financial planning is a positive service. It is an approach from the other side of our emotions. We no longer have a common enemy. In fact, we may perceive the enemy to be ourselves if we do not do everything just right.

3. For the most part, our regular services could only be provided by us or another professional like us. We knew who our competitors were and how we compared to them. With financial products, there is a new level of competition where we are not totally convinced of our superiority.

4. The complexity of tax law and accounting rules kept our clients at ''a comfortable distance.'' We were comfortable in knowing that they did not know what we were doing. With investments, the client gets right in the middle of our business. It is much more personal and pushes us out of our comfort zone.

5. Because of our preconceived stereotypes of salesmen, we have a distorted view of how our clients will perceive us if we actually start offering positive services and the products that go with them.

Sounds like I am reinforcing the argument that CPAs will never sell. Far from it! The first step in overcoming your resistance to selling is to admit that there is a problem, identify its cause, and then find a way to solve it. That is where TOPS comes in.

WHAT IS TOPS?

Most sales courses and books today focus on closing techniques and prospecting. When I read and attended these, I came away with ideas that I tried to put into practical use. However, I could never bring myself to ask a redundant question or use any of the standard closing techniques. I did not like to have these used on myself, so why should I use them on my clients? I did not have an *ethical* problem with using them because I felt that my clients needed to take the steps I was recommending. I had a *comfort* problem with it. I just could not do it. So I started using approaches that seemed comfortable to me. That is where TOPS figured into my sales presentation.

Step #1. Gaining Your Client's *Trust*

People will not buy from someone they do not trust. Fortunately for us CPAs, our clients already trust us. However, they may need a little reassurance in order to trust us all over again in our new roles. In regular sales training, you would be told to spend a good deal of time perusing the client's office looking for things he might be interested in such as sports, family, awards, etc. But this will not work in your situation. You will be seeing most of your clients in your office.

Since you already know a good deal of information about your clients, you need not spend a great deal of time on typical trust type questions. For the CPA, these are just preliminaries. A typical trust question might be, "I noticed from your tax return that your income was up last year. Congratulations! How did you accomplish that?" This (a) tells the client that you are interested enough to notice; (b) reminds him that you are his tax advisor and that you understand his financial situation; and (c) makes him feel good. Another even lighter question to remind him of your close relationship could be, "I noticed that Jane [his wife] went to work at the University last year. How does she like it?" Another tougher question might be, "When do you plan on retiring?" This is also a good time to ask typical tax planning questions. It solidifies the client's trust and you are comfortable with them. But remember to listen to the answers!

This trust session primarily should be to gather data and to get relaxed. Ideally, you should have already obtained one or more of these tools to help you. These include:

1. A preliminary questionnaire indicating the areas in which the client needs.
2. A goals sheet completed by the client.
3. The client's tax return.
4. A completed financial plan.

You could make it through the interview without these tools, but they will make your chances of success much greater.

Another important point is not to linger too long on this section of the sales presentation. If the interview takes too long, your client will do one of two things:

1. If he is busy, he will get fidgety and cut short the more important steps.
2. He will get comfortable and start telling you stories so long that you will not ever get to Steps 2, 3, or 4.

For a long-term client who you have a great relationship with, spend only two minutes on trust questions. For others, you might want to ask as many as three questions to ease any tension that might be present.

Step #2. Take Advantage of the *Opportunity*

The questions you asked in Step #1 point out problems. The client has to be made aware of any problems he has. If he does not have any financial problems, then you should be talking to another client. A typical question might be: "Bob, your income last year put you in the top 10 percent of Americans in terms of earnings last year. However, I also noticed that you don't have much saved. How much is your retirement plan at work going to provide when you retire?" Then, *listen!*

You should already know the answer to this question. The typical retirement plan is going to pay in a range of 20 to 60 percent of current salary. Most fall in the lower range. You have now pointed out a problem. However, your client may still consider it to be *your* problem, not his. After all, he did not have it when he came in your office.

If your clients do not have any money, do you not feel somewhat responsible? Who is their primary financial advisor, after all? If your client gives you this excuse, then I see a minimum of three opportunities.

1. Client needs an emergency fund—Start a bank draft.
2. Client needs a goals funds—Start a bank draft.
3. Client may need health, life, or disability insurance. He certainly cannot afford any uninsured losses.

Step #3. Inflict Some *Pain*

You must now personalize the problem by making your client uncomfortable. Do not worry, it is for his own good. Ask, ''Bob, from what you tell me, your income could drop from $175,000 to $50,000 when you retire. Since you don't have much in the way of investments to add to your income, are you prepared for a 70 percent drop in your standard of living?'' Now, *listen!*

If this does not phase him, ask him another pain type of question. ''Yes, I understand that your mortgage will be paid off by the time you retire, but what do you think will happen to maintenance, insurance, and taxes during the next 10 years?'' Again, *listen!* ''That brings up the subject of inflation. What do you think the inflation rate will be for the next 10 years?'' *Listen!*

Pull your financial calculator out and calculate what his equivalent earnings will be 10 years into retirement. ''If inflation does run at 4 percent during those 10 years, the value of your $50,000 will have decreased to $33,778. Do you feel comfortable with that type of income?'' *Listen!*

If he is not bleeding all over the floor by now, ask him some specific lifestyle questions such as: ''I see you on the golf course a lot and I know that you love to travel. I also know that you enjoy driving a nice new Cadillac. I think that it is wonderful that we get to enjoy the fruits of our labors. As your financial advisor and friend, I see it as my obligation to do everything possible to help you to continue to enjoy what you have worked so hard for. But will you be able to keep up the membership in the club, drive Cadillacs, and travel on this fixed income? Which items are not all that important to you?'' *Listen!*

Step #4. Propose a Solution

You have now:

1. Reinforced the trusting relationship that you enjoy with your client.
2. Pointed out a problem that he may have only been vaguely aware of or chose to ignore.
3. Personalized the problem by making the client feel pain. He knows what may happen to him if he does not fix the problem. He should now recognize that it is *his* problem, not yours.

It is now time for the knight in shining armor to arrive. You will ask some solution or comfort questions such as: ''How important is it to you to maintain or even improve your current lifestyle when you retire?'' *Listen!* ''Would you feel more secure about your future if you knew that you were going to be able to protect yourself against inflation?'' *Listen!* ''If there were a way to do this without severely affecting your current lifestyle, how important would that be to you?''

By this time, your client should be giving you the benefits he wants from retirement. Most clients will throw you at least one curve ball. A typical curve ball is: "I know I've got a problem, but my mortgage is so high because I do want it paid off when I retire. I also have two kids in college who are draining me. There is just not enough to go around." Do not let him get away with this excuse. You just change tactics and say: "If I could show you a couple of adjustments you could make in your lifestyle that could possibly free up the funds you need to protect yourself from that 70 percent drop in living standard, how important would that be to you?" You have again reminded him of the pain and positioned yourself as the solution.

It is now time for the *close*, but let us not use that word. It builds a wall in your mind. Your client should already have his mind made up. All you have to do is present the solution. "Bob, as I see it, you could build a retirement fund of approximately $350,000 by investing only $2000 per month in a couple of quality mutual funds. I don't know what the rate of return will be in the next 10 years, but I have used an assumed rate of 8 percent in my calculations. Although that $350,000 will not make up the shortfall in your retirement income completely, it may put you back on the golf course and throw in a little travel. The longer you wait, the more per month is going to be required, so I suggest that you start with the program today. I can get the paperwork done before you leave. How does that sound?" *Listen!* It is critical that you do not speak before the client does at this time. Let him answer.

The client should be ready for you to call in your assistant now. The assistant should take the client to another office to complete the applications. Notice that *no product* has been mentioned yet. When the paperwork is finished, your assistant will go over the product in detail with the client. You will step in at the very end and make sure that the client fully understands the product. Most clients are not product oriented; they buy on emotion. The visit with your assistant as the paperwork is being completed will give him plenty of time to justify his decision using logic. If he wants to discuss product more, by all means do so. Just never let the product be the main element of the sale. The client's need or problem, his pain, and your comforting solution are the driving points of the sale. If you *live* by selling product and performance, you will also *die* on product and performance.

Too easy, you say? Maybe, but this is the way that 80 percent of your interviews will go. It works if you believe in yourself and in what you are doing for your client. That belief will shine through any mistakes you make in presentation or objections your client may have.

SUMMARY OF TOPS QUESTIONS

Trust

Use these questions to get relaxed and establish rapport. Use light questions about personal situations and other questions to casually ask about goals. This is to cement your trusting relationship with your client and help him to start seeing you as more than a tax advisor.

Opportunity

Use opportunity questions to point out problems that the client has in reaching his financial goals, reducing taxes, etc. You are going to try to get him to think more clearly about his financial goals. Oftentimes, this may be the only time he has ever given clear thought to where he wants to go financially. Most people go through life aimlessly without goals. Your job during the opportunity questioning is to ask questions that will get the client to open up to you and to see some problems that he may have. A good questioning technique in this step is to repeat the client's statements back to him. Use phrases such as, ''In other words, you want to retire early enough to enjoy some travel while your health is good.''

Pain

This is where you must make the client uncomfortable. Do not worry; it will be good for him. When you point out the problems with questions, they are still your problems, not his. When you personalize them by naming names and giving amounts, they become his problems. Use a lot of visual imagery such as a picture of the first child going off to the wrong college, or going to work flipping burgers instead of going to college.

Solution

Now you can be the hero. Position yourself as the solution. Questions are not as important in this segment as solutions. This is where you make the sale. Your client should be feeling the problems emotionally, so he wants to get rid of the pain and find comfort. Give him the solution. Then be quiet and listen!

OTHER TOPS TIPS

KISS

Genius has been defined as the ability to reduce the complex to the simple. Do not use industry buzz words. They just cause your client pain and you are the source of the pain, not the solution. Do not be afraid to present seventh grade solutions to a Ph.D. He may know a lot about his field, but he may know nothing about yours. If he is very astute, you will pick it up very early in the conversation and can adjust accordingly. Use the KISS theory—Keep It Simple Stupid!

Use Stories and Anecdotes

Particularly during the pain questions, throw in a story or two about cases you know about or have read about where a client had a similar problem but failed to solve it. Then throw in where you helped the client to solve it. Of course, you cannot divulge client information, so you can use stories you have heard from other colleagues, read about, etc. I have even used composite stories of various clients to emphasize my point. If a client has given me permission, I may even use names to emphasize success in the solution questioning phrase.

Try on Your Client's Shoes

Take note of everything about your client. Is he or she a slow talker, nervous, high strung, laid back, etc.? What does her risk profile say? Try to get inside her head and think like she does. If you were her, would this seem like a good deal? What would bother you about it? What would you want your financial advisor to say or do? Could you make a decision based on the facts given?

Tell Them What To Do

Do not go overboard on the questioning, especially in the solution stage. Many sales trainers will tell you to always ask open-ended questions so that the client will give you feedback. However, there is a time to get some yes or no answers. That time is in the solution step. If you keep asking open-ended questions, both you and the client will tire of them. Most of my clients want me to tell them what to do. After all, you have positioned yourself as the trusted financial advisor. Now act like it.

Of course, not every interview will go smoothly. Some clients will reject your advice for numerous reasons. Here are a few of the most *common* objections:

Do You Not Have a Conflict of Interest When You Sell a Commission-Based Product?   Yes. Almost every delivery of a service has a built-in conflict of interest. Consider the thousands of lawsuits that should not have been filed. How about the tonsillectomies, mastectomies, and ear tube operations that were unnecessary? From auto mechanics to audits, conflicts of interest are present. The question becomes one of integrity. As a financial advisor, you want to build a long-term relationship with your clients. Putting them in the wrong product because it pays a fee will work in the short term, but not in the long term. You must be someone they can trust and who has integrity. If they do not trust you, then they will not want to be your client.

Would Not the Conflict of Interest be Solved by a Fee-Only Planner?   Perhaps. There are many fine fee-only planners. However, there are many fine products with loads out there that a fee-only planner may not be able to offer without doing a rather delicate dance around offsetting fees with commissions. Also, does a fee-only planner not trust his own integrity enough to deal with the conflict of interest issue? I do not have a problem with it, because I never select a product based on a commission. I select it based on my clients' needs. Finally, is there a conflict when a planner increases his fee without increasing his work?

I Want to Think it Over.   When this happens, one of two things has taken place:

1. You have not reached the decision maker.
2. You did not make the pain severe enough.

If someone wants to think it over, do not try to talk them out of it. Although you wish they would make the decision then and there, you must appreciate their desire to "sleep on it." Here are four possible solutions:

Solution 1—"I understand. This is a big step. Before you leave to make your decision, would you let me make some final notes to be sure that I will have everything ready when you give me your decision." At this point, go back over your pain pointers to be sure that the client leaves feeling uncomfortable.

Solution 2—"No problem. We would not hold you to any decision made today, anyway. We always like to give our clients at least 24 hours to think about it. Since the plan is fresh in our minds now, however, would you mind going over the paperwork with my assistant so that we do not have to reinvent the wheel? You may even want to sign everything today under the condition that no action will take place until you give us the complete go-ahead."

Solution 3—"That is perfectly understandable. Is there any particular concern that you would like me to go over before you leave? If there is a question later, please give me a call. Please bear in mind that some of the numbers and facts used in our projections are based on today's market conditions and that those can change rather quickly."

Solution 4—"Certainly. Could I just ask one favor? We think we have arrived at a solution that is as close to perfect as we can get for your needs. If you decide not to implement, would you give me a call and let me know what you didn't like?"

HOW TO SELL WHEN YOUR CLIENT INSISTS ON TALKING PRODUCT

Most CPAs who get into this profession are sucked immediately into the product pit. There will be more about products later in this book. For now, select no more than two or three mutual fund families and insurance companies and concentrate your business. You will do yourself, the product sponsors, and your clients a favor.

When you client wants to talk product, let him. By this I mean let *him* do most of the talking. If he asks you a question, feed him back a question such as, "Why is that important to you?" Rephrase his questions and statements and feed them back to him. Let him know early on that you are not trying to locate the world's greatest product because that is a foolish quest. Sooner or later, if you keep quiet, he will have to show that he does not know much about product. If he does, then you do not want to argue with him.

When he settles down, attempt to describe the *perfect investment*. State that the advantages of the perfect investment is that it:

1. Has a high yield and rate of return.
2. Has tax benefits.
3. Has no commission.
4. Has complete liquidity.
5. Has no risk.

Then inform him that the perfect investment obviously does not exist. Ask him which of these advantages is most important to him and proceed from there.

CLOSING TECHNIQUES

Selling is not selling, it is asking! Never mind the future close, the Ben Franklin close, the puppy close, the small matter close, the balancing close, the authority close, the positive alternative, the sense of loss, etc. Use TOPS. Ask TOPS questions in the right places. Listen to the answers and take notes. When you have let your client get into an emotional state of pain, you simply take him to a point of comfort and pleasure by solving the problems and taking away the pain. In this phase, you simply say things like, ''Does this solution seem sensible to you? If it does, I do not think we should delay any longer. We would like to prepare the paperwork today. My assistant needs to go over the details with you now.'' Call in your assistant and congratulate the client on going forward. Then be quiet! Do not keep selling pain. You will talk yourself out of the sale.

5

Designing a Marketing Plan—Finding Your Niche

"People with goals succeed because they know where they're going."

Earl Nightingale

"Finding your niche" sounds better than "designing a marketing plan" does it not? That is because the words "planning" and "marketing" usually have negative connotations. They translate into words and phrases from the academic world and huge corporations, where marketing plans are prepared by folks who never implement them. But think of a marketing plan as a tool that can *save you work* and *make you money*. Suddenly it becomes a working tool rather than just a huge report slightly above the rank of a policy and procedure manual. Also, the term "marketing" is broad—what is the difference between selling and marketing? *Selling* is getting a client to buy a product or service, while *marketing* is finding a client to whom you can sell.

Begin your marketing plan with a few basic steps:

1. Decide that a marketing plan is not a dust gathering document, but a useful tool that will save you time and work, reduce your stress, and make you money by allowing you to serve more people.
2. Set aside at least one day, preferably two, when you will work away from the office to prepare the plan.
3. Set up a folder titled "Marketing Plan."
4. Write down all the topics and ideas that start coming to mind *when* they enter your conscious mind. These are messages from your subconscious. Take them seriously. Stuff the notes into your folder.
5. On the scheduled planning days, prepare a rough outline of your plan. Figure 5-1 shows a sample list of opportunities.

Figure 5-1 is not meant to be a complete list—there are dozens (probably hundreds) of marketing opportunities not included. You may want to concentrate on only one or two or attack most of them due to the nature of your clientele. Specialization probably is more efficient and profitable if it works, but specialization cannot work in a very small market. Try to practice holistic financial planning. It is better to have a working knowledge of all areas of the financial and estate planning spectrum.

Figure 5-1 Master List of Major Marketing Opportunities

1. Retirement Plans and Planning:
   (a) 403(b)/ORP tax-sheltered accounts for employees of tax-exempt organizations who qualify under IRC 501(c)(3) (primarily schools and colleges).
   (b) 457 plans for tax-exempt organizations that are not 501(c)(3)—primarily cities and counties.
   (c) 401(k), and other qualified plans for non-tax-exempt organizations.
   (d) Non-qualified plans and private pensions.
   (e) IRAs.
   (f) SEP and Sar-Sep.
   (g) Planning for early retirement, lump sum distributions, etc.
2. Payroll Deduction Group Sales:
   (a) Savings by payroll deduction.
   (b) Group health and disability.
   (c) Group life.
3. Business Continuation Planning:
   (a) Buy/sell agreements.
   (b) ESOPS.
   (c) Business interruption and disability insurance.
   (d) Business valuation for estate planning and business succession.
4. Cafeteria Plans:
5. Traditional Insurance:
   (a) Life insurance marketing to individuals.
   (b) Disability insurance for individuals.
   (c) Insurance in business:
       I. Split dollar.
       II. Executive bonus.
       III. Non-qualified retirement plans.
   (d) Health insurance:
       I. Individual health.
       II. Medicare supplement.
   (e) Long-term care insurance.
6. Estate Planning:
   (a) Wills, powers of attorney, living wills, living trusts, credit shelter trusts, life insurance trusts, etc.
   (b) First to die, second to die, survivorship life insurance.
   (c) Charitable giving.
7. Insurance as an Investment:
   (a) Annuities:
       I. Fixed.
       II. Variable.
   (b) Variable life.
   (c) Universal life.
8. Financial Planning from the Tax Return:
   (a) Post-tax interviews.
   (b) Plans from the tax return.
   (c) Off-season interviews.
9. Selling Financial Products through Banks:
10. Financial Counseling and Training Through Businesses.
    (a) Fee based workshops.
    (b) Executive financial plans.
11. Education Funding.
12. Planning for the Elderly.
13. Other Investment Products Marketing.
    (a) Mutual funds.
    (b) Unit investment trusts.
    (c) Individual securities.
    (d) Others.

CHOOSING YOUR PRIMARY TARGET AREAS

So how do you choose what areas in which to concentrate? Begin by setting up a rating system:

1. Rate each category that appeals to you on a scale of 1 to 10. *Appeal* refers to level of interest and excitement about the possibilities.
2. Rate each category where you have existing knowledge and experience on a scale of 1 to 10.
3. Rate each category as to the level of need that your present clients have for the service on a scale of 1 to 7.
4. Rate each category as to the level of need in your marketing area for the level of service on a scale of 1 to 5.

Total the score for each category. Concentrate your efforts based on the total scores. For example, the highest score possible for a category would be a 32. If something scores a 25 or better, it is time to get on with the plan.

DEVELOPING AN ACTION PLAN

After selecting the areas where you wish to concentrate your efforts, you must first develop specific action steps to implement your plan. (See Figure 5-2.) Next, define your target market (who needs this type of service?) Use the rules of goal setting and time management including delegation. Although a marketing plan should be developed even when you are alone, it is a much more effective tool when the responsibility is shared with staff who share your goals.

SUMMARY OF THE STEPS INVOLVED IN DEVELOPING A MARKETING PLAN

1. Develop a master list of marketing opportunities.
2. Rate each opportunity using the criteria provided.
3. Discuss the various categories listed with staff members, mentors, or others who may be able to provide guidance.
4. Set up a goals, responsibility, and an action plan for each marketing opportunity.
   (a) Decide who your target market is.
   (b) Set your goals (the revenue you want to achieve for each target market, for example) with due dates.
   (c) List the action steps necessary to reach your goals with due dates for each step.
   (d) Assign responsibility for each marketing opportunity and for each step.
   (e) Input each major marketing opportunity as a project and each task under that project into your time management system.

What happens to the other marketing opportunities that did not make the favorite list? Keep them as part of your marketing plan—it serves to sharpen your

Figure 5-2   Sample Action Plan for a Marketing Opportunity

Current Update _____ 1993

Marketing Opportunity _____

Target Markets:

_____

_____

_____

Goals: 1. _____   Due Date _____

2. _____   Due Date _____

3. _____   Due Date _____

Steps necessary to achieve goals (arrange as close to sequential order as possible, although many steps may be going on simultaneously). Do not be afraid to go into detail, making the steps smaller bits of a larger project.

1. _____   Due Date _____   Proj. Assigned _____

2. _____   Due Date _____   Proj. Assigned _____

3. _____   Due Date _____   Proj. Assigned _____

awareness of these opportunities. Also, list some activities that let you "test the water" for these areas to see if they deserve more of your attention. See Figure 5-3 for a sample marketing plan.

IMPLEMENTING A MARKETING PLAN

At this point, the hardest part of your work is over. If you have devoted the time and creative thought to determine what niche you are going to go after, what goals you hope to achieve, and what steps are necessary to meet these goals, then all you have to do now is to follow these steps. You should "own" the plan. You should believe in it. The project and task management system will remind you if you meet or miss deadlines, but belief is what will make the plan work. Just follow these simple steps:

1. *Own* the plan: Believe in it!
2. Be sure that each opportunity is input to your time management system as a project.
3. Input each task with due dates under its project.
4. Meet monthly at first to discuss and update the plan—no less than quarterly thereafter. This should be on everyone's calendar and should be assigned as a task with due dates.

Figure 5-3   Sample Marketing Plan for the 1990s

Current update *May 1994*
Major Marketing Category *403(b) and ORP*

Primary Responsibility   *Leslie C. Killgore*
Secondary Responsibility   *Mary Lambert*

Goals   1. *Increase 403(b) clients by 25*   Date *12/31/95*
            (incr. sales by $5000/mo and comm by $225/mo)

          2. *Increase ORP clients by 10*   Date *12/31/95*
            (incr. sales by $7500/mo and comm by $300/mo)

          3. *Add 6 new schools to current active list*   Date *12/31/95*

          4. *Get total monthly sales to $75,000 per Month*

Target Market: Faculty and staff to public and private schools in northeast Texas area within 100 miles radius of our office.

Steps Necessary to Achieve These Goals

1. Send letters to all current 403(b) and ORP clients advising of current balance, projection in 20 years, new products and ask to increase. Also ask for referrals on P.S. Mary and LK—due 6/30/94.

2. Prepare referral letters for presentation when we increase—7/1/94.

3. Host a brunch/workshop at _____ office for teachers at _____, _____, _____, _____, and _____. Projects:

    Obtain lists of teachers from Superintendents—LK—6/15/94.
    Send out flyer/invitation—MCC—7/5/94.
    Hold workshop 7/30/94.

4. Contact TSTA groups by mail for programs in school in fall or spring of next year—Mary—due 6/15/94.

5. Schedule appts with Jr. Colleges in area, including _____, _____, _____, _____, and _____—LK—due 7/15/94.

6. Call _____ to see if he can get us in Schools. Get names of persons to see in each location—LK 9/1/94.

7. Follow up 8/15/94 for new personnel at _____—LK due 8/15/94.

8. Get list of all people retiring at _____. Send letter offering free financial consultation.

9. Schedule visit for one faculty/week about conversion to _____.

---

5. Revise the plan as necessary and no less often than semi-annually.
6. Reward yourself and staff when goals are met and tasks are completed.

Remember that *activity* (doing the tasks) *will* lead to meeting the goals!

THE TOOLS OF A MARKETING PLAN

One of the many advantages of developing a marketing plan and assigning responsibility for completion of its tasks is the development of expertise within your staff. Add a *responsibility chart*. You'll find that as you begin to implement your action steps, the steps will generate a lot of business. Your emphasis will change from marketing to selling and servicing. Assign responsibility for various "tools" that are used in the different aspects of the marketing program. For example, the person implementing a 403(b) sale might uncover a need for a complete financial plan that is beyond the scope of his abilities. The natural inclination is to overlook that opportunity. In order to prevent this, assign responsibility for various areas of expertise or tools. If a prospect needs a complete financial plan, consult your responsibility chart and find the person who has primary responsibility for developing financial plans. Do not discard this step because it sounds like I am talking about a big staff. It is especially useful with a staff of 14 or so, however, it is just as valuable with a staff of three. This is a list of some of the tools and areas of expertise to develop.

1. Individual and business financial plans.
2. Prospectuses and product material.
3. Seminars.
4. Portfolio monitor reports (periodic reports to clients on the status of their investments).
5. Newsletter and promotional mailings.
6. Media advertising.
7. Speaking engagements.

Add this list to your marketing plan and assign a person to have primary responsibility for each tool or area of expertise. Develop a "general" marketing category. Use this list for items that do not fit readily into another category or are applied to several categories—things like writing general articles about the firm for the local press, obtaining premium prizes for gifts to clients, etc.

CONCLUSION

Let us review the reasons for doing a marketing plan:

1. *It gives you focus.* With several marketing opportunities available to you and the need to keep several other balls in the air, the natural tendency is to get unfocused. Often, we freeze into a state of inaction because there are just too many things to do. When your attitude improves, you want to get back to work on the opportunities, but you forgot where you left off and you do not know where to start.
2. *It reduces stress.* When your mind cannot recall all the good ideas that you had, when you cannot figure out where you are or who was supposed to do what, you can find relief by knowing that the marketing plan is your road map. Even if you get completely off-track, it can be rebuilt from the rubble.
3. *It saves time.* You do not have to keep reinventing the wheel. You just improve on the wheel already built and keep the wheel rolling.
4. *It allows you to leverage yourself with staff.* The plan is a written guideline for your staff. They know what your goals are, what has to be done to reach the goals, who has to do it, and when it has to be done. You do not have to keep telling them.
5. *It develops expertise within your staff and yourself.* When you decide to focus on certain areas, then you will improve your expertise accordingly.

6

Selling Financial Planning During Tax Season

"I do not think there is any other quality so essential to success of any kind as the quality of perseverance. It overcomes almost anything, even nature."

John D. Rockefeller

Tax season is the busiest time of year for CPAs. It is also the most productive. Most CPAs would never consider pursuing financial planning sales during this hectic time but consider these questions:

1. When do your clients come to see you without your even having to ask them?
2. When will your clients sit still long enough for you to discuss their financial status and plans for the future?
3. When do your clients treat your telephone calls as if they were as important as a call from the President?
4. When is your advice most sought and most revered?
5. When do you get your most inspirational ideas?
6. When is your adrenaline at full throttle, allowing you to put your best foot forward with your clients?
7. When are you and your staff the most efficient, approaching productivity levels at 500 percent above the remainder of the year?

Unless your practice is different from most, you will answer "tax season" to at least five of these questions. Most CPAs are at their best during tax season. Why not use that energy to implement your marketing plan?

SETTING UP A POST-TAX FINANCIAL PLANNING INTERVIEW SYSTEM

In order to implement your marketing plan effectively, you must follow up throughout the year. Begin with the pre-tax season.

Use the Pre-Tax Season to Do Your Legwork

During the off season, have your staff prepare a *Financial Planning Cover Sheet* for each tax client. (See Figure 6-1.) They will complete only the name and whether or not the client is an existing investment client.

During breaks in work or at your leisure, complete the cover sheets using your knowledge about the client. I found that I could complete the forms for 98 percent of my clients without pulling the file. If you have clients who you do not know that well, you may have to have a staff member who knows the client assist you. The cover sheet is used for:

1. Rating the client as to investment or financial planning potential.
2. Rerouting clients who are not profitable, enjoyable, or necessary for you to see in order to prepare the tax return.
3. Providing all staff members including your receptionist with directions as to what is to be done for this client.

FIGURE 6-1.   Financial Planning Cover Sheet for Tax Return

POST INTERVIEW DATE _____

CLIENT _____   EXISTING INVESTMENT CLIENT _____

DATE _____

1. Pre-interview by: Partner _____   Staff _____

2. This client will need:

   A.   _____ No Post Appointment _____ Ask Client _____ Urge Client
   B.   _____ Goals/Investment Philosophy-Temperament (Include Prudent Investor Piece)
   C.   _____ Planning From the Tax Return
               To Be Prepared By   _____ Preparer
                                          _____ Financial Planner-Ptr
                                          _____ Financial Planner Staff

   D.   _____ Data Gathering   FIN. PLNG.   FIN. PLNG.
                                          PREPARER   PTR.   STAFF

        _____ Entire Package   _____   _____   _____
        _____ Financial Data   _____   _____   _____
        _____ Income/Expense   _____   _____   _____
        _____ Policy Listing   _____   _____   _____
        _____ Estate Planning   _____   _____   _____
        _____ Advisor/Document   _____   _____   _____
               Listing

   E.   _____ Social Security Benefit Report or Completed Application
   F.   _____ Investment/Financial Plan Modules
               _____ Basic
               _____ Advanced (Use Check Sheet)
   G.   _____ Client Investment Form
   H.   —Post Interview Form—To Be Prepared By _____ Ptr.
                                                _____ Staff

               Note: Post Interview Package Will Include Each Item Checked Above.
   I.   _____ Other _____
               _____

                              AMM, Inc.

4. Insuring that you are fully prepared before tax season, and before the client's visit to your office with all the necessary information to properly present all the services you have to offer.

Setup line-by-line instructions for the cover sheet as follows:

Line 1: Tells staff who will do the pre-interview.

Line 2: Lists all the information you will need before this client sees you after his return is prepared. This information should list:

(a) *Conduct a post-tax interview or not?* Instructions as to whether a post-tax interview is needed and whether the client should be urged to set up an appointment. I recommend simply setting one up after the return is prepared for all high potential clients. Do not ask before the return is done. Just have your receptionist call and set one up after it is prepared. There are some clients you will not want to see before *or* after the return is prepared except possibly to say hello.

(b) *Discover your clients' goals/investment philosophy and temperament.* These forms should be completed by every client, whether you see them or not. You need this basic information before you can even begin a basic conversation about investments or planning.

(c) *Begin planning from the tax return.* This form is to be completed after the return is prepared. It is designed to allow your staff to identify potential financial planning needs from entries on the tax return. Have your staff highlight high potential items. The cover sheet allows you to give instructions as to whether you are going to complete the form or you want someone else to.

(d) *Start data gathering.* Data gathering packages will be discussed in more detail in the chapter on preparing financial plans. These are usually prepared when you see a definite need for a financial plan to be prepared for the client. If you can catch the client during tax season, it is an excellent time to get as much information as possible.

(e) *Complete a Social Security Benefit Report.* Get your clients to regularly complete the Social Security Benefit Report form. Have a standard cover letter that alerts the clients to the inadequacies of Social Security and positions you as the person who is thinking about their retirement. This letter and the report from Social Security stimulates clients to begin thinking about retirement.

(f) *Setup investment/financial plan modules.* If you are fairly certain that you will be preparing a financial plan for this client, ask your staff to pull the necessary forms in order to do the plan. The basic package includes forms necessary to do a very basic or short plan. If an advanced plan is anticipated, use the module directory to check off the forms you need. This part of the cover sheet is useful because you can work on plans in a variety of locations including a home office and another branch office. When away from available forms, it is very convenient to know that the forms are already with the file. This is also an excellent way for you to save time. You should not be using your time to pull forms.

(g) *Use a Client Investment Performance Report.* For clients who already have funds invested with you, it is wise to have a performance report available on those investments and to be prepared to discuss and reaffirm the quality of the decision that the client made. This can also lead to more sales.

(h) *Complete the Post-Interview Form.* This form is simply a series of TOPS questions to ask the client. Most are pain questions. Use a few points in the tax return or supporting data to reestablish trust and to get the client comfortable with what you are going to talk about. Then ask a few opportunity questions about reducing taxes for next year and problems you have noted from last year. Most of the other questions are pain questions: Personalize the problems found, affirm your good intentions and desire to help as the reasons for causing the pain, then offer a solution. This may just lead into getting the clients permission to help him solve those problems, a completed sale, or permission to proceed with a complete financial plan. *At the very least, it will reposition you as more than just a tax preparer.*

After the cover sheets are checked as required for each client, they are placed on top of the client's tax file. Prior to tax season, you may want to advise your clients of changes you have made in your practice to adjust to changes in tax laws, the economy, and in response to client requests:

(a) Send them a letter with general information about your new services and how they can be beneficial to clients. (See Figure 6-2.)

(b) You may want to consider a video of yourself explaining the changes. It can be played in the reception room for clients while they wait.

(c) Train your staff thoroughly about how to handle the new procedure. A sample of our internal procedure and instructions to your staff is included in the pages that follow.

Implementing this procedure should free up about 60 percent of your time during tax season to do financial planning. Who absorbs that 60 percent? In most cases, it is absorbed by staff who had previously been performing well beneath their capabilities. Most are pleased with the new opportunities for client interaction.

DURING TAX SEASON

When clients come in, your staff should greet them and direct them in accordance with your instructions on the cover sheet and the written procedure. (See Figure 6-3.) Your staff should know the story by heart. Remember that even though *other staff* will be doing the pre-interview, *you* will visit with them after the return is prepared. If you have a video, play it for them. Keep copies of your letter announcing the changes to refresh their memories. (Unnecessary for clients who simply drop off or mail their tax data.)

Ask each client to review and complete the goals sheet and risk profile questionnaires. Have the receptionist perform this task.

FIGURE 6-2.   Sample Letter to Clients about Adding Financial Planning and the Post-Tax Interview.

Dear Client:

We are pleased to announce a series of new services available from our firm, as well as some changes to our prior methods of delivering services. We think you will like the additional services you are going to receive. Don't worry; if you are happy with the way things have been done in the past and don't want any changes, we are flexible enough to continue our services just as before for all clients who request it. We know that most of you will want to take advantage of the changes we have implemented.

We have more computer power in our offices than we could possibly have dreamed of only a few years ago. Combined with tax law changes, sophisticated software and hardware have shifted tax return emphasis away from the interview *prior* to preparing the return to the need for an interview *after* the return is prepared. There is now more need to plan for *next* year and the future than to talk about what happened last year. Accordingly, I will be spending some time with you after your return is prepared this year. There is no extra charge for this service.

Changes in tax laws, an ever-changing global economy, and requests from clients make it necessary for any forward thinking financial services firm to adapt quickly in order to meet client needs. We know that it is no longer adequate to just prepare tax returns. Clients need assistance not only in lowering taxes, but in reaching financial goals of a secure retirement, educating children and grandchildren, and investing wisely.

I am now a Registered Representative of 1st Global Capital Corp. This affiliation allows me to provide the assistance that my clients need and demand. What do we need from you in order to provide these expanded services? A little bit of your time and some information. We look forward to seeing you soon. Please call me if you would like to discuss our new services.

FIGURE 6-3.   Sample Procedure for Financial Planning and Tax Returns

TO: POLICY & PROCEDURE MANUAL

ROUTE TO: ALL STAFF

SUBJECT: FINANCIAL PLANNING & TAX RETURNS

DATE: _____

Our Goals:

1. Obtain basic data gathering packages on each client.
   A. Goals/investment philosophy—temperament
   B. Financial data
   C. Insurance policy listing
2. For high potential clients—all financial data.
3. Put together post interview packages for partners or financial planning staff for each client.
4. Post interview all clients.

(Continued)

FIGURE 6-3. (*Continued*)

Our Tools:

1. Planning from the tax return.
2. Data gathering packages.
3. Asset allocation software.
4. Post-interview questionnaire.
5. Financial/investment planning modules.
6. Social Security benefits report.
7. Investment performance reports.
8. Financial planning software.

TAX DEPARTMENT will produce a list of all tax clients. For each client, a "Financial Planning Cover Sheet" will be forwarded to the partner in charge or a financial planning assistant.

PARTNER OR ASSISTANT will identify items required for each client by checking appropriate boxes.

ALL STAFF WITH CLIENT CONTACT

1. Emphasize the difference between the pre-interview for tax and the planning interview to discuss ways to solve client tax problems and meet client financial needs.
2. Try to set up each client with both pre- and post-appointments.
3. Emphasize the post-(planning) interview only if client wants one.
4. Partner will only do pre-interview *if client insists*.
5. Refer to cover sheet to determine what information is to be gathered for the client.
6. During the pre-interview:
   A. Refer to cover sheet and gather data as required.
   B. Give client letter and request for data to bring to planning meeting.
   C. Ask for assistance from Financial Planning Department if needed.
7. If no pre-interview, make request to client for data to bring to post-interview.
8. After return is prepared:
   A. Complete "Planning From the Tax Return" (Preparer)
   B. Investment Performance Report (Financial Planning Staff) (For Existing Investment Client).
   C. Other items required for post-interview as indicated on cover sheet. NOTE: Some items to be prepared by financial planner will be done during post-interview.
   D. Partner will (A) Use "post-package" and prepare post-interview questionnaire in preparation for meeting with client. (B) Complete Financial Plan if required.

EMPHASIZE

1. That complete financial plans are available free of charge.
2. There is never any cost for the post-interview.
3. The need for *TOTAL* financial planning.

Special handling for existing Personal Financial Planning or Investment clients should be noted on the cover sheet.

_____

Partner Signature

If there is a pre-interview, have the *preparer* gather as much data as possible in accordance with instructions on the cover sheet. You are primarily looking for financial data, goals, and risk tolerance. *Remember*—most of the financial data will be available from the tax return data, so conducting an in-depth interview with the client is not necessary at this stage.

Sample questioning technique: "I see from your 1099 that you had interest income from Bank X. When Jim goes over your return with you later, he will want to know some additional information about your entire financial situation so that he can advise you properly. Could I ask you some more information now about these investments and other matters so that we can have it ready for him to do an in-depth review of your tax return and its relation to your financial goals?"

If there is no pre-interview, the receptionist must be responsible for gathering the basics from the client when he drops it off. If it is mailed in, then the interview can be conducted over the phone.

The important thing is to be sure that as much information as possible is obtained. *This is not an audit. Do not expect to get exact figures.* In many cases, values of client accounts were estimated based on interest income shown on the 1099s. The client will correct you if you use the wrong amounts. That is a good way to get the information you need.

After your staff has prepared the return, it should be returned to you for final review with most of the information requested on the cover sheet. If everything is not there, that is OK. Complete data is not necessary to start the process, just very nice to have.

If a "Financial Planning from the Tax Return" form was completed, your staff has already highlighted the areas to review. (See Figure 6-4.) If not, then this could be a good place to start. I have found that this form and the post-tax interview are excellent ways to review the return for accuracy, completeness, and tax planning. You will uncover many ideas for reducing taxes in future years as well as possible ways to prepare the return differently in order to reduce taxes for this year.

Using the forms, tax return and data gathered by your staff, you can sit down with the return and go over opportunities already evident and discover many more. I have never found a tax return that could not generate at least one opportunity question. Using the post-tax interview as your lead, highlight all of the *trust* (status), *opportunity* (problem), *pain* (personalization of the problems) you can find on the form itself.

After you are satisfied that the return has been completed correctly, have the staff process the return for pick-up by the client. (If you have uncovered opportunities in the return that warrant the preparation of a plan, then you can prepare the plan prior to seeing the client. This could be a mini-plan or a full blown plan. I prepare mostly mini-plans during tax season. If the plan calls for action on investments, I have applications ready for the client's visit.)

After the return is ready for delivery, your receptionist should call the client, advise that his return is ready to be discussed with you and set an appointment to do so.

When the client comes in, have the receptionist present the return and the bill to the client in your normal procedure. Take the client into your office for the post-tax interview. Have a copy of his return ready to go over. I usually have my copy marked in red ink on the lines that I want to emphasize.

Be sure to use TOPS. The post-tax interview is perfect for its application.

FIGURE 6-4.   Financial Planning from the Tax Return

NAME(S) _____ AGE _____ DATE _____
_____ AGE _____
(PLEASE HIGHLIGHT PRIORITY ITEMS)

1040 LINE REFERENCE		(X)	(X)

6c	DEPENDENTS
	1. Clients have pre-college age children
	2. Need Form SS-5 for dependent Social Security #
	   Recommend:
	     A. Adequate Life Insurance
	     B. Adequate Disability
	     C. College Funding Plan		

7	WAGES
	1. Highly Paid? (Above $40,000 Single)
	            (Above $50,000 MFJ)
	   Recommend:
	     A. Salary Deferral Options
	     B. Charitable Giving
	2. Owner or Part Owner of Business?
	   Recommend:
	     A. Salary Reduction Plans—
	        401(k), SAR–SEP
	     B. Key Person Insurance
	     C. Split Dollar
	     D. Disability
	     E. Buy–Sell Agreement
	     F. 80% Dividend Exclusion
	3. Employee of Tax Exempt Organization?
	   Recommend:
	     A. 403(b)
	4. Employee of State or Local Government?
	   Recommend:
	     A. 457		

8a	TAXABLE INTEREST AMOUNT
	Client has CDs
	Client has Individual Bonds
	Client has Mutual Funds
	Client has Low Yielding Bank Savings or MMA
	   Recommend:
	     A. CD Roll Over Program
	     B. CD Rate Finder Service
	     C. Change of Broker/Dealer
	     E. High Yield MMA
	     F. Start Monthly Savings Plan		

FIGURE 6-4. (*Continued*)

1040 LINE REFERENCE		(X)	(X)

	G. If High Tax Bracket:
	   Tax Exempts
	   Tax Deferreds
	Comments _____		

8b	TAX EXEMPT INTEREST AMOUNT
	Taxable Equivalent Yield
	   Recommend:
	   A. UITs, Mutual Funds vs. Individual
	   B. Switch to Taxable if After Tax Return is Higher		

9	DIVIDEND INCOME
	   Recommend:
	   A. Value Line Analysis
	   B. Discount Brokerage
	   C. Diversification Plan
	   D. Mutual Funds
	   E. Higher Income Investments		

12, 18, 19	BUSINESS INCOME, WORKING PARTNERSHIP, OR FARM
	   Recommend:
	   A. Retirement Plan		

13	CAPITAL GAINS OR LOSSES
	Unused Capital Loss
	   Recommend:
	   A. Sales of Capital Gain Investments to Offset
	Capital Gains:
	   Recommend:
	   A. Reinvestment of Proceeds		

16a	IRA DISTRIBUTIONS
	   Recommend:
	   A. Plan to Avoid Premature Distributions
	   B. Consolidation to Avoid Complexity of Mandatory Distribution		

17a	PENSIONS AND ANNUITIES
	   Recommend
	   A. Roll-Over to IRA
	   B. Lump Sum Distribution Analysis		

21a&b	SOCIAL SECURITY BENEFITS
	   Recommend:
	   A. Single Premium Whole or Universal Life to Avoid Tax
	   B. Annuities to Avoid Tax		

(*Continued*)

FIGURE 6-4. (*Continued*)

1040 LINE REFERENCE		(X)	(X)

24 & 25	IRA DEDUCTION
	Nondeductible IRA
	  Recommend:
	    A. Tax Deferred Annuities
	    B. Our IRA Products Transfer
	    C. Contribution for this Year
	    D. Early Contribution Next Year
	        (Bank Draft)		

27	CLIENT HAS SEP OR KEOGH
	CLIENT QUALIFIES BUT HAS NO PLAN
	  Recommend:
	    A. Our 3rd Party Administrator
	    B. SEP
	    C. Proposal from Mutual Fund
	    D. Transfer of Assets		

Schedule A	NONDEDUCTIBLE INTEREST PAID
	  Recommend:
	    A. Budget Planning/Savings
	        Program
	CHARITABLE GIFTS
	    A. Charitable Remainder Trusts
	    B. Contribution of Appreciated
	        Assets
	OTHER SPECIAL
	CONSIDERATIONS
	
	_____
	
	_____
	
	_____
	
	_____		

(See Figure 6-5.) If all goes according to plan, the client should be in your assistant's office signing implementation paperwork after the interview.

FOLLOW UP ON LEADS DEVELOPED DURING TAX SEASON

If you are like I was, you will develop all sorts of projects and leads during tax season. As hard as you try to "strike when the iron was hot," circumstances often prevent you from closing at that time. Perhaps a client had just renewed a CD or was leaving on a trip and wanted to discuss it when he returned, etc. A lot of these leads get away because you do not have an efficient follow-up system.

FIGURE 6-5.   Post-Tax Interview.

Date _____

(Opportunity and Pain Questions)

Name(s) _____   Age _____
_____   Age _____

HIGHLIGHT EACH ITEM REQUIRING SPECIAL ATTENTION!

1. YEAR _____   TAX EXPENSE _____   ☐

   TOO HIGH _____
   ABOUT RIGHT _____
   REDUCTION TECHNIQUES: 403(b) ___ 457 ___ 401(k) ___ IRA ___
           SEP ____ OTHER RETIREMENT PLAN _____
           TAX DEFERRED _____ TAX EXEMPTS _____
           LTD P/S _____ OTHER _____
   _____

2. YOU LOST $_____ IN INTEREST DEDUCTION LAST YEAR ☐
   (CAN YOU START PAYING CASH?)

3. WHAT ARE PLANS FOR YOUR REFUND? $_____   ☐

4. IF YOU OWN A BUSINESS, ARE YOU EMPLOYING CHILDREN?
                                                    ☐

5. ARE YOU MIXING NON-DEDUCTIBLE WITH DEDUCTIBLE
   IRAs?   ☐
                                          EST.

6. INVESTMENT INCOME   YIELD   VALUE   ☐
   INTEREST—TAXABLE $_____ _____ $_____
   INTEREST—NONTAXABLE $_____ _____ $_____
   DIVIDENDS $_____ _____ $_____

   TOTAL $_____ $_____

   DOES THIS MEET EMERGENCY FUND NEEDS? _____   ☐

   IS THIS YOUR ONLY SOURCE OF RETIREMENT? _____   ☐

   IT WILL GENERATE ABOUT $_____ PER MONTH. CAN ☐
   YOU LIVE ON THAT?

   IS IT IN LOW YIELDING ACCOUNTS? RATE? _____%   ☐

   IS IT INCREASING OR DECREASING EACH YEAR?   ☐

   DO YOU KNOW ABOUT THE 4 TREASURE CHESTS?   ☐

       1. EMERGENCY CHEST (3–6 MONTHS TAKE HOME).
       2. RECURRING (NONEMERGENCY) EXPENSE FUND.
       3. MID-RANGE GOALS (EDUCATION, HOUSE,
          INVESTMENTS).
       4. LONG-TERM GOALS AND RETIREMENT.

7. ARE INVESTMENTS TOO CONCENTRATED?   ☐

   IS THE MIX APPROPRIATE FOR YOUR AGE?   ☐

8. ARE YOU DOING EXCESSIVE TRADING TRYING TO   ☐
   OUTGUESS THE MARKET?

(Continued)

FIGURE 6-5. (*Continued*)

9. WHAT ARE YOUR FINANCIAL GOALS? ☐

    WHAT ARE YOU DOING TO REACH THESE? ☐

10. YOUR NET WORTH IS _____. YOUR TARGET ☐
    NET WORTH SHOULD BE _____ AT AGE _____.

11. WHAT ARE YOUR PLANS FOR EDUCATING: ☐

    NAME _____ AGE _____ EST. COSTS _____
    NAME _____ AGE _____ EST. COSTS _____
    NAME _____ AGE _____ EST. COSTS _____

12. YOU HAVE SEVERAL SCATTERED IRAs. ARE YOU ☐
    AWARE OF MANDATORY DISTRIBUTION RULES AT
    AGE 70 1/2? CONSIDER CONSOLIDATION.
    ARE YOU PAYING FEES ON EACH ONE? ☐

13. WHEN DO YOU PLAN TO RETIRE? _____ (AGE) YEARS _____. ☐

    WHAT PERCENTAGE OF YOUR CURRENT INCOME ☐
    WILL YOU REQUIRE AT RETIREMENT? _____%

    CURRENT INCOME _____ X _____% = $_____ ☐
    YEARS TO RETIREMENT _____
    INCOME IN FUTURE DOLLARS $_____ ☐

    HOW MUCH WILL YOUR COMPANY PENSION
    PLAN PAY? $_____ ☐
    HOW MUCH WILL YOUR IRAs AND OTHER
    RETIREMENT FUNDS PAY? $_____ ☐

    TODAY'S BALANCE _____ ANNUAL CONTRIBUTION $_____
     ☐
    FOR _____YEARS.
    HOW MUCH SOCIAL SECURITY DO YOU EXPECT? ☐
     $_____

    TOTAL $_____
    BALANCE (WHERE IS THIS GOING TO
    COME FROM?) $_____ ☐

14. YOU ARE 4 TIMES MORE LIKELY TO BECOME ☐
    DISABLED FOR SOME PERIOD THAN YOU ARE TO DIE
    BEFORE YOU RETIRE.
    WHAT WOULD YOUR FAMILY LIVE ON IF YOU ARE ☐
    DISABLED?
    WHAT WOULD PAY FOR YOUR CHILDREN'S ☐
    EDUCATION?

    WE CALCULATED YOUR INCOME CONTINUATION ☐
    COVERAGE REQUIREMENT TO BE $_____. HOW MUCH
    DO YOU HAVE?

15. WE CALCULATED YOUR LIFE INSURANCE NEED AT: ☐

    HUSBAND _____WIFE _____

    HOW MUCH DO YOU HAVE? ☐

    IS ANY OF IT PERMANENT? ☐

FIGURE 6-5. (*Continued*)

WHAT HAPPENS IF YOU HAVE A HEALTH PROBLEM ☐
AND BECOME UNINSURABLE?

WHAT HAPPENS IF YOU CHANGE JOBS? ☐

16. THE LIFE INSURANCE INDUSTRY HAS COMPLETELY ☐
CHANGED DURING THE LAST 10 YEARS. DO YOU HAVE
POLICIES OVER 5 YEARS OLD?

THEY MAY BE ANTIQUATED AND NO LONGER FILL ☐
THE PURPOSE. DO YOU KNOW WHY YOU BOUGHT THEM?

WILL THEY BE TAXABLE IN YOUR ESTATE? ☐

17. DO YOU KNOW THAT LONG-TERM CARE IS NOT PAID ☐
FOR BY MEDICARE?

ARE YOU INTERESTED IN FILLING THIS GAP IN ☐
COVERAGE?
YOU CAN PROTECT $_____ IN ASSETS FOR ☐
ONLY $_____ PER MONTH.
DO YOU HAVE PARENTS WHO MAY NEED THIS ☐
COVERAGE?

IF THEY HAVE SUBSTANTIAL ASSETS, YOU MAY WANT ☐
TO PROTECT YOUR INHERITANCE OR <u>ONE</u> OF YOUR
PARENTS FROM BECOMING DESTITUTE IF THE OTHER
REQUIRES LONG-TERM CARE.

18. DO YOU OR YOUR PARENTS NEED MEDICARE ☐
SUPPLEMENT INSURANCE?

19. HOW MUCH ARE YOU PAYING FOR YOUR HEALTH ☐
INSURANCE?

20. YOU OWN ALL/PART OF A CLOSELY HELD BUSINESS: ☐

DO YOU HAVE A PLAN FOR DISPOSITION? ☐

DO YOU HAVE BUY–SELL AGREEMENTS WITH ☐
PARTNERS/SHAREHOLDERS/FAMILY?

DO YOU NEED HELP IN SELLING? ☐

HAVE YOU CONSIDERED WAYS TO AVOID CAPITAL ☐
GAINS TAX WHEN YOU DO SELL?

    CHARITABLE REMAINDER TRUST _____
    ESOP and CRTs   _____

DO YOU HAVE OVERHEAD PROTECTION IF ☐
SOMETHING HAPPENS TO YOU OR YOUR PARTNER SO
YOUR BUSINESS CAN KEEP GOING?

21. WE ESTIMATED YOUR ESTATE TO BE WORTH: ☐

$_____ TODAY. $_____ IN 10 YEARS.

WE ESTIMATE YOUR ESTATE <u>TAXES</u> TO BE:

$_____ TODAY. $_____ IN 10 YEARS.

DO YOU WANT TO "WILL" THIS MUCH MONEY TO THE ☐
IRS OR WOULD YOU RATHER YOUR HEIRS OR CHARITY
HAVE IT?

(*Continued*)

FIGURE 6-5.   (*Continued*)

WILL THERE BE ENOUGH "MONEY" IN YOUR ESTATE TO PAY THESE TAXES?   □

IS YOUR LIFE INSURANCE GOING TO ADD TO THESE PROBLEMS?   □

22. DO YOU HAVE A WILL?   □

    DID YOU KNOW THAT PROBATE COULD COST YOUR HEIRS OR YOU $_____ .   □

    DID YOU KNOW THAT A WILL IS PUBLIC INFORMATION?   □

    DID YOU KNOW THAT PROBATE CAN TAKE UP TO 2 YEARS?   □

    DID YOU KNOW THAT WILLS ONLY ARE VALID WHEN YOU <u>DIE</u>?   □

    WHAT HAPPENS TO YOUR ASSETS IF YOU ARE DISABLED?   □

    WHOM DO YOU THINK A COURT WOULD APPOINT AS YOUR GUARDIAN?   □

23. DO YOU HAVE A LIVING WILL?   □

24. DO YOU HAVE A DURABLE POWER OF ATTORNEY?   □

25. ARE YOU PLEASED WITH OUR SERVICES?   □

26. WOULD YOU RECOMMEND US TO FRIENDS?   □

27. WOULD YOU SIGN A LETTER OF INTRODUCTION?   □

28. NAMES OF FRIENDS AND ASSOCIATES YOU BELIEVE COULD BENEFIT FROM OUR SERVICES. (GIVE FORM IF THEY WANT TIME TO THINK.)   □

    (1) NAME _____
        ADDRESS _____
        _____
        PHONE # _____

    (2) NAME _____
        ADDRESS _____
        PHONE # _____

SUMMARY OF RECOMMENDATIONS: □

1. _____
2. _____
3. _____
4. _____
5. _____

PREPARER'S COMMENTS _____   □
_____
_____

FIGURE 6-6.   Investment Prospect Report

Prepared by: _____

Date: _____

Rating: _____
(Hot, warm, good)

Client: _____

Date Contacted: _____

Method of Contact: _____

Route to: _____

Summary of Discussion: _____

_____

_____

_____

	Action Steps	Product	Resp.	Due Date	Task Assigned
1.	_____	_____	_____	____	_____
	_____	_____	_____	____	_____
	_____	_____	_____	____	_____
2.	_____	_____	_____	____	_____
	_____	_____	_____	____	_____
	_____	_____	_____	____	_____
3.	_____	_____	_____	____	_____
	_____	_____	_____	____	_____
	_____	_____	_____	____	_____
4.	_____	_____	_____	____	_____
	_____	_____	_____	____	_____
	_____	_____	_____	____	_____
5.	_____	_____	_____	____	_____
	_____	_____	_____	____	_____
	_____	_____	_____	____	_____

The time and project management system should help to alleviate this problem, but adding financial planning and investments can bring the problem roaring back. Each financial planning or investment prospect usually generates *several tasks*.

Solve this problem with the *Investment Prospect Report*. (See Figure 6-6.) Using this form, you can make all the notes you need regarding discussions you had with the client, tasks that need to be assigned, products mentioned, etc. This form can be used to trigger entry of tasks into the time management system under this project for this client. The form itself is placed in the clients investment file. When the time management system reminds you that it is time for follow-up, you can pull the file and review everything that was discussed. That makes you a lot smarter when you discuss this with your client. They will be impressed by your thoroughness.

7

SELLING FROM THE
FINANCIAL PLAN

When you are organized, you have a special power.
You walk with a sure sense of purpose.
Your priorities are clear in your mind.
You orchestrate complex events with a masterful touch.
Things fall into place when you reveal your plans.
You move smoothly from one project to the next with no
wasted motion.
Throughout the day, you gain stamina and momentum as
your successes build.
People believe your promises because you always follow
through.
When you enter a meeting, you're prepared for whatever
they throw at you.
When at last you show your hand, you're a winner.

Mark McCormack, Author of What They Don't Teach You at
Harvard Business School

Financial plans are tools that can be used for selling rather than just regurgitations from boiler plate programs. Rather than being strictly academic in nature, they add sizzle and stick to the sales process. They add sizzle because they tell a story that most clients have never seen before and they add stick because the clients are reluctant to leave the professional who has "their plan."

WHY CPAs SHOULD USE FINANCIAL PLANS

CPAs, in particular, should use financial plans for the following reasons:

1. *We need something tangible to sell to our clients.* We are used to presenting our clients with a product. Even though the services we sell are intangible, almost all of our bills are for a tangible product of some kind. Think about it. Tax returns, audit reports, and financial statements are all tangible. We deliver something tangible that our clients can see and touch when we send them a bill. Without a written plan, you will have a hard time selling.

2. *They give us an education.* Only after I had completed my first plan for a client did I feel truly qualified to assist clients in this profession. The creative process that is required to complete a plan will force you into creative thought about the particular client and the financial planning process.

3. *They give us something to talk about besides product.* When I used to try to sell from product illustrations, my tongue would get tied in knots and I would lose my train of thought. When the client throws you a curve, you can get back on track by referring to the plan.

4. *They provide good documentation for your files.* When your client calls for an appointment after a long absence to discuss his investments, you can review the plan to remember exactly why he is invested the way he is. You cannot keep all of those things in your memory if you have more than 25 clients. A plan also provides a good defense if a competitor tries to steal your client with the latest hot product.

5. *Plans distinguish us from the competition.* Few, if any, of your competitors ever prepare financial plans. If they do, they are generally ''canned'' plans.

6. *They help us to close the sale.* By the time we have gone through a creative process to arrive at a road map for our clients, we ''own'' the plan. When the client comes in to discuss it, you are convinced that it is the right thing to do. That conviction will come through in all aspects of the presentation and your client will sense it.

7. *They enhance client retention.* Clients are extremely reluctant to leave the professional who designed their road maps to financial security.

8. *They attract continuous business.* Plans are both events and processes. They must be monitored and changed as circumstances change. They become an evolving instrument. When circumstance or events demand changes, then you are the one with the plan. Changes often bring more sales.

9. *A plan creates a sense of obligation in the client's mind to at least listen to what you have to say.*

10. *Everyone should have one.* We all know that. Why fight it?

WHY CPAs DO NOT USE FINANCIAL PLANS

With all these reasons for preparing financial plans, why is it that most CPAs do not do it?

The Fee Issue

CPAs are used to getting paid directly for all time expended on behalf of a client. Of course, most do not get paid for all this time, but we like to think that anyway. How do you charge for a financial plan when a learning curve is involved? ''Better to not do one at all'' becomes the excuse.

The Audit Mentality

We do not think we can do a plan unless the numbers are exactly right. ''Well, Mr. Client, exactly what is the balance of your CD and how much of that is accrued interest?'' Forget the audit—you are dealing with projections that go out as far as 50 years sometimes. This is not an exact science, but an educated projection is better than no plan at all. If your client could provide you with exact figures for this financial statement, chances are he would not need you at all.

The Projection Freeze

Most of our training is anti-forecast. Forecasts have to be documented. We have to place disclaimers on every page and assumptions have to be clearly documented. They are dangerous. But projections are necessary in financial planning. Remember, these are not going to be reviewed by the general public. They are for your client's use in planning his future.

We Are Not Creative Thinkers

''Where are the rules for filling in the forms? Where are the answers so I can see if I did this right?'' Sorry folks, there are no correct answers. There are too many individual circumstances, personalities, etc. involved to arrive at a perfect solution. That is one of the things that makes this profession so exciting and rewarding. You can become a creative thinker with practice.

GETTING DOWN TO BASICS

If you are starting to agree that plans are good and that CPAs can prepare them, where should you start? In order to prepare a plan, you must have certain information from the client. It must be reasonably accurate, although not necessarily perfect. So how do you get it? The essential ingredients necessary for the smallest of financial plans are:

1. *Goals*. This does not necessarily mean that you have to have all of the client's financial goals, but you must have at least the one or more that relate to the subject at hand. Finding out goals is the easiest and most rewarding part of the process. Most clients are both surprised and pleased when you ask what their goals are. Even if you are just asking for their goals in relation to one particular investment, they are still pleased. If they do not know what their goals are, provide them with a goals sheet to spark their imaginations. (See Figure 7-1.) Ask them to rate their goals in order of importance. (See Figure 7-2.)

2. *Risk Tolerance*. Risk measurements are available from several sources including product sponsors, The College for Financial Planning, and The American College. Figure 7-3 is a shortened version used to evaluate your client's tolerance for risk. This short form along with some probing questions will determine the client's true risk. Statistics indicate that most people say that they will take more risk than they actually will. I have found that most of my clients will take more risks if they understand the nature of risk. Most do not understand purchasing power risk or the risk reward principle.

3. *Financial data (information for a personal financial statement)*. Getting financial data sheets completed is often a stumbling block to getting a plan com-

Figure 7-1   Data Gathering—Goals/Investment Philosophy

CLIENT _____

DATE _____

COMMENTS _____

_____

_____

_____

_____

pleted. I use to send forms home with a client to complete. I never had a set returned. I now assign the data gathering process to my staff who are tenacious in getting the necessary information without offending the client.

Most financial data sheets are either too lengthy and cumbersome or too short. Try to design something in between that will provide most of the information you need, yet still be easy to complete.

(a) Except in rare cases, do not rely on the client to complete the forms.

(b) The most efficient way to gather data is to do it when you can get the client's complete cooperation. That usually means doing it during tax season. If he is unable to provide the data at that time, send him a list of things to bring or send to you. Then keep following up until you get what you want.

(c) Do not forget that you have the most valuable piece of information about the client you can possibly have—his tax return. Use it to gather data. A major portion of the information you need can be determined from the return.

If you can gather these three basic items, you are ready to prepare a financial plan.

MAXI OR MINI PLANS

Another common misconception about financial plans is that they are all "small books" and too cumbersome with which to work. If you keep to the basics, eighty percent of the plans that you prepare will be less than 12 pages in length. Length and complexity do not a good plan make. What makes a good plan is clarity, congruency with the client's goals and risk tolerance, and implementation. If you do not have these qualities, you may have an academically correct, long, complex plan; but a poor one.

How do you decide if a client needs a full blown plan or a small one?

1. *How many opportunities does the client have?* More problems usually mean a bigger plan.

Figure 7-2   Financial Goals Worksheet

CHECK YOUR GOALS—THEN RANK THEM BY PRIORITY

	IMPORTANT (CHECK)	YOUR RANKINGS
FINANCE CHILDREN'S COLLEGE EDUCATION	☐	☐
BUY A NEW HOME (PRIMARY OR VACATION)	☐	☐
BUY A NEW CAR/BOAT/FURNITURE/OTHER PERSONAL PROPERTY	☐	☐
TRAVEL EXTENSIVELY	☐	☐
REACH THE PROPER LEVEL OF INSURANCE PROTECTION FOR MYSELF AND MY FAMILY	☐	☐
SAVE FOR RETIREMENT	☐	☐
REDUCE/ELIMINATE DEBT	☐	☐
SET UP A RESERVE/EMERGENCY FUND	☐	☐
BE FINANCIALLY INDEPENDENT AT AGE _____	☐	☐
SUBSTANTIALLY CONTRIBUTE TO FAVORITE CHARITY/INSTITUTION	☐	☐
INVEST IN THE STOCK MARKET	☐	☐
HELP SUPPORT ELDERLY PARENT(S)	☐	☐
INVEST IN REAL ESTATE (LAND, RENTAL PROPERTY)	☐	☐
START/BUY/EXPAND OWN BUSINESS	☐	☐
START A FORMAL RETIREMENT PLAN FOR MY BUSINESS	☐	☐
LEAVE LARGE ESTATE FOR CHILDREN	☐	☐
OTHER	☐	☐

2. *How much information will the client provide?* If he will not sit still or provide the information to do a complete plan, then do a mini plan with a cover letter and agreement that he needs a bigger one, but has elected to go with a partial plan at this time.

3. *Plans for a particular investment or problem.* You can do a specialized plan that addresses only one investment that the client owns or a specific problem. This should lead to more comprehensive plans later. Should you do a plan

Figure 7-3   My/Our Investment Policy

INVESTMENT PHILOSOPHY

ATTITUDE TOWARD RISK (CHECK ONLY ONE)	YOU	SPOUSE
VERY CONSERVATIVE (COMFORTABLE ONLY WITH LOWEST RISK)	☐	☐
CONSERVATIVE (WILLING TO ASSUME ONLY LIMITED RISK)	☐	☐
AVERAGE (WILL ASSUME MODERATE LEVEL OF RISK)	☐	☐
MODERATELY AGGRESSIVE (ACCEPTS HIGHER-THAN-AVERAGE RISK)	☐	☐
AGGRESSIVE (RISK TOLERANCE IS VERY HIGH)	☐	☐
OVERALL, I RATE MY TOLERANCE TOWARD RISK AS (1–10 WITH 1 = RISK AVOIDER AND 10 = RISK TAKER)	_____	_____

INVESTMENT TEMPERAMENT

(CHECK ONLY ONE)	YOU	SPOUSE
VERY CONSERVATIVE AND MORE INTERESTED IN CONSERVING CAPTIAL THAN IN MAKING IT GROW. WILLING TO ACCEPT MODERATE INCOME AND NOMINAL CAPITAL GAINS POTENTIAL IN EXCHANGE FOR MINIMUM RISK.	☐	☐
INTERESTED ONLY IN HIGH QUALITY INVESTMENTS AND WILL BE QUITE SATISFIED WITH A REASONABLE CURRENT RETURN AND SOME GROWTH POTENTIAL.	☐	☐
LIBERAL CASH RETURN WITH A CHANCE FOR CAPITAL APPRECIATION.	☐	☐
CAN ACCEPT A LOWER LEVEL OF INCOME NOW IN ORDER TO AIM FOR CAPITAL APPRECIATION AND GROWTH OF INCOME IN THE FUTURE.	☐	☐
WILLING TO ACCEPT RELATIVELY HIGH RISKS IN EXCHANGE FOR THE POSSIBILITY OF ABOVE AVERAGE CAPITAL GAINS AND APPRECIATION.	☐	☐

even when you are only talking about changing a CD to a mutual fund? Yes. Look back at the advantages to doing plans previously listed for the reasons why. Even if your plan consists of only a cover sheet and a recommendation, do the plan!

PLANS PREPARED FROM THE TAX RETURN

Is it possible to prepare plans from a tax return? The answer is ''yes.'' The plan may not be accurate to the last detail, but how many plans are? Financial statements prepared that are accurate to the penny on a certain date will change before you can get them in front of the client.

Other than the client's goals, the most valuable source of information about the client can be taken from the tax return. This is a sample of what you can obtain from the return:

1. Personal data such as addresses, children's names, and ages.
2. Client and spouse salary.
3. Interest income and approximate value of interest-bearing investments. If you have two years' tax returns and 1099s, a lot of principal invested information can be obtained. Just by division, using current and historical interest rates or yields, you can estimate the value of holdings that bear interest.
4. Stock or mutual funds (dividend yielding investments). Using dividend yields, you can estimate the value of stock.
5. You know if the client has a business, what kind it is, whether it has a retirement plan.
6. Whether or not a client trades stocks from Schedule D.
7. Whether or not he has rental property, what he paid for it and when he bought it, how much income it brings in, and what is owed against it.
8. Whether he has a farm, what he paid for it, when he bought it, what livestock or equipment is on it.
9. Whether he has an IRA or Keogh.
10. What his mortgage is on his personal residence (from Schedule A).
11. Most other debts that he has from Schedule A.

These are just a few of the items that you can glean from current and prior tax returns. You can prepare a rough plan that will get your foot in the door for a more accurate plan if needed.

Should you do a rough plan from the tax return? If that will get the client's attention and cause him to take some needed course of action, you bet! Often the rough plan from the tax return will inspire the client to provide you with more complete information to do a more complete plan.

HOW PRODUCTS FIT INTO THE PLAN AND THE SALES PROCESS

As we have discussed, product is the least important part of the sales process. That does not mean that product is unimportant; it just means that a well-prepared plan is like a puzzle with a few missing pieces. When you know the shape of the pieces, it is easy to plug them into the puzzle. Products, of course, represent the missing pieces.

Do not mention a specific product in financial plans. Product recommendations can be decided before you present the plan to the client, but do not include them in the plan except in a generic fashion. A standard financial plan format has an implementation sheet that lists all of the products to be used. On the implementation sheet, list the products by amounts and in accordance with goals by number. Try to list the source of funds for each product investment. That implementation sheet provides your staff and you with a nice paper trail to use when completing the transaction. It also is a good referral source when you are trying to trace where funds came from at a later date.

After the client has accepted the recommendations presented in the plan, discuss products that will be used to implement the plan. My discussion is limited to a discussion of the particular features and a reiteration of the risks involved. These have usually been discussed generically during the discussion about the plan. After you have discussed the plan to the client's satisfaction, turn the client over to your assistant who can go through the application, prospectus, and check-writing procedures. The client will again be reminded about risk and will have ample opportunity to ask any additional questions he may have.

What if a client insists on buying a product that you do not recommend? If it is a product that you simply cannot live with, then just refuse to implement using this product. Better to lose the sale than to have an unhappy client tell others that you sold him something that did not meet his needs. If the client insists on buying a product that you can live with but would not recommend in this particular situation, go ahead with implementation as long as you get to implement the major portion of the plan using products that you recommend and with which you are comfortable. Get a disclaimer letter to avoid future misunderstandings.

Do not try to sell based on yield or product. You are giving your client every reason to beat you up with the same information later when conditions change. Sell only long-term solutions! Figure 7-4 through 7-8 are sample forms that you can use to both educate your clients and protect yourself.

GETTING APPOINTMENTS AFTER THE PLAN IS PREPARED

Do not fail to get a client to meet with you after a plan has been prepared. Follow this procedure:

1. After the plan is prepared and ready for presentation, ask the receptionist or other assistant to call the client and report that the plan is prepared and ready for his review. Tell the client that you are going to mail it to him and would like to schedule an appointment to discuss it with him. Do not try to set the appointment before the plan is ready. You cannot take the risk of not giving the client time to review the plan before you go over it with him. You give him an automatic excuse to delay implementation if he has not had the plan for at least a couple of days before your appointment.

Figure 7-4 Personal Investment Plan

Client _____

Date _____

<u>Plan Implementation Steps</u>
<u>(Internal Use Only)</u>

Client Authorization Date _____

Project	Due Date	Comp. ( )
_____	_____	_____
_____	_____	_____
_____	_____	_____
_____	_____	_____
_____	_____	_____
_____	_____	_____
_____	_____	_____
_____	_____	_____
_____	_____	_____
_____	_____	_____
_____	_____	_____
_____	_____	_____
_____	_____	_____
_____	_____	_____
_____	_____	_____
_____	_____	_____

_____   _____
                    (Date)

_____

_____

(Continued)

Figure 7-4 (*Continued*)

We recognize that our clients often desire to make investments that suit their particular personal needs. These investments may not coincide or may even conflict with basic financial planning concepts and principles. You have elected to make such an investment and we have agreed to process the transaction for you and we will be compensated for our services.

To avoid any future misunderstandings between ourselves or other interested parties, please sign below to indicate that you are making the following investment(s):

_____ against our recommendations

_____ without any recommendation by any member of our firm

Investment Description: _____

_____

Amount: _____   Date: _____

_____   _____
Client Signature   Date

2. Allow him about a week, no longer than two, for review time between mailing time and appointment time. If you allow longer, the plan gets cold. Do not mail the plan until an appointment has been set up. If you are doing the plan for free, you own it, not the client. If he will not give you a date right away for an appointment, tell him you will call back when he has a better handle on his schedule.

3. The day before the scheduled appointment, review the major points of the plan.

4. When the client comes in, ask him if he has had a chance to review the plan. You may get a strong clue if he brings in the plan in the same envelope you used for mailing with the seal unbroken. *That is not your problem.* If you try to present it to him on the same day of this appointment, then it *is* your problem. If he has not reviewed it, approach it in a straightforward manner as follows:

   (a) Repeat the goals and make sure he understands the goals are his, not yours (trust and opportunity questions here).

   (b) Repeat any problems he has in reaching his goals. You can take this from the financial statement and the ''assets required'' section of the plan (mostly pain questions here).

   (c) Go directly to your recommendations for meeting his goals. Turn with him to the recommendations page and go over them item by item (solutions and comfort here).

   (d) If the client has reviewed the plan extensively, start by asking him if he has any questions. Then start with the same process as stated previously.

Figure 7-5   Memorandum of Understanding Mutual Fund/Other Investments

Client _____   Date _____

Investment Description _____

DO YOU UNDERSTAND?

   I. The principle of risk and the degree of risk involved with the investment I am making with your firm has been explained to me. My investment is primarily subject to the following types of risk:

     Interest   Market   Purchasing   Credit and
     Rate _____ _____ Power _____ Financial _____   _____
                                                        Initial

  II. I understand the risk/reward principle and I have been shown the "Investment Pyramid."   _____ Initial

 III. The difference between liquidity and marketability. My investment is considered to have _____ liquidity and _____ marketability.   _____ Initial

 IV. I understand that because of possible movements in markets or interest rates and the effect of commissions or surrender charges, I should consider this investment as long-term allowing a period of at least _____ to _____ years for it to perform properly. This holding period is not mandatory, but highly recommended.   _____ Initial

  V. Commission and/or surrender charges applicable to this investment have been explained to me. My investment may be affected by a:

    _____ Front Commission (%)   _____ Back Commission
    _____ Surrender Charge— Year 1 _____%   Year 4 _____%
                       Year 2 _____%   Year 5 _____%
                       Year 3 _____%   Year 6 _____%
    _____ Other
    _____ N/A   _____ Initial

By signature below you are attesting that this sheet has been explained to you. You have been asked to sign it as indicated in the interest of full and complete disclosure. This is for your protection as well as ours.

Thank you for your cooperation!

_____   _____
Client Signature   Registered Representative
                                 1st Global Capital Corp.

(e) State that you have the paperwork ready to start him on the road to-ward reaching his goals.

(f) Be quiet!

(g) Bring in the assistant to do the implementation.

(h) After the checks are written and paperwork signed, you should step in to congratulate the client on his decision and ask if he has any more questions on the products used. Make sure that he understands principal fluctuation, risks involved, and the long term nature of the investment he is making. These will have been explained again by your assistant using a form called *Memo of Understanding*. (See Figures 7-6 through 7-8).

Figure 7-6   Memorandum of Understanding Insurance Annuity Purchases

Client _____   Date _____

Investment Description _____

DO YOU UNDERSTAND?

I. The principle of risk and the degree of risk involved with the investment I am making with your firm has been explained to me. My investment is primarily subject to the following types of risk:

Interest   Market   Purchasing   Credit and
Rate _____   _____   Power _____   Financial _____

I understand the risk/reward principle and have been shown the   _____
"Investment Pyramid."   Initial

II. I understand that while my investment is considered marketable because I can get my money out at any time by electing my choice of annuity options available, it is considered to have low liquidity. If I take my money out in a lump sum within the next _____ years, my earnings will be subject to the following surrender charges by the insurance company:

1st year _____ %   5th year _____ %
2nd year _____ %   6th year _____ %
3rd year _____ %   7th year _____ %
4th year _____ %   8th year _____ %
                                                    _____
                                                    Initial

III. I understand that the earnings rate of _____ % should be guaranteed for the first year(s) after which time the money will go in with other larger sums to earn at a rate that will fluctuate on a _____ basis.
                                                    _____
                                                    Initial

By signature below you are attesting that this sheet has been explained to you. You have been asked to sign it as indicated in the interest of full and complete disclosure. This is for your protection as well as ours.

Thank you for your cooperation!

_____   _____
Client Signature   Registered Representative

_____   _____
Date   Date

Figure 7-7   Memorandum of Understanding for 403(b) Insurance Annuity Purchases

Client _____   Date _____

Investment Description _____

DO YOU UNDERSTAND?

I. The principle of risk and the degree of risk involved with the investment I am making with your firm has been explained to me. My investment is primarily subject to the following types of risks:

| Interest Rate _____ | Market _____ | Purchasing Power _____ | Credit and Financial _____ |

I understand the risk/reward principle and have been shown the "Investment Pyramid."

_____
Initial

II. I understand that while my investment is considered marketable because I can get my money out at any time by electing my choice of annuity options available, it is considered to have low liquidity. If I take my money out in a lump sum within the next _____ years, my earnings will be subject to the following surrender charges by the insurance company:

1st year _____ %   5th year _____ %
2nd year _____ %   6th year _____ %
3rd year _____ %   7th year _____ %
4th year _____ %   8th year _____ %

_____
Initial

III. I understand that effective January 1, 1989, IRC Section 403(b) (11) prohibits the distribution of post-1988 salary reduction elective deferrals and earnings from my 403(b) contract, except in the event of one of the following:

(1) attainment of age 59-$\frac{1}{2}$
(2) separation from service
(3) death
(4) total and permanent disability
(5) financial hardship (in which event only the contributions may be withdrawn).

_____
Initial

IV. I understand that per Section 403(b) (11), if I take my money out prior to age 59-$\frac{1}{2}$, I will be subject to a 10% penalty by the IRS. I will also be taxed on the money as income in the year in which I take it out.

_____
Initial

V. I understand that the earnings rate of _____ % should be guaranteed for the first _____ year(s) after which time the money will go in with other larger sums to earn at a rate that will fluctuate on a _____ basis.

_____
Initial

By signature below you are attesting that this sheet has been explained to you. You have been asked to sign it as indicated in the interest of full and complete disclosure. This is for your protection as well as ours.

Thank you for your cooperation!

_____   _____
Client Signature   Registered Representative

_____   _____
Date   Date

Figure 7-8   Plan Summary

Client _____

Date _____

These are the steps you should take in order to achieve your goals.

                                                                    Dates

1. _____   _____

   _____

   _____

2. _____   _____

   _____

   _____

3. _____   _____

   _____

   _____

4. _____   _____

   _____

   _____

5. _____   _____

   _____

   _____

6. _____   _____

   _____

   _____

TO CHARGE OR NOT TO CHARGE

Most CPAs consider themselves commission and fee-based planners, but 95 percent of our revenue comes from commissions. Our clients are very fee resistant. This comes from the nature of the area we serve. There are no fee-based planners in our area. People are not used to paying fees for financial planning. They do not like to write checks to professionals unless they are paying for a service they have to have. Others areas will be different. We do not charge fees for our plans. We like to think that we are confident enough in our plans that our clients are going to implement through us.

I usually set some standards for medium and large plans that will take a considerable amount of time. I ask for the client's assurance that if she likes my suggestions, she will implement through me. If she implements elsewhere, I will bill for time expended at my standard rate. Rarely, I will agree to offset any fees with commissions earned. If commissions earned are sufficient to pay my fee, then there will be no fee charged. One other seldom used procedure is to give the client a minimum amount of fee for the plan, regardless of whether or not it is implemented. I use this for clients who I have not had dealings with before and when the plan is fairly large. This gives me some protection for at least a recovery of direct costs. The key is *full disclosure*. Make sure the client understands the arrangement before you start.

8

Selling with Mailers and Tangibles

"Character is the ability to follow through on a task after the enthusiasm has waned."

We have said several times that you should not attempt to sell by using products themselves. Can you sell by mailing things to clients and potential clients? Can you sell by using product illustrations and hypotheticals? Yes and no. Everything counts in the sum total of your ability to sell but it is impossible to measure the impact that mailers, illustrations, and hypotheticals have on sales. They are a minor component in the entire sales process, but they also are tools that may complement the TOPS process for certain clients.

A few cautions for CPAs using products to make a sale:

1. Do not hide behind the product. The only true effective way to profitability in this business is to get face to face with clients. Most tools will not sell a thing for you.
2. Selling is a numbers game. The more presentations you make, the more sales you will make.
3. If you sell by product and performance, your relationships will be based on product and performance. We all know that products do not always perform like we hope they will.

USE PRODUCT SPONSOR MAILERS

Make use of these mailers. They are inexpensive and often free. Some of the sponsors will even help you with postage. They are professionally designed and may add to your professionalism. They will position you with your clients as being in the investment business. Will they sell much directly? No. But if they get the clients interested, then you can use TOPS and financial plans to cement the sale and the relationship.

TAKE ADVANTAGE OF PRODUCT SPONSOR WHOLESALERS AND STAFF

Product wholesalers have a vested interest in your success. If you make money, they make money. They will assist you in client meetings, often pay for seminars, assist in advertising, and provide help on technical questions. They are a very valuable resource. Get a clear understanding of how the wholesaler makes money so that you can help her as she helps you.

Limit your products to only a few major sponsors. The more business you send to a product sponsor, the more she can afford to help you. Is this in the best interest of the client? Actually, I think it is. You can usually find a wide range of different types of products in only one or two mutual fund families. You only have the ability to be thoroughly familiar with a few products. The more you limit your offerings, the more familiar you will be. That seems to be in the client's best interest. If you develop a strong relationship with a product sponsor, you can get quick action on client requests or in the event of errors in their accounts.

MAKE USE OF HYPOTHETICALS AND ILLUSTRATIONS

Use hypotheticals as much as possible. These are past performance illustrations that show what a particular hypothetical investment would have done over varying periods of time in the past. Software to do hypotheticals can be obtained from the particular mutual fund companies usually at minimum or no cost. They are also available from companies like Morningstar and CDA. Using hypotheticals is a good way to learn about the historical performance of funds. You can take your client's current situation back to the past and see what would have happened if she had made a particular investment one, three, five, ten years or other selected periods of time. Most software also allows you to use a combination of funds, different withdrawal strategies, etc. They are good for giving comfort to yourself and your client about the historical performance of the particular investment products. Be sure that appropriate warnings are given to your clients about past performance not being a guarantor of future performance. Past performance is just one way of evaluating a product.

But do not sell the client based on the hypothetical illustration alone. Sell him on how the product is the vehicle that allows him to solve his problem and to reach his long-term goals. Always emphasize the long-term nature of the investment.

Insurance illustrations are a different matter. They are not based on past performance but on current interest rates. They are a fairly ineffective sales tool because they are too confusing for the client to properly understand. Again, when selling insurance, you must use TOPS. You are selling solutions to problems, not illustrations.

Be cautious when using illustrations. Drop the interest rate a point below what is currently being paid so that your client can see the effect on his insurance if the yield drops. This is especially important for interest-sensitive products. You do not want your client to run out of insurance and cash value when your original illustration shows him with plenty of death benefit and a hefty cash value.

Put a couple of cover sheets on your illustrations. One should explain the terms used in the illustrations in simple language (something apparently not available to insurance companies). The other should be a ''caution'' piece that basically says that you or anyone else can do almost anything with an insurance illustration by using different assumptions.

USE A PERSONAL LETTER

If you are going to communicate with your client using the mail, nothing is more effective than a personal letter from you. Even if you are mailing the same letter to a lot of clients, personalizing is effective. Here are some rules for effective communication:

1. *Keep it simple.* If a seventh grader cannot understand it, it is too complicated. CPAs need to be repeatedly warned about this. We have this need to be sure that the client knows how smart we are and often put that need ahead of the need to communicate effectively.
2. *Keep it focused.* Do not try to cover every available topic in one letter. Do not let your reader wonder what the letter is really about after he has already read it.
3. *Talk solutions or benefits.* Get to the point in plain English. Offer comfort and reassurance to the pain and problems that the client has.
4. *Read the letter as if you were the client.* How do you feel when you get home from a hard day's work and find a three-page, difficult-to-read letter? What is your reaction?
5. *Write like you talk.* That is assuming you use good grammar. Do not break the basic rules.
6. *Keep the trust.* Remember that clients buy from you because they trust you. Make it as personal and friendly as possible. Remind them of how much you know about them.
7. *Make it as short as possible.* People are short on time. Get to the point as quickly as possible.
8. *Be sure your letter matches your reader.* Do not write something that is appropriate for one type of client but inappropriate for another.
9. *Do not assume what your client knows, feels, or likes.* He may not know what you are talking about, and may not share your love for the Dallas Cowboys.
10. *Do not use business buzz words.* Leave out the acronyms and terms peculiar to the industry. Your client will appreciate it.
11. *Watch the details.* Spell the names right, get the address right, do not misspell words.

Feel free to duplicate the ''Penny Pincher'' (see Figures 8-1 through 8-4) for your clients. It is very basic and has special appeal for parents with children in their twenties.

Figure 8-1   The Penny Pincher—Overview

Many of you have heard people described by the old adage as "Penny Wise and Pound Foolish." That truly describes a lot of people's money habits. However, most people who are penny wise are also pound wise. They know how to turn their pennies into dollars. In the following pages we will try to tell you how to be penny wise and dollar wise. We will tell you:

HOW TO KEEP YOUR MONEY
(Keep it from slipping through your fingers)

HOW TO SAVE YOUR MONEY

WHERE TO PUT YOUR MONEY

We hope you can use these helpful hints in your savings and investment program. These are only broad based hints to be used as reminders and as a part of our overall financial planning program. Please contact us about our other services.

Sincerely,

Registered Representative

Figure 8-2   Penny Pincher #1

HOW TO KEEP YOUR MONEY
(keep it from slipping through your fingers)

1. *Do Not Be a Big Spender*

Stop having guilt feelings because you do not spend enough. Overspending is often related to insecurity. However, some of our social standards have made it the other way around. Savers and wise spenders are usually more secure than folks who overspend regularly. You have nothing to prove by overspending.

2. *Keep Minimal Cash*

Stop carrying so much cash in your pocket. Money in your jeans makes you feel "flush." It is just too darned easy to spend. Make spending money a little more troublesome by carrying less in your pockets.

3. *Wants vs. Needs*

Establish your priorities. Is something that you want just a "whim" or is it a really valid want? What is it really worth to you? Ask yourself those things every time you buy a "want purchase" rather than a "need purchase." Learn how to distinguish wants from needs. If you sincerely desire or want some product or service that you do not necessarily need, make a list of those items and put it aside. Sometimes that want will disappear entirely or at last will not become quite so nagging. This will save you from lots of impulse purchases, but will not deny you all of your wants. Use that want list as a motivation to save for what you want rather than using credit to buy it.

Figure 8-2   (*Continued*)

4. *Cheap Saturday Nights*

If you think that a good way to spend a cheap Saturday night is to visit your local discount store and shop—forget it. That can be one of the most expensive forms of entertainment because you will buy things that you do not need. If you do not buy them on the spot, you will make a mental note to go back and get them later. Most of the things you buy, you probably could have done without.

5. *Stop Chasing Sales*

Do not be a sale chaser. Do not go all over town searching for the cheapest item or chasing items that are advertised as being on sale. Only watch for sale items that you truly need and would have purchased anyway. Also, remember the cost of traveling from one place to the other or to an out-of-the-way location. I have seen people travel 40 miles to save two dollars. With the cost of gasoline and automobiles today, that is truly ''Penny Wise and Pound Foolish.''

6. *Do Not Buy on Impulse*

Do not use impulse purchases to scare away the doldrums. Instead, reward yourself occasionally with one of the items on your want list after you have saved adequately for it. That way, your thriftiness is rewarded and you will feel better after the purchase. Did you ever notice what some people refer to as the ''post-purchase blues'' or ''buyer's remorse?'' You usually suffer these after you have made a purchase that is impulsive and something that you did not necessarily need. That is not always true but it often is. If you find yourself suffering from this often, then you are doing too much impulse buying.

7. *Avoid Credit Card Whiplash*

Do not get caught in a credit card ''whiplash.'' That is caused from whipping out your credit card every time you want something, rather than waiting until you can afford to pay for it. Try to avoid using your credit card totally on ''snowball purchases.'' These are purchases that tend to melt away or get used up in a relatively short period of time. A good example is vacations. Save for your vacations ahead of time. Everyone deserves a vacation, but they are often ruined when you are left with a credit card bill when you get back. I do not advocate tearing up your credit cards unless you are a chronic overbuyer, but I do advocate using credit wisely.

8. *Use Credit Wisely*

On the subject of credit—some folks believe that you should pay cash for everything. That is not necessarily a bad habit, but it often leads to bad financial management. Sometimes, I recommend borrowing for two reasons: 1) leverage (that allows you to use other folks' money instead of your own). It works when you wisely invest your own funds. 2) Borrowing can often be self-inflicted discipline for *saving*. Sound strange? I have found that my clients will generally pay the bank or other creditors. If they do not, the consequences of not paying will be made very evident to them by their creditors. However, if you do not pay yourself back for savings that you have dipped into, there will be no one to cry foul.

9. *Be Your Own Banker*

Pay your own insurance and taxes on your personal residence or other real estate. Do not let your mortgage company hold your funds in escrow without paying you interest. Establish your own interest-bearing escrow account that you use to pay

(Continued)

Figure 8-2   (Continued)

insurance and taxes. Caution: Be sure that you fund your own escrow account and that you have money available to pay your insurance and taxes when they come due.

10. *Keep it in the Family*

Make budgeting, saving, and financial management a family matter. Discuss it with your spouse and your children. If everyon does not know what the common goals are, everybody suffers.

Figure 8-3   Penny Pincher #2

HOW TO SAVE YOUR MONEY

1. *Pay Yourself First*

I know that is a tired old saying, but it works. Every time you get paid, put part of it back for yourself in a savings account or other savings investment. If you put it in your checking account or in your pocket, you can "color it gone."

2. *Let it Ride*

If you have your money in a money market, CD, or mutual fund, let your interest accumulate. Do not withdraw it unless you need it for an emergency or if you are retired and are using it for living expenses. Let it accumulate. You will be amazed at how large sums of money can be accumulated on small investments.

3. *Separate Your Savings*

Do this either mentally or physically for specific wants and needs. For example, you may have one money market fund for vacation and another for college education. Do not be upset if you do not have enough funds to practice this type of segregation. You can do it using a simple note pad to segregate one account. If you do not have enough money now to have a minimum balance for a bank money market account, see us about a "no minimum" money market fund. You do need to segregate either mentally or physically the funds that you have available for discretionary spending and those that you consider long-term growth funds.

4. *Consider Yourself to Have* <u>*Two Jobs*</u>

One is for your employer that pays for living expenses. The other is for yourself. That makes it a little simpler to put back a small amount of your paycheck each month. Some people look upon saving as punishment and therefore very difficult to do. Remember that the funds are still yours and still available for expenditure; you just segregated them to make future purchases or for other specific reasons.

5. *You Should Establish Goals*

Do not be ultra-sophisticated when you do it. It is one thing to say that you want to save for your children's education or to provide funds for retirement. Be more specific and segregate your bigger goals into shorter ones. For example, you may want to save $5,000 for a down-payment on a new car. You may want to save up to six months of your salary as an emergency fund. Most financial advisors agree that you should have at least six-months salary as an emergency fund. I call that "sleep money." Read, update, and re-read these goals often.

Figure 8-4   Penny Pincher #3

WHERE TO PUT YOUR MONEY

This is a big subject that cannot be covered in a simple one-page letter, but I will give you a short listing of the more common generalized types of investments and savings accounts available to you.

1. *Checking Accounts That Pay Interest*

Ask your banker about NOW accounts and Super NOW accounts. The banking market is much more competitive and open than it was just a few years ago. Many banks offer varying competitive rates of interest on different types of checking accounts. Be sure you understand the interest rates that are being paid and the restrictions regarding minimum balances, etc., on the account before you take the plunge.

2. *Passbook Savings Accounts*

In most cases, passbook savings accounts are poor investments, but they often provide a good method of saving small amounts of money until you can move it into something with more competitive rates. Most passbook accounts pay the lowest rates available anywhere and several banks now have minimum balance requirements.

3. *Money Market Accounts*

Money market accounts are usually segregated into mutual funds and accounts offered by banks. Mutual funds can best be described as a group of investors with "mutual interest" who pool their money and hire a manager to invest it for them in the money market. This manager will usually buy larger certificates of deposit and other money market instruments than you could afford to buy yourself. I consider them to be an excellent, safe method of investing at a fairly good interest rate. This is an excellent place to keep your money while you are waiting to invest in more aggressive or growth-oriented types of investments.

4. *Certificates of Deposit*

These are also available from bank, savings and loans and some brokers. You usually have to invest your money for a specified period of time at a fixed rate.

5. *Savings Bonds*

This method of investment has long been overlooked by savers, but is now very much back in favor because of the competitive interest rate and the tax deferral feature. Do not overlook these as part of your savings program.

6. *Stock Market or Equity-Type Investments*

Investing in the stock market requires a considerable amount of thought and planning. You usually need the help of a good broker or investment counselor to buy stock in various companies that are traded on the various stock market exchanges or over-the-counter markets. You should always consider the cost of commissions as they relate to the size of your account before taking the plunge into the market. Equity investments can also be made through mutual funds. This is a good way for the small investor to enter the market and achieve diversification.

7. *Tax Favored Investments*

Real estate.

Real estate is favored with many provisions of the internal revenue code including depreciation. Be sure that you understand these and the property

(Continued)

Figure 8-4   *(Continued)*

that you are investing in, or the partnership that you are buying a part of, before you take the plunge. Real estate investment trusts provide the small investor with a means to invest in real estate and still have liquidity.

Equity investment or stock market.

See above.

Individual retirement accounts.

If you do not have an individual retirement account, get one. I consider them to be one of the best tax shelters available now. There are a myriad of ways that you can invest in individual retirement accounts and you may need to seek counseling.

8. *Tax Exempt Investments*

These usually pay a lower rate because they are not taxable. Learn how to calculate your effective after-tax yield on investments like this before you make an investment. Ask your financial planner how this works and how it relates to your tax bracket.

9. *Shifting Income to Other Family Members*

This is a good tax tactic for moving earning on invested funds from your large tax bracket to your child's small or nonexistent tax bracket. It can be an excellent way to fund a child's education. Seek guidance.

10. *Annuities*

Annuities are another good way to build a retirement fund and have some of the earnings or contributions tax-deferred. Again, seek counseling before you invest.

11. *Your Personal Residence*

The home that you live in is a shelter in more ways than one. Be sure you understand the tax implication of buying and selling a personal residence. Call us before you make major decisions on house purchases.

These are just a few general descriptions of the methods available to you to build a nest egg for retirement. We can explain or expand upon any of these suggestions at your request. Call us.

Finally, do not get so caught up in pinching pennies that you do not enjoy your money. You can enjoy it better with a plan.

A WORD OF CAUTION ABOUT INSURANCE ILLUSTRATIONS

It is often said that an insurance professional had better be the first and only, or the last person to prepare an insurance illustration. Unfortunately, this is true. If given the opportunity, we can also beat any competitive quote. This is true not only because we have a variety of insurance companies and products to choose from, but an infinite variety of ''assumptions'' that we can make regarding future interest rates, and so on.

What does this mean to you, the consumer? It means that you must ask each professional you are dealing with what assumptions were made to arrive at the numbers in your illustration. The cheapest policy is not always the best policy! Be sure that your insurance professional has made realistic assumptions that are in your best interest. Always deal with professionals who you know and trust.

9

Marketing to Small Businesses

"I only do what only I can do."

Jim Ainsworth

If your firm is similar to mine, approximately 25 percent of your clients are small businesses. They represent a way to grow your business exponentially. Here are some of the opportunities available and some hints on how to take advantage of them.

PAYROLL DEDUCTION PLANS

This represents a great opportunity that is under utilized and under marketed. The program can be done without IRS approval, costs the employee nothing, and is a great fringe benefit. The program simply offers employees a way to save by payroll deduction. Numerous surveys have shown that employees would rather save through their employer rather than anyplace else. Even though the employer is out almost no trouble and no expense, it is perceived by employees as a benefit. Several product sponsors offer a program that allows the employer to simply withhold funds from the employee's paychecks and submit one check to the product sponsor.

RETIREMENT AND CAFETERIA PLANS

Many of us are reluctant to sell retirement plans because of administration complexity and a perceived resistance by employers to any kind of contribution on behalf of employees. However, through our tax knowledge, CPAs can show employers how it can be very cost effective to establish a retirement plan for employees in order for the owner to save on his own taxes. A good retirement plan will also reduce turnover and make recruiting new employees easier.

The administrative complexity and plan selection problems can be solved in a variety of ways. Third party administrators are available to handle administration. Also, these administrators or product sponsors will prepare proposals for your client complete with recommendations as to the type of plan to be implemented.

The possibilities for income for the registered representative in retirement planning are enormous. For example, a 25 employee business with average contributions of 6 percent on average salaries of only $30,000 would yield annual commissions of approximately $1,800. If you set up only two small plans like this for 10 years, your annual revenues would be approximately $80,000. This would be an almost ''automatic'' revenue. This does not count the possibilities opened for new relationships with 5,000 employees including approximately 100 executives.

So How Do You Sell Retirement Plans?

Use TOPS. Remember TOPS stands for:

1. *Trust.* Ask only one or more trust questions such as: ''Joe, your business is continuing to show good profits, and Uncle Sam seems to keep right on taking a larger and larger share. How long have you and I talked about doing something about it? Tax laws limit our choices, but sheltering income and putting off the taxes on the income it earns is still available to businesses like yours.''

2. *Opportunity.* If he already has a plan, ask: ''Do you completely understand the costs and benefits of the plan you currently have? What information were you provided to help you in your choice? Do your employees understand the plan and its benefits? Do they perceive it as a benefit that would be difficult to leave? What kind of participation do you get?''

   If he does not have a plan, ask: ''Is turnover costing you money? Do you know about what it costs to train a new employee and to absorb new employee errors? How are you going to make this business provide you with a comfortable retirement without taxes cutting too big a slice?''

3. *Pain.* Ask: ''How many years have you owned this business? Do you have other sources of retirement? How do you feel about getting hit for social security taxes last year of about $_____ as well as unemployment taxes of about $_____? And that is just on your employees. What about the taxes you paid on your own earnings? How important is it to you to assist your employees in reaching a comfortable retirement? How important is it to you to make this business provide you with a comfortable retirement? Under your present conditions, how is it going to do that?''

4. *Solution.* Ask: ''What does retirement mean to you in terms of income, activities, etc. What do you want to do and how much do you think it will take to do it? If you could find a way to sock away some of your hard-earned dollars and keep the IRS away from it, how important would that be to you?'' Now, sit back and listen!

Here are some other questions you could ask. Remember, do not push. Ask the question and then sit back and listen:

''What about if I could also show you how to lower your social security taxes on employees' wages [cafeteria plan] and provide them an income tax break as well?''

''Which is more important, providing for your own retirement or providing employee benefits and reducing turnover and costs?''

''Would you be interested in a plan that allows you to receive the lions share of the contributions?'' (Age weighted plan, nonqualified plan.)

"If you do not want to contribute anything for the employees, would it be important to you to set up a plan that provides only for you?" (Charitable trust, nonqualified plan.)

"What about a plan that uses only employee money?" (401(k).)

"If I could show you a way to contribute to the plan and use it as a way to provide for employees' retirement plans, take a tax deduction, while incurring only administrative expense, would that be of interest to you?" (401(k) with ER contribution substituted for raises in one period. Good deal for employees who do not have to pay income taxes on the raise; employer gets a deduction without substantial out of pocket costs.)

Of course, you generally would not have to ask all of these questions of every employer. Usually one of them will be the hot button you are looking for.

BUY–SELL AGREEMENTS

Sounds like something that an attorney sells does it not? If your small business prospect has two or more owners, chances are it needs a buy–sell agreement that provides for either disability or death of any of the primary owners. So how do you make money on this? You sell the disability and life policies on both. Who writes the agreement? Either the client's attorney or one with whom you work. Most insurance companies will provide prototype plans to be reviewed by attorneys.

How Do You Sell Buy–Sell Agreements

Again, use TOPS. Here are some sample questions using the four elements of TOPS. Remember to stop and listen after you ask each question.

Trust. "How long have you two been partners? I see from your tax return that the ownership is 50–50? Are any of your family members involved in the business at this time?"

Opportunity. "Does anybody know how to do the part of the business that Joe does? How about Tom? Do you have any kind of agreement that specifies what happens if one of you is disabled? Dead?"

Pain. "Joe, would you be comfortable being partners with Tom's wife? Does she know as much as Tom does about running the business? Tom, since Joe is not married and his only heir is his thirteen-year-old son, how are you going to deal with being partners with Joe, Jr.? Since he is under-age, who will be his guardian? None named? Then your partner will be a judge and a lawyer? Do you have time to report monthly to the court on operations of the business? You'll buy them out, you say? Without strapping the business for cash? What about the tax consequences of drawing that much money?" Aren't these easy pain questions?"

Solution. "How important is it to you to be able to draw money from the business if you are disabled? Do you want your wife to get a fair price for her share of the business? Is it important that the business continue? If I can show you how to avoid all these problems with a relatively painless plan today, are you prepared to do it?"

This is one of the easiest sales to make because the pain questions are so practical and real. Yet, most financial professionals do not make the sale because they get hung up on the issues of cross-purchase or entity (stock redemption) agreements. I have found that circumstances usually dictate which method is more appropriate. You have to consider who has the funds to pay the premiums, how many owners there are, and the possibility of alternative minimum tax. But these can be handled easily with assistance from the attorney, your broker-dealer's technical support, or the insurance company. See Part 3 for more details.

KEY EMPLOYEE BENEFITS

If your client wishes to provide benefits for key employees without providing for all, or expensive reporting to the IRS, you can assist him with a nonqualified plan providing excellent retirement benefits for key employees. See Part 3 for more details.

BUSINESS SUCCESSION

Most small business owners do not have a plan to take the benefits of a lifetime of work out of their companies. They may want to pass on the business to children, sell it to employees, or to an outside buyer. They may not realize that estate and or income taxes may prevent their dreams from being realized. Estate taxes may require the forced sale of the business in the event of death. Income taxes may prevent the owner from receiving the income he expects from the sales proceeds. It is often a shock to see taxes take from 30–50 percent of your proceeds. This opens opportunities for charitable remainder trusts, ESOPS, life insurance to provide estate liquidity, key employee insurance, and disability insurance.

A typical TOPS pain question about business succession would be: "Did you know that the IRS is going to take up to 55 percent of your estate that exceeds $600,000, when you die? That they will get more than any heir you have designated? If the tax amounts to $550,000, will your business be able to take that kind of cash hit? Could your children or wife sell it quickly? Would it bring full value if it had to be sold within nine months of your death?" (I know that there are certain relief provisions for family owned businesses, but I have never had a client to meet these provisions.)

GROUP, LIFE, HEALTH, AND DISABILITY INSURANCE

Does having a large group of employees buying these commissionable products automatically every month by payroll deduction appeal to you?

FINANCIAL PLANNING AS A COMPANY BENEFIT

For medium-size or large companies, offering financial planning is a great way to provide a low cost benefit to your employees that they will be grateful for. If you do the planning workshops right, the employees will receive a value that will be a permanent part of their lives. You can either charge a fee for the workshops paid by the employer or shared by employee and employer. You can elect to do the workshops for free just to get prospects for your services or products.

CONCLUSION

We have listed only some of the opportunities available to you in the small business market. You will discover many more in the next chapter.

10

Success with Seminars

"Most great leaders I've met are simple men. People like Sam Walton and General Schwarzkopf—they're far from stupid, but they are basically very simple. I hate complexity. The world is already complex enough without me making it more so. The principles of management and leadership are simple. The hard part is doing them, living up to them day after day, not making lots of excuses for ourselves."

H. Ross Perot

Seminars are an effective method of prospecting and getting clients familiar with your new services. Other than the post-tax interview, seminars are the most effective way to position yourself as more than just a tax accountant. They are especially effective for CPAs, because they have an established client base from which to draw. If a CPA gives a seminar, then some of his clients will almost always show up.

Are they cost effective? Ninety-nine percent of seminars pay for themselves within the first month after presentation. There is no way to measure the pay off for years afterward, but I am convinced they continue to pay for years. I have had many seminar participants visit me for the first time years after the seminar was held. Also, seminars can be held at little or no cost. Product sponsors will often assist you. It is not necessary to go to huge expense because you already have an audience in your client base. Most of the huge expenses associated with seminars are for advertising and mailings to large numbers of people in order to get a few attendees. You do not have to buy a mailing list. Just start with your clients if you want to keep costs down.

OVERCOMING THE FEAR OF PUBLIC SPEAKING

Pick a Friendly Audience for Your First Attempt

Most people fear public speaking more than they do death. If you are one of those people, I suggest beginning your public speaking in front of friendly audiences. People will forgive you if you are a little nervous. If you are a member of a service club, ask to speak on a subject that you are comfortable talking about. A natural, of course, is taxes.

Study the Subject of Public Speaking

There have been many books written on public speaking. Try these: *I Can See You Naked* by Ron Hoff, *How to Write and Give a Good Speech* by Joan Detz, *The Eloquent Executive* by William Parkhurst, and *How to be a Good Speaker*, Research Institute of America, Inc.

Join Toastmasters or a Similar Teaching Organization

The benefits of joining a group will reach into many areas of your life. Your confidence will increase, interpersonal skills will improve, and you will learn to stand in front of a group without being so self-conscious that you feel naked.

You Are Still Not Ready to Stand Up in Front of a Group?

Can you still use seminars as a way to attract business? Yes. However, I believe that your success will be limited unless you are the focal point of the seminar. You must come across as the person in charge. If you get others to give the seminar, be sure that they position you and your staff as the experts on the subject.

WHERE TO GET SPEAKERS

Product Sponsors

Most wholesalers have to be pretty good presenters in order to survive. They will be happy to assist you with presenting. However, suggest that they talk generically and not go too much in detail about their products. If they are going to assist you, it is only fair that some credit be given to their companies and products, though. They will often help you with costs of the seminar, as well.

If you have clients in attendance who are considering investing in or have already invested in the products being mentioned, having a third party reaffirm their choice can be very effective. Just do not use a hard sale during the seminar.

Your Staff

Even if you are a coward when it comes to seminars, maybe your staff is not. If not, let them show their stuff. Maybe it will motivate you to get over your irrational fears.

Use Authors and Professionals

Many people may want to plug a book that has a relationship to a seminar that you are giving. For example, we are planning a seminar on responsible investing. We will invite the author of a book on the subject to speak on the environment and social issues. We also have had psychologists speak on adjusting to life after work at seminars on retirement planning.

A FEW SIMPLE TIPS FOR MAKING A GROUP PRESENTATION

1. Tell them what you are going to tell them; then tell them, then tell them what you told them. Repetition is key. That is a good outline for any speech. People have short attention spans and low retention levels. This makes it necessary to say the same things in detail and summary format.

2. Use a conversational tone. Talk to your audience, rather than at them. Unless you are a practiced orator, it is best not to try to ''preach'' to an audience. Talk to them as you would in a normal conversation.

3. Involve your audience. Remember the rule: ''Tell me and I will forget; show me and I will remember; involve me and I will understand.'' Ask questions. Use members of the audience as illustrations. Tell stories of personal experiences involving your subject matter.

4. Read from any text sparingly. If you are going to read, you may as well hand out your prepared speech and leave the room.

5. Use various voice inflections, facial expressions, and your hands and body to illustrate points. It is good to show some emotion if you feel strongly about your subject, but this is not the time for faking it.

6. Get out from behind the lectern occasionally.

7. Forgive yourself. If you lose your place, do not know the answer to a question, just admit it. The audience will forgive you.

8. Keep it short and simple. Only the most gifted orator can keep an audience's attention for more than half an hour. In a seminar, you can go for an hour and a half if you are able to provide relief breaks for your audience and if you can break your presentation into digestible parts.

9. Use visual aids. Be sure they can be read from anywhere in the room. We like to use overheads. They are easy to make and the equipment is inexpensive. Most people are primarily visual learners. Be sure to keep them simple and understandable. Do not try to impress them with your ability to put together rows of numbers. You will just put them to sleep.

10. Handouts—Use them, do not abuse them. I hate to go to a seminar, have the presenter show some wonderful overheads or wave a great information packet before my eyes, then fail to hand it out. ''Sure wish I had some of these to give to you guys'' is a sure sign of a poorly prepared or thoughtless speaker. If you are going to show something, be prepared to give it to your audience.

    When should you deliver handouts? That depends on your type of presentation. If you are using overheads that require analysis or worksheets that need filling in, have someone hand them out just before you use them. However, be cautious about giving handouts that will steal your show. If you give them out in advance, your audience may read them rather than listening to you. They will almost certainly get ahead of you or stay behind you unless you exercise a great deal of control and relate your presentation to your material very effectively. If you are going to hand them out and refer to them, number the pages! How many times have you been in a seminar and had a speaker say that he was working off page 42 of Section 7, when there are no tabs to identify sections and no page numbers.

SEMINAR CHECKLIST

Because I hate reinventing the wheel and trying to remember what mistakes I made last time, I recommend a checklist. Break it up into preliminary preparation, site preparation, on-site duties, presentation, and follow-up. (See Figure 10-1.)

Figure 10-1   Seminar Checklist

Preliminary Preparation	Resp.	Due Date	Complete
1. Identify target audience	___	___	___
2. Select sites and times	___	___	___
3. Prepare client and nonclient lists	___	___	___
4. Prepare mailouts and invitations	___	___	___
5. Complete mailing two weeks prior for receipt on Monday or Tuesday	___	___	___
6. Prepare advertising copy	___	___	___
7. Arrange for ads to run in appropriate media (be sure to specify ad size and location)	___	___	___
8. Prepare and mail news releases if seminar is designed to be for general public education	___	___	___
9. Notify local Chamber of Commerce and give handouts	___	___	___
10. Follow up if response to mail and ads is not adequate. Follow up with phone calls beginning three days prior to date of seminar.	___	___	___
11. Confirm reservations on day prior and day of seminar	___	___	___
12. Select handouts and group into order	___	___	___
13. Prepare rough outline of seminar topic	___	___	___

Site preparation	Resp.	Due Date	Complete
1. Room temperature 5 degrees below normal	___	___	___
2. Shades drawn and distractions removed or hidden from view	___	___	___
3. Lighting and glare checked	___	___	___
4. Seating (short); space (adequate); chairs arranged for best view of presenter and visual aids (have extra chairs hidden but ready for use)	___	___	___

Figure 10-1 (*Continued*)

Preliminary Preparation	Resp.	Due Date	Complete
5. Visual aids in working order			
(a) grease board, markers, erasers	___	___	___
(b) overhead projector and screen	___	___	___
(c) slides and projector	___	___	___
(d) lighting monitor assigned	___	___	___
(e) other materials needed	___	___	___
6. Handouts readily available but under our control	___	___	___
7. Evaluation and appointment sheet ready	___	___	___
8. Business cards on hand for presenter	___	___	___
9. Name tages for staff and participants (staff tags should have firm name)	___	___	___
10. Refreshments arranged	___	___	___

On-Site Duties   Responsibility

1. Greeting participants   ___

2. Registering participants (we write names, address, and phone number if person is not an existing client)   ___

3. Issuing name tags   ___

4. Refreshments   ___

5. Break and group "control"   ___

6. Facility "tour" director   ___

7. Handouts (include business cards) (Be sure all handouts are properly stamped   ___

8. Evaluation sheets and setting appointments ***(Extremely important!)***   ___

9. Calendars for setting appointments   ___

Note: In scheduling appointments with seminar attendees, schedule their beginning appointment time 15 minutes in advance so that staff can interview and gather as much information as possible regarding where their investments are (use form). Have Office Management set up files.

Presentation Reminder List

1. Introduce yourself or have staff member do it   ___

2. Introduce other staff members—always refer to as *associates*, not employees. Staff should not group together. Aisle seats are good to assist with handouts.   ___

3. State the purpose of the seminar
(a) Goals for participants   ___
(b) Goals for us—state why we are doing it; why we are qualified; what we are trying to specialize in   ___

4. Have two staff members hand out your business cards   ___

(*Continued*)

Figure 10-1 (*Continued*)

Presentation Reminder List

  5. Announce break times, restroom locations, etc.   _____

  6. Tell them handouts will be available   _____

  7. Follow seminar outline   _____

  8. Use only ''audience participation'' type handouts during seminar   _____

  9. Summarize your presentation. (Reinforce the need for audiences to act on our suggestions.)   _____

10. Ask for questions   _____

11. Have at least two staff members give handouts (describe the handout prior to physically passing it out). Distributions should be quick to keep flow going   _____

12. As handouts are distributed, repeat our qualifications, goals, and no cost services   _____

13. Hand out *evaluations* and appointments—ask them to complete *now*! Have pads or clipboards for writing on   _____

14. Staff should collect all evaluations, introduce themselves, set up appointments on calendar, if possible   _____

15. Thank you and close   _____

Follow-up

	Resp.	Due Date	Complete
1. Review evaluation sheets next day	____	____	____
2. Call to schedule appointments for people who responded positively next day	____	____	____
3. Send thank you for attending notes with additional marketing data in three days (send goals sheet)	____	____	____
4. Call to confirm day prior to appointment—remind to bring tax returns, IRA, CD, and other investment statements, etc.	____	____	____
5. Add to potential client list (Q & A)	____	____	____
6. Financial planner must then follow through with a plan or suggestions for the client—if we do not, why even have it?	____	____	____

Notes: *Follow-ups are as important as the seminar itself.* Your best and most experienced staff should be used. Assume clients are interested and want to talk to you and let them know you sincerely think you can help them to achieve their goals stated in seminar.

Preliminary Preparation

After stage fright, the second most common reason for not having seminars is the fear that nobody will come. The preliminary preparation is to be sure that does not happen. Could it happen anyway? Yes, but it is highly unlikely. Of approximately 75 seminars we have held, we only had to cancel one for lack of interest. When we reviewed our list, we had not done all of the preliminary steps. We have had sparse attendance several times, however. What to do? Go ahead as if you had a packed house. Try to give everyone special attention and make it a workshop environment rather than just a group presentation.

On-Site Duties

This checklist is to insure that no details are overlooked in greeting the participants, getting name tags, evaluation sheets, and so on.

Presentation Reminder List

Review this list just before you present so that you do not forget important things like introducing yourself, your staff, special guests, and the like. Exercise caution with handouts.

Follow-Up

If you are not going to follow up, then why give the seminar? It is absolutely essential. Yet, this is where most fail. Follow-up is more uncomfortable than speaking. We may get rejected.

11

Other Marketing Tips

One of the most important qualities that distinguishes winners from losers is the ability to adopt a long-term perspective.

PROSPECTING

Most of this book is directed to CPAs who already have an established client base. What about those who do not have clients? You can use the same techniques for gathering clients with only slight modifications. Use the rules of good time management, use seminars and the other tools, keep prospecting all the time, set goals, and position yourself differently from the competition.

BIG ELEPHANTS OR SITTING DUCKS

Most CPAs want to go after the big elephants. They also chase the most esoteric products and schemes. I do not know what drives this tendency unless it is the basic human desire to get rich quick with minimal effort. It is especially ironic because most of our practices were built "one tax return at a time." If your client base is small and wealthy, then elephant hunting may be for you. If not, then go after the sitting ducks. The elephants will present themselves between ducks.

SERVICE AFTER THE SALE

All through this book, we have talked and will continue to talk about building relationships. If you want long-term success in this business, you will be relationship-oriented rather than transaction-oriented. That means you will maintain contact with the client after the sale. More will be mentioned on this in the next part of the book, but it is important enough to mention twice.

1. Return your phone calls promptly.
2. Report to your clients regularly on the status of their investments.
3. Consider it a race to call your clients first before they call you in the event of a negative happening.
4. Send thank you notes or letters after the transaction is completed.

MORE CLIENT SERVICE IDEAS

As a CPA, you have spent many years building relationships with your clients. You should use that same commitment to service in providing financial planning and investment services to your clients. Do not be fooled into thinking that *performance* of investments is the key to client retention. *Communication* is the key to keeping clients, generating new business from existing clients, and getting referrals for new ones. People do not care how much you know until they know how much you care. Let your clients know that you care by keeping in contact on a regular basis.

Status and Performance Reports.   In good or bad times, you must send your clients reports on the status of their investments. It does not matter that they are getting reports from a mutual fund or insurance company; they bought the investment from *you*. You are the person from whom they want to hear. This is doubly important when performance has been poor. Write your clients a personal note on their reports to let them know you are watching the investment and remember the goals set by you and your client. Supplement this with periodic phone calls.

Use a data-base system that tells you which clients are invested in which areas. If something happens of significance in that particular area, give the client a call. If there are too many to call quickly enough, prepare a letter to go to all clients affected by certain events.

Call for No Reason.   Set up a system of reminders so you can call on birthdays or other special occasions.

Take All Phone Calls and Return All Phone Calls.   Make it a rule that no phone call goes unreturned for more than 24 hours.

Improve Listening Skills.   Ask your clients questions about what they are saying. Write down their comments. Rephrase and repeat what they say. Practice being quiet at least 50 percent of the time so that your client can talk.

Do Things for Nothing.   Do things for clients when there seems to be nothing in it for you. The rewards will come. Help enough people and money will come.

Call Their Names.   Instruct your staff and remind yourself to call the client's name at least three times when he visits your office.

Know Their Habits.   Have your receptionist keep a card file on the special things about the client such as how he likes his coffee, if he/she prefers tea, and the like.

Do More Than is Expected.   If a client has an error on a transaction and you correct it, send him a small gift or thank you note apologizing for the inconvenience and asking if it was resolved to his satisfaction. Make a personal delivery of a late check or statement.

Send Interesting Articles.   When you read something of interest to your client, copy it and send it with your card and comments. It does not have to be about investments.

Buy Books. Send your clients complimentary copies of books that might be of interest to them about financial planning or about their industry or business.

Appreciate Referrals. Send thank you notes for referrals. Accompany them with tickets to the theater, complimentary dinners for two, a tree planted in the front yard, etc.

Ask Clients How You are Doing. Ask them what you could do to make your service better. Do not ask them if you are doing alright. They will be too embarrassed to say no.

Appreciation Events. Host an annual client appreciation night. We usually invite our clients to an annual outdoor stew. It is relatively inexpensive considering the response we get.

Do not Hide. Keep in personal touch and keep pressing the flesh with your clients. Do not hide behind subordinates, the computer, *The Wall Street Journal*, or any of the other myriad of excuses we use to avoid meeting clients face to face.

Keep the Plan Current. Keep their financial plans updated and refer to them consistently. Plans are the ''ties that bind.''

Send for Social Security Benefits. Fill out a social security benefit card and send it in for the client.

Invite Service Clubs. If you have the room, invite service clubs to your office for lunch and a short presentation from you. They will welcome the lunch and the program.

Invite a Friend. Take a client to a sporting event, and ask him to bring along a friend.

Get Testimonial Letters. Get clients to write letters of referral for you.

Get an 800 Number. If you have clients who must call long distance, get an 800 number for them.

Put a Welcome Sign in the Lobby. Put client's name on the sign before they arrive.

Offer New Services. Provide elderly planning, estate planning, mediation, etc. Provide clients with written ''helpful hints'' on planning for a secure financial future.

Here are a few more handy marketing tips:

Send out reminder cards for appointments
Confirm meetings by phone
Produce a newsletter
Send gifts for holidays or special occasions
Provide subscriptions to business publications

Make house calls

Send a thank you note after a client makes an investment

Offer CD rate comparison services

Write newspaper columns, clip them, and send to clients

Give educational seminars

Do post-tax interviews even after the sale is made.

CONCLUSION

You now know:

How to use TOPS

How to find your niche and design a marketing plan

How to sell during tax season

How to arrange your office and use the proper equipment and tools

How to sell from the financial plan

How to use mailers and tangible sales aids

How to market to small businesses

How to use seminars

How to prospect

How to service after the sale

So what are you waiting for? Stop procrastinating. Stop regarding procrastination as harmless. It is a deadly enemy that you must overcome or it will overcome you. Do not let things like mailers or brochures give you an excuse for not getting person to person with your client. Do not duck selling because you perceive it as difficult. The rewards are far greater than the small price.

PART III

Technical—The Tools of Financial Planning

12

Retirement Plans

"The inability to delay instant gratification is a predictor of failure. People do what is "fun and easy" rather than what is hard and necessary."

Retirement plans conjure up visions of mountains of paperwork, dealing with several layers of federal bureaucracy, liability, and loads of technical expertise requirements. It is our job as advisors to change our own perceptions as well as our clients. We must recognize that the government almost always attempts to destroy the viability of every measure passed for our "benefit" by attaching regulatory "hoops" to jump through. These "hoops" are supposed to keep the system from being abused. However, the hoops themselves are abusing the system far more than the few who would use the law to their own advantage. They generally hurt most the very people they are supposed to help. Those with the resources, expertise, and inclination to abuse the system will always find ways to either circumvent the law or simply break it. The ones without such assets or attributes wind up getting hurt by the rules that are supposed to protect them.

So what can we do in such a system? While working to change it, we must learn to use it to our benefit while we have it. The alternative of simply not participating may leave us out in the cold at retirement time.

Many aspects of life today (including retirement planning) are like a ball game. If you do not play, you will always be a spectator and have to pay the price of admission. I choose to play in the game of life, even when I do not like the rules. When I come to the game, I bring the best ball, bat, and glove I can find (education and advice about retirement planning). Before it is my turn to bat, I want to know where the bases and fences are located, how many strikes I get, how I can be called out, and what the other rules are. Then I step up to the plate with a plan for getting a few base hits. Whether we like them or not, we must recognize that the retirement plan options we have today *are* today's rules. They do provide opportunity if we know how to use them.

Stop thinking of retirement plans as legal documents. Do not visualize the 5500 forms and mounds of legalese. Think of retirement plans as tools for yourself and your clients to reach financial security faster. In spite of the clumsy way Congress camouflages the benefits of retirement plans, there are usually good ideas or benefits lurking behind everyone of them if we can ferret them out. There should always be a tax benefit. Otherwise, why have the retirement plan at all? Never underestimate the power of compound interest on deferred taxes. What are deferred taxes? They are taxes that we do not send to the government today to be dropped in a black hole. They are taxes that we keep to invest. Many downplay the advantages of tax deferral citing the possibility of higher tax rates in the future. They say that we should pay taxes now. If you can invest your deferred taxes for a period longer than five years, then deferral usually pays off, even if tax rates go up. The longer the time period invested, the more tax rates can rise with deferral still paying off. The power of compounding will inevitably catch up to all but the most horrendous increases in tax rates. Hopefully, some type of reason will prevail and tax rates will not go through the roof again. Also, you will still have some control over when the funds are removed in order to spread out your tax burden and to wait until tax rates come down.

The purpose of this chapter is to locate tax and other benefits present in those retirement laws and to show you how you can maximize them while minimizing the negatives. It is not intended as a primary technical source for every aspect of retirement plans. Unfortunately, that is a book in itself. I hope to show you that you do not have to be an expert on retirement plans in order to "play ball."

In the following pages, we will cover:

1. Marketing retirement plans.
2. Types of retirement plans available.
3. Selecting the right retirement plan for an employee and employer.
4. How to effectively participate in a plan.
    (a) How to put money in and how much.
    (b) How to get money out.
5. The mechanics of retirement plan administration.
    (a) Set up.
    (b) Administration of regulatory rules.
    (c) Accounting for investments.
    (d) Investment selection and monitoring.

MARKETING RETIREMENT PLANS

Finding The Perfect Retirement Plan

All self-employed, employers, and employees want to set up and participate in the perfect retirement plan. Self-employed individuals and employers both want:

1. All contributions to the plan to be income tax deductible for both the employer and employee.
2. All contributions not to be subject to FICA, FUTA, or SUTA.
3. Contributions to be heavily skewed toward owners and any employee contributions to be based on merit or other selective measurements controlled by the employer.
4. No set up or administrative costs.
5. A high rate of return on all investments.
6. No commissions on investments.
7. All statements to be easy to understand, prompt, and accurate.
8. Employees and employers to understand the program and to be motivated by it to increase performance and lower turnover.

9. If the employer elects to contribute funds on the employees' behalf, all such funds should not be vested until the employee retires at a time selected by the employer.

10. Employees perceive the plan as an excellent benefit provided by the employer even if he contributes nothing to it.

The perfect retirement plan for employees would include the following aspects:

1. Employers make all contributions which are nontaxable to employees when the contribution goes in and when it comes out.

2. Employees may make as much in tax-deductible contributions to the plan as they wish in order to supplement the employers contribution. Employers will match such contributions dollar for dollar.

3. Employees have option of choosing their own investments or allowing another to choose for them.

4. Statements come every month or quarterly depending on the employee's choice.

5. Statements are easy to read and understand.

6. Money can be withdrawn at any time for reasonable expenditures free of penalty or taxation.

7. All contributions are immediately 100 percent vested.

8. High rate of return on all investments contributed without risk.

9. No costs associated with set up, administration, reporting, monitoring, or selecting investments.

Why list the perfect investment for both the employer and employee? Because you will represent both sides in effectively marketing retirement plans. You must be able to balance the things most wanted by both sides with the real world. If you show your client the perfect retirement plan as it is shown here, he will usually recognize the unreasonableness of his own expectations. Both you and he will start to see some of the reasons why we have so many rules attached to retirement plans. Hopefully, both will more fully understand the reasons for some of the rules. If the reasons behind the rules are understood, then hopefully there will be some forgiveness for the administrative burden they impose.

After your client has been shown the perfect plan, then you can start asking him to prioritize which of the items are most important. Ask your client to rate them in order of importance or rate each item from one to ten. Then convert them to a numerical sequence. More than one item, of course, may be essential to the consideration of a plan.

USING TOPS

We covered how to use TOPS in selling retirement plans to small businesses in Chapter 9. Asking your client about his/her ''perfect retirement plan'' is a good way to lead into TOPS questions. For example, asking your client to rate each characteristic of the perfect retirement plan as to its importance would be opportunity questions. They help you find out what the client's primary criteria are for evaluating retirement plans (i.e., what are his "opportunities" or problems?).

Pain questions would probably relate to the answers he gives to the opportunities questions. By the time you get around to the pain questions, you should know something about the client's personality and what is important to him in selecting retirement plans. If you find that he is concerned about providing for his own retirement, but feels he cannot afford administrative costs, you may want to ask "What happens if you do nothing because of administrative costs? Are you going to be able to take the money you need for retirement out of the earnings of the company if you are not here to run it?"

For solution questions, try something like this: "Would you be willing to sacrifice some of the items in a perfect retirement plan and make a decision to go ahead if I could design one that allows you to make adequate contributions to provide for your own retirement, make larger contributions for your key employees, and provide for your other employees at minimum cost to you?" How can he say no? Sounds great, but can you deliver on such a promise? Yes. This describes a combination of a nonqualified plan with a non- or low-contributory 401(k). I like contributory 401(k)s, so I often ask the employer who is reluctant to contribute to just lower a planned wage increase and put what he was planning to add to salaries into a 401(k). The employer is out no extra money other than set up and administration, gets a long-term incentive plan in place, and is able to provide a disproportionate share for himself and key employees.

SELLING TO EMPLOYEES

Selling retirement plans may involve dual selling. After you have sold the employer on participating in the plan, you have to deliver on your promise to get his participation high. This is not a problem if employees are not putting in any money. But it can be a problem if they are. That means meeting with employees either in groups or one on one. I prefer small groups or one on one if it is possible. Selling to employees at any level is usually easy, especially if the employer is contributing.

Many product sponsors provide videos and sales materials to assist you in enrolling employees. However, nothing is as effective as the personal touch. You need to try and establish a relationship with as many employees as possible. In small groups of fifty or less, you or a member of your staff should meet individually with each employee, even if they are not eligible yet. If you are an experienced group meeting presenter, then this can be very effective, but it can also be a problem if one employee who is a leader makes trouble for you by displaying a negative attitude toward you or the plan in general. People are likely to be much more open and honest and make their own decisions in private personal meetings with you rather than as part of a group. Group mentality can be excellent if it is favorable toward you, but it can be a stampede if it goes the other way. Here are some tips:

1. Allow at least 15 minutes to meet with each employee. Enrollment forms should be ready prior to the meeting. If the employee elects to enroll, you may want a staff member to handle the paperwork so that you can continue selling.

2. Point out the excellent benefits that the employer has elected to provide to the employees. Concentrate on the benefits to the employee and try to show him how this step is going to make his life and his workplace better.

3. Talk about retirement in general. Project the employees' current salary to planned retirement age using a normal rate of inflation with your financial calculator. When they see the principal needed to support their current lifestyle at retirement and the inadequacy of social security to support such a lifestyle, they will listen more attentively to the retirement plan being offered.

4. State emphatically that the program is entirely voluntary. However, the higher the participation, the better the success of the program.

5. Explain the basics of the program. How much each employee can contribute, how much (if any) the employer is contributing, and investment options available.

6. Show the ways that an employee can gain from participating in the program:

    (a) Show how her own contributions grow with the benefit of tax deferral versus growth outside the plan in a regular savings program. Use the same projected rate of growth for both investments; just use tax deferral for the plan investments.

    (b) Show how the employer contribution will grow.

    (c) Show how she can benefit from forfeitures if they are reallocated under the program. Forfeitures are the nonvested portions of employer contributions left by exiting employees. This is extremely impressive for higher level employees and encourages longevity.

    (d) Summarize the ways that an employee's retirement plan can grow by numbering them.

        I. Employee contributions
        II. The earnings on employee contributions
        III. Employer contributions
        IV. Earnings on employer contributions
        V. Forfeitures
        VI. Earnings on forfeitures
        VII. Earnings on taxes not paid until retirement.

    (e) Estimate each of the contributions and earnings to a value at the employee's date of retirement using conservative estimates. Be sure to explain fully that these are estimates and how you arrived at the assumptions for growth.

    (f) Point out the investment choices (keep them limited) and assist the participant in selection.

    (g) Sign up the participant.

FINDING PROSPECTS

Use the "Acres of Diamonds" Rule

If you have not heard Earl Nightingale's tape on this story, you should obtain it. It tells the story of a farmer in South Africa who is unhappy farming and has dreams of striking it rich by striking gold. He sells his farm and uses the proceeds to seek his fortune. He dies in poverty without making his discovery. The purchaser of his farm accidentally discovers literally acres of diamonds on the farm. The lesson to be learned is to look in your own back yard for your "Acres of Diamonds" before you go elsewhere. Here are a few places to start:

Your File Cabinets.   When brokers and insurance agents are receiving training on marketing, guess what the most recommended method for getting new retirement plan clients is? Ask for referrals from CPAs! If you are a practicing CPA, you have a file cabinet full of diamonds. Look at your client list to see who needs a retirement plan. Who *does* need a retirement plan? Everyone who is not already financially independent. Even they may need one for employees or to avoid taxes. Rate your own clients as to need. Small businesses are obvious targets, but do not overlook individuals who may need IRAs, insurance as a retirement plan, or nonqualified annuities as a substitute for nondeductible IRAs.

Your Business and Home Neighborhoods.   Ever do a tax return for an employee of a local business establishment and notice a retirement plan indicated on her W-2? Does it make you feel a little embarrassed to know that a business a few blocks away from you set up a retirement plan with someone else right underneath your nose? Then do something about it! Visit them directly and ask them if they have a plan. Use the TOPS questions detailed under the sales and marketing curriculum.

Have a coffee and donut breakfast at your office for your business neighbors. Tell them about your ability to coordinate all aspects of a retirement plan through your connections to product sponsors, third-party administrators, trust companies, and your broker–dealer. Ask them for a meeting to discuss their special needs.

Prepare Proposals.   Most third-party administrators and product sponsors will assist you in making proposals for prospects as to the proper type of retirement plan, projections for individuals within the business, estimated costs for set up and administration, and so forth.

Use Your Tax Clients as Leverage.   If you have a client who is an employee of a business, ask the employee for an introduction to decision makers. You can tell the decision maker that you are the employee's financial advisor and have been working on his retirement plans. Ask what type of plan they have (you may already know from the W-2). Ask if the owner sees a need to provide for himself. Do not spend too much time on your client's needs. You are not there as your client's representative; you are trying to help the new prospect reach his goals.

Prospect Where You Spend.   If you are using the services or purchasing tangible goods from a firm, ask if they have a retirement plan. Do not spend all of your time looking for the "perfect business" or the huge one-shot retirement plan that will provide a permanent retirement for you. Somehow, even though we are small business people ourselves, we overlook the local garbage disposal company, the dry cleaners and laundry, auto repair shop, building cleaning services, etc. These are the same folks your competition is overlooking. As a group, they are often more receptive to your suggestions than the "glamour" business will be. Often, they are flattered that somebody finally asked them about their finances.

Prospecting Outside Your Neighborhood and Client Base

After you have found success in your neighborhood and file cabinets, you may find that the retirement plan area is an excellent specialty for you. If so, you may want to purchase outside sources for information such as the *Redbook* of retirement plans. You may want to hold seminars and use purchased mailing lists. Look at the local Chamber of Commerce list of business and professional members. These are traditional methods of prospecting, however, and you will find that is exactly what your competitors are doing. If you are going to beat them, you have to ''be good, get better, and become the best.'' You have to have more tenacity and be willing to take more rejection. Persistence and patience pay off.

If you have been successful with your own clients, ask them for referrals and testimonial letters. Tell product sponsors, third-party administrators, and trust companies to whom you have referred business that you wish them to return the favor. Think about specializing in one or more industries. You may want to become a specialist in women's clothing manufacturers, for example. Most small business groups have trade associations. Subscribe to their magazines. Attend their conventions. Ask to write articles or to provide a newsletter for their members.

Remember, retirement plan contributions have a tendency to grow like compound interest. They also attract other business from executives, other employees, and their referrals.

TYPES OF RETIREMENT PLANS

My fingers literally freeze at the keyboard when I start to classify retirement plans. I have seen them classified as pension versus profit-sharing plans, defined benefit versus defined contribution, qualified versus nonqualified, contributory versus noncontributory, deductible versus nondeductible, salary deferral plans, individual versus business plans, corporation versus partnerships and sole proprietorships, private pension plans, and so on. The purpose of this section is to simplify what has been made needlessly complex. It is not intended to be a comprehensive guide to retirement planning types or their intricacies.

Individual Retirement Accounts

IRAs have been called the little guy's tax shelter. When originally passed, the law that allowed a tax deduction for these arrangements seemed to herald a new approach and new thinking for Congress. Only a few years later, they came back and crippled the excellent legislation. I think individual retirement accounts should not only be deductible, but *mandatory* for individuals above a very low minimum income limit who do not have vesting in a verified retirement plan. Although this goes against my usual thinking about government interference in the private sector, think of the benefits: Increased savings rate, economic stimulation, less pressure on the social security system, increased capital for economic investment, and most important, the feeling of security to be felt by Americans who have a sense of financial security. The feeling of dependence on the government that tears at the very fabric of our society might decrease. Does it not make sense that everyone would have his own individual retirement account, funded every year that the individual has income above a predetermined amount, with administrative costs paid by the private sector, funds invested in the private sector rather than the government black hole, no Congressmen deciding how the funds can be spent, no funny bookkeeping, no wasteful bureaucracy?

What we really have for IRAs include:

1. Someone must act as a trustee or custodian to an individual retirement account. I call them the tattle-tales. They are banks, credit unions, investment companies, S&Ls, insurance companies, and so on. A trustee's job is to keep records of contributions, and report to the government any withdrawals, prohibited acts, and so forth.

2. Contributions cannot exceed $2,000 per year or 100 percent of compensation, except for spousal IRAs when the contribution can go as high as $2,250 for both spouses when only one has earned income. Excess contributions draw a 6 percent excise tax. Rollover contributions from other retirement plans can be any amount.

3. IRA contributions cannot be made during or after the year that a taxpayer reaches the age of 70-$\frac{1}{2}$.

4. IRA funds cannot be commingled with the taxpayer's other assets.

5. IRA funds cannot be used to buy a life insurance policy or collectibles.

6. No loans can be made from IRAs.

7. Anyone who has earned income and is under the age of 70-$\frac{1}{2}$, or who has a rollover from another plan can make a contribution.

8. Deductible or nondeductible? If you *or your spouse* is an active participant in an employer sponsored retirement plan, then your contribution will be deductible only if your adjusted gross income falls under certain limits. (That is a great rule right? It assumes that if your spouse has a retirement plan at work, you do not need one. You probably are not going to eat much in your retirement years, after all.) These income limits are as follows:

	Deduction		
Filing Status	*Full*	*Reduced*	*None*
Single or Head of Household	< $25K	25K to 35K	> $35K
Married Filing Jointly	< $40K	> 40K to 50K	> $50K
Married Filing Separately	None	< 10K	> $10K

Should your client make a contribution if it is not deductible? The advantage is tax-deferred compounding. Because of the onerous rules for reporting deductible versus nondeductible IRA contributions, I believe that tax-deferred annuities are an attractive alternative to nondeductible IRAs because of the lack of limitation on contributions and the absence of reporting requirements. I foresee a major quagmire of problems when nondeductible and deductible IRAs start being distributed on a large scale.

9. Distributions:

(a) *Maximum Age.* You must begin taking distributions from your IRA by April 1 of the calendar year following the year that you reach the age of 70-$\frac{1}{2}$. The minimum distribution is based on a formula designed to have the entire amount withdrawn by the time of your death based on mortality tables. If you withdraw less than the minimum, you will be hit with a 50 percent penalty on the amount that should have been distributed.

(b) Distributions because of death or disability are not penalized, but are taxed.

    I. If distributions have already begun at time of death, then they must be continued at a rate just as fast as they were prior to death. The beneficiary can elect to take the entire distribution and pay tax on them.

    II. If distributions have not already begun at the time of death:

        (A) No beneficiary—must be distributed within five years.

        (B) Nonspouse beneficiary—funds can be distributed at once or over the life of the beneficiary but must start *one year* after the taxpayer's death.

        (C) Spouse beneficiary can take distribution immediately or simply take the same position as the deceased spouse.

    III. Premature distributions
Distributions prior to age 59-$\frac{1}{2}$ incur a 10 percent excise tax penalty unless:

        (A) Made in the form of a life annuity or its equivalent for a minimum of five years.

        (B) Death or disability.

The Potential Market for IRAs

Virtually everyone! Use the sales and marketing skills you learned in the last part to reach your clients. See Figures 12-1 and 12-2 for contribution limits and deductions.

SEP–IRA Plans and SAR–SEP Plans

SEP started out being SEPP or *Simplified Employee Pension Plan*. It is a fairly simple plan as compared to its cousins, but the bureaucrats could not resist justifying their jobs by tinkering with it. SAR is an acronym for *salary reduction*.

Think of the SEP as an IRA set up for employees. SEPs are alternatives to a profit-sharing plan or a 401(k). SEP contributions are ordinarily made by an employer. SAR–SEPs may be funded by salary reduction agreements by employees.

Major Advantages of SEPs:

1. *Simplicity.* A SEP is easy to set up and administer. If salary reduction is not involved, almost no administration is required other than to be certain that all employees who are eligible receive a contribution, that all contributions are in equal percentages, and that contributions do not exceed the indexed limits. If salary reduction is involved and the owner participates, then nondiscrimination tests must be made. If the owner does not participate and at least 50 percent of the employees participate in the SAR–SEP, then discrimination tests are not necessary. No 5500 requirements are involved.

Figure 12-1   Individual Retirement Account (IRA) Limits and Features and the Importance of Tax-Deferred Compounding

Contribution Limits	Ideal Investor	Special Features
The lesser of $2,000 or 100 percent of eligible compensation. $2,250 for individual and spouse who earns less than $250.	Every wage earner who wishes to save for retirement with dollars that grow tax-deferred. Ideal plan for individuals interested in planning ahead for a secure future.	• Full flexibility of contributions Additional full service features: • Full government reporting • Social Security integration • Vesting • Comprehensive record keeping

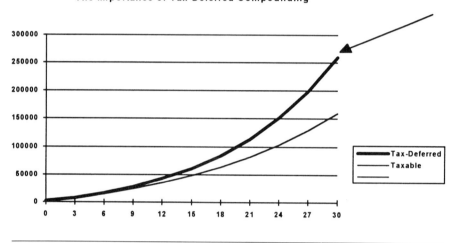

2. *Substitute for a 401(k) with less administrative costs.* The SAR–SEP can be marketed as a substitute for a 401(k) plan for businesses with 25 or less employees. It has less administrative costs than the 401(k) and can still be funded in a similar manner.

3. *Discretionary contributions.* Your client is not locked into contributions every year. The amount of the contribution and the frequency is completely at the discretion of the employer. This is probably the most important marketing point to employers.

4. *Plans may be established after year-end.* SEPs can be a planning tool at tax time, because they can be funded and a tax deduction taken on the prior year's tax return if contributions are made by tax filing deadline including extensions. Exercise caution, however, and set up the employees' IRA accounts prior to April 15.

5. *May be integrated with Social Security.* This means that the employer may consider the contributions he makes to Social Security when calculating the

Figure 12-2   Is Your IRA Contribution Deductible?

Tax Filing Status	Are You (or your spouse) Covered by a Retirement Plan at Work?[1]	Adjusted Gross Income[2]	You are Entitled To[3]
Single	No	No limit	Full deduction
	Yes	$25,000 or less	Full deduction
		Over $25,000 but less than $35,000	Deduction is reduced by $10 for every $50 of income above $25,000[4]
		$35,000 or more	No deduction
Married, filing jointly	No	No Limit	Full deduction
	Yes	$40,000 or less	Full deduction
		Over $40,000 but less than $50,000	Deduction is reduced by $10 for every $50 of income above $40,000[4]
		$50,000 or more	No deduction

Source: Internal Revenue Service, Publication 590. Of course, this chart provides general information for determining an IRA deduction.

[1]Coverage by a retirement plan includes, but is not limited to, qualified pension, profit sharing and annuity plans as well as certain self-employed retirement plans.

[2]Adjusted gross income is your total income excluding such items as IRA deductions, and foreign income or housing exclusions, as reported on the annual federal tax return (Form 1040).

[3]For most individuals, a full deduction is the lesser of $2,000 or 100 percent of compensation.

[4]Do not reduce below $200.

If you are married and filing a joint return you will want to figure an IRA deduction for each spouse separately. In this case the deduction is reduced by $10 for every $50 of your combined income above $40,000.

minimum contribution required for each employee. If the employer is well above the Social Security maximum salary level, this can be a factor that allows him to slant contributions more toward himself.

Major Disadvantages of SEPs:

1. Employees are 100 percent invested immediately. There are no golden handcuffs with these plans.
2. They are overly generous to nonkey employees. Even part-time employees must be covered.
3. Employees who met the requirements during the year, but left before contributions were made will still qualify and contributions must be made on their behalf.
4. SAR–SEPs were almost on target for small employers, but the 50 percent requirement and the nondiscrimination test make them unwieldy.
5. Because the plans are discretionary, employers may stop making contributions and employees may be left without an adequate retirement plan.
6. No lump sum distribution benefits (ten- or five-year forward averaging) benefits are available.

SEP Features That Can Be Advantages or Disadvantages:

1. Younger participants are favored over older ones.
2. There is no accelerated funding for those near retirement.
3. There is no vesting schedule, and therefore no forfeitures.
4. There are no loan privileges.
5. There are no hardship distributions.

The market for SEPs and SAR–SEPs would include small employers who want simplicity and low administrative costs. See Figures 12-3 and 12-4 for more information about SEP and SAR–SEP plans.

Keogh Plans (HR 10)

Keogh plans, once the mainstay of partnerships and self-employed sole proprietors, are less important today because legislation has largely erased the difference between corporate plans and plans for partnerships and sole proprietors.

Figure 12-3   Simplified Employee Pension Plan (SEP)

Contribution Limits	Ideal Investor	Special Features
The lesser of 15 percent of eligible compensation or $30,000.	Small firm seeking to minimize filings and paperwork. One short form sets it up and investments are made to an IRA. May exclude employees with less than three of previous five years of service and those under age 21.	• Easy to establish • No government filings • Extended deadline for setup • Full flexibility of contributions

Figure 12-4   Salary Reduction SEP (SAR–SEP)

Contribution Limits	Ideal Investor	Special Features
Salary reduction arrangement up to the lesser of $8,994 (1993 limit) or 13.04 percent of compensation. Three percent contribution from the business is required in top-heavy plans.	Business with 25 or fewer employees wanting to offer employees a way to invest through convenient salary reduction in *before tax* dollars. Limited contribution by the business. May exclude employees with less than three of previous five years of service and those under age 21.	• Simple, inexpensive 401(k) • IRA replacement • Promotes employee participation • Special nondiscrimination tests

Keogh rules were a separate and distinct body of law. Keogh is derived from the last name of Congressman Eugene Keogh who sponsored the law, and HR 10 refers to the number assigned the bill in the House of Representatives.

Keogh sponsors today can have most of the same types of plans as corporate sponsors (i.e., defined benefit, defined contribution, etc). Only two distinctions remain:

1. Keogh plans are not permitted to have loan provisions for owner employees.
2. The self-employed contribution or benefit is based on net earnings instead of salary.

401(k) Plans

The acronym CODA is often used in describing 401(k) plans. CODA stands for *cash* or *deferred arrangement*. A 401(k) is probably the best known IRS code section. More than any other type of plan, these are status symbols. Whether you mention 401(k) at an elegant business lunch or a beer bust, most people will recognize what you are talking about.

All 401(k)s are profit-sharing plans. They are the answer to the old thrift plans where employees kicked in their own money to supplement employers pension plans. Employee contributions were after taxes in thrift plans, however. With 401(k)s, employees can contribute before tax dollars up to 15 percent of their salaries subject to stated indexed maximums. They are subject to antidiscrimination rules and the pension administrator will have to conduct tests to see if these rules have been met. If your participation among rank and file is low, and there is a large variance between upper management and the rank and file employees, then it is easy for upper management to over contribute and have to refund. Work with your third-party administrator to stay on top of the testing formula and make estimates as to maximum contributions that should be attempted by upper management when the program begins. If they want to contribute more, but cannot because of the rules, it is time to suggest a nonqualified plan.

Contributions to these plans are income tax deferred, but do not dodge Social Security taxes. Employer (matching) contributions can be subject to vesting rules. Loan privileges are optional with the plan document, but withdrawals cannot be made except for:

1. Retirement.
2. Death or disability.
3. Separation from service.
4. Attainment of age 59-$\frac{1}{2}$.
5. Hardship (defined as anything that is necessary in light of immediate and heavy financial needs of an employee).

Be sure to tell employees that 401(k) plans should not be considered their personal banks. If they are not making a retirement commitment, I do not recommend them for capital accumulation.

The 401(k)s are excellent door-openers for prospecting retirement plans. They can be used as the only plan or a complementary plan to an existing profit-sharing or pension plan. They can be structured to allow contributions by the em-

Figure 12-5   401(k) Plan

Contribution Limits	Ideal Investor
Funded from three sources: 1. Employee pre-tax salary deferrals (1993 limit of $8,994). 2. Matching contributions made by the business. 3. Profit-sharing contributions made by the business.	Larger firm where the majority of employees wish to defer a portion of their salaries. Ideal for business desiring to contribute on a match basis. Special nondiscrimination test for deferrals. May exclude employees under age 21 and those with less than one year of service.

ployer, or to have the plans funded only by employee contributions. They are also excellent side-kicks for nonqualified plans.

Major Advantages of 401(k)s:

1. They are well known and easy to introduce to employers and employees.
2. They encourage employees to become partners in retirement savings.
3. They attract key employees to the firm.
4. When employees send their own money into the plan, they get involved. They watch management's contributions closer, and they take the time to find out how the plan works. That makes it a lot more attractive as a method of reducing turnover.
5. Can be marketed as IRA substitutes since Congress shut the door on deductions for IRAs for most. You can contribute more to them than an IRA and you can get tax-favored treatment when you withdraw.
6. Can be used as part of a cafeteria plan while other profit-sharing plans cannot.
7. Vesting schedules can be used to encourage employees to stay with the firm.
8. Forfeitures can be used to reduce employers contributions or reallocated among the active participants.

Major Disadvantages of 401(k)s:

1. Employee contributions are limited by the indexed maximums and may be under desired amounts (currently $8,993 in March 1993).
2. Antidiscrimination rules can cause over-contribution problems for upper management.
3. Administrative costs can be too high for some small companies. However, go back to the perfect retirement plan scenario and see what is really important to your client. If this plan achieves his goals, then administrative costs should be a secondary consideration.

The 401(k) Market

Almost every company is a prospect for a 401(k) because it can be companion plans for other types. The employee deferral options make them different than almost any other plan other than the SAR–SEP. The 401(k) can be an attractive option for any company with 25 employees or more, although I have set them up in companies with less. I generally recommend the SAR–SEP if employees number less than 25. Look for companies who:

1. Want low over-all costs and wish to pass on some of the retirement funding obligation to employees.
2. Want maximum flexibility in making contributions (the optional matching is an excellent feature).
3. Have a plan in place that employees neither understand or appreciate.
4. Want employees to choose their own investments.
5. Want to reduce employee turnover with a vesting schedule.

403(b) and 403(b)7 Deferred Compensation Plans

Although not as well known as the 401(k), the code section that describes 403(b) is still popular. These are unique retirement programs available to employees of certain tax-exempt organizations, such as hospitals and schools. Known only for allowing tax-sheltered annuities for many years under 403(b), 403(b)7 added mutual funds and other packaged products to the available products list. Virtually any 501(c)(3) nonprofit organization, public and private is eligible for these plans as well as Public Educational Institutions—IRS Code Section 170(b)(1)(A)(ii).

These code sections were enacted to try to place employees of tax-exempt organizations on a level playing field with taxable corporations. While taxable corporations have tax incentives for setting up retirement plans for employees, nontaxable entities do not. Employees of the organizations named above can contribute before tax earnings into such plans. Employers can also contribute to such plans, but minimum coverage, participation and Average Deferral Percentage tests may apply. Most plans have only employee elective salary deferrals.

Contributions can generally not exceed 20 percent of reduced salary (after the contribution) or $9,500, although special catch-up provisions for employees with over 15 years of service can increase this level. Plans may be established at any time during the year. Only elective deferrals, not earnings, can be withdrawn due to financial hardship.

Major Advantages of 403(b) Plans:

1. You may "piggy-back" on an established plan. That is, you may sell an individual employee your investments while other employees use another company.
2. Employers have little or no administrative costs in plans that do not make employer contributions.
3. No 5500 forms to be filed unless employer contributions are involved.
4. Plan can be established at any time during the year.
5. No or minimal set-up cost.
6. Participants choose their own investments.
7. The plan is easily understood by participants.

Major Disadvantage of 403(b) Plan.   Most plans do not include employer contributions, so there is less opportunity for more accelerated growth of retirement funds.

Marketing 403(b) Plans.   With the exception of the IRA, the 403(b) is probably the easiest to market. It is usually sold to employees rather than employers. Since most of the plans are salary deferral only, there are few administrative hurdles and little cost. Most 501(c)(3) nonprofit organizations already have a plan in place. As a registered representative, all you have to do is find out what products are on the approved list. Most product sponsors do not grant exclusive marketing privileges. If your broker–dealer has an approved selling agreement with one of the products, you can start selling to employees immediately. Getting a new product approved is often just a function of getting one employee to agree to buy the product. Then take that employee's request to the appropriate authority within the organization for approval. Often, this can be handled by a payroll clerk, principal, or superintendent.

For school districts, I suggest asking permission to conduct generic seminars as part of the teachers pretraining programs. Also, ask for permission to place a brochure in teachers' mailboxes and to set up a table in the lobby when teachers are on campus prior to the time school begins. Once you get one or more teachers, ask for referrals. Figure 12-6 offers more information on 403(b) plans.

Optional Retirement Plans (ORP)

Before we leave our discussion of 403(b)s, we should mention Optional Retirement Plans or ORPs. Many states, including Texas, have plans that allow certain staff and professors in colleges and universities to elect an out-of-state retirement program and allow their own contributions and that of the state to go into an optional retirement program. The employee who elects to participate in the optional retirement program is allowed to select his own investments. Traditionally, these investments have been fixed annuities, then variable annuities. Now with 403(b)7 in place, mutual funds and other packaged products are also available. This is potentially a more lucrative market than just salary deferral under 403(b) because of the added state contribution, and the higher salaries in higher education institutions.

Figure 12-6   Tax Sheltered 403(b)(7) Plan Custodial Account

Contribution Limits	Ideal Investor	Special Features
Salary reduction arrangement calculated under special rules or $9,500.	School teachers, employees of universities, colleges, hospitals, churches, and other nonprofit organizations wishing to reduce their personal taxes and save for retirement with tax-deferred dollars.	• Available only to select group of individuals. • Can usually contribute more than an IRA allows. • Loan provisions available.

There is also a very large potential market for rollovers out of this program. Many college and university personnel need counseling when taking retirement funds. Often, they only consider a noninflation protected guaranteed lifetime annuity, rather than properly exploring all options.

This market may be more difficult to enter, because you usually have to get approval for your product through an insurance committee or other university organization that tends to be very protective of its staff. However, once you can get yourself and your product on the approved list, marketing your services to participants can be easy, especially if some are already your clients. You need to be able to compare yourself and your firm as well as your product to the competition. This is a sale where product is more important than in most others. Professors are looking for high return, safety, flexibility, low expenses, and service. Show them that through personal visits, phone calls, seminars, and mailings. Be knowledgeable about the ORP system in your state. Offer to assist in planning at retirement time. Emphasize your tax expertise and the necessity of maintaining flexibility during retirement years.

457 Deferred Compensation Plan

A 457 deferred compensation plan is a salary deferral plan available to state and municipal employees. Contributions made by the employees are with before tax dollars (reduce the employees taxable income) and earnings on the contributions are also tax deferred. These 457 plans are not considered to be qualified plans, and therefore do not have all the discrimination and coverage requirements typical of those types of plans.

Employers are not permitted to contribute to an employee's 457 plan, but often carry some type of qualified retirement plan in addition to offering a 457 plan. Employees can generally contribute up to one-third of their net compensation (after the elective deferral) or 25 percent of gross compensation before the elective deferral.

Major Advantages of 457 Plans:

1. No or little cost to employers in set up or administration. All they have to do is process payroll deductions.
2. Participants choose their own investments.
3. Participation does not affect IRA deductibility.
4. Not subject to discrimination testing.

Major Disadvantages of 457 Plans:

1. Plans cannot be rolled to IRAs prior to retirement. When an employee leaves the employer, he can transfer only if she goes to another state or municipality that has a 457. Otherwise, contributions must be distributed and taxed.
2. The employer is the applicant, owner, and beneficiary of the plan until the employee leaves. Funds are technically subject to creditors of the employer.

Marketing 457 Plans.   These plans are not as difficult to market as some might think. Since the employer does not have to incur any additional expense to bring

Figure 12-7   457 Plan

Contribution Limits	Ideal Investor	Special Features
The lesser of 25 percent of gross income or $7,500.	Employees of state or local government agencies or a select group of management or highly compensated employees of nonprofit organizations who want to save through payroll deduction in pretax dollars which grow tax deferred.	• Available only to select group of individuals. • Convenient payroll deduction. • Pretax contributions and tax-deferred growth.

a valuable fringe benefit to employees, 457s should be easy to sell. Also, because most registered representatives do not understand them, there is little competition.

Most registered representatives are also not comfortable with the bureaucracy of a municipality. If you can make a presentation, getting on an agenda for a city or county commissioners meeting is not that difficult. Since they have everything to gain and little to lose by participating, the presentation should go well.

After getting approval to establish a 457 plan for the city, county, or state, you must enroll employees using the rules mentioned under 403(b). However, you must make clear the unique disadvantages of a 457 including the inability to rollover prior to retirement if they no longer work for an employer who qualifies for a 457. This can cause a tax burden at an inopportune time. However, a tax deferral is usually still a winning formula if there is a good chance that the employee will continue working with a 457 qualified employer for a reasonable period of time. Figure 12-7 offers more information on 457 plans.

Profit-Sharing Plans

Profit-sharing plans are classified as defined-contribution plans. They permit the employer to contribute up to 15 percent of pay to all eligible employees. Contribution levels may vary from year to year. Although they are called profit-sharing plans, contributions are not always based on profits. More often, they are based on cash flow.

Contributions may be made by an employer up to 15 percent of eligible compensation. Final benefits will be based on the employee's account balance at retirement.

Major Advantages of Profit-Sharing Plans:

1. Employers can vary size of contributions from year to year, or may choose not to contribute in a particular year.
2. Favors younger employees.
3. Easy to understand and appreciate.
4. Since theoretically based on profit, may help employees to be more conscious of expenses.

Major Disadvantages of Profit-Sharing Plans:

1. Even though theoretically understood by employees, the plans are often seen as a "right and privilege" rather than a valued fringe benefit.
2. Since employee funds are not usually involved (although voluntary after tax contributions are allowed) employees who do not choose investments are not as "involved."
3. Contributions are limited to 15 percent.

Marketing Profit-Sharing Plans. Ordinarily marketed to companies who do not wish to be stuck with a fixed annual contribution. They want flexibility in contributions. These companies feel an obligation to provide retirement for employees or feel that this must be provided in order to attract and keep qualified people. They are companies who need tax deductions and whose management has retirement planning needs. Figure 12-8 offers more on profit-sharing plans.

Money Purchase Plans

A money purchase plan is similar to a profit-sharing plan in that the employer makes pro-rata contributions to all eligible employees. Its unique feature is that the plan permits contributions as high as 25 percent of pay, but the percentage contribution limit is *fixed* and cannot easily be changed.

Since these plans are also defined contribution plans, the employees retirement income is dependent on the balance in his retirement account. The term money purchase arose because the money in the participant's account was traditionally used to purchase an annuity that provides monthly retirement benefits.

Figure 12-8   Profit-Sharing Plan

Contribution Limits	Ideal Investor	Special Features
The lesser of 15 percent of eligible compensation or $30,000.	Small firm where business and income are somewhat variable. Ideal plan for firm wanting a flexible contribution with a maximum of 15 percent. May exclude employees under age 21 and those with less than two years of service. A full-service plan is ideal for a firm seeking a variety of options in the plan provisions. (One year of service if vesting applies.)	• Full flexibiilty of contributions. Additional features: • Social Security integration. • Vesting.

Major Advantages of Money Purchase Plans:

1. Large percentage contributions can be made allowing a larger tax deduction.
2. Provides a better ability to accumulate large sums for younger employees.
3. Participants in the plan have individual accounts.
4. Administrative costs are relatively low.
5. Predictable costs.

Major Disadvantages of Money Purchase Plans:

1. Contribution rate is fixed and cannot easily be changed, regardless of profitability.
2. Cannot provide for past service.

Other Features   Forfeitures may be allocated among active participants or used to reduce employer contributions.

Marketing Money Purchase Plans:

1. Companies with a steady cash flow.
2. Young, well-paid key employees.
3. A stable work force (low turnover).
4. Companies with plans in place that employees do not understand or appreciate.
5. Companies who indicate that tax deductions and predictable costs are high in importance.

Money purchase and profit-sharing plans are often combined to maximize contribution amounts while maintaining some contribution flexibility. They are actually two plans. The contributions to money purchase plan are usually fixed at 10 percent. The profit-sharing contribution is discretionary and may vary from 0 to 15 percent in any year. Figure 12-9 provides more information on money purchase plans.

Target Benefit Plans

Target benefit plans are hybrid plans, combining the best features of both defined contribution and defined benefit plans. Like a defined benefit, contributions are based on pay, years of service, and investment earnings assumptions. Like a defined contribution, participants' retirement incomes vary based on the actual earnings of the plan's investments.

Employers may make contributions up to 25 percent of eligible compensation. A contribution level is determined by using a defined benefit formula. This contribution will only change if forfeitures are received by the plan. An actuary or knowledgeable plan administrator must be used to make this initial calculation. Contributions are made regardless of profits.

Figure 12-9   Money Purchase Pension Plan

Contribution Limits	Ideal Investor	Special Features
The lesser of 25 percent of eligible compensation or $30,000. Required annual contribution.	Small firm where income is substantial. Ideal plan for firm wanting to maximize contributions at a fixed percentage. May exclude employees under age 21 and those with less than two years of service. A full-service plan is ideal for a firm seeking a variety of options in the plan provisions and wishing to maximize contributions at a fixed percentage. (One year of service if vesting applies.)	• Maximizes deductible contributions. Additional features: • Social Security integration. • Vesting.

Major Advantages of Target Benefit Plans:

1. Predetermined contribution levels.
2. Good investment performance can increase retirement benefits.
3. Larger contributions may be made as compared to some other plans.
4. Can provide for speedy accumulation of retirement benefits for older employees.

Major Disadvantages of Target Benefit Plans:

1. Higher administrative costs.
2. Complexity—not easily understood by employees and thus not easily appreciated.
3. Contributions must be made each year regardless of profitability.

Marketing Target Benefit Plans:

1. Companies with older owners and younger rank and file with older owner–employees well paid.
2. Strong earnings and cash flow.
3. Desire to have a defined benefit plan but without resources to fund it.

Defined Benefit Plans

Defined benefit plans accomplish just what the name implies. They start with a defined benefit for an employee and work backwards to determine what contributions will be required to reach that level of benefit based on certain actuarial assumptions. This type of plan allows a company to provide a higher level of benefit for its older highly compensated employees. Tax-deduction limits can be much higher than under any other type of plan.

Benefits may be expressed as a percentage of compensation, or as a percentage of compensation multiplied by a participant's years of service. When years of service are combined with compensation, this is called the *unit-benefit formula*. When based on a percentage of earnings, the formula is called the *fixed-benefit formula*. The amount that an employee can receive each year is indexed with $110,000 being the approximate maximum in 1992.

Major Advantages of Defined Benefit Plans:

1. They provide accelerated retirement benefits for older, highly compensated employees. Since past service can be considered, they can also reward longevity with the company.
2. Usually, they provide the highest tax deduction available because the contribution limits are higher (if they are not higher than other plans, then they may have selected the wrong type of plan).

Major Disadvantages of Defined Benefit Plans:

1. Employer must meet funding requirements regularly regardless of earnings.
2. Without individual accounts, most employees will have a difficult time getting involved with the plan and appreciating its benefits.
3. Highest administrative costs of any plan. Actuaries must be used annually.
4. Employers' future costs are not precisely known.
5. Employees' future benefits may change annually, because of changes in salary and years of service, so the employee does not know what his future benefits might be.
6. Superior investment performance does not enhance retirement benefits.

Other Features:

1. The employer assumes responsibility for preretirement inflation, income adequacy, and investment results.
2. Superior investment performance in one or more successive years could leave a plan over-funded in a year when tax deductions are needed.
3. These plans are usually covered by the Pension Benefit Guaranty Corp. which may increase reporting requirements and costs.

Marketing Defined Benefit Plans:

1. Companies with defined benefit formulas may be excellent candidates for other types of plans. They have become increasingly unpopular in the last several years because of the disadvantages shown above. Also, millions

of plans were put in place with companies who a) did not need this type of plan, or b) committed themselves to a large contribution when profits were good, but could not meet the commitment in a recession. They are excellent candidates for termination of the DB plan and setting up something more suitable. Note, however, that companies who have had DB plans can never install an SEP. Amazingly, I have seen several companies that needed an SEP and had DBs.

2. Companies with older owner–employees with long years of service. They need to accelerate their retirement benefits and have the largest share of company contributions to go to their benefit.
3. Companies with strong, steady earnings and cash flow.
4. Sophisticated management and staff.

Age-Weighted Plans

Age-weighted plans combine the best features of a defined benefit plan with the advantages of a profit-sharing plan and allow older business owners to contribute more to their retirement. (Have we heard that before?) They were created in May of 1990 under IRC 402(a)(4). They are defined benefit plans without the actuary and with lower limits of contribution, or profit-sharing plans that allow you to give larger contributions for older owner–employees.

In a profit-sharing plan, contributions are allocated based on income. In an age-weighted plan, contributions are allocated based on age and *compensation*. The employer first chooses a contribution, between 0 and 15 percent of eligible payroll. The contribution is allocated using three steps called *cross testing*. (The nice thing about these three steps is that either you or the product sponsor can do them without an actuary.) The three steps are:

1. Accumulate each employee's allocation at interest to normal retirement age. Current regulations allow use of 7.5 to 8.5 percent.
2. Convert the accumulation for each employee to a straight life annuity benefit using one of five approved annuity tables at the chosen interest rate.
3. The ratio of each employee's annuity benefit to current pay is expressed as a percentage called the EBAR or equivalent benefit accrual rate. If the EBAR for any highly compensated employee does not exceed the EBAR for any non-highly compensated employee, the plan is nondiscriminatory.

Contributions to the plan do not have to made every year, but must be substantial and recurring. That means that you can get by without a contribution if you have a lousy year, but you cannot just set it up and let it die.

Major Advantages of Age-Weighted Plans:

1. Has some benefits of defined benefit without the actuary, high expense, and required annual funding.
2. Can benefit older owner–employees.
3. Easier to sell than the defined benefit.

Major Disadvantages of Age-Weighted Plans:

1. Contributions still limited to 15 percent, much less than defined benefit plans.
2. Will not yield as high a tax deduction.
3. Formulas to cross test are somewhat complicated, but still can be done with the aid of tables.

Marketing Age-Weighted Plans:

1. Companies who want owner–employees to have a larger share of the contribution, but a) cannot afford administrative costs of a DB plan, b) do not want to be locked in to annual funding.
2. Since this program is relatively new, it makes a good presentation to companies who have been turned on to the advantages of defined benefit but turned off by its disadvantages.
3. Companies who give high marks on the perfect investment to providing income for owners and low marks for income to rank and file.

Nonqualified Plans

As we have seen in the preceding pages, employers have been limited by law in the amount they can contribute on behalf of their key employees or owner-employees. However, that is exactly what many corporations still want to do. Enter the nonqualified plan. Nonqualified plans allow a company to provide excess benefits for these employees. They are used to attract and retain certain highly skilled and highly paid employees. Nonqualified plans, in fact, are required to discriminate in favor of key individuals.

Tax benefits, of course, are less under this type of arrangement. I like this type of plan used in conjunction with a profit-sharing plan or 401(k). It is particularly suited to a 401(k). You can have flexible employer contributions, employee participation, and thus involvement and appreciation, and golden handcuffs.

Unfortunately, nonqualified plans have many names. For marketing purposes, they have been called private pension plans, top-hat plans, SERPs (Supplemental Executive Retirement Plans), SERP–COLI (Company Owned Life Insurance), and excess-benefit plans.

Top-hat plans are just salary reduction plans used to defer taxes. They are usually unfunded so no need to worry too much about them. An excess benefit is usually maintained by an employer solely for the purpose of providing benefits for certain employees in excess of the amounts allowed under the Internal Revenue Code. Private pension plans and SERPs are usually the same thing, just the method of funding may differ.

If you read the marketing data associated with nonqualified plans, they often sound too good to be true. Taken verbatim, that may be true. We accountants, for example, have a problem with saying that contributions to the plan are tax deductible when the very word nonqualified implies that they are not. However, tax deductibility is obtained by paying bonuses that are fully taxable to the employee and deductible to the employer. Marketing ploys aside, these plans can be very effective and can make your sale of a 401(k) much easier. In addition, financial rewards for this type of plan are usually higher and paid sooner. SERPs are usually funded with life insurance.

Major Advantages of Nonqualified Plans:

1. Employer:
   (a) Rewards key executives.
   (b) Allows selective participation.
   (c) No or little administration.
   (d) Set up is simple.
   (e) Amount can vary from employee to employee.
   (f) No IRS approval for implementation or termination.
   (g) Vesting schedule can create golden handcuffs.
2. Employee:
   (a) If the employee owns the insurance, he can accumulate savings tax deferred.
   (b) If company owned life insurance is used, taxation on benefits being provided is deferred.
   (c) Participant or employer can choose retirement age.
   (d) No penalty for early withdrawal.
   (e) May be able to receive retirement income tax free through policy loans.
   (f) Tax-free survivor benefit.

Major Disadvantages of Nonqualified Plans:

1. Although the plans are relatively simple in concept, the many names used and somewhat deceptive marketing make the plans ''too good to be true'' in the client's eyes. I prefer to market them with advantages clearly shown and with details as to tax deductibility clearly explained.
2. Insurance illustrations using split dollar arrangement and industry buzz words work against the accountant who will not take the time to keep it simple in client presentation.
3. Resistance to insurance because many people cannot associate the product with a life benefit and ''loans'' conjure up a negative image at retirement time.

Marketing Nonqualified Plans:

1. Use your perfect investment questions. If a client or prospect has high disdain for the regulatory requirements of a qualified plan, wants to do more for key executives, then he may be a candidate for nonqualified plans.
2. Find out what benefits key personnel want, when they want to retire, and prepare insurance illustrations to support those needs. Either universal life or participating whole life policies are used. Plans are usually designed to be paid up at the retirement age selected by the client. Extend the illustration to show loans being withdrawn from the policy to supplement income in the retirement years.
3. Decide who will pay the premiums and who will own the policies. If employees pay the premiums and own the policies, then the company can pay tax-deductible bonuses to them for the premiums. If the company is

to pay, then employees will pay taxes only on the pure life insurance cost of the product. Premiums will not be deductible by the company, but tax-free build-up inside the policy will be allowed.

SELECTING THE RIGHT PLAN

Oftentimes, it is difficult to choose the correct plan for prospects. Problems stem from trying to make the perfect selection. That is similar to trying to be perfect in selecting investments. It may very well not be possible. You must weigh as much information as you can gather, analyze the situation currently, and project future conditions as closely as possible, then ACT!

Use Product Sponsor Proposals

Ask them for fact sheets to be completed on your prospect. Using these fact sheets, the product sponsor can provide you with recommendations as to the proper type of retirement plan and an illustration of benefits and costs for this particular client.

Concentrate on Your Client's Stated Goals

You can determine these goals by asking him to describe the perfect retirement plan if he had complete freedom to choose. He will need your help to describe its features, but asking TOPS questions should get you down to his key criteria. Try to find out what is really important to the client. A plan that may seem to be a perfect match for a company may not be suitable if it does not match the goals of the owner of the company.

Perfection May Not Be a Worthy Goal

You may not be able to select the perfect retirement plan for your prospect. If it is perfect today, conditions next year may make it a little less than perfect. The key question is whether or not the company, the owners, and employees are better off with a retirement plan or not. If they are, then progress has been made.

Use Product Sponsor Promotional Materials

Most product sponsors have field materials that allow you to compare advantages and disadvantages of the various types of plans in easy to read formats. Use them. See Figures 12-10 and 12-11 for some examples.

PLAN DESIGN CONSIDERATIONS*

1. Contributions:
   Employees only—401(k) or SAR–SEP (if 25 or less eligible employees).

*Courtesy of Colonial Group of Mutual Funds.

Figure 12-10   Making the Right Plan Selection for Individuals

	Individual Retirement Account (IRA)	*Rollover IRA*	*403(b) Custodial Account*
Features	Allows tax-favored accumulation of a retirement "nest egg." Investor must be under age 70-$\frac{1}{2}$ and have earned income.	Allows distribution from an existing qualified retirement plan to be "rolled over" to an IRA. No age limits.	Salary deferral plan for employees of educational, charitable, scientific, or religious organizations defined under IRC 501(c)(3).
Tax Benefits	Contributions may be tax deductible. Earnings compound tax deferred until withdrawn.	Taxes on amount rolled over and subsequent earnings are deferred until withdrawals are made.	Salary deferrals reduce employee's current taxable income. Earnings compound tax deferred until withdrawn.
Maximum Annual Contribution	$2,000 or 100 percent of earned income, whichever is less.	No dollar limit. Rollover amount must be a distribution of at least 50 percent of plan balance and due to a qualifying event.	Lesser of $9,500 or 25 percent of salary (adjusted for amount of deferral).
Deadline to Set Up/Contribute	April 15 (tax filing deadline, not including extensions) for prior year deductibility.	Rollover must be completed within 60 days from date of receiving the distribution.	Salary deferrals only on a calendar year basis.

Employer only—money purchase pension (MP), profit sharing (PS) or SEP.

Both employer and employee—401(k) or a SEP/SAR–SEP combination.

2. Employer tax deduction:

0–15 percent of participant's compensation—SEP, 401(k) or profit sharing.

Up to 25 percent—Money purchase pension or combinations of MP and PS or MP and 401(k).

3. Employee pretax deferrals:

Available only on SAR–SEP and 401(k) plans.

Maximum is $8,994 for 1993 (indexed annually).

4. Vesting:

SEP and SAR–SEP plans require 100 percent immediate vesting.

Employee contributions are always nonforfeitable and not subject to a vesting schedule,

Figure 12-11   Making the Right Plan Selection for Business Owners

	Simplified Employee Pension Plan (SEP–IRA)	*Salary Reduction SEP (SAR–SEP)*	*401(k) Plan*
Maximum Annual Contribution	Lesser of $30,000 or 15 percent of earned income on behalf of each eligible employee.	Lesser of $8,728 or 15 percent of salary (adjusted for amount of deferral).	May defer the lesser of $8,728 (indexed) or 15 percent of salary (adjusted for amount of salary deferral). The overall contribution limit (including employer discretionary and employer matching contributions) is the lesser of $30,000 or 25 percent of employee's earned income.
Deadline to Set Up/Contribute	Employer's tax filing deadline plus extensions, for prior year deductibility.	Salary deferrals apply to salary earned in the same calendar year. Past earnings may not be deferred.	Plan must be adopted by employer's year end. In general, the deadline for employer discretionary and employer matching contributions is the employer's tax filing deadline.

	Profit-Sharing Plan	*Money Purchase Pension Plan*	*Defined Benefit Plan*
Features	Flexible employer-funded plan. May be used in conjunction with Money Purchase Pension Plan to increase contribution rate.	Fixed annual contribution rate. May be used with a profit-sharing plan for added flexibility.	Annual contributions are required to fund a predetermined annual retirement benefit. Generally works in favor of older employees.

Figure 12-11 (*Continued*)

	Profit-Sharing Plan	Money Purchase Pension Plan	defined Benefit Plan
Tax Benefits	Contributions are 100 percent deductible by the plan employer. Distributions may be eligible for special tax treatment. Earnings compound tax deferred until withdrawn.	Contributions are 100 percent deductible by the plan employer. Distributions may be eligible for special tax treatment. Earnings compound tax deferred until withdrawn.	Contributions are 100 percent deductible by the plan employer. Distributions may be eligible for special tax treatment. Earnings compound tax deferred until withdrawn.
Maximum Annual Contribution	Lesser of $30,000 or 15 percent of earned income on behalf of each eligible employee.	Lesser of $30,000 or 25 percent of earned income on behalf of each eligible employee.	Targeted annual benefit cannot exceed the lesser of 100 percent of earned income or $112,221 (indexed).
Deadline to Set Up/Contribute	Must be adopted by the employer's year end. In general, the deadline for contributions is the employer's tax filing deadline plus extensions.	Must be adopted by the employer's year end. In general, the deadline for contributions is the employer's tax filing deadline plus extensions.	Must be adopted by the employer's year end. In general, the deadline for contributions is the employer's tax filing deadline plus extensions.

Money purchase pension, profit sharing, and 401(k) employer contributions can be subject to a vesting schedule. Forfeitures are usually reallocated to remaining participants.

5. Eligibility:
SEP and SAR–SEP plans can require an employee to work for an employer three of the last five years.
No 1,000 hour rule under SEP and SAR–SEP.
Money purchase pension and profit sharing plans allow an employer to exclude employees for up to two years of service (401(k) one year). A "year of service" is a 12-month consecutive period beginning on the employee's date of hire, in which he works at least 1,000 hours. If you use greater than a one-year service requirement you must provide 100 percent immediate vesting.
Note: In most situations use age 21 with a one-year service requirement and select a vesting schedule so forfeitures can be reallocated.

6. Optional features (including loans, hardship withdrawals, and life insurance company products):
   Available only on money purchase pension, profit sharing, and 401(k) plans at employer's discretion.
   Not allowed on SEP or SAR–SEP plans since they are funded by participant IRAs.
7. Plan administration:
   SEP and SAR–SEP plans require little or no administration.
   Money purchase pension, profit sharing, and 401(k) plans require full administration in order to maintain the plans' qualified tax status. The employer usually designates an administrator who carries out the required duties for a fee.
   Does the employer currently have other plans? If so, they must be considered so that contributions will be made in conjunction with IRC 415 limits.
   Does the employer own or control any other businesses? If so, he may be required to include those employees in any plan he establishes.
   What is the employer's fiscal year end? Plans must be established by the last day of the employer's fiscal year in which he wants a tax deduction.

MAXIMIZING PLAN PARTICIPATION BENEFITS

Plan participants including owners and owner–employees will ask your guidance in getting maximum benefits out of the plan established. This will include how much to put in, where to invest, and how the money should be withdrawn. Providing these answers can be critical to getting other referrals and increasing your business from existing clients.

How Much to Put In to the Plan

There is no pat answer for this question. What an employee puts in should depend on his goals, other investments he has, income level, dependents, education, etc. In other words, treat any employee who asks your assistance the same as you would any client. Try to determine as much as you can about the participant and advise accordingly.

Generally, the quality of the plan itself is a major factor in the decision of how much to put into the plan. If an employer is matching 100 percent for example, the employee should almost always put in as much as he is allowed. Where can you get 100 percent return on investments, plus whatever he earns from the investment return, plus allocated forfeitures if applicable, and with tax deferral? This is a great investment unless the participant plans to leave before he gets any vesting.

How to Invest Contributions

Generally, choices are somewhat limited in retirement plans. However, regulations require that a reasonable number of choices be available. If you have a chosen product sponsor who assisted you in setting up the plan, then their products will usually be on the menu. I suggest limiting the selection to no more than six funds offered by the company. If an insurance company is involved, you will probably want to use a fixed annuity and/or a variable annuity. Remember that retirement plan contributions are almost always long-term investments, so use short-term investments sparingly depending on the client's age.

TAX ADVANTAGES: THE MOST COMPELLING REASONS TO CONSIDER A RETIREMENT PLAN

Choosing a tax-deferred investment, such as an IRA, business retirement plan, or a variable annuity, can substantially increase the growth of your earnings. At the end of 30 years, annual $2,000 tax-deferred investments earning a fixed 8 percent would be worth $99,936 more than the same taxable investment. Earnings on tax-deferred accounts are taxed as the money is withdrawn, when most people are in a lower tax bracket.

Also, even with Tax Reform, up to 87 percent of all Americans are still eligible to deduct contributions made to an IRA. Check the chart in Figure 12-12 to see if your IRA contribution is deductible.

Figure 12-12   Is Your IRA Contribution Deductible?

Tax Filing Status	Are You (or Your Spouse) Covered by a Retirement Plan at Work?[1]	Adjusted Gross Income[2]	You're Entitled to:[3]
Single	No	No limit	Full deduction
	Yes	$25,000 or less	Full deduction
		Over $25,000 but less than $35,000	Deduction is reduced by $10 for every $50 of income above $25,000[4]
		$35,000 or more	No deduction
Married, Filing Jointly	No	No limit	Full deduction
	Yes	$40,000 or less	Full deduction
		Over $40,000 but less than $50,000	Deduction is reduced by $10 for every $50 of income above $40,000[4]
		$50,000 or more	No deduction

Source: Internal Revenue Service, Publication 590. Of course, this chart provides general information for determining an IRA deduction.

[1] Coverage by a retirement plan includes, but is not limited to, qualified pension, profit sharing, and annuity plans as well as certain self-employed retirement plans.

[2] Adjusted gross income is your total income excluding such items as IRA deductions, and foreign income or housing exclusions, as reported on the annual federal tax return (Form 1040).

[3] For most individuals, a full deduction is the lesser of $2,000 or 100 percent of compensation.

[4] Do not reduce below $200.

If you are married and filing a joint return you will want to figure an IRA deduction for each spouse separately. In this case the deduction is reduced by $10 for every $50 of your combined income above $40,000.

Withdrawing Contributions

If the participant is not retiring, the simplest answer is ''don't withdraw funds from your retirement plan.'' If retirement is at hand, then be prepared to advise your client.

Regular Retirement.   If the client has reached normal retirement age, your financial advice is more critical than ever. Possibly for the first time, the client is talking about really living off the income from her investments. Accumulation time may be over and harvesting time is at hand. Be sure to advise the client of the various options available which usually include lump-sum distributions, periodic annuity type payments, etc. Prepare projections for her showing the various options available. Remember that the client may still have more than one stage left in her life. The stages remaining depend on the age of the client at retirement. The stages are:

1. Pre-social security—the client may need to receive enough income to compensate for the lack of Social Security benefits until she reaches the qualifying age.
2. Stage 2 may be from age 62–65 to 75. Clients are usually traveling during this time period and are healthy. They should try to live off their income, hopefully leaving something to reinvest.
3. Stage 3 may be from age 75 to 90. Health may be declining, inflation could have taken its toll. The client may have to use 100 percent of income and even start drawing principal from some investments.

When you talk to your client about the remaining stages, they are usually surprised. They had thought of retirement as one last stage. If they make decisions without considering the fact that we are living longer than ever and that inflation is still a culprit, then they may find themselves short in the final stages. In other words, they may *outlive their money*.

To avoid this, some clients will opt for the lifetime annuity. They are comfortable in the assurance that they will receive a fixed income for the remainder of their lives. I almost always caution my clients against this. I use illustrations about inflation. They do not want all of their assets tied up in one single monthly payment. They may need to take occasional distributions of principal to make large purchases, make gifts, etc. For these reasons, I seldom advise clients to leave money with their companies at retirement. Company retirement plans are not usually meant to be financial advisors for people after they leave employment. They are for people who are still working.

Preretirement Distributions.   Preretirement distributions often come from elected or forced early retirement, leaving one company to take a position with another, etc. . . . Do not let your clients fall into the trap of spending their retirement funds just because they have access to them. They will be hit with ordinary income taxes and a 10 percent penalty. In some states, income taxes may consume up to 50 percent of their retirement accumulations.

If the client must have some income from the distribution, then work with the client to show how distributions can be taken without penalty prior to age $59\text{-}\frac{1}{2}$ if taken for a minimum of five years and based on life expectancy.

Under current IRS rules, distributions made directly to the employee will be subjected to a 20 percent withholding for taxes. Even if you elect to rollover your distribution into an IRA within 60 days, you must replace the 20 percent withheld with other funds or be taxed on the 20 percent. If this sounds like a double trap, you are correct. Advise your client about forward averaging rules if applicable, then assist her in making a decision before she takes distribution. If the funds are transferred directly into a rollover IRA, then no taxes will be due and no withholding will be required.

Lump-Sum Distributions.   If the client wants some or all of the money now, it will cost the client the regular income taxes plus a 10 percent penalty plus whatever state income taxes and penalties are due unless he is:

1. Over age $59\text{-}\frac{1}{2}$.
2. Disabled.
3. Leaving his job and is over 55.
4. Making regular withdrawals in substantially equal amounts over the client's life expectancy.

You may be eligible for *10-year forward averaging*, if you were at least 50 on January 1, 1986. This allows your distribution to be taxed in one year as if it were your only income over a 10-year period. The worst rate is usually around 20 percent unless your distribution is over $300,000. The 1986 rates are always used.

You may be eligible for *five-year averaging* if you were over $59\text{-}\frac{1}{2}$ at time of distribution. It is based on the applicable tax rate for the year you receive the distribution. In almost all cases, your taxes paid under either method will be less than regular income taxes. In order to qualify for any averaging, these requirements must be met:

1. Distribution must come from a qualified plan.
2. Distribution must be because:
   (a) Client left job.
   (b) Disability.
   (c) Death.
   (d) Reached age $59\text{-}\frac{1}{2}$.
3. Full distribution paid within one calendar year.
4. Must have participated in the plan for five years.

Forward averaging can be used only once in a lifetime.

If your client wants to defer all taxes, have the retirement plan distribution transferred directly into a roll over IRA. Or, leave it in the current employer's plan (if that option is available). A roll over IRA is separate from any other IRA you may have, but also grows tax deferred.

Portions of the distribution may be rolled over, but any nonrolled funds will be subject to the 20 percent withholding rule. If part or all of the distribution is distributed in the form of stock, you may open a self-directed IRA and roll the shares into it, or sell the shares, pay the tax on the appreciation, and roll the proceeds into a regular IRA. See Figure 12-13 for a breakdown of lump-sum distributions.

Figure 12-13 Lump-Sum Distributions Before Age 59-$\frac{1}{2}$

Name: _____

Date: _____

Age to begin distribution	55
Life expectancy based on single life	28.6
Life expectancy based on joint life	37.1
Present value of account or projected value when distribution is to begin	$145,000.00

MINIMUM DISTRIBUTION:	Annual	Monthly
Minimum distribution with single life	$ 5,069.93	$ 422.49
Minimum distribution with joint life	$ 3,908.36	$ 325.70

This method can be recalculated eary year using the new
life expectancy. The amount shown is for the first year.

MAXIMUM DISTRIBUTION*		
Maximum distribution with single life	$12,283.48	$1,023.62
Maximum distribution with joint life	$11,496.74	$ 958.06

The maximum method uses an assumed growth rate—   7.36%
currently the 10-year T-note rate.

OPTIONAL DISTRIBUTION*
Optional method using 5 percent assumed growth rate.

Distribution with single life	$ 9,637.55	$ 803.13
Distribution with joint life	$ 8,668.47	$ 722.37

The distribution must be continued for five (5) years or until age 59-$\frac{1}{2}$, whichever is later.
*Under the maximum and optional methods, the amounts cannot be recalculated each year.
This chart estimates the amount you can withdraw per month and avoid the 10 percent IRS early
withdrawal penalty.

THE MECHANICS OF RETIREMENT PLAN ADMINISTRATION

Retirement plans have four types of administration:

1. Set up.
2. Administration including IRS and DOL reporting requirements.
3. Accounting for investments inside the plan.
4. Investment selection and monitoring.

Many CPAs are excellent plan administrators and regularly prepare 5500s forms and the like. I did some of all the functions listed above, and the only one I made money at was number 4. I try to leave the others to the experts who do this exclusively.

Turn-Key Retirement Plans

Many product sponsors offer turn-key programs for all of the first three phases. Your client will incur charges for the first two, may incur small charges for number 3 and no charges for number 4. Third-party administrators usually handle number 1 and 2 in an agreement with the product sponsor. Often, prototype plans developed by product sponsors are used for setting up the plan.

Using Third-Party Administrators

Your broker–dealer has relationships with third-party administrators that will handle any size or type of plan. Contact them for assistance in pricing your proposal. They will work with you, the product sponsor, and the client to assist you in making the sale and in assuring that all regulatory requirements are met.

Investment Accounting

The product sponsor may charge your client a small per-participant charge for maintaining separate accounts, regular reporting, etc.

Investment Selection and Monitoring

You should be involved in this process with every client and participant. The investments in the retirement plan should be monitored using the same system that you use to monitor other investments. These investments should be included in the clients regular reports.

13

Education Funding

**Failure is not the worst thing in the world. The very worst
is not to try.**

College education funding can be one of the most rewarding aspects of personal
financial planning. It is rather easy to do, relatively painless, and is mostly positive. I have been in business long enough to have clients actually thank me for
helping them to prepare for their education. It is especially nice to have a college
or high school student recognize you for your assistance in making her life better
by advising her parents about the need to save for college.

College funding should be one of the easiest and least technical subjects involved in financial planning. However, the IRS, Congress, and clients insist
on making it difficult. It should be a four-step process:

1. Assume that the parents want their children to attend college and determined today's approximate costs of the college she will probably attend.
2. Project the cost to the time for entering college using an assumed inflation
   rate.
3. Calculate the lump-sum investment required today or the monthly investment required to meet the goal.
4. Select the proper investment vehicle and get started.

I usually limit my college planning to these four steps. However, there are other
circumstances to consider. Just don't let the complications carry you away from
your main purpose.

HOW MUCH WILL IT COST?

During the 1980s, college tuitions grew by 10 percent annually, more than twice
the rate of inflation. How much your client will have to pay is dependent on
where the child will go to college and how many years before the child is of college
age. Fortunately, there are a multitude of sources to determine current costs
for any college in America. Colonial Funds, for example, offers free copies of
a LIMRA International (Life Insurance Marketing and Research Association,
Inc.) publication showing college costs for all accredited colleges and universities in the United States using data supplied by the College Entrance Examination Board. College Board Publications also publishes *The College Hand-*

book, *Index of Majors*, and *The College Cost Book*. If you need the information quickly and cannot put your hands on these books, call Oppenheimer at 1-800-525-7048 and they will provide you with information from the *College Cost Book*.

Other recommended readings for parents and yourself are *Dollars for Scholars: Barron's Complete College Financing Guide* by Marguerite J. Dennis, *How to Pay for Your Children's College Education* by Gerald Krefetz, and *Don't Miss Out, The Ambitious Student's Guide to Financial Aid* by Anna Leider.

Armed with all the information you need regarding today's college costs, most mutual fund and insurance companies have one or more college cost planning worksheets. These are usually accompanied by a chart providing factors for projecting today's costs into future costs using assumed rates of inflation. Most are currently using 6 percent. I recommend using a financial calculator. By pushing about three buttons, you can do all the calculations you want and impress the client more. Also, those tables are never around when you need them. Read the section on using your financial calculator. After you have calculated the future cost, you can use the tables or your financial calculator to determine the lump sum investment requirement today or the monthly savings required to provide for a child's education.

FROM WHERE DOES THE MONEY COME?

Financial Aid

Most financial aid situations occur because your client has waited too late to seek your advice or you waited too late to offer unsolicited advice. If college funding is going to be a source of fee income for you, you should become expert on how to qualify for financial aid, what aid is available, and in what amounts for different institutions. I usually provide my clients with the toll free number for Federal Student Financial Aid Information Center, 1-800-333-4636. I also recommend becoming acquainted with financial aid officers at Universities in your area. I usually include a short period on financial aid in college planning seminars.

However, planning for financial aid seems like an oxymoron to me. Funds available for scholarships and financial aid have decreased at a faster rate than college costs have increased. It appears rather easy to forecast that this trend will continue. It is likely that qualifying for financial aid will also be more difficult. The federal government has shrunk its financial aid budget by 16 percent during the last 10 years.

One final word of caution on financial aid. If you do plan for college, placing funds in the child's name can often be a detriment to qualification for aid. As usual, the government punishes initiative and planning. I have not found this to be a detriment to planning except in very isolated cases. You can usually tell in advance whether your client is going to qualify for financial aid. If I have more than five years before college and clients with stable incomes, I do not plan to quality for financial aid. I plan to have funds available. If your client simply cannot accumulate adequate funds, then we consider loans.

Loans

Perkins Loans (formerly National Direct Student Loans or NDSLs) are need-based, low-interest loans made through a school's financial aid office. Stafford

Loans (formerly Guaranteed Student Loan or GSLs) are low-interest government loans offered by banks, S&Ls, or credit unions. Supplemental Loans for Student (SLSs) and Parent Loans to Undergraduate Students (PLUSs) are also made through banks, savings and loans, or credit unions.

Loans may be the only alternative for families who fail to plan or who are affected by circumstances beyond their control. Loans will either saddle the student with debt burdens in the early years of his career, or saddle the parents with debt during the years when they should be preparing for retirement.

Scholarships

Seems like there is no planning involved here. If you qualify, go for it. Scholarships are wonderful and most parents assume that their children will all qualify when they are young. They will either qualify based on merit, grades, talent, or athletics. Unfortunately, only a few qualify for scholarships. However, scholarships may be available for the enterprising parent willing to search. Hundreds of organizations offer scholarships—alumni associations, school clubs, service clubs, foundations, religious, ethnic, fraternal, civic, patriotic, veterans organizations, and employers. Many companies offer work-study programs. The client's employer may be a good source. These are usually awarded based on merit, grades, or talent. Many, however, are awarded based on need and many are awarded to those who most aggressively pursue them. Scholarships for anything other than tuition and fees may be taxed.

Work

Ever had a client say, ''My kid will work his way through college just like I did?'' A worthy goal, but it just may not be realistic. Jobs in college towns are not always plentiful. The child's course of study may preclude him from holding a steady job. Worse, the child just may not be mature enough to hold a job and go to school. It happens. Prepare your client for it by telling him stories of people who thought the same thing but were disappointed. This is a good time to use a pain question. ''Maybe little Jim will get a job flipping burgers and work his way up if you can't afford to send him to college and he can't get a part-time job to send himself.'' Be careful with that one.

Planning

This is the only alternative that I spend much time on. It is my philosophy that my service is more valuable here than in any of the other areas. My job is to see that the children of my clients are able to attend college and that my clients do not have to mortgage their retirement in order to do it.

Getting Your Clients to Plan.   How to get your clients to plan? Use TOPS. Opportunity questions will be obvious. ''How important is it to you that your children go to college?'' What college would you like for them to attend? Do you know what the current costs are at this college for tuition and fees, room and board? Are you aware that inflation for college costs has been averaging 50 percent above the normal inflation rate for the last 10 years?'' Use the figures in Figure 13-1 to bring home your point.

Figure 13-1   College Cost Projections

Age	1	4	8	12	15
#Yrs Till College	17	14	10	6	3
5 Yrs @: Public School	$70,000	$59,000	$46,000	$37,000	$31,000
Monthly Savings Required	$145	$175	$236	$387	$748
Private School	$186,000	$156,000	$124,000	$98,000	$82,000
Monthly Savings Required	$385	$463	$636	$1,024	$1,978

Now for the Pain Question.   ''My calculator [or this chart] shows that it will cost $84,000 for little Sally to attend State University in 15 years when she graduates high school. How did you plan on paying for that ?'' If client resists or has lame excuses, ask ''I assume you are already drilling Sally on the need for education. What are you going to say to her when she's 18 and she says, 'Dad, I'm ready to follow your advice. After visiting State U. I've decided I'm really going to love college. I plan on entering pre-med. They say I will need a check for $10,000 for the first semester.' Are you going to tell her she'll have to get a job at the Dairy Queen for the summer and put together the 10 grand?''

Solution.   ''The key to any education funding plan is to start early. By putting back only $241 per month or a lump-sum investment of $24,251 starting today, you can reach your goal of $84,000 by the time Sally reaches college age. If she qualifies for scholarships, so much the better. She will have an education fund that can be used for higher education, for med school or just to get her started in life. Isn't this better than mortgaging her future or yours at a time when you need to be preparing for your own retirement?''

WHAT INVESTMENTS ARE APPROPRIATE?

The Kiddie Tax

Any discussion of suitable investments for college funding must be preceded by a discussion of the kiddie tax. Congress, peopled largely by folks who have never had to live under the rules it imposes, decided to punish the infinitely small number of the very rich who were transferring money to children in large amounts in order to avoid taxes. In their zeal, they have punished the vast majority of Americans who simply want to plan ahead for college educations so that they will not have to depend on the government for aid. The kiddie tax punishes such planning. College education expenses are not deductible, but funds accumulated for college are. Besides writing Congress, we as planners must help our clients sidestep this ridiculous tax.

This silly part of the tax code taxes children under 14 differently than children over 14. Generally, for children under 14, the first $500 of unearned income is tax free because it can be offset against the standard deduction. From $501 to $1,000 is taxed at the child's rate. Unearned income over $1000 is taxed at the parent's highest marginal rate. For children over 14, all interest and dividend income is taxed at the child's rate.

Rules of thumb for selecting investments for education funds in the child's name include:

1. Do not select based on taxes until the child's investments are enough to create at least $1,000 in taxable income
2. Goals and time period are more important than taxes. But tax frees can be considered for the child under 14 who already has a substantial college fund. If they are over 14, you consider tax equivalent yields and the same factors in college funding that you would use selecting investments anytime.

State and Local Tax-Free Bonds

Although in limited supply, the bond department of our broker–dealer will be able to locate any available bonds designed for college savings plans.

IRA and Tax-Deferred Accounts

If the client is going to be over $59\frac{1}{2}$ and retired with a good chance of a lower tax bracket than he is in today when his children attend college, then IRAs, SEPs, and Keogh accounts could be appropriate for saving for college because taxes on the earnings are deferred.

Tax-Free Savings Bonds

Congress recently made available special Series EE savings bonds, for families with incomes under $60,000 and tax-reduced for families earning $60,000 to $90,000. However, there are restrictions and the usual regulatory hoops to jump through.

Life Insurance

I do not usually recommend life insurance for college funding. However, it can be effective when the client has a need for coverage and the need to fund for college. Money can be obtained from the policy through loans.

Guaranteed or Prepaid Tuition Plans

Many colleges and universities allow you to lock in tuition rates by paying four years in advance when your child is very young. These guarantee only tuition costs and not room and board. The disadvantages are obvious:

- What if your child or you change your mind on this college?
- Would you not be better off doing your own investing rather than having the college do it for you?

Education Charitable Remainder Trusts

These are charitable trusts funded with appreciated assets. The parents or grandparents who set up the trust bypass capital gains tax and get a charitable deduction for the future value of the asset that will go to charity. The trust is established for a period of time (up to 20 years) in order to generate income while the kids are in school. When the income is paid out, it is taxed to the kids at their rates since they will be over 14. When the payout period is over the assets go to charity.

Zero Coupon Municipals and Treasuries

With these bonds, you know the maturity dates and amounts. The Treasuries are taxed as the income accrues. The advantage is in knowing what the maturity value will be. The disadvantages are lack of diversification and interest rate risk. The longer the maturity date, the more the risk. They are still appropriate in a lot of cases where the client has a lump sum to invest and wants to invest it and forget it.

Individual Stocks and Bonds

Not enough diversification.

Mutual Funds

These provide the best diversification and flexibility. Also, you can switch between funds when the kiddie tax necessitates a switch. The younger the child, the more aggressive the fund, if the client has a high enough risk tolerance. You should evaluate risk tolerance and time period just as you would any other investment with a stated goal. As your time period shortens, (as college time gets closer), the more your risk decreases.

For time periods longer than 10 years, use aggressive growth funds. As the time period shortens, move to total return, equity income, and balanced funds when college time is at hand, move the first year's cost to a money market fund.

Who Should Own the Investments?

Much talk has been devoted to stories of recalcitrant children who take their college funds and drive away in a new automobile, never darkening the doorway of a college classroom. In all my years of practice, I have never had such a case. With few exceptions, I believe that it is still prudent to place college funds in the child's name. Just because he owns the funds does not mean that he has to know how to get to them or even where they are. There will be plenty of time to judge his maturity before turning over the funds to the child. Yes, at the age of majority, the child could force the control of his investments. He does legally own the funds. A good financial advisor should be able to easily protect his client from such a happening.

UGMA vs. UTMA

These acronyms stand for Uniform Gifts to Minors Act and Uniform Transfers to Minors Act. Their advantages are

1. Easy to open and administer.
2. Offer tax advantages in spite of the kiddie tax.
3. Make your goal of education funding more concrete and easier to monitor

What is the difference? Some states have UGMA, some UTMA.

1. UGMAs can only be funded with bank deposits, securities including mutual funds, and insurance policies. UTMAs can also be funded with these things, but also with most kinds of property, including real estate, paintings, and collectibles.
2. The age of majority when the children come into control of the assets is usually 18 for UGMAs, 21 for UTMAs.

14

Insurance—Do CPAs Really Need to Sell Any?

> There is nothing better for a man than that he should make his soul enjoy good in his labor
>
> *Ecclesiastes*

IS THERE ANYTHING GOOD ABOUT INSURANCE?

During my 20 or so years in the accounting profession, I cannot recall ever reading anything positive about insurance. Everything that a CPA subscribes to in periodicals, everything we are taught in school, basically says that insurance is bad. I know that many people will adamantly refute that statement, so let me explain. Many articles have appeared in the accounting press with well-intentioned authors talking about both positives and negatives of insurance. They seldom say that we should not own any insurance. Quite the contrary. In academic terms, they extol the necessity of providing for our families, being sure that our cars, business and homes are insured, etc. However, the lion's share of space is devoted to warnings about buying the wrong kind or amount of insurance and to the evils of insurance salesmen earning commissions. Not only is the lion's share of each article devoted to warnings, but the overwhelming majority of articles and speeches are negative in overall content. What is ignored is that most of us reading such articles over a period of several years develop a negative thinking pattern. We start to ignore the need for insurance planning and start to think of it as the enemy or, at best, a necessary evil. Journalists and academics add fuel to the fire. They see it as their duty to find flaws and make news under the guise of ''consumer protection.''

WHAT ABOUT THE INSURANCE COMPANIES?

How about the responsibility of the insurance companies? They have to share an equal if not larger portion of the blame. Their contracts and illustrations are impossible to understand. They add insult to injury by even making the pages of a typical insurance policy different sizes and even different thicknesses of paper. There may be all sorts of excuses given for this, but there can be only one reason—to confuse the consumer and to protect the insurance company.

Whenever someone in the industry tries to defend their defenseless position, I simply point out that highly successful businesses have been launched just to make better insurance illustrations. Insurance companies *purchase* services to explain their own products. They blame the legal profession for the incomprehensible nature of their contracts and illustrations. Attorneys do usually lurk behind most of the damage done to industries, professions, and consumers. The solution? Produce understandable illustrations and contracts without legalese, all on the same size and type of paper.

ARE THERE ANY GOOD INSURANCE AGENTS?

How about the folks who sell insurance? I have the highest regard for the insurance professional who is trying to make sales in an environment that is made hostile and is littered by incompetents. Insurance companies continue to recruit and turn loose on an unsuspecting public legions of people who have not the slightest training in financial matters of any kind. Many have only the most rudimentary knowledge of the product they are pushing. That kind of activity makes it tough on the professionals who are providing a very badly needed service. Products are continually presented in a "too good to be true" context. When we see these too good to be true products, we CPAs are immediately on guard and may dismiss a product or turn our clients away from it because it is too good to be true. This often leaves our clients with incorrect or inadequate insurance coverage. We go away feeling smug with having protected our client from himself. However, in many cases, we have turned our clients away from a wonderful product that meets their needs but was over zealously presented.

The better approach would have been to present the product as it really is. Emphasize the good features but also bring out the weaknesses. Relate the product to how it fits into the overall client picture. In particular, show how the particular insurance product solves the client's need. Insurance salesmen are often taught to create such a "feel good illusion" that the client will buy whether or not he understands it. We want the client to understand as much as possible about how the product meets his needs and why he is purchasing it.

WHAT ABOUT THOSE HIGH COMMISSIONS?

What about those high commissions earned by insurance people? Do not they amount to highway robbery? Unfortunately, the industry has to plead guilty again. Not that insurance salesmen do not earn their pay. The insurance sales field has been made such a tough one by ill-trained salesmen, poorly designed illustrations, and poorly drafted documents mentioned above, that high commissions are necessary to attract and keep anyone in the profession. Turnover is tremendous. Also, commissions are structured to award new business, not for business retention. Although a competent and ethical insurance professional has learned not to do this, the compensation structure is often designed to encourage the pursuit of new business, often at the expense of service to existing clients. The solution? Structure the commissions to pay less on the front and more for renewals. Both consumers and the industry will be better served.

SHOULD YOU BUY TERM AND INVEST THE DIFFERENCE?

Do we stick with our own self- and client-limiting philosophy of always buying term and investing the difference? What is wrong with it? Nothing, from a purely academic point of view. It just ignores basic human nature and the differing needs of different people. For example, over 80 percent of people do not really "invest the difference." It also ignores that some people have a need for permanent insurance. It ignores that term insurance often becomes unobtainable or unaffordable at the point in the client's life when he needs it the most. Many people will also never save *except* inside an insurance policy. These are real-world facts, not just academic postulations.

HOW DO WE SERVE OUR CLIENTS?

Our choices are:

1. Let them alone and stay out of the insurance part of their lives.
2. Work with their insurance agents and try to protect them from the bad deals and also the ones that are too good to be true.
3. Learn about the deals and advise them ourselves. Be a real participant in the process.

If you decide on number 1, many of your clients will continue to have the wrong kind or amount of insurance. Will this bother you if one of them becomes disabled or dies prematurely leaving his family and business unprotected?

If you decide on number 2, then you may be an ill-informed advisor and could almost be as guilty as the salesman with the deal that is too good to be true. What happens if your client dies or becomes disabled after you have advised him right out of any coverage? Also, you will continue to prepare tax returns for insurance salesmen who make a lot more money than you do. You will continue to send referrals to other professionals without getting many referrals in return.

I think number 3 is the most attractive alternative. The best way to advise your clients is to become licensed and learn enough about insurance and how it relates to the clients' needs to properly advise them. Learn *both* sides of the story.

THE REST OF THE INSURANCE STORY

Why do people need insurance and how can the CPA help them to obtain the right kind and amount? Why cannot I just leave it to others? If you are going to provide *investment planning* properly to your clients, you must do *financial planning*. If you are going to provide financial planning, you must also provide estate planning. Although the industry and some professionals continue to refer to them as separate disciplines, they are inseparable. If you are going to properly advise your client, you must include insurance planning as well.

I think working with other insurance professionals is excellent. You will need their assistance, especially in the earlier stages. However, I can almost guarantee that there will be cases where you do not need the professional, cases where the client and the professional do not get along, cases where the professional sells your client something later that you did not recommend, and cases where the insurance professional does half the work that you do and gets compensated in multiples above your own compensation. Also, I do not think that you can be a complete financial advisor for your client on insurance matters unless you understand the products. Are you going to understand the product if you do not sell it? We are not going to get the training and exposure to product from the insurance company unless we are an agent. Why miss out on the valuable resource of the insurance company's training and staff?

MAKING THE MOST OF INSURANCE PLANNING

Insurance planning, like estate planning, can be complicated. However, also like estate planning, it can be reduced to certain common denominators that will help you to determine your client's needs and to find the solutions to those needs. The following is intended to do just that. They should be a referral source to help you remember how to see the forest when you get all tangled up in the trees.

Why Do People Need Insurance?

Notice I did not say *buy* insurance. They often buy insurance for reasons varying widely from their needs. In my own practice, I had a standard question in post-tax interviews about why clients purchased insurance. Most could not remember why they bought the policy. Many bought because the selling agent had stirred guilt feelings in them. Others bought because having their families protected made them feel good. Many times, those people had protection for death, but not for their most valuable resource, their earning power. Families might have their automobile and homes protected with credit insurance, but have no protection for the *value* of the home or auto.

People need insurance to manage or limit risk. Although we have been taught to believe otherwise, many people also buy insurance as an investment because of the tax deferral advantage. Risk is the possibility of loss or the possibility of any outcome other than the one that the client hoped for. Your clients generally insure against:

1. Personal risks:
   (a) Death.
   (b) Health.
   (c) Disability or loss of earning power.
2. Property risks.
3. Taxes.
4. Financial insecurity.

So how can a CPA provide valuable service to his clients in determining how to control this risk? Most people already know how to buy property insurance, right? Wrong! Millions are being made by astute marketers selling books, newsletters, and memberships to people who want to know such simple things as when to increase the deductible on their car insurance or when to drop everything except liability on the old car. This just identifies a need not being served. Clients need the assistance of their primary advisor (usually you) to help them in the most basic of decisions about insurance.

DELIVERING THE SERVICE

How does a CPA who has practiced avoiding insurance all these years suddenly start serving client needs in this area? Use TOPS. Ask questions during your visit with the client.

Trust

Since the insurance area is newer to you, you need to spend slightly more time acquainting your client about your ability to serve his insurance needs. "John, I have been preparing your tax returns for many years. Since you have been coming back each year, would it be fair to say that my service has been satisfactory? How many financial advisors do you have? Do you see me as one of the primary advisors? Who is your insurance advisor?"

"As a CPA, I get a chance to deal with lots of clients on a personal basis every year. I have had clients die, become disabled, have wrecks, divorces, business failures, etc. You name it and I have probably seen it. During those years of experience, I have noticed a lack of preparedness for many of my clients. I was hurt by this. Although I was unaware of it myself, I was considered the only financial advisor for many of these clients. I am sure they or their family members may have wondered why I failed to give them advice or protecting themselves and their families better. I am asking a lot more questions of my clients so that I can make sure that my job as a professional is done completely and well."

Opportunity

"How long since you have had a needs analysis done on your insurance? What types of policies do you have? (Do not get hung up and end the conversation if the client does not know. You have just uncovered a need. He does not know!) Are you comfortable with the amounts and types of coverage on these policies? Has your situation changed any since the policies were purchased? Are you aware of the new mortality tables prepared as a result of increased life expectancy today? Many old policies have high mortality costs based on outdated mortality tables. Also, the insurance industry has changed dramatically in the last ten years. Many new types of policies are available that meet customized needs of clients that were unheard of even fifteen years ago."

Pain

"I noticed that you have $500,000 in life insurance, but no disability insurance. Did you know that you are four times more likely to be disabled for some period of time than you are to die prematurely? What happens to the business if you are not there to run it for an extended period of time? Will your wife's income be adequate to support the family lifestyle *and* send little Julie and Bob to college?"

Solution

"Why not let me examine each of your policies and compare them to your current needs? I will design a program allowing you to control all of your risks at the least possible cost and to provide for your other goals, too."

It is hard to put insurance training into a chronological sequence. I have already shown you the TOPS solution to identify needs and provide solutions. These questions get you to the point of the client allowing you "in the door." He has allowed you to look at his policies. You will return to TOPS when you are ready to present the specific solution. If you previously gathered the data necessary during the tax interview, then you can present the solution the first time you use TOPS. Otherwise, you will need a return appointment to use TOPS for the actual sale.

Now that you have positioned yourself as a more complete advisor in your client's eyes, what do you do now? Many CPAs do not take the steps outlined above under TOPS because they are afraid the client will say yes and they will not know what to do. Your next steps are to determine these questions:

1. For what reasons does the client need insurance?
2. How much insurance does the client need?
3. What type of insurance is best?
4. What products will fill the needs?

WHY DOES YOUR CLIENT NEED INSURANCE?

Go back to the basics of why people need insurance. They need it to control risks and to meet specific goals they want to accomplish. For purposes of this book, we will ignore property insurance needs, so the personal risks are death, health, disability, or loss of earning power. Ask the following questions.

Death

What happens if the client dies prematurely? Who would be left unprotected? Use the insurance needs worksheet in the financial planning section to determine what would happen and how much insurance is needed. Income required to support the family is relatively easy to estimate. It can be taken from the tax return. Remember, this is not exact. Will the income needs drop if a spouse dies? Some expenses will go away, but others will crop up to take their place. Generally, the lifestyle is set for a family and the death of a spouse will not reduce it dramatically. I usually estimate 80 to 85 percent of the family's adjusted gross income less any above average savings. Should all savings be taken out when estimating? I do not think so because savings will be required even if a spouse dies. The rest of the form is self-explanatory. You may want to do a conservative estimate and a liberal estimate of insurance needs or a minimum or maximum. Be prepared to explain to the client in personal terms what each of these needs mean to him personally.

Health

Determining health insurance needs may be unnecessary if the client has an excellent group policy with his employer. However, if he is self-employed or is employed in a small business, health insurance needs may need more analysis. Purchasing more coverage than is required can be prohibitively expensive. In this case, I believe that clients should insure against major losses and not worry too much about losses for which they can pay. My major concern is to see that the client will not be ''wiped out'' by a prolonged illness.

Disability or Loss of Income

Many clients will have disability insurance at work. Usually, this is short term. Most clients think of disability only in terms of crippling accidents that leave them permanently disabled. Most disabilities are not permanent and result from illness, not injury. If the client has his own business, he also suffers from risk of the business collapsing because of his absence. Business interruption should be proposed to pay the overhead until the client can get back to work and generate revenue. Remember, the client's most important resource is often his earning power. If he loses his car, he can get another as long as he can work. If he loses his ability to earn a living, he cannot replace anything.

Use the disability needs worksheet in the financial planning section to determine the amount of income protection needed by each spouse.

Protection From Taxes

Insurance contracts enjoy many tax benefits because insurance is determined to be in the public interest. Why is it in the public interest? Because if private insurance is not purchased, many more people would become the responsibility of the public (the government). So how does this aspect of tax shelter or deferral affect your planning for the client? Always refer back to the client's needs. Is tax advantaged investing a primary goal? Does he have retirement planning needs in addition to insurance needs? If so, then an insurance product that covers both needs may well be the answer.

HOW MUCH INSURANCE DOES YOUR CLIENT NEED?

For disability and life insurance needs, refer to the worksheets in the financial planning section and in the Appendix. For health insurance, get at least $1 million in coverage for catastrophic illness. Find out what the client's maximum loss is on current coverage. What kind of maximum loss can he tolerate? Get coverage for anything above that loss.

The disability and life insurance worksheets will provide you with an educated estimate of the amount of coverage needed to cover risks. However, they do not address the needs for retirement planning or tax deferral or investment. These should be considered at the same time. If you can meet a portion of the client's retirement needs at the same time, they you may be able to reduce the amount of coverage required for risk needs. However, exercise caution when completely offsetting one against the other. Be sure that risk needs are met with the proper type of coverage. Then determine if the investment types of policies are adequate to offset the risk type of coverage. In other words, will they be in force as long as the need for risk protection is around?

Somewhere between 51 to 74 percent of a person's income is the amount that is replaced under most disability policies.

WHAT TYPE OF INSURANCE IS BEST?

What type of need does the client have?

1. To manage risk.
2. To provide for retirement and use tax shelter.
3. Is the need short term or long term (i.e., when does the risk go away? For example, if your child is 18 and you are going to send her to college out of current earnings, your risk is that you will die and she will be unable to go. That need should go away in four to five years. Income needs for a disabled spouse or child, however, are usually a definite long-term need.
4. What are the financial constraints? Some clients simply cannot afford the premiums that are required to get the level of coverage required. Then you must compromise on type of coverage or amount.
5. What is the health status of the individuals to be insured? This can have a profound effect on the type and amount of coverage.
6. What is the client's tolerance for risk?

The problem with this book or any other is that it never gets around to giving you specific answers to every question you will eventually have concerning insurance types. That is because every situation is unique. There is no pat answer to the right type of insurance, unfortunately. However, with practice, you can eliminate a lot of types. Do not be afraid to ask for assistance from our insurance department or from the insurance company itself. Even an expert can often use a second opinion. The problem with selecting types of insurance is that many insurance agents only know the products of one company. Products are complicated, so they often only know one or two products within one company. It is only natural that they recommend this product for *every* situation. It does not matter if the client has a short-term need or a long-term one, is looking for risk control or investment, one of their products is the answer because that is the product they understand. You can avoid this trap by going through the type selection first, then evaluating products from a couple of competing companies. See if the illustrations match your client's goals. If you cannot read the illustrations, do not be afraid to ask for help.

What are the types of insurance? I will not attempt to list all the types of insurance here, but will list those most widely used today. The problem, again, is that the insurance industry has attached several names to the various basic types and added several features to contracts that make them have characteristics of each other. Again, *go back to the client's need and goals sheet*. Ask the questions for each type of policy—does it meet the goals and needs of my client?

Term

This is pure insurance for short-term needs. It provides protection against financial loss resulting from death during a specified period of time. The premiums may be level or increasing during the specified period of time. The death benefit may also decrease during the time period in decreasing term.

Renewable Term

Most term policies are guaranteed renewable (at a higher premium) after the end of the specified time period.

Convertible Term

This is term insurance that may be exchanged for permanent insurance without physical examination or other evidence of insurability within a specified period of time.

Whole Life

Also known as straight life and ordinary life, it usually provides insurance protection at a level premium for the lifetime of the insured. Thus the term *whole* life.

Limited Pay Whole Life

This is a form of whole life where premium payments are adjusted to pay for lifetime protection but premiums stop after a specified period of time.

Participating or Non-Participating Insurance

Participating policies pay annual dividends to the policyholder. Usually the premiums are higher because of a built in overcharge that increases the insurance company's margin. If the company performs well, then dividends are returned to the policyholder. Nonparticipating policies have premiums that more closely reflect the actual cost of insurance. No dividends are paid.

Variable Life Insurance

The premiums are fixed, and the death benefit is guaranteed, but the cash value fluctuates with the performance of the portfolio invested in by the insurer.

Adjustable Life Insurance

This may provide lifetime protection like whole life or limited protection like term life depending on the face amount and the premium at the insured's attained age. The policy can be changed during its duration from term to whole or vice versa. When the premiums paid exceeds the cost of protection, the policy cash value increases; when the premiums are less than the cost of protection, the cash value decreases. If the policy is for a limited period (term), increased premiums will extend the period. If it is lifetime, increased premiums may shorten the time period when premiums must be paid. The relationship between the initial face amount and the premium determine the nature of the policy issued.

Universal Life Insurance

This is a lot like adjustable life insurance in that premiums, coverage, and cash values may be adjusted during the term of the policy. However, universal life augments this by a variable rate of earnings on the investment element of the policy. Interest credited to the cash value is geared to current market conditions, but is usually subject to a minimum. Cash values are invested in medium- and short-term instruments rather than the traditional long-term investments of life insurance. Policyholders may make withdrawals from the cash value without terminating the contract. If current interest rates are above the expected rates set when the policy began, more money goes into cash value. However, if interest rates fall below expected projections and premiums are not enough to make mortality payments, then money may have to be withdrawn from cash value. When there is no cash value, then premiums may have to be increased or the policy will lapse.

Variable Universal Life Insurance

All aspects of this type of contract—the premium, the level of protection, and cash value or investment component—are all flexible. The cash value is invested in a variable family of mutual funds.

Survivorship Life Insurance

Insures two lives, pays death benefits at death of second. Usually cheaper premiums because two deaths have to occur before benefit is paid. Used primarily to pay estate taxes or furnish liquidity at second death.

First to Die

This insures two lives, but pays at the death of first one. Usually cheaper premiums than individual policies, but used when income or liquidity is needed at first death. Also works well when one spouse is in poor health. See Figure 14-1 for more about different types of insurance.

WHAT PRODUCTS WILL BEST FILL YOUR CLIENT'S NEEDS?

After determining what problems your client has that may be solved by insurance, the amount of insurance required, and the type of insurance required, one problem still remains. What product best fits the needs of my client? Even after becoming familiar with the other phases, this final task can be much more challenging to a CPA than picking a mutual fund. Mutual funds have independent rating services that rate them by almost every possible measure. Insurance companies have rating services that rate them also, but not so much the individual products. That is because products are so diverse, it is impossible to compare apples to apples.

So where does that leave us? I highly recommend that you limit your insurance company carriers to no more than three. Most companies have products that really "shine" in a particular area. Find out what those products are. For life insurance, you will need a good term, whole life, universal life, second to die, and first to die product. Try to stick with one product for each need. You should be able to find all in no more than three companies. Do not worry too much about finding the perfect product for each situation. Everyone has a perfect product if you hear the sales pitch. Just be sure that it is a good, competitive product. Also, of course, be sure that the insurance company has the best ratings from independent rating services such as A.M. Best, Duff and Phelps, Standard and Poors. You do not have time to worry about insurance company stability. Simply rule out all companies that do not meet safety criteria.

Four or five products should provide you with most of the traditional insurance coverage your clients will need. Once you decide on these products,

Figure 14-1   A General Guide to Selecting an Insurance Plan

Type of Need	Type of Insurance
Short term	Term
Long term or permanent	Term with conversion privilege Whole life Universal or variable universal
Ability to pay premiums is limited; need is short term	Term
Ability to pay premiums is limited; need is long term	Term with guaranteed conversion
Client is risk averse	Whole life
Protection from inflation is more important; willing to take risks	Universal variable or variable life
Flexibility to change premium, face amount, and increase cash value	Universal
Retirement income with ability to withdraw cash value as opposed to borrowing	Universal
Retirement income with no risk	Whole life
Tax deferral combined with death benefits	Whole life, universal, or variable universal
Client has health problems or family history of health problems	Whole life, universal life
Liquidity to pay estate taxes	Survivorship life, second to die
Liquidity at death of first spouse, lower premiums, or health problems with one spouse	First to die
Permanent insurance need client wants to pay premiums for limited time	Limited pay whole life, universal life, or variable universal life

get all the information from the insurance department of 1st Global on these products. I recommend that you also obtain the software to run proposals for clients. If not, then have your proposals run by the insurance department. Learn to read the proposals in spite of what you think of them. Consider designing your own cover sheet showing what each part of the proposal means in layman's terms. Reduce the proposal (also called an illustration or ledger) to the needs expressed by the client. Incorporate the proposals into your financial plan showing how each type of insurance will solve the problems expressed by the client.

When presenting the proposals as part of an overall plan to the client, use TOPS.

Trust.   "Do you recall that we discussed my desire to be your advisor in all phases of your financial life including insurance needs?"

Opportunity.   "Do you agree that estate liquidity, insuring that your children's college education is paid for, and providing income for your spouse were your primary goals?"

Pain.   "When we discussed this before, you indicated that you did not remember why you had purchased the existing insurance. Our calculations showed that funds set aside for college would run out in Julie's second college year if you were to die. Your wife's income would not be adequate to maintain lifestyle and pay for college."

Solution.   "Does a term policy costing $_____ per month for 10 years in the amount of $150,000 sound like a reasonable solution to meet the education funding need? For the income needs of Jane, I recommend a variable universal life because of your expressed need for protection from inflation and your risk comfort level. These numbers show what the cash value would be at the end of 10 or 20 years and the projected income to Jane."

You now know why people need insurance and why CPAs should get involved in the insurance planning process. You know how to determine the needs that may be solved by insurance, how to determine the right amount of coverage, the right type of coverage, and how to select the right product. You also know how to reintroduce yourself to your client as an insurance advisor. You know how insurance planning is related to overall estate, investment, and financial planning. You know how to present proposals for coverage. What are you waiting for?

INSURANCE IN BUSINESS

Most of our previous discussion referred to the individual needs for insurance and to generic insurance analysis. Although the products are usually the same when insurance is used in business situations, the needs are somewhat different and the methods of paying for insurance are often different. That's because you are throwing in a third party and sometimes several other parties into the picture. The third element is the business, the corporation, the partnership, etc. Other elements could be other shareholders, multiple partners, and so on.

Identifying Business Insurance Needs

The Buy–Sell Agreement.   This is probably the easiest need to identify. If you have clients who have business partners or fellow shareholders, they need protection in the event of a dispute, disability, or premature death. If one of the partners dies prematurely, there may not be enough money to buy out his heirs. That could mean that the surviving partners become partners with heirs with whom they never intended to be in the business. It could lead to lawsuits by heirs to get a fair price, a sale by the heirs to a third party that is not satisfactory to the original partners, or worse.

How does the CPA get involved in solving this potential problem?

1. It is your responsibility to point it out. Even if you are not in the insurance business.

2. Assist in setting a value for the business (more fee income).

3. Work with attorneys and your clients to structure the arrangements of the buy–sell. They are usually surprisingly easy. When a partner dies or becomes disabled, the others usually buy his interest from him or his heirs. This is true even in family or retirement situations.

4. Fund the agreement with insurance for:

   (a) The stock redemption/entity plan—An entity buy–sell plan is a contract between a business owner and the business. It obligates the business entity to purchase his interest. Stock redemption is the term for corporations, entity plan for partnerships. The estate receives the purchase price income tax free, because the estate's stock basis is stepped up at death. The company pays the insurance premium, only one policy is needed per owner, and the company has the liability to purchase the deceased owner's share. The surviving owners do not get a step up in basis, insurance proceeds may be subject to the claims of corporate creditors, and insurance proceeds may be subject to AMT.

   (b) Cross purchase—Individual shareholders or partners buy policies on each other. The agreement specifies that the surviving party will purchase the deceased owner's share from his estate. The life insurance is owned by the individual parties on each other. The surviving owners realize a stepup in basis, attribution rules are avoided, alternative minimum tax rules are avoided, and the death proceeds are not subject to claims of creditors of the corporation.

   Multiple insurance policies may have to be purchased on each owner if there are more than two owners. This can cause unfair cost distribution because of the difference in ages, but this can be solved through corporate bonuses or split dollar agreements discussed later.

Key Man Insurance.   People are usually the most valuable assets in a business. The main cause of business failure has been lack of good management. Losing key people can cause business to fail. The solution is to purchase insurance on key personnel. It:

1. Covers any losses experienced during readjustment.
2. Protects the firm's credit situation.
3. Protects surviving owners from losing control of the business.
4. Strengthens firm's credit position.
5. Cash value of policy can be used as emergency or opportunity fund.
6. Policy can be used as collateral for loan.
7. Policy can be used as a sinking fund for special projects.
8. Can inspire confidence in potential investors in the company.
9. Policy can inspire loyalty and enthusiasm in insured officers.
10. Premiums are not tax deductible.
11. Death proceeds are received income tax free.
12. Policy can be structured to become a SERP (supplemental executive retirement plan). This is accomplished by an agreement to pay benefits from the policy at the employee's retirement, or to heirs at death.

13. Proceeds can be used to redeem a portion of a decedent's stock without it being considered as a dividend distribution through IRC 303 under certain conditions if the value of the stock exceeds 35 percent of the gross estate.

Marketing key man insurance is relatively easy. Virtually every business has one or more key persons.

NONQUALIFIED PLANS AND PRIVATE PENSIONS

This topic was covered under retirement plans, but is mentioned again here to emphasize how insurance is applicable in the small business market. As with almost all products or marketing concepts involving insurance or attorneys, several names are used to describe the same concept or very similar concepts. These include private pension, top-hat, golden handcuff, excess-benefit, and SERP-COLI (the acronym for Supplemental Executive Retirement Plan using Corporate Owned Life Insurance). Although these types of programs can be unfunded or funded with other types of investments, the tax-deferred build up of cash values and death benefits available with cash value life insurance are the only practical means of implementing these types of plans.

The advantages to the owner and key employees include:

1. Participation may be limited to select employees.
2. Tax-deferred growth on plan assets.
3. Disability benefits.
4. Preretirement death benefit.
5. In a deferred salary arrangement, employee defers current taxation on salary.
6. An excellent way to supplement other retirement benefits which often discriminate against key employees.

The advantages to the business include:

1. Ability to attract and retain quality employees.
2. Allows retirement benefits to be deductible when paid out.
3. Exemption from IRS approval.
4. No plan administration.
5. Improves morale and loyalty of key employees.
6. Golden handcuffs to retain key employees if vesting schedules are used.

The possible disadvantages are:

1. No current deduction for premium payments.
2. Corporate alternative minimum tax considerations.
3. Assets are available to corporate creditors.
4. Death benefits are taxable to the employee's beneficiary when paid because the employer is deducting them.

How Does It Work?

1. A written agreement is made between employer and employee which is usually referred to as a salary reduction and/or continuation agreement.

2. Plan contributions are made by the employer and grow on a tax-deferred basis (contributions are not deductible when made by the employer). Contributions are usually made in the form of an insurance policy purchased on the employee that builds up cash value. The employer is the owner, premium payer, and beneficiary of the policy.

3. The insurance policy is an *unsecured general asset* of the employer, and available to the employer's creditors in the event of a liquidation. Plan benefits are supported by an "unsecured promise to pay with a substantial risk of forfeiture." These words allow tax deferral in the salary reduction program, however, the promise to pay is actually backed up by the insurance policy. The only way the employee is not going to get paid is if the insurance company folds and guarantees are not there, or the company liquidates.

4. When the employee retires, benefits are paid to the employer by the insurance company who then pays the employee in a prescheduled amount for a specified number of years. The payments are tax deductible to the employer as retirement benefits under IRC 162(a)(1) and IRC 404(a)(5). Benefits are taxable to the employee when paid. These are considered wages subject to employment taxes of FICA and FUTA. However, in some cases, it may be wise to withhold the taxes on the wages during working years when the employee is over the FICA limits. "Wages" paid under the nonqualified plan after retirement will not disqualify the recipient for Social Security benefits (Section 203(f)(5)(c) of the Social Security Act).

   There may be a $5,000 death benefit exclusion for amounts paid to the employee's beneficiary for income in respect of a decedent in the year after death *only* if the employee's rights in the living benefits are subject to a substantial risk of forfeiture at the time of death (IRC 691(a) and IRC 101). At this point, the employer has several options. He can cash in the policy, continue it until a later date or until death of the employee.

5. If the employee dies prior to retirement, the employer can provide the employee's family with income from the interest earned on the death benefit, while permitting the employer to keep the death benefits on the assets of the corporation.

6. The increasing cash value of the insurance policy is an asset on the corporate balance sheet to offset the liability that must be booked for the future benefit owed to the employee.

7. The discounted value of the future benefits will be includable in the employee's gross estate, IRC 2039(a). Benefits passing to the surviving spouse, however, qualify for the marital deduction and are not taxed.

8. Employees may be 100 percent vested or not and still qualify for tax deferral as long as the promise to pay continues to have substantial risk of forfeiture (i.e., the insurance policy is subject to claims of creditors).

Who are the prospects for these plans?

1. Employees of sole proprietorships.

2. Employees of partnerships.
3. Shareholder—employees, independent contractors, and directors of C corporations.
4. Nonshareholder employees, independent contractors, and directors of S corporations.

What I originally found confusing about the nonqualified plan market were the different descriptions found for what was supposed to be the same thing. That was until I discovered that the nonqualified plan may take many forms. For example, nonqualified plans are consistently referred to as nonqualified deferred comp plans. Yet, I seldom saw a nonqualified plan that involved deferred comp. They are usually supplemental compensation that is not taxed. Here is how:

1. *Pure deferred compensation.* The employee just elects to take less salary today in exchange for more in the future when he will theoretically be in a lower bracket.
2. *Supplemental salary continuation.* These are SERPs. Employer makes contributions to plan over and above existing compensation levels. This is easiest to market because employees are all in favor of it. Some will not be in favor of pure deferred compensation unless there is protection under a *Rabbi Trust.* This is in irrevocable trust which prevents an employer from using salary continuation funds for any purpose other than funding the salary continuation agreement. Trust funds are still general assets of the employer, and subject to the claims of its creditors, GCM 39320, PLR 8113107, and PLR 8325100.
3. *Hybrid or 401(k) look alike.* Employee salary reduction with employer match. The employee and the employer both contribute money toward purchase of an insurance policy. Employee's contributions are made on a before tax basis as salary deferral. These plans allow a larger retirement benefit to build up because employer and employee are both contributing. Also, the employee gets tax deferral on a portion of his salary.

METHODS OF PAYING FOR INSURANCE

I am not at all surprised when clients or even attorneys and CPAs tell me they bought some *split dollar insurance.* Many people think that split dollar is a type of insurance because it is poorly marketed and explained. Actually, split dollar is a method of paying for insurance. The basic split dollar plan involves the allocation of premium costs and benefits for a permanent life insurance policy between an employer and employee. The employee usually has the need for additional coverage, and the employer has the means and motivation to help finance the purchase as a selective employee benefit. The arrangement divides or ''splits'' the death benefit, the living benefits (withdrawals and loans), and possibly the premium between two parties. In case you have not already guessed, this method of payment is a perfect match for the nonqualified plan market, key employee plans, and buy–sell funding arrangements.

In the traditional split dollar plan, the employer pays for and owns the investment part of the plan (cash value) and the employee or his designate, has a right to the death benefit. Many plans, however, allow the employee to own any cash values in excess of the employers cumulative premiums. In other words, the employer will get his money back first, then everything else may belong, to the employee under this type of arrangement.

Split dollar arrangements are used most frequently in these situations:

1. Providing immediate death benefit and income protection needs of key employees.
2. Nonqualified deferred compensation discussed earlier.
3. Insurance on the *spouses* of key employees.
4. Funding buy–sell agreements.
5. Substitute for group life insurance.
6. Executive benefit for nonemployee directors.

The above list refers to employer–employee arrangements. Split dollar can also be used in private situations where a C corporation is involved for:

1. Equalizing estate distribution when another heir is to receive business interest. The business can pay for life insurance on the owner with the proceeds to go to the other heirs to balance out the estate when one heir is to receive the business. The insurance is usually owned by the insured or by a trust.
2. Allowing parents, grandparents, etc. to assist children and grandchildren in getting started in insurance.

Split dollar plans will not work in S corporations because all of the premiums paid pass through to the owners as taxable income. But if you are like me, you are still wondering what the big deal is. Where is the sizzle of split dollar plans? The following benefits may make it clearer.

Employer Benefits

1. All costs for premiums paid are recovered at plan surrender or termination (roll-out) or death.
2. There is no IRS involvement. This is a way for an employer to provide a benefit without involving the IRS.
3. It provides a selective benefit. The employer can choose which employees to reward with this benefit *and* what level of benefit to reward each one.
4. It attracts and keeps key employees.

Employee Benefits

1. *Inexpensive protection*—While the employee contribution to the plan varies with the type of split dollar arrangement selected by the employer, it is generally a fraction of the cost of buying the policy personally. Although the employee's share of premiums may be substantial in the early years, it will decrease each year as the cash value grows faster. In many cases, the employee's share drops to zero in a relatively short time.
2. *Retirement benefits*—Structured properly, the plan can provide excellent post-retirement benefits

3. *Withdrawing funds from the corporation with tax benefits*—In many cases, the employer and insured employee are the same person. Split dollar represents an effective way to transfer corporate dollars to the owner's pocket on a favorable basis.

Income Tax Treatment

Neither the employee nor employer can take a deduction for the premiums paid. Since no deductions have been taken, the cost basis in the policy will be income tax free if cash value is withdrawn. Also, death proceeds will be income tax free. Under some plans, the employer pays for all of the premiums through a bonus to the employee for his part of the premiums. The bonus is taxable to the employee and deductible to the employer.

The insured employee must be taxed on the economic benefit derived from the employer's premium contribution. This "economic benefit" is equal to the one-year term cost of the employee's share of the death proceeds, *less* any premiums paid by the employee in that year. The applicable one-year term rate is the lower of the government's PS 58 rate or the insured's one-year term rates. Do not use split dollar programs in S corporations because the premium paid by the corporation will flow through to the shareholder as taxable income.

Split Dollar Systems (Policy Ownership)

Collateral Assignment.   The insured employee or a designated third party such as a spouse applies for, is the owner, and designates the beneficiary of the policy. In a separate agreement, the employer obligates itself to lend the employee an amount of money each year equal to the annual increase in cash value. The *collateral* for the loan is the policy. The employee assigns it to the employer as security for repayment of the loan.

Endorsement System.   The employer owns the policy and is primarily responsible for premium payments. The employee agrees to reimburse the employer for the portion of each premium payment that exceeds the annual increase in the cash value of the policy. The employer is named the beneficiary for that portion of the proceeds equal to the cash value. The employee's rights are protected by an endorsement on the policy that modifies the employer's rights as a policy-holder.

Which one to use? If the employer wants to draw down the cash value for use in business, then the endorsement system is better. When the parties are funding a nonqualified plan, then the collateral assignment is preferred. When key person policies are used for golden handcuffs, then use the endorsement method. The collateral assignment system is the simplest and most often used.

15

Taxes for NonTax Pros

My Father had only a third-grade education, but he taught me what I think is the most important principle in business: You don't make money unless you help other people make money.

Armstrong Williams

This chapter is not intended to make you expert at preparing income taxes or as a reference point for tax questions. I know better than to attempt that in a book for tax professionals. Almost every statement I could put in print about taxes could be successfully refuted by a knowledgeable professional. My purpose is to introduce very basic information about income taxes and to reemphasize points I made earlier in Chapter 6 on selling during tax season.

THE "PARTS" OF A TAX RETURN

Most people have never noticed that tax returns are in sections. The parts are as follows:

1. Name and address label section
2. Filing status
3. Exemptions listing
4. Gross income
5. Adjustments
6. Adjusted gross income
7. Deductions
8. Exemptions amounts (see item 3)
9. Taxable income
10. Income tax
11. Total taxes
12. Credits
13. Other taxes
14. Payments
15. Refund or amount due

Is this just trivial information? No. If a nontax professional can get familiar with these parts and what they mean, he can more readily understand other's tax returns and various tax planning situations.

Gross Income

This section has 22 lines that allow you to list wages, interest income, net income from businesses and farming, net capital gain or loss, alimony, and the like. All items of income, even though reported first on a supplemental schedule, wind up here.

Adjustments to Income and AGI

This section provides the ability to deduct IRAs, self-employed pension plan deductions, alimony, and so on. Adjustments have some significance because adjusted gross income is used in several calculations to determine deductibility of other things such as medical expenses, miscellaneous itemized deductions, and overall itemized deductions.

The lower your adjusted gross income (AGI), the more you may get to deduct for certain other things.

Deductions

Everyone is entitled to some deductions, whether you have any or not. That is, everyone gets a standard amount that they can deduct from AGI, no matter what their actual deductions total. That amount was $6,000 in 1992 for married couples filing jointly, for example.

If you can get your *itemized deductions* to total more than your standard deduction, then you will want to use schedule A and take the larger amount. Itemized deductions are listed on schedule A as *certain types* of medical and dental expenses, taxes, interest, charitable gifts, casualty and thefts, moving expenses, and miscellaneous. Each of these items is subject to a plethora of rules describing what parts of which expenses under what circumstances, subject to certain limitations, will be deductible.

Deductions should be distinguished from credits, which will be described later. Deductions are subtracted from adjusted gross income to arrive at a number that has no description, so we will call it ''AGI less deducts.''

Exemptions

Everyone who files a tax return is entitled to at least one of these. The amount for 1992 was $2,300 for each exemption. Exemptions, generally speaking, are those folks including yourself for whom you provide more than half of the support.

Taxable Income

Subtracting exemptions (and AGI less deducts) from gross income finally gives us the amount of our income subject to income tax. Going to an appropriate set of tables, we can arrive at our income tax based on this taxable income with rates applied.

Income Tax and Total Income Tax

Of course, there are some other types of taxes not included in the tables such as the tax on lump-sum distributions that are not calculated in the regular way. After adding them in, we arrive at total income tax before credits.

Credits

Credits are items that come directly off your income *taxes*, not off income that is going to be taxed. That is quite a difference. If you are in the 30 percent tax bracket, then a deduction or exemption is worth only 70 percent of the total amount. A credit is worth 100 percent. Of course, it may have already had a few percentages applied to it before it ever gets to the 1040. Subtracting credits from your total taxes gives you tax after credits.

Other Taxes and Total Tax

The IRS collects various other taxes that are not really income taxes. Some are income taxes: they just could not figure out where else to put them on the form. These include Social Security and self-employment taxes, taxes on distributions from qualified retirement plans, recapture of investment credit when you sold something before you were supposed to, and the alternative minimum tax or AMT. The AMT is the IRS's last parting shot. If you outsmarted them all the way through line 46 (Total Tax), they are waiting for you with this last bullet. Adding Income Taxes After Credits to Other Taxes you arrive at Total Taxes.

Of course, there is also the payments section which should be self-explanatory, right? Wrong. In this section, we have credits that are called *refundable*. That means we can get money back even if we have not paid any in. The credits section above only includes refundable credits. If you do not have a tax liability to use them against, you do not get to use them this year. I know that this explanation was extremely elementary, but I hope it serves as a reference point. By the way, if you think our tax rates are high today, take a look at Figure 15-1 for an historical look at tax rates on unearned income.

USING THE TAX RETURN IN FINANCIAL PLANNING

The IRS uses the taxpayer's return to analyze his personal financial circumstances. Why are CPAs not able to do the same? The IRS also selects approximately 1 percent of unfortunates for its TCMP (Taxpayer Compliance Measurement Program). I call these guinea pig audits. Every line of the return is examined and entered into a statistical bank that compiles DIF scores. These DIF scores are used to set parameters or norms under which taxpayers at a certain income level should fall. If a return is out of these norms, it will be pulled from the system and visually reviewed. If the reviewer feels the return is worthy, it will be audited.

Right to Access and Review

Section 7216 requires any person who is engaged in preparing or providing services in connection with the preparation of tax returns to obtain the taxpayer's written consent before the return or other information gathered to com-

184

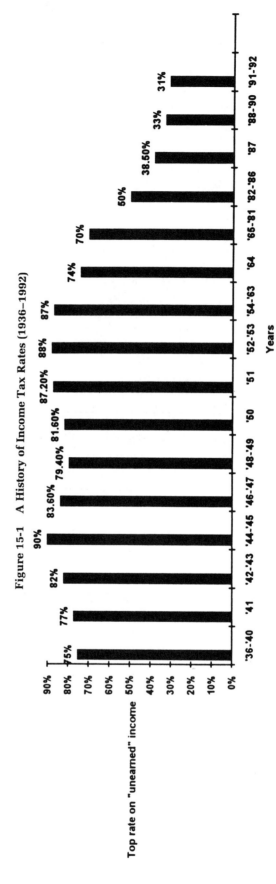

Figure 15-1   A History of Income Tax Rates (1936–1992)

Source: Internal Revenue Code.

plete the return are used to solicit additional services. The Code requires that the consent form contain:

1. The name of the preparer and taxpayer.
2. Purpose for which the consent is being furnished.
3. Date consent is signed.
4. Statement that the tax return information may not be disclosed or used by the preparer for any purpose (not otherwise permitted) other than that stated in the consent.
5. A statement by the taxpayer that he consents to the disclosure and use of the information for the purpose described herein.

Sounds intimidating, does it not? However, if you routinely present these contracts for all of your clients when they come in, they will sign without hesitation.

Planning Opportunities on the 1040

Use the form titled Financial Planning From the Tax Return and the Post-Tax Interview provided in Part 2 and the Appendix to review your client's tax returns. What will you find? Let us take a look just using the sections referred to earlier:

1. Name and address label section.
   (a) The address will give a clue as to the taxpayer's lifestyle attitudes and overall wealth which may indicate something entirely different than the numbers shown on the 1040. For example, if you have a client living in an exclusive, expensive area with poverty level wages, then you know that there may be an inheritance involved.
   (b) A change in address may tell you that a change in estate planning may be needed if the client moved from a community property state to a noncommunity state, for example.
2. Filing status.
   (a) Along with the mailing label information, this tells you whether the client may have children who are not shown as dependents.
   (b) Changes in marital status may affect estate planning or insurance needs.
3. Exemptions listing.
   (a) Income shifting opportunities.
   (b) Employing children in business if there is a schedule C, E, or F.
   (c) Education funding.
   (d) Life insurance.
   (e) Disability insurance.
4. Gross Income.
   (a) Wages.
      I. Is there a protection for this income stream in the form of disability and life insurance?
      II. W-2s will tell you if the client contributes to a retirement plan, participates in one but does not contribute, has over $50,000 of life insurance at work, whether or not the employee is key or not, and may be eligible for a deferred comp arrangement.

     (b) Interest and dividends.
          I. Interest income is listed on schedule B and is segregated by taxable and nontaxable. Is the client diversified? Does he have an emergency fund? Are the investments in line with his goals and risk tolerance? Are the investments primarily low yielding? Are they too risky? Are they illiquid? Too liquid? Is there an opportunity for tax deferral on earnings (annuities) or tax exemptions?
          II. Are the stocks held yielding high dividend rates? Have you pulled a Value Line or other analysis?
     (c) Schedule C, E, and F.
          I. Are buy–sell agreements in place?
          II. Business insurance coverage should show up on these forms. Do they have business interruption insurance or disability?
          III. Are children working in the business?
          IV. Is a retirement plan in place?
          V. Would PIGS or PALS be appropriate to offset suspendable (taxable) passive activity losses (income)?
          VI. Are subchapter S or partnership income or losses reported on E suitable for this taxpayer?
     (d) Schedule D and Form 4797.
        Are there opportunities to offset unused capital losses with more capital gains? Is the client consistently trading and incurring losses?
     (e) What type of IRA or other retirement plan distributions were taken and why? Where are the funds now?
     (f) If Social Security benefits are taxable, would annuities reduce income low enough to avoid it?
     (g) What is the source of other income?

5. Adjustments.
     (a) Does the client have an IRA; need one?
     (b) Does he have an SEP, Keogh, or other plan for his self-employment income?
     (c) If paying alimony, when does it end and what is he going to do with the funds when payments end?

6. Adjusted gross income.
     (a) Any opportunities to reduce this number can help in itemizing deductions, etc.

7. Deductions.
     (a) Any opportunities for paying off nondeductible interest type loans?
     (b) Any need to tap into home equity?
     (c) What is investment interest for?
     (d) If taxpayer is charitably inclined, perhaps have a conversation about a charitable trust to obtain estate tax as well as current tax benefits.
     (e) Are casualty losses covered by insurance that has not been received yet?

What is Not Found on the 1040

I have prepared personal financial statements many times using only the information taken from the 1040 and my knowledge of the community. I can estimate house values by looking at addresses, and I can estimate home mortgage and other liability balances by looking at interest paid. I can also estimate values for stocks and interest income instruments by looking at dividend and interest income on schedule B.

What I cannot tell from the 1040 is:

1. If there are any annuities.
2. The cash value of life insurance.
3. Gifts or inheritances received recently unless they have been reinvested for dividends or income.
4. Life insurance proceeds unless reinvested.
5. Personal injury awards unless reinvested.

My clients will almost always mention every one of these items during our interview.

16

Estate Planning

When a man feels throbbing within him the power to do
what he undertakes as well as it can possibly be done, this
is happiness, this is success.

Orison Swett Marden

Although I have used the term estate planning as the title for this chapter, I
suggest that you limit your use of this term in seminars and when talking to
clients. The word "estate" conjures up visions of death or great wealth. Most
of your clients will associate themselves with neither. "Life planning" or "controlling your financial destiny" and "leaving the IRS off your list of heirs,"
are all nicer phrases.

Why should a CPA get involved in estate planning? When you are scanning
your weekly or monthly updates to your tax services, you probably stop when
you reach the section about estate planning. They make you think of the dreaded
form 706—the Estate Tax Return. Even though the typical 706 is less complicated than a lot of 1040s, I never liked them. Since I only did two or three
a year, I never got into the flow that I achieved with 1040s or even 1120s. I had
to stop and read instructions on the 706. How degrading! I would never want
anyone to catch me having to actually read instructions for any tax return. I
am supposed to know those things by heart. In addition, there always seems
to be some piece of missing information and the client is no longer around to
answer your questions.

Fortunately, estate planning is much more than preparing estate tax returns.
It is much more than helping people avoid estate taxes. I have heard attorneys
and CPAs tell their clients that current laws do not provide much ability to plan
any more or that since their estates are below $600,000, there is no need to plan.
I cannot believe my ears when I hear remarks like these. First, the law does leave
a lot of room for reducing taxes. Second, as this is being written, the specter
of reducing the exemption to $200,000 is hanging over us. Congress could do
this. They love to tax dead people. They can no longer vote. Third, too many
people equate estate planning with estate tax planning. It is about much more
than reducing taxes. Everyone needs to do some estate planning. That means
great opportunity for us financial planners to do good for clients.

Is not estate planning complex? Should we just stay out of something we do
not fully understand? After all, maybe we have never set up or even been involved in a trust of any kind. We do not understand legalese. This type of thing
is best left to attorneys, right? Wrong!

Yes, estate planning can be complex, but it can also be filtered down to its most basic terms for your client if you are willing to help. I am not an estate planning expert, but I have educated myself and involved myself in enough client situations to recognize needs when I see them. I have a network of attorney and other relationships to call on when I need expert help. You do not have to be an estate planning expert to recognize needs and to find answers to those needs. Build up a network of referral sources to call on if you need them. Those referral sources will turn out to be a two-way street for you. They will refer business to you and everybody wins. Estate planning, besides helping clients, is an excellent way to expand your network of contacts.

If you stay out of the picture for your client, who is going to help them? Answer for most—nobody! "Hey, that's not my fault," you say. Whose fault is it? That is "stinkin' thinking," as Zig Ziglar would say. You are ignoring the indisputable fact that most people (70 to 85 percent) die and leave their families and heirs without instructions. Even the wealthy fail to plan. More than half of the wealthy die without adequate planning. Elvis Presley, for example, lost over 70 percent of his estate to administration and taxes. Groucho Marx was forced to go through an excruciating court battle in a struggle over his care and his estate after he was incapacitated. John Q. Average Client needs help also. Chances are you may be his only financial advisor. He can become disabled, and he most certainly will die. He probably has family who will need instructions and help. If you are not providing that help, strangers will.

Start the estate planning process the same way that you approach a financial plan. Ask the client what his goals are in the area of planning for death or incapacity. If one of his goals is not to plan, then you may not be able to help him. However, if you ask a few TOPS questions, you may find that he does, indeed, have certain goals and certain definite things that he does not want to happen. You can find out these things without knowing much at all about estate planning. In fact, when asking these types of questions, I would avoid using any of my estate planning skills. Just talk to your client as you would any friend, and see what he would like to accomplish and avoid. Then you have the basics of a plan.

In the first part of this book, I stated that if you help others, money will follow. Nowhere is that more true than in estate planning. Follow me through this chapter, and I think you will begin to see what I mean.

If estate planning is about more than taxes, what is it about? In my practice, estate planning involves planning for death, disability, or incapacity. It is all about making your own life or death decisions. It is about writing instructions now while you can so that the decision is yours. Actually, estate planning and financial planning are interchangeable. I consider both to be integral parts of the same process. For example, one of the most important parts of the estate planning process is to determine where the assets are. This is one of the first steps in preparing a financial plan. I think of estate planning as the "preparation for death or incapacity" part of financial planning.

These are the most common decisions to be made in estate planning:

1. What do I have, where is it, and how is it titled?
2. Who gets what when I die and when do they get it?
3. Who is responsible for carrying out my wishes and who are their advisors (if any) in the event of death or incapacity?
4. What happens to my assets if I become incapable of making decisions anymore and who decides if I am incapable?

Figure 16-1   Estate Tax Rates

Estate tax rates start at 18 percent and go as high as 55 percent. Because of the silly way that the Unified Credit is figured, rates below 37 percent have no effective meaning. Below is a general guideline for figuring estate taxes:

Taxable Estate After Marital and Other Deductions	Tax	Rate
$600,000 or less	0	37%
$750,000	$55,500	39%
$1,000,000	$153,500	41%
$1,250,000	$255,500	43%
$1,500,000	$363,000	45%
$2,000,000	$588,000	49%
$2,500,000	$833,000	53%
$3,000,000	$1,098,000	55%

These amounts are after subtracting the $192,800 credit. A $192,800 credit is equivalent to excluding $600,000 in taxable estate value from taxation.

The benefits of the graduated estate and gift tax rates and $600,000 exemption are phased out for estates/gifts over $10 million and everything is taxed at a flat 55 percent.

5. How are my heirs to be provided for in the event of my death or disability?
6. What kind of process should be used in the carrying out of my wishes?
7. How do I provide for the orderly transfer or continuance of the family business?
8. How can I be sure that there is enough liquidity to pay estate taxes and avoid forced liquidation of some assets?
9. How much do I want to leave to heirs and how much to the IRS?

If those are not nine good reasons for helping your clients, look at Figure 16-1. Most of them are interrelated and affect each other in some way. Trade-offs are involved, but with good planning, you can help your client to make the right decisions.

WHAT DO YOU HAVE, WHERE IS IT, AND HOW IS IT TITLED?

These are probably the three most important questions about the estate planning process for the average client. In Texas, for example, the probate process is not considered to be a problem. Probate and administration in Texas averages about 2 percent of the total estate value. California and Alaska, by contrast, average between 7 and 12 percent, depending on whose statistics you believe. When I started giving living trust seminars back in 1988, most of my attorney friends went on the attack. ''Probate is not a problem in Texas,'' they shouted. ''Why go through this business of a living trust when we have independent administration in Texas?'' The problem is not with the probate process in Texas as much as it is with lack of planning and poor communication between CPAs, attorneys, and their clients. I have seen many simple estates with no estate tax problems take years to settle. I have seen fees and expenses run as high as 20 percent or even 30 percent of the estate.

CPAs do not advise their clients to answer these three questions while alive and the attorneys do not properly advise clients after death. Clients do not know that *they* can be a major cause of delays or expense because the attorneys and CPAs are searching for property, making lists, etc. that the client, his heirs, or administrators could be doing much more inexpensively.

If your client does not have a detailed personal financial statement, then this is just one of the reasons for you to prepare one. This may result in fees as well as financial planning opportunities for you, but the client will pay much less than if the search has to go on without his help or instructions.

Your preparation of a personal financial statement should be supplemented by an individual listing of each category of asset. That is why the data gathering forms in the Appendix are supplemented by detailed schedules. Also, you should have lists that show *where* assets are located. Finding assets, titles, notes, and other documentation can be a very expensive and time-consuming process.

What significance does titling have? Titles can take precedence over your will or trust (your instructions). For example, if you own something with your spouse or someone else in joint tenancy with right of survivorship, that property passes to the surviving owner, regardless of instructions to the contrary. Be sure that your clients' assets are titled in accordance with their wishes. Joint titling can have the beneficial effect of avoiding probate on that particular asset, but be sure that title does not interfere with your clients' wishes or instructions in a will or trust.

WHO GETS WHAT WHEN YOU DIE, AND WHEN DO THEY GET IT?

Many people are apathetic about what happens to the distribution of their assets at death. That apathy is often due to ignorance of the problems that can be caused by the failure to leave proper instructions in a will or trust. In Texas, I tell my clients who do not have instructions that they have a will whether they know it or not. I tell them that they have a ''governor's will.'' I usually fill in the governor's name. That means that the state will decide what happens to your assets when you die. Do you want the state legislature or governor to decide or do you want to decide for yourself? Decisions involve:

1. *Personal bequests.* Everyone has special items with special meaning. These items should be left to someone who will appreciate them and treat them as you would. Some things are masculine or feminine in nature and may naturally go to heirs in that order. However, you may want to leave some of your masculine things to a daughter or vice versa to a son.
2. *The family business.* I have lots of clients who own their own businesses. I have none that do not have special feelings for those businesses. Passing on the business may be made impossible or difficult without instructions and planning.
3. *Special needs.* If a client has children or heirs with special needs, he has an obligation to provide for those needs in the estate plan.
4. *Equaling things out.* After special bequests are made, things may be very unequal. If one child is to inherit the family business because she is the only one who wants it or knows anything about it, that asset may comprise 80 percent of your estate. Does your client want to provide equally for all

the other heirs? If so, then you must help him do so. This often means that insurance must be purchased for either a buy–sell arrangement on the business or just to provide equal amounts for the other children.

5. *Settling disputes.* Many clients will tell you, ''Each member of my family gets along well with the others. They will be able to divide my assets without dispute,'' Right! In the overwhelming majority of cases like this, disputes do arise. Many are only hurt feelings, but many wind up in court. Did you ever hear, ''Dad would have wanted me to have this'' by one child while another is telling you that ''Dad gave me that when I was 13.'' They are both talking about the same item. Putting your wishes in writing and possibly the reasons for those wishes is better.

6. *Irresponsible heirs.* If you have a spendthrift or ne'er do well on your list of heirs, you may want to control *when* they come into their share. You can only do this through written instructions.

7. *Income needs.* Some heirs, usually your spouse, may need income from your assets but it does not make tax sense to leave the assets to the spouse outright. You can provide for this with a plan. The same goes for income needs for other heirs.

WHO CARRIES OUT YOUR WISHES AND WHAT ADVISORS ARE NEEDED?

Without a written estate plan, disputes may arise as to who is in charge. In fact, they will almost always arise. Either everyone wants to take charge or nobody will take responsibility. That is when lawyers and the state start taking over. If your client has a trusted advisor or family member he would like to be in charge at his death or incapacity, have him say so in writing.

Whether a client leaves a will or not, a formal procedure must generally be followed after death. Called the *probate procedure*, it serves the purposes of identifying proper heirs or legatees, satisfying debts, and computing or paying estate taxes. Someone has to manage the client's affairs while this process is taking place and see that all necessary procedures are followed. This person, if named by the client in his estate plan, is called an *executor* or *executrix*. If the court makes the appointment, then they are called an *administrator* or *administratix*. Does your client want to name this person or have the court do it? What will the fees be for a court-appointed administrator? Will he be competent? Will he have your client's best interests at heart?

Even if your client does name someone to represent him, that person may not be competent to handle all the affairs. You should help your client select someone trustworthy and help him name advisors to the executor as required. These advisors can be CPAs, financial planners, or attorneys.

Naming the proper individuals as executors and advisors can save the client's heirs money and grief. Make sure your executor is willing to serve, and consider paying a reasonable fee for his services, even if he is a family member. Provide for an alternate executor in case conditions change and your primary one is unable or unwilling to serve.

In the event of incapacity, there is often a formal procedure called *guardianship* that may leave your client's affairs in the hands of a court-appointed guardian if he is declared incompetent to deal with them anymore. Better to have your client make this decision ahead of time.

DEALING WITH INCAPACITY

If the statistics on the number of people who do not plan for death are staggering, they pale in comparison to the lack of planning for incapacity. In spite of the fact that incapacity is more of a problem today than ever before, Americans are still failing to plan. The fastest growing age group in America today is the over 85 set. Medical science has shown us how to prolong life, but in many cases, they have failed to show us how to prolong the quality of life. Many of the elderly are totally incapable of handling their own affairs but did not plan for such an event. Of course, incapacity does not just strike the elderly. Here are some ways to protect your clients.

1. *Living trusts.* Although *living trusts* (sometimes called *loving trusts*) are not necessarily the panacea that some have claimed them to be, they are excellent estate planning tools. I particularly favor them because they can spare your clients the expense and embarrassment of a court-appointed conservator. The living trust can sidestep this with a provision that permits your successor trustee to take over for you if your physician (or group of physicians if preferred) certifies that you are incompetent.

2. *Standby living trusts.* As explained later in more detail, in order to be effective, all probatable assets must be transferred to the living trust. If a client's circumstances will not allow that for any reason, you can set up a standby or convertible trust in conjunction with a durable power of attorney. This *durable power of attorney* gives your trustee (a trusted friend, relative, or advisor) the power to act as your financial representative in shifting your assets into your trust for management by the successor trustee named in the trust. (The successor trustee is someone your client has previously named to be his trustee when the client is no longer able to serve in that capacity himself.) If you die suddenly while you only have a standby trust, your assets will go through probate.

3. *Durable powers of attorney.* This is a legal document that allows a family member or friend to take care of the affairs of the incapacitated person.

4. *Living will (directive to physicians) or health care powers of attorney.* In my home state of Texas, the living will is usually referred to as a *directive to physicians* and its form is set by state law. As for the *durable power of attorney for health care*, it can be structured to provide the same benefits as the living will. Traditionally, the living will stipulates in advance whether or not the person wants to be kept alive artificially if they are not expected to recover. The durable power of attorney for health care can cover this eventuality but also can authorize the person holding the POA to make health care decisions for you that may not necessarily be life or death in nature.

PROVIDING FOR YOUR HEIRS AND LOVED ONES

A proper estate plan will help your client to insure that his assets are properly invested, distributed, or held in trust for care of his family members or to meet whatever special needs he may have. As mentioned earlier, many of the benefits of preparing an estate plan are at cross purposes. For example, a client may want all of his assets to go to his spouse when he dies and to his children when his spouse dies. However, that may cause estate taxes to rise sharply at the second death. Proper planning can usually help your client to achieve both goals through the use of a credit shelter or by-pass trust.

Minor Children

Guardians.   Providing for minor children is one of the most prominent reasons for having a will and an estate plan. Even clients who do not have substantial estates need a will to name guardians for minor children in the event that both parents are dead or incapacitated. The children's personal guardian may have to manage some, or all, of their financial affairs, depending on whether or not a minor's trust has been set up for them. But, of even more importance, the guardians must see to the care and raising of the children. They must see them through the childhood diseases, the trauma of adolescence, and all the rest. In short, they must be the parent's substitute. Choosing them should not be left up to an indifferent legal system. They should be people who share similar opinions and beliefs with your client on raising children, religion, and so on.

Minor's Trust.   Unfortunately, the best person to raise your children may not be the best person to handle their inheritance. To safeguard your client's legacy, you can create a minor's trust in the will. In these trusts, the client's trustee is in charge of investing and spending the trust's assets on behalf of the children. This type of trust can also help your client to control the assets until the kids are old enough to manage it.

Spouses

Of primary concern to most clients is that their spouse's needs are properly met. A spouse may actually own half the estate, helped in building the estate, is usually the guardian of minor children, and is the most dependent on the other spouse. Many couples have *I love you* or *sweetheart wills* simply leaving everything to the other with the children as alternate beneficiaries. These may meet their individual needs, but may cause the estate to be severely depleted by estate taxes at the death of the second spouse.

Marital Deduction.   If the surviving spouse is a U.S. citizen, all assets passing to that spouse will pass tax free, no matter how big the estate. However, those same assets will be subject to taxes when the second spouse dies. That means that the first spouse did not get to take full advantage of the $600,000 exclusion.

Credit Shelter Trust.   These trusts are also called A/B trusts, family trusts, and by-pass trusts. Lawyers do that to confuse us. Brokers and marketing people use different terms to make them sound more appealing. This type of trust allows you to leave assets totaling the amount of your exclusion directly to your children or secondary beneficiaries, while allowing the spouse to receive lifetime income from the assets and to withdraw principal if needed to maintain the spouse's lifestyle. (Be careful on the wording of the trust so as to allow spouse to withdraw principal. If it is too loose, it may be drawn back into the estate.)

Q-TIP or GPA.   The by-pass trust can be of the Qualified Terminable Interest Property (Q-TIP) variety or the General Power of Appointment (GPA) type. Under the Q-TIP, the client decides who the ultimate beneficiaries are. This may be used when the client wishes to keep assets out of the hands of a future spouse or to be sure that they wind up in the hands of children of a first marriage, for example. The GPA lets the surviving spouse decide who will be the trust's ultimate beneficiary.

Disabled Heirs.   Property left directly to handicapped heirs might disqualify them from social service programs such as Medicaid, which are generally reserved for people of modest means. You may be able to dodge this by setting up a discretionary spendthrift trust which is designed to supplement, not replace, government assistance. These trusts should give the trustee the right to distribute income and principal to beneficiaries besides the disabled child, such as other relatives and charities. The trust should also stipulate that the principal remaining in the trust pass to other heirs upon the death of the handicapped heir. Also, there should be a clause that terminates the trust if the state successfully challenges it in court. The principal, in this case, should go to beneficiaries other than the disabled heir. In this case, be prepared to ask the other beneficiaries to spend some of the inheritance on the handicapped heir, because they are not legally obligated to do so.

Spendthrift Heirs

Most types of trusts can be designed to distribute income to heirs in accordance with special needs. Ongoing administration of the trust is usually required to do this, so fees must be considered. The trust can be designed to distribute income only, various parts of the principal at various times or ages, and the distributions can based on circumstances such as earned income, longevity on the job, and so on.

Sprinkling Provisions

These allow the trustee to allocate income and principal to heirs based on changing needs. For example, one child may be a starving artist while the other becomes a famous star or highly paid professional.

THE PROCESS OF CARRYING OUT YOUR WISHES

Estate and financial planning are all about making choices and writing instructions about what those choices are. One of the important choices in estate planning is what process is going to take place in the event of death or incapacity. The primary selection of process is to elect probate or avoid probate. If probate is elected, it can be made less painful by good planning.

The Probate Process

Probate is the process of ''proving'' the validity of a will in court. When your client dies, his representatives will have to submit his will to the probate court and an inventory of all his assets and liabilities. The forms involved are seldom called what they really are by attorneys but are called by antiquated and ridiculous terms developed by the legal profession to keep clients from knowing what is going on. (I say that with tongue-in-cheek only slightly.) If an executor has been named in a will, he is usually free of further court supervision in Texas.

The court will admit the wills to probate and issue Letters Testamentary to the executor (usually through his attorney). When the list of assets and liabilities is presented to the court, then the world is invited to come forward and make any claims against the estate. After all claims are settled including filing a federal estate tax return and a state tax return, and final individual tax returns for the decedent, then the assets are allowed to pass through probate to reach their intended destination (the heirs).

In Texas, small estates can often circumvent the probate process by having *muniments of title* issued, where the will is merely recorded as a link in the chain of title from the decedent to his heir.

Think of the probate process as a funnel through which most of the probatable assets must flow before they ultimately reach the destination that the client intended. Depending on the state, the bottom of the funnel can be small or large. If it is small, that means more procedures are necessary to get the assets through the funnel and consequently, it takes longer. The longer assets stay in the funnel, the more they shrink due to administrative costs and professional fees. All the while, everything is a matter of public record.

Assets Not Subject to Probate

Many assets may pass outside of the will or the probate process. These include:

- Joint Accounts with right of survivorship
- Assets held in a trust
- Life insurance
- Pension plans
- Profit-sharing plans
- IRA and Keogh plans with named beneficiaries.

These assets may be dropped into the probate funnel if your client names his estate as the primary beneficiary.

Easing the Pain of Probate

1. Make adequate financial plans.
   (a) Be sure there will be readily available cash.
   (b) Knowing where the assets are and how they are titled will reduce time and expense.
   (c) Have plans in place to deal with special assets such as a business with buy–sell agreements, etc.
2. Create confidence in yourself with your clients by patiently explaining what will happen. Death causes enough stress without adding the burden of complexity.
3. Avoid handwritten wills and poorly written documents. Do not use mail-order or canned documents. Find one or more good attorneys to assist your clients.
4. Act promptly. I have found that simple poor time management is the worst culprit in poorly managed and expensive estates. Most estates should be concluded within one year. Push attorneys to meet this deadline and never be a bottleneck in the process yourself.

Avoiding Probate

Even in states like Texas where independent administration is allowed, *people*, not laws, still drag out the probate process and make it degrading and painful for the survivors. For this reason, many of your clients should probably elect to avoid probate.

Nonprobate Assets.   Using *joint titling* to allow assets to pass directly to a joint owner can avoid the probate process. Assets with *beneficiary designations* other than the estate or trust will pass outside of the probate process. Exercise caution when using titling or beneficiary designations to avoid probate. Be sure that this direct passage of title and full ownership is in accordance with the whole estate plan. For example, if the asset is listed as approximately 50 percent of a total estate, and the estate plan calls for three heirs to share equally in the total estate, the heir who receives the jointly titled property will already own more than his share. Also, owning everything jointly with a spouse can cause heavy taxation when the second spouse dies. Joint ownership can also diminish control over the property during one's lifetime.

A *totten trust*, or a pay-on-death bank account is another way to avoid probate. The client can open a bank account in his own name, as trustee for the benefit of his beneficiary. The name beneficiary will then receive the proceeds when the client dies.

Revocable Living Trusts.   When I first started attending seminars on living trusts in the late 1980s, they seemed to meet the needs of many of my clients. However, I could not find an attorney who would help me establish such trusts for my clients. In fact, most got downright rude when the subject was brought up. I realized that living trusts had not been taught in law school for most of these lawyers, so they did not know anything about them. This made them the enemy—the province of a "fanatic fringe element."

So-called financial planners, such as insurance companies, did not help my case by over-zealously promoting the living trust as the Utopia of estate planning. Today, many of the same attorneys who invited me to leave when I mentioned living trusts are now promoting them heavily in their practices. The best attorneys know that living trusts are not necessarily for everyone, but they certainly fit a need.

Since living trusts will be covered in more detail in a later chapter, I will only cover the highlights here. Living trusts keep your property under your control during your lifetime and provide direct transfer to your named beneficiaries after your death. Living trusts bypass probate, because the assets have already been transferred into the trust prior to death. Note that I said that the assets had been transferred prior to death. If you set up a trust and do not transfer the assets into the trust, then they will pass through the probate process.

Living trusts contain the client's instructions as to what should happen if the client dies *or becomes incapacitated*. Wills function only in the event of death. The client generally serves as his own trustee, saving administrative costs. A successor trustee is named in case of incapacity or death.

A living trust files no tax return and usually has no need for a tax identification number. Since it is revocable, it has no income tax advantages or estate tax advantages unless estate planning features are designed in the document.

A living trust can be designed to save taxes just as a will can, but has no particular tax savings without these added planning features. A living trust usually avoids the publicity of probate. If this is important to your client, study his privacy concerns and see if the trust will meet them. The trust may avoid multistate administration if assets, particularly real estate, are held in different states.

TRANSFERRING THE FAMILY BUSINESS

The family-owned business may be the most valuable asset in the owner's estate. Two out of three family-owned businesses do not survive the first generation due to poor planning. Begin the planning process with your business–owner client the same way you begin other processes. Ask what the owner wants to happen.

Who Will Take Over the Business if You Die?

Is there anyone trained and ready to take over the reins? Entrepreneurs often run autocratic shops and do not pass down enough knowledge. There may be no successor management ready.

Who Should Inherit the Business?

Do family members currently work in the business? Should they inherit it? What about other family members? How will the estate be equaled out if one member inherits the business?

What is the Value of the Business?

Clients usually go to two opposite extremes when asked this question. They have a highly inflated sense of the worth of the business, or they are shocked when you apply IRS formulas to the calculation of net worth. Arriving at an educated estimate as to the value of the business is critical to the plan. The IRS formulas, although not foolproof, are relatively easy to apply. This will give your client an idea of the estate tax problem he may be facing and will allow you to work on equalizing the distribution of the estate.

Estate Tax Breaks

If the closely held business value exceeds 35 percent of the adjusted gross estate, the estate may qualify for a deferral of tax payments. No payment other than interest need be made until five years after the normal due date for taxes owed on the value of the business. The remaining tax can then be paid in ten equal annual installments. This means that a portion of the original tax can be delayed for as long as 14 years. This sounds good on the surface, but how many businesses can generate enough cash flow to pay for as much as 55 percent of their value over a 14-year period if the principal owner dies?

The Buy–Sell Agreement

This agreement controls what happens to the company stock or partnership interest in the event of death or disability of a shareholder or owner. The agreement might provide that the ownership interest be bought back by the corporation or by other shareholders or partners. These types of agreements:

1. Provide a ready market for the shares.
2. Set a price for the shares, and can fix the value for estate tax purposes.
3. Provide for a stable continuance of the business by avoiding unnecessary disagreements caused by unwanted new shareholders or partners.
4. When funded by insurance, can provide the means for the deceased or disabled to be paid for his ownership interest without crippling the company or other owners.

Gifting the Family Business

Since the family business can be the fastest appreciating asset your client owns, giving away ownership can keep this appreciation from being taxed in your estate.

ESOP (Employee Stock Ownership Plan)

The ESOP is a type of qualified plan similar in many respects to a profit sharing or pension plan. It is designed to invest in the stock of the company. The corporation sets up a trust and makes tax deductible contributions of its own stock to the trust or cash which can be used to pay off a loan which was used to buy the corporation's stock. Stock in the ESOP is allocated according to qualified plan rules for employee participants.

Used in conjunction with a charitable trust, this method can be used to transfer ownership to a family member or other successor with substantial tax advantages. However, there is a high cost of administration and this method is usually reserved for businesses with relatively high values.

SOLVING THE LIQUIDITY CRISIS

The largest and most frequently encountered problem for my clients was having enough liquidity to pay estate taxes. This was particularly true for small business owners. Clients inevitably failed to recognize the value of their businesses and that the government was going to take a large chunk of them (up to 55 percent) in taxes when they were transferred. Entrepreneurs often do not see themselves as rich. In fact, their businesses with high estate tax values often suffer from chronic cash shortages. Other assets purchased long ago may also be undervalued in the client's mind. It is embarrassing for a CPA to have to announce a huge estate tax liability to a client's successors and have them be surprised. It is your job to keep them informed about such matters. It is also troublesome when clients have to sell assets under forced circumstances because inadequate planning was done.

It is our job as financial planners to keep this problem from being exacerbated at death or disability with proper planning. You can do this for your client by preparing a simple liquidity analysis showing what cash expenses will be due within one year of death, what expenses will be paid in the event of disability, and calculating the shortfall based on current cash flow of the client. Who is more qualified to do this than the CPA?

After quantifying the estimated liquidity shortfall, you can design insurance coverage to allow the client to be sure that his business continues in accordance with his goals and that assets will not have to be subjected to ''fire sale'' type liquidations.

Our primary goal in the first stages of estate planning is to identify problems. We take the personal financial statement of the client, which should include all assets at an estimated fair market value, and simply add in the face value of any insurance policies that the client owns (not included in a life insurance trust or owned by someone other than himself) to arrive at an estimated gross estate value. We apply the rates above to this estimated gross estate. This may not be technically accurate because the taxable estate is after administration expenses, but remember that this is not an audit or an exact science. Your estimates of fair market value may be off enough to compensate.

You are trying to identify a problem and look for solutions, not prepare an estate tax return. A lot of CPAs believe that in order to do estate planning, they must first arrive at an exact tax by filling out a form 706 before death. Result—inertia. No planning gets done. Which is worse, educated planning using forecast and estimates or no planning at all?

After arriving at an estimated estate tax liability, we use our estate liquidity test form (included in the financial planning section and the Appendix) to identify liquidity problems. The liquidity test is simple to complete. It identifies the assets available to pay the estate tax, assets needed for other needs, and points out to the client the need to solve the problem.

Solving the Problem

These are the essential two steps in solving the problems:

1. *Reduce the estate tax by planning; and*
2. *Purchase insurance to provide liquidity.*

REDUCING ESTATE TAXES BY PLANNING

How Much Do I Want to Leave to Heirs and How Much to the IRS?

Although this is a very complicated problem with a lot of answers for every client, it can be reduced to only a few simple steps:

1. Use the marital deduction in connection with the unified credit.
2. Giving away assets now or as bequests in your will or living trust.
3. Giving up control of assets.

Do not show the last two methods to your clients without some type of explanation. They do not have much sales appeal. However, they can be effective tools that are not as distasteful as they first sound. There are ways to "give away the cake and have it too."

Using the Marital Deduction Without Losing the Unified Credit

The A/B, Credit Shelter, By-Pass, Marital Deduction Trust.   Any assets passing to a surviving spouse pass tax free at the time that the first spouse dies if the surviving spouse is a U.S. citizen. This is only a deferral, however. If the surviving spouse does not remarry, she cannot take advantage of the marital deduction when she dies. In other words, the first spouse's estate will be taxed when the second spouse dies. In this case, the first spouse only deferred taxation;

he did not avoid it. He also failed to take advantage of his $600,000 exclusion, because he buried it (pardon the pun) in his marital deduction. You can show your client how to avoid this using the A/B or credit shelter, or by-pass trust. The terms are used by attorneys interchangeably to describe the same type of trust. The A/B refers to two trusts. One goes to the spouse and one goes to the children. The A trust that goes to the spouse is set up for ease of administration and management of assets. The B trust goes to the children and qualifies the estate to use the $600,000 exemption.

Since most clients have *sweetheart* or *I love you wills*, they typically leave everything to each other. If their estate including taxable insurance proceeds is $1.2 million, then their estate taxes will approach $250,000 when both of them die. Remember, the marital deduction will defer all taxes at the first death. By setting up a testamentary trust provision in their wills, they can reduce their taxes to $0 and effectively use both their exemptions instead of just one. The by-pass, credit shelter, marital deduction, A/B trust (by whatever name) is a *testamentary trust*, so it does not come into existence until the first spouse dies. You simply leave assets equivalent to the $600,000 exemption to your children in a trust. The spouse is entitled to income from the assets in the trust for life and may even invade the principal under certain conditions. This trust is not subject to estate taxes at the death of the second spouse. It passes to the ultimate beneficiaries.

This change to the will is inexpensive, quick, and easy to make. By this simple step, you can easily show your clients how you have already saved them a *quarter of a million dollars*. They will usually be eager to go on with the estate planning process.

Giving Away Assets

Use the gift tax exclusion and unified credit during the client's lifetime. The *unified credit* is called unified because it is a credit that includes both gift and estate taxes. Under prior law, there was a credit for estate taxes alone. Under the unified credit, the $192,800 is applied to estate taxes and to any lifetime taxable gifts that you make. Notice that I said *taxable* gifts that you make.

You can still give away $10,000 per year without any reporting or tax. A married couple, if both consent, can give away $20,000 to the same person per year. If a married couple has three children they can give away $60,000 per year free of any reporting or tax requirements. If your clients can afford to do this, it is a simple way to remove taxable assets from the estate.

When should you make such gifts? That's when good planning comes in. You have to take into account several factors, both psychological and financial. Are the gift recipients responsible? Will gifts have an adverse impact on their ambition? Can your clients afford to do without the assets permanently? Many advisors are telling clients to take advantage of the $600,000 exemption while we still have it. Rumors of reducing it to $200,000 by a hungry Congress feed this advice. You cannot control when you die, but you can control when you use the credit through gifts. What are the mechanics of using up the credit through gifts? You simply give assets exceeding the $10,000 exclusion, file a gift tax return on form 709, and report the use of the credit. When death occurs, the estate tax return has provisions for reporting all of the credit previously used. If you use it up through gifts, there is nothing left to offset the estate tax. If part is left, then you can use what is left. That is why they call it the unified credit.

You may want to consider giving away not only cash but assets that have highly appreciated in the client's hands or assets that are expected to continue appreciating. The appreciation that has already taken place will escape taxation in the client's estate. Future appreciation will also escape taxation in the client's estate. For example, a $10,000 gift that can be given without any tax can have the effect of reducing the taxable estate by $20,000 if the asset is expected to double through appreciation. There can also be income tax advantages to making gifts of appreciated assets. The client will escape income taxation on the gain in the assets, although the donee will have to take the client's low basis. In the case of charitable gifts, the client can often get a current tax deduction for the fair market value of the asset.

Charitable Bequests

Your client can make a bequest in his will to qualified charities that will reduce his taxable estate. This is a very simple and effective way to reduce estate taxes with little administrative bother. Be sure that the charity qualifies for estate tax deduction. Many clients either cannot afford to do this because of income needs of survivors, do not have the charitable inclination, or simply want their estate to go to family members. However, remember to bring it to the client's attention.

Giving Up Control of Assets

Do not use these terms when beginning conversations with clients. For most clients, particularly elderly ones, the words ''giving up control'' will get you thrown out the door before you get a chance to explain the benefits. However, before your presentation is complete and your client is ready to look into trusts in order to reduce estate taxes, they must know that control has been given up. That is the key ingredient to getting the estate tax benefit.

There are many types of irrevocable trusts that can be used to reduce estate taxes and achieve your client's goals. I will not attempt to cover them all here. I have already covered the most simple A/B, credit shelter, by-pass, or family trust. All names used interchangeably to describe a trust for making sure that the clients both use their $600,000 exemption. I will cover only GRITs, CRUTs, CRATs, and ILITs here.

GRITs. No, this is not something you order with ham and eggs in Texas. These are *grantor retained income trusts*. Married couples with assets in excess of $1.2 million or singles with assets in excess of $600,000 should consider these, especially if they own property that is appreciating rapidly. With a GRIT, you place the property in the trust, which is irrevocable, and then receive all the income from the property for up to 10 years. When the trust terminates at the end of 10 years, the property passes to the beneficiaries the client has chosen. It does not sound great so far, does it? What makes it worth looking at is the fact that the IRS uses special tables to calculate the value of the income interest that your client will receive and the trust's remainder interest. This remainder interest is going to be well below the current value of the assets contributed and this is what the IRS considers to be the value of the gift you made to the trust. If it is below the $600,000 exclusion, then there is no tax. If the assets appreciate at only 7 percent during the 10-year period, they will double in value allowing a large chunk of assets to pass to the heirs tax free.

One catch—your client has to live 10 years or the assets will go back to the taxable estate. However, you can sell the beneficiaries insurance on the client to cover the estate tax if they know they are going to receive the assets.

CRATs and CRUTs (Charitable Remainder Annuity or Unit Trusts). I consider these to be relatively simple, yet excellent planning tools. They will be covered in more detail in the chapter on charitable giving, so I will only cover the major points here. Both are charitable remainder trusts. One is an annuity trust which provides for lifetime income at a fixed amount, and one is a unit trust which provides for income that changes each year based on the fluctuating value of the trust. These trusts can be used to provide income to your client during his lifetime or to his beneficiaries at his death. I will primarily focus on providing income during life. I call these trusts *five win* trusts.

Win No. 1—A Current Income Tax Deduction. Your client gets a current income tax deduction for the value of the assets contributed less the value of the income stream that your client will receive. Therefore, the client's age and the rate of return selected for income will affect the amount of the deduction. Tables and software are available to figure this deduction.

Win No. 2—The Tax on Gains for Appreciated Assets is Avoided. If the client donates appreciated assets to the trust, he does not have to pay taxes on the appreciation that has taken place in the assets.

Win No. 3—The Asset is Removed from the Taxable Estate. Since the asset eventually winds up in the hands of charity, it is not taxed as part of the estate.

Win No. 4—The Client's Income is Usually Increased. If the client had to sell the asset in order to get income from it, capital gains would reduce the amount he would have to reinvest and his income would be lower. Under the CRT, he gets to reinvest the entire amount and receive income from a larger investment. Also, the minimum amount of income he can elect to receive is 5 percent, but he can elect to go higher. The higher he goes, the less his charitable deduction in win #1, but that may be less important than getting more income.

Win No. 5—You Get to Replace the Asset with Insurance. One of the things that bothered many of my clients with the charitable trust was that the asset eventually goes to charity and that their children may feel cheated. You can correct this by having the children or the client purchase insurance to replace the asset. Not only would the children usually rather receive cash, the savings from Win #1 and 2 are often enough to pay the premiums. If not, # 3 and #4 will almost certainly cover the cost.

If you have not caught on already, the ideal asset to put into a trust of this type is an appreciated one that is yielding low income—stocks or real estate, for example. You probably have many clients sitting on such assets who need income but cannot stand the capital gains tax if they sell a highly appreciated asset.

PURCHASING INSURANCE TO PROVIDE LIQUIDITY

Life insurance is often an important part of an estate plan. It is often necessary to accomplish the following:

1. Provide the necessary cash flow to maintain the lifestyles of heirs.
2. Provide the amounts necessary to pay estate taxes.
3. Provide for other liquidity needs so that assets do not have to be subjected to forced liquidation.
4. Provide for the continuity of the family business.
5. Provide funds for possible disability of the owner of a family business and other partners or major shareholders.
6. Fund buy–sell agreements.

What Type of Insurance is Required?

This was covered in more detail in the chapter on insurance, yet still there is no set answer to this question. Individual circumstances vary widely. Second-to-die or joint and last survivor and even first-to-die contracts are the types of insurance most often thought of in estate planning situations. Under these types of policies, two people are named as insureds but the proceeds become payable only when one dies, either at the first death or at the second death. Second to die is more frequently used, because that is when most of the estate taxes come due. However, there may be significant liquidity needs at the first death. This is particularly true for a buy–sell agreement, where proceeds are needed at the first death. Because two lives are being insured, costs are usually lower. Also, a policy can often be issued when one spouse is in poor health and even un-insurable.

ILITs (Irrevocable Life Insurance Trusts).   Irrevocable life insurance trusts are used to keep life insurance proceeds out of your client's estate. They are also known as wealth replacement trusts. I use that term when explaining the concept to the client. Many middle income clients do not realize that they have purchased up to 55 percent of their life insurance in order to provide funds for the government to squander. If your client has an estate over the taxable exclusion, then be sure that he does not own his life insurance policies when he dies.

In a life insurance trust, the trust owns the policies and pays the premiums. When the client dies, the proceeds pass into the trust to be distributed in accordance with the client's instruction and are not included in the estate.

How does money get into the trust to pay the premiums? Your client can usually use his annual gift tax exclusion to make gifts to the trust. The amount of the exclusion he can use is dependent on the number of beneficiaries in the trust and the powers of the beneficiaries.

What about gift tax on the value of life insurance policies transferred to the trust? Gift taxes will be due on the value of the policy transferred if it exceeds the exclusion allowed. When I say due, I do not necessarily mean that you have to send a check to the IRS. I only mean that you have to file a gift tax return and possibly use up some of the $600,000 exclusion. Transferring policies into the trust also has one more caveat. If your client dies within three years, the value will be pulled back into the estate. Be sure that the attorney includes a clause in the trust document that allows the insurance to be paid directly to the spouse or to a marital deduction trust if death takes place within three years.

I try to get around the three-year rule by putting *new* policies into the trust. Be sure the trust is set up and signed before the policy is. Often, your client can take reduced paid-up insurance on existing policies and use the money previously paid on them to purchase new ones inside the trust.

WHICH IS BEST—WILLS OR LIVING TRUSTS?

The controversy over whether clients should have wills or revocable living trusts (RLT) began in the late 1980s and continues today. Living trusts are gaining in popularity because more attorneys are going back to school to learn about them. Still, many come down flatly on the side of one or the other. I think both have places in your clients' estate planning. Both have advantages and disadvantages. Let us consider features or goals your client might find important in the perfect estate plan.

Incapacity

I consider this to be the most important value to a living trust. Wills only take effect at death. With a living trust, a successor (meaning one who takes over after your client) trustee can be appointed to manage the client's affairs after he becomes incapacitated. Without such a trust, someone has to ask the court to declare the client incompetent and appoint a guardian for him. This process can be expensive, time-consuming, and embarrassing. It also may not turn out with the guardian the client wanted.

Probate

Wills are subject to probate. Living wills are touted to avoid probate, and sometimes they do, but not always. Not all living trusts provide for direct distribution to the beneficiaries, but instead provide for distribution to the client's estate. Unless there are other reasons for the trust, do not use one for avoidance of probate when the assets will not be distributed immediately. There are also other disadvantages to trusts when the assets are left in the trust after death (e.g., throwback rules). However, the primary reason that living trusts do not avoid probate is because all assets subject to probate are not put into the trust prior to death. Advise your clients accordingly.

Pour-Over Will

There is a short will called a pour-over will that should be used to complement your living trust. This will provides that any property you never got around to retitling to your RLT will ''pour-over'' into the RLT at death.

Is probate worth avoiding? In my opinion, yes. Even in Texas, where we have independent administration, the probate process can be painful, long, and expensive because of incompetence on the part of judges, attorneys, and lack of cooperation by descendants. In some other states, attorney and executor fees may be fixed by law and run from 5 to 10 percent of the total estate. Once you have had to work with a client in petitioning the court to get income while an estate makes its way through the process, you will know why the process should be avoided when possible.

Publicity

Wills are public information. When they are filed for probate, the wills and other associated documents are subject to public scrutiny. Living trusts generally are not filed since they are not subject to probate. However, some states require estate tax returns, which typically include copies of the trust documents to be filed. The trust documents may also become public when the trustee asks the court to interpret the trust's instructions (this should not happen) or when any of the beneficiaries sue the trustee. Some jurisdictions also require the trust documents to be filed when there is a pour-over will.

Multistate Administration

The living trust avoids administration in multiple jurisdictions when assets, particularly real estate, are held in different states. A will does not.

Family Disputes

Family members who are not beneficiaries do not have to be notified about an RLTs terms. All family members are notified about the terms of a will. Probate provides an opportunity for family members to argue over the terms of a will. The RLTs are also not subjected to challenge as much based on the grantor's lack of capacity, fraud, or duress than a will. In many jurisdictions, nobody has access to a will's assets until disputes are settled, but a trustee can usually use the RLTs assets to defend the trust.

Disinheriting a Spouse

Although this may not be a wise course of action, an RLT may be effective in doing it. In many states, spouses can elect to take action against a will and receive a statutory share. That same option may not be available under a trust.

Tax Returns

Much confusion exists in the CPA and attorney community about whether or not a living trust is required to file a tax return. There is no tax return for a trust as long as the grantor–settlor (the person who owns the assets and sets up the trust) is also the trustee and primary beneficiary. All items of income, deductions, and credits will appear on his return unless there are assets located outside the United States. The RLT does not require an employer identification number.

When the settlor is not the trustee but is primary beneficiary, you must file a 1041. However, since there is no income taxed to the trust, the form will be blank with a statement attached showing the name and social security number of the person to whom the income is taxed.

Cost

Establishing a trust and retitling property can be much more expensive than a will. If a professional trustee is used, professional fees can also run from 1 to 2 percent of the trust assets.

Property Titling

RLTs that do not work usually fail because property is not transferred into them. Some financial institutions may not allow retitling if they hold a mortgage. This can usually be overcome with a letter from an attorney, but it can be a problem.

Retitling is an additional expense, but quit-claim deeds are often used and expenses are kept to a minimum.

Insurance

Some insurance companies may not insure property owned by a trust. Again, this can usually be avoided, but not without delay and some cost.

Taxes

Having already said that the trust does not file a tax return except under unusual circumstances, the trust may have to file a return after death if assets are not distributed. This can put the trust at a disadvantage when compared to estates.

- Trusts must elect calendar years while estates can elect fiscal years, using an important tax deferral option.
- A deceased probate estate can elect to file a joint return with the surviving spouse for the year of death, while a trust cannot (usually not relevant).
- Estimated tax payments must be made by a trust.
- Trusts are subject to IRC section 665-668 regarding throwback rules while estates are not. Although the accumulation of an income in an estate is not in the best interest of the client under current law, it could be a factor in the future.
- Losses are disallowed when trust assets are distributed to beneficiaries. Estate losses are allowed.
- The $25,000 rental loss allowed to offset other income under a probate asset is not allowed in a trust.

Claims by Creditors

With a trust, there is no deadline for filing claims by creditors. With wills, creditors usually have four to six months to file a claim. However, since assets are already distributed by the trust, the creditor will usually have to come after all the beneficiaries individually.

Estate Tax Savings

This is where most confusion arises. Promoters of living trusts tout the estate tax savings of living trusts. In fact, trusts by their nature do not save taxes. The same can be said about wills. They start out even. It is the way they are designed through the use of estate tax savings trusts, optimal use of other tactics, bequests that save taxes.

So which should your client choose? What are his goals? Which come closest to satisfying the ones that are most important to him? Also, consider the estate planning comfort zone sheet shown later in deciding what will work best for your client. Remember, even if your client will not sit still or pay the fees for the perfect estate plan for him, it does not mean that nothing should be done. Do the best you can to improve his situation even if you do not make it perfect.

ESTATE PLANNING CHECKLIST

If you are like me, you wonder if the client has everything he needs when the estate plan is complete. A complete checklist would be too long, but certain basics may help you to insure that the major bases have been covered. They include

- Wills for both spouses.
- Living trust if applicable.
- Pour-over will.
- Durable power of attorney—Especially applicable to a living trust because it allows agent to transfer assets to the trust if client becomes incapacitated. The durable POA can serve as a temporary and expedient substitute for the RLT.
- Living will or directive to physicians.
- Minor's trust.
- A/B, by-pass, credit shelter, family trust.
- Irrevocable life insurance trust (wealth replacement).
- Power of attorney for health care or designation of a health care representative.
- Charitable bequests.
- Q-TIP trust.
- Is property titling going to work with your plan or does it need to be changed?
- Estate liquidity needs met.
- Charitable trusts.
- Advisors, executors, trustees, and guardians selected.
- Family business succession plan in place.
- Buy–sell agreement.
- Incapacity instructions:
  —Living trust.
  —Power of attorney—general.
  —Power of attorney—limited.
- Special needs considered:
  —Handicapped.
  —Spendthrift.
- Equal sharing needs of client met.
- Personal bequests.
- Organ donor instructions.
- Funeral and similar arrangements.

COMMUNITY PROPERTY SYSTEMS

Nine states have community property systems—Arizona, California, Idaho, Louisiana, Nevada, New Mexico, Texas, Washington, and Wisconsin. Under such a system, a spouse usually has a one-half interest in property acquired during marriage. Also, through commingling of assets, personal property brought into the marriage may become community property. Community property statutes may have some advantages to your estate planning strategies, but, in other cases, they may require changes in your plans. Some strategies discussed in this chapter depend on property ownership. Keep that in mind when planning strategies.

One of the advantages of community property is that the surviving spouse gets a stepped up basis in his half of the property as well as the deceased spouse share that was inherited. Another advantage is that many couples have 100 percent community property. That eliminates the need to prepare separate schedules for each spouse. However, it does not obviate the need to seek out information on how the property is titled.

THE IMPACT OF POOR PLANNING

I first recognized the urgent need to do estate planning when I had to tell a widow that she was going to have to write a check for $23,500 in estate taxes. Obviously, this was not a huge estate and the bulk of it had been in a small business. However, $23,500 was a huge check for this client to write. She asked if there was anything she could have done to avoid it, and I had to answer yes. The second impact was when a surviving daughter had to write a check for $450,000. Although her father had not been my client, he could have avoided virtually all of the tax with a minor amount of planning. Figure 16-2 shows how estate taxes and administration costs have affected some celebrities. Show this to your clients and you may get their attention.

Figure 16-2 Effect of Estate Taxes and Administration Costs on Some Well-Known Estates

	Gross Estate	Total Net After Subtracting Costs	Shrinkage	%
Marilyn Monroe	$819,173	$370,426	$448,750	55%
W. C. Fields	884,680	554,887	329,793	37%
Humphrey Bogart	910,146	635,912	274,234	30%
Franklin Delano Roosevelt	1,940,999	1,366,132	574,867	30%
Clark Gable	2,806,526	1,705,488	1,101,038	39%
Gary Cooper	4,984,985	3,454,531	1,530,454	31%
Elvis Presley	10,165,434	2,790,799	7,374,635	73%
John D. Rockefeller	26,905,182	9,780,194	7,124,988	64%
Walt Disney	23,004,851	16,192,908	6,811,943	30%
Dean Witter	7,451,055	5,620,338	1,830,717	25%
Howard Gould	67,535,386	14,985,704	52,549,682	78%
A. C. Ernst, CPA	12,642,431	5,518,319	7,124,112	56%

MARKETING ESTATE PLANNING SERVICES

Some of you still may not see the potential in marketing estate planning services. If you are one of those, you are probably looking at estate planning from a fee-for-service point of view. Since estate planning is fairly complex, you are comparing it to other fee-for-service areas of your practice. Here is how you should be marketing it:

1. Financial planning and estate planning are interchangeable terms. To prepare a financial plan without considering preparation for death and/or incapacity is to prepare an incomplete estate plan. Incomplete plans are alright if your client will not allow anything else, but your loyal clients are going to ask your advice on these matters sooner or later. If they do not, you have an obligation to ask them if they are prepared.
2. Estate planning is a great way to find out everything about a client. You can gather all his assets for the plan.
3. If you are the estate planner, it will be difficult for you to properly monitor a client's portfolio if assets are held elsewhere. Clients will see the advantage of investing through one source.
4. Estate planning cements relationships.
5. Estate planning leads to other sales of investments.
6. Heirs appreciate a well-prepared plan that leaves more money in their hands and less in the hands of the IRS or attorneys. They may show their appreciation by letting you invest their inheritances.
7. Insurance is needed in many estate plans in order:
   (a) To provide for income needs of the descendants.
   (b) To pay estate taxes.
   (c) To fund the continued operation of a family business.
   (d) To equalize the estate among heirs.
   (e) To fund buy–sell agreements.
   (f) To fund disability payments in a family business.
   (g) To provide other liquidity needs and prevent forced sale of assets.

Here is how to market estate planning services.

1. Conduct seminars primarily for your client base and prospective client list.
2. Integrate estate planning into your financial planning process by asking estate planning questions of your clients.
3. Use the post-tax interview to ask questions about preparation for death and incapacity.
4. Use terms like life planning or death and disability planning rather than estate planning.
5. Use TOPS. Here are some sample TOPs questions to use:
   * *Trust Questions*—"Any idea what your estate would be worth? From looking at your tax return and the returns for your business, it looks like it could be well over the exemption amount. Would you say that I am right? What types of wills do you and Joe have?"
   * *Opportunity Questions*—"Do you have a plan of succession for your small

business? Who do you want to have it when you die or retire? What type of disability do you have in place?''

- *Pain Questions*—"My calculations show that you will owe $787,000 in estate taxes if you die. You only have $500,000 in liquid assets, where is the shortfall going to be made up? With your present disability policy, there is no provision for payment beyond 90 days. Will the business be able to pay you in the event of a prolonged disability? What about your partners? If Bill dies, you have no buy–sell agreement. That means that you are going to be partners with Lucille. Will that work?''

- *Solution Questions*—"Shouldn't we have a plan in place to provide disability payments to you and your partners without strapping the business? Wouldn't it be nice if we could pay for the estate taxes with discounted dollars today without increasing your current insurance expense by more than 10 percent. Would you rather keep 100 percent of the insurance proceeds on this policy or 45 percent?''

6. Start with the perfect estate plan and find out what makes the client tick. What is most important to him? Ask him to rate each of the items on the

Figure 16-3   The Perfect Estate Plan

1. Provides income to my family when I die.
2. Provides income to me if I am disabled.
3. Provides cash to meet all liquidity needs of my estate.
4. Reduces estate taxes to nothing.
5. Has small set-up cost.
6. Has small administrative costs.
7. Provides for the orderly succession and continuance of my business.
8. Prevents the forced sale of any of my assets to meet liquidity needs.
9. Provides for the continuation of business if I am disabled.
10. Names competent, willing executors, guardians, and advisors who are willing to work for free.
11. Provides for my favorite charity as well as my family.
12. Provides high income for me while I am alive and high income for my family when I am gone.
13. Provides current tax deductions.
14. Allows my assets to flow to my designated beneficiaries according to my wishes.
15. Little time or complexity is needed to implement my wishes.
16. Provides for all my heirs with special needs including handicapped or irresponsible heirs or ones with other special needs.
17. Allows me to donate my body parts to research or for transplants.
18. Assures that all my heirs get the equal or unequal shares that I designate.
19. Insures that all my personal belongings go to the people who will appreciate and care for them as I would.
20. Leaves instructions as to how my final funeral and other arrangements should be carried out.
21. Leaves detailed instructions and legal documents providing for my care if I am incapacitated so that no court proceedings are necessary to name a guardian for me.
22. Assures that current income needs are met for my spouse while assuring that my assets wind up in the hands of my intended heirs.

Figure 16-4   The Estate Planning Comfort Zone

1. Would you consider the use of trusts to distribute your assets if it would reduce estate taxes?
2. Are you comfortable with your spouse's ability to handle large sums of money?
3. Would you consider transferring assets to others if it would reduce estate taxes?
4. Would you be willing to make lifetime gifts if it would reduce estate taxes?
5. Do you want your estate equalized among your children, or should they be distributed based on individual needs?
6. At what age should your children be entitled to receive their inheritances outright, free and clear of any trusts?
7. Who would you want to serve as trustee(s) of any trusts that may be established?
8. Who would serve as your trustee or guardian if you were incapacitated?
9. Who would you want to raise your children if both spouses were dead or incapacitated? Can they manage money?
10. Who would serve as executor and alternate executor to your will?
11. Do you wish to leave any money to charity? If not, would your answer be different if you could save current income taxes and estate taxes by doing so?
12. What specific items of property do you want left to what individuals?

perfect estate plan on a scale of one to ten. Then ask him to rank his top ten choices in order.

7. Find the client's estate planning comfort zone. Use the analysis in Figures 16-3 and 16-4 to help.

17

Asset Protection

The pain of sacrifice is much lighter than the pain of regret.

The legal system for awarding damages for private injury is out of control. Anybody can sue anybody for anything! And there is no punishment for those who file frivolous suits. Lawyers say there is, but they really know that there is not a system that causes attorneys and their clients to pay when they file a groundless lawsuit. This lack of punishment for abusing the system tilts the scales of justice heavily in favor of those with deep pockets. They can usually intimidate those of us who had just as soon never enter a courtroom into doing their bidding by just suing. Most people without deep pockets cannot defend themselves properly, so the bad guys often win through intimidation, not justice.

What does this mean to CPA planners? It means that it is no longer enough to just help our clients *build* wealth. Now we have to help them *preserve* wealth. I have done many financial plans where the primary objective was to hold on to what the client had accumulated. But what are the goblins that await us to attack and devour our hard-earned assets? They include:

- Divorce
- Lawsuits for anything
- Liability on loan guarantees
- Suits by employees
- Malpractice suits
- Government civil actions

Lest you think that your clients are safe because they keep good records and do not take chances, consider the case of a judgment of over a million dollars against a 96-year-old woman whose adopted grandson got into a accident driving a car for which she had cosigned. I could go on, but you get the point.

WHAT CAN YOU DO?

Carry Adequate Malpractice, Property, Casualty, and Personal Umbrella Coverage

I have found the personal umbrella coverage to be the best buy. However, many professionals say that the more insurance coverage they have, the more likely they are to be sued. Again, the insurance companies will settle out of court because it is cheaper and that encourages more groundless suits. I am not saying that people should not be allowed to sue. I am just saying that frivolous, groundless suits should be punished. Convene an impartial group of professionals (not just lawyers) to evaluate lawsuits when they are lost. If they are lost, make the lawyer and his client pay all court costs for both sides and a penalty.

Malpractice and liability insurance policies are often woefully inadequate. They often cover you ''if someone falls off the roof, but not if he hits the ground.'' Many malpractice and liability insurance policies could be summed up as follows: ''We will let you know what is covered after you file a claim. Don't count on much before then.''

Watch What You Sign!

I had at least five clients who did not understand the term ''jointly and severally'' when they cosigned notes as part of a group of shareholders or partners. They were not particularly concerned because the other shareholders and partners had significantly more assets than they did and they were just a ''small fry.'' When the loans defaulted, the big fish were all bankrupt. Only small fry was left and they were liable for the whole enchilada.

Several clients also owned real estate with mortgages that were sold with the old ''wrap-around.'' Two received calls five to seven years later advising that the loans were in default and guess who was liable for the balance? Bankruptcy!

Try not to cosign notes for your corporation. Cosigning notes does away with a lot of the benefits of having a corporation in the first place. Your bank will want you to guarantee all corporate notes, even if the corporation is strong on its own. Try to convince them that the corporation should stand on its own.

Use the Proper Form of Business Organization

For liability protection, most businesses should probably be set up as corporations. However, in a lot of small businesses, the corporation and the owner are so close that it is hard to distinguish which is which. For many of my smaller clients, incorporation just brings on another set of rules, another tax return, and another layer of bureaucracy. However, if the business is large at all, I recommend incorporation and keeping the owners and the corporation as separate as possible. It is probably not a good idea for the husband and wife to own shares in the family business, because if the corporate veil is pierced, then all of the family assets are exposed.

Piercing the Corporate Veil

Lawyers can try to prove that your corporation is really not a corporation for liability protection at all; that it is just a ''sham'' through which you do business. The more you commingle your personal and corporate assets and affairs, the easier you make it to do this. Treat the corporation like the separate entity it is.

Choose Investments Wisely

Some assets appear to offer more protection than others. Check with your attorney network to see which assets are protected from creditors. Some examples include:

Homesteads. Florida and Texas place no limits on the value of homesteads that are protected from creditors.

Annuities and Cash Value Life Insurance Policies. Texas Art. 21.22, Texas Insurance Code leads us to believe that clients may prudently stash considerable assets into an insurance policy or annuity with protection.

Qualified Plans. Texas Property Code Section 42.0021 provides protection for qualified retirement plans with specific mention of IRAs, SEPs, and 403(b)s.

Giving Up Control

You would think that a sure-fire way to avoid losing your assets would be to not own them anymore. That works in some cases, but not all. There is something called a "fraudulent conveyance" that will take away the very protection you seek. If you transfer assets just to get them out of the reach of creditors, the transfer will not likely be honored. You must have another legitimate motive for the transfer, such as estate planning. The longer the transfer is made before problems arise, the better.

Should clients give up control to protect assets? I have found that most will not, at least until it is too late. If trouble is eminent, they are more than happy to give up control in order to salvage them, but not before.

To whom should the assets be given? If the marriage is sound, the spouse is possibly a good answer. Making large gifts to the spouse may foul up estate planning, however. Making large gifts to children may subject you to gift tax and use up the lifetime exclusion. It also may place too much money into the hands of the inexperienced.

Using Trusts

Trusts are probably the best bet for ironclad asset protection if you elect to give up control. Gifts to trusts can remove assets from clients' taxable estates as well as from exposure to creditors. Trusts require the loss of control and are irrevocable. Therefore, clients should be sure that they have enough "safe" assets (those in retirement plans, annuities, and life insurance policies) outside of the trusts. The client cannot be the trustee or beneficiary.

Spendthrift Trusts. Since the client is giving up control, these types of trusts offer some type of protection by limiting the ability of the beneficiaries to transfer their interests or borrow against them.

Lifetime Q-TIP Trust. Assets go into an irrevocable trust, with the maker's spouse entitled to all the income for life. At the spouse's death, all the assets go to beneficiaries selected by the maker.

Megatrusts. Assets are transferred to a trust where the grandchildren are beneficiaries (married couple can put up to $2 million in such a trust before running afoul of the generation-skipping transfer tax). Megatrusts give the trustee the right to buy residential real estate and provide it to the beneficiaries, rent free.

Foreign Sites Trust. Now we are really getting exotic. Some jurisdictions, such as the Isle of Man and the Cook Islands, are known as asset protection havens, where a court may say that a creditor cannot collect from the trust. Be careful, however, because you may have trouble if you want to bring the assets back home. Some trusts may allow you to put the assets into an offshore trust and keep the assets in the United States, but such trusts are expensive to set up and administrate.

Keeping It In the Family

One of the best ways I have seen to protect assets besides repositioning assets into insurance products is using the *family limited partnership*. Using the family limited partnership may have significant estate tax-savings features, as well as minimizing probate. This may insulate it from the fraudulent conveyance rules. How does it work?

1. Set up a limited partnership with 5 percent or fewer general partner interests and 95 percent or more limited partnership interests. (Can be 1 and 99 percent.) The client initially owns all interests (100 percent).
2. Virtually all of the client's unprotected assets are transferred into the limited partnership.
3. Over the years, the client starts giving away the limited partnership interests to family members using the $10,000/$20,000 annual gift tax exclusion or the lifetime exclusion.

At this point, the client has his assets inside a limited partnership primarily owned (95 to 99 percent) by his family limited partners. Since the client controls the general partnership interest, he still controls the assets. So how does this insulate the assets from creditors?

If a creditor wins a judgment against a limited partnership, the creditor becomes an assignee, not a substitute LP or GP. This means that the creditor cannot force cash distributions or the sale of assets from the partnership. In fact, the GP, your client, retains the power to withhold distributions from the limiteds. This can stick the creditor with taxable income from the limited partnership without the cash flow to pay the taxes. Ever have a client get "phantom income" from a K-1? This type of income can discourage a creditor.

Sounds great, does it not? However, it does have some drawbacks. For example, if the assets inside the limited partnership are generating income, then the limited partner family members are going to be hit with taxes on their share of that income. That means distributions to them to pay the taxes—distributions from your client's assets. That may or may not be OK with the client.

The partnership can loan money to your client or to family members and pay the general partner a management fee when your client needs to have access to some money. Also, the partnership is revocable at any time, although it may be more than a little difficult to unwind.

This plan can possibly be improved by making the general partner a corporation that is owned by the client and his family. With this arrangement, the partnership can:

1. Pay the corporation a management fee.
2. The corporation can pay the client a salary and provide tax-deferred retirement plans.

HOW ASSET PROTECTION PLANNING BENEFITS THE CPA-FINANCIAL PLANNER

Now that we have learned how to assist the client in protecting his assets, how do we make money at doing it? First, remember the rule that "if you help enough people, the money will take care of itself." However, for you skeptics:

1. Asset protection is part of financial planning for many clients. If you are known as a financial planner who knows how to protect assets, you will get referrals for financial planning.

2. Asset protection plans require that you know where all assets are. They require the preparation of a financial statement and should always include a financial plan. A protection plan without a financial plan can lead to trouble when the client needs assets to meet his goals and objectives and they are not there or are unavailable. You must consider estate planning consequences before setting up a protection plan.

3. Many of the easier asset protection plans involve repositioning assets into insurance products. Who sells insurance products?

4. Asset protection is a hot topic for seminars targeted to professionals.

5. Clients who need asset protection are usually wealthy clients.

6. Much of the work for attorneys in setting up the plan will be billable on a fee basis.

18

Asset Allocation

Common sense is genius with its working clothes on.

Thomas Jefferson

Asset allocation has been a hot term in the financial services industry for a few years now. In prior years, most registered representatives competed to see who had the hottest product. Studies have now shown that diversification and tenacity are the two qualities that lead to success in investing.

The proven concepts of *modern portfolio theory* (MPT) were conceived by Dr. Harry Markowitz in the early 1950s. He won a Nobel Prize for his research in 1991. Markowitz held that an investment manager should evaluate the interrelationship among assets as opposed to analyzing each asset in isolation. His approach emphasizes the collective importance of all an investor's holdings.

When selecting assets for your client's investments, you have to broaden your perspectives from individual asset selection to portfolio balance. This approach emphasizes diversification and how the attributes of each portion of the portfolio work with other portions to achieve the goals of the client.

TO DO "NOTHING" OR "SOMETHING" (EVEN IF IT IS NOT PERFECT)

Beginning CPAs want a formula for diversification. Is that a realistic goal? Yes and no. Formulas do exist and I believe that they provide excellent guidelines, especially for the beginning financial planner. But is not asset allocation more complex than just putting a client's assets into various asset mixes based on their ages? Yes, but do not let that stop you from doing something for your clients. When the typical analytical CPA starts delving into modern portfolio theory and the efficient frontier, he often sees something more complex than he wants to attempt. The result is inertia. He does nothing for his client for fear it will not be technically correct. Is his client better off with:

1. Some diversification based on age;
2. The latest hot product; or
3. Exactly where he is (with 100 percent of his investments in CDs)?

I think he is better to start moving along the path to perfect investment allocation. In all probability, he will never reach it, however, if he is continually on the path, he is better off than to be nonallocated.

BECOME AN EXPERT—PRACTICE!

You will never become an expert on a subject by just reading and studying. You have to practice. You have to become involved. If you start using asset allocation in its simplest forms, you will start to learn how to adjust and work with your clients to reach the best possible combination of assets to meet their goals. My friend and partner, Tony Batman, is a Chartered Financial Analyst who knows portfolio theory backwards and forwards. He certainly studied it for many years and has the awards, articles, and certifications to prove it. He will tell you that he learned more from applying the concepts to real client portfolios and having personal impact on their lives. Tony also has the gift of being able to reduce highly complicated research to its simplest terms. As a CPA financial planner, you need to begin with those simple terms. Most clients will never understand the more complicated ones. They may appreciate your technical presentation and your depth of knowledge, but they may not give you their money to invest because they do not understand what you are going to do with it.

DETERMINE THE CLIENT'S GOALS

Most CPAs will heartily embrace the concept of diversification because it fits our training and our conservative natures. However, when I began applying the concepts, I often got tangled up in details and became frustrated. I screamed ''Where is the software to help me untangle this?'' The problems were caused when I would make what I thought was a textbook solution for asset diversification, only to have my client ask me a question that threw the whole plan out of kilter. I would fluster and sometimes fold because I had not considered the question. The questions almost always related to his goals. I had forgotten to ask him enough questions about what he wanted the portfolio to do for him. All the software and textbook solutions in the world will be worthless if the client needs checks every month for $4,000 that is 50 percent free from tax and your plan will not provide it.

The Treasure Chests Approach

I started using the *treasure chest approach* to asset allocation in order to be sure that I had met all of my client's goals. This started out as a way to help myself keep things straight, but developed into a method of explaining asset allocation to clients. Although it is so simple that I was embarrassed the first few times I used it, I find that it works very well. I use this approach to explain plans I have prepared but also as a basic primer on financial planning. It is especially effective for younger clients. Here is how it works: Think of your money as being saved in four basic treasure chests:

Chest #1 is Your Emergency Fund.   It should contain from three to six months of take-home pay at all times. Whether you use three or six months or longer depends on job stability, other savings, education and ability to find employment. Money in chest #1 should be readily available. That usually means a mutual fund money market account or similar short-term account.

Chest #2 is the "Big Expense" Fund.   Everyone has big recurring expenses that are paid annually, quarterly, even every three years. You are incurring those expenses every day and every month. You should be putting aside money that can earn some small return until the funds have to be used. Big expenses would include car and home insurance, vacations, automobile expenses, and regular auto purchases. Again, a money market account is probably your best bet until the fund is adequate to pay most recurring expenses for one year. Then you may want to consider a short-term bond fund or even an income growth fund for the excess.

Chest #3 is for Goals.   Goals can include whatever the client wants. This could be anything from a new home to an education fund for the children. This is the chest that requires the most work in asset allocation. Segregate these chests into boxes a, b, c, for each goal the client wants to accomplish.

Chest #4 is for Retirement Funds.   Although retiring financially secure is certainly a goal, keep retirement funds separate because they are often in the hands of an employer. They are also likely to be tax deferred even if not in a qualified plan.

As elementary as they may seem, these chests will help you keep focused on your client's goals. Chest #3, for example, might contain a bond fund that provides checkwriting privileges and a monthly check to meet the client's particular need. Also place equity investments here that provide protection from inflation to reach longer term goals. The key is to match the assets to the client's objectives, preferences, and constraints.

WHAT ARE THE CONSTRAINTS AND PREFERENCES?

Risk Tolerance

You can design a textbook portfolio for your client that meets all of his goals and have him turn it down because it scares him. Worse, he will implement it and drive you crazy because he cannot sleep at night. Determine his risk tolerance and educate, educate, educate him about principal fluctuation and the necessity of being a long-term investor if you put money into a long-term investment. How do you find out his risk tolerance? See the section on data gathering in Part 2. The risk profile is essential to any data gathering process. If you feel that your client needs further analysis, use a longer form and take him through a thorough analysis.

Caution! Explaining risk can be frustrating. If your client is unsophisticated, do not use terms like principal fluctuation. These are camouflage terms used in old-fashioned sales schools. I have been through many presentations about principal fluctuation, the different types of risk, and all the industry buzz words for losing money, only to have my client say at the end:

"All of these things you're recommending are insured, aren't they?"

Come right out and say, "You have indicated to me that you want to achieve _____ goal. In order to do this in the time frame you have outlined, we are going to have to invest in things that have traditionally outperformed CDs, Treasury bills, and similar investments that are generally considered risk-free. However, even these investments are subject to purchasing power risk. For example, can you remember when stamps were 2 cents and gasoline was 20 cents a gallon? If you stay in investments that do not grow, you are unprotected from inflation. Do you understand that? The assets that I am recommending are not insured nor guaranteed by the government or the FDIC. Any investment that is subject to growing is also usually subject to shrinking. That means that your investment could be worth less in one year, two years, or any time period you name than it is today. If history is any indication and our plan works, it will be worth much more if you hold it in accordance with our plan. If that is going to make you lose sleep or feel uncomfortable, please tell me now.''

Liquidity

I have been through many long presentations only to have my client say, ''I don't want to tie my money up.'' Find out the client's liquidity needs in advance. Most people are drowning in a sea of liquidity. Explain the cost of liquidity by comparing a short-term money market fund rate of return to your proposed investment over a period of time. Compare taking the money out of each at various periods. Ask the client which pile of money he would rather have, the nonliquid pile or the liquid pile. You pay dearly for liquidity. Show how your emergency fund and big expense fund provide the liquidity needed.

Marketability

You can often overcome liquidity concerns by explaining the difference between liquidity and marketability. Most mutual funds are highly marketable by their very nature. However, clients who have never invested have this feeling that their money is going to a place far, far away never to be seen again. They do not have the comfort of seeing your ''vault'' like the bank has where they think all their money is stored. If you can explain that they can sell any part of or all of their investment on a given day, their liquidity concerns usually go away.

Income versus Growth

Many clients will have income needs from their investments. Make very sure that those needs are met. Often, those income needs will be more imagined than real. Question the client carefully about whether he wants income to be paid regularly from the investment. If he does, then you are probably going to have to invest in an income producing investment that produces the income he desires. One of my first mistakes as a financial planner was to *not* provide that income would be distributed to a client. He did not need the income. He just wanted the pleasure of going to the mail box and picking up his check monthly. In his mind, unless the investment could produce a check monthly, it was worthless. My mistakes were two-fold.

1. I did not spend enough time explaining how reinvestment of dividends was better than getting checks you did not need to support your lifestyle.
2. I assumed I knew better than the client what it was he wanted. Even though I did know better on an *academic* level, I did not know better on an *emotional* level.

Taxation

Many clients are downright paranoid about paying taxes. I tried to talk an elderly client out of municipal bonds because she barely had any tax liability. She finally convinced me she wanted *no* tax liability. She recognized that a taxable investment might leave more money in her pocket, but she wanted her taxable income to be below the filing requirement level. I had her sign a statement that we did not recommend the investment and implemented her investment the way she wanted. If you hand your client a goals sheet, then avoidance of taxes is listed there. Also, as his tax advisor, you know whether or not he needs tax avoidance. Factor that need into your recommended asset allocation.

Explain carefully the difference between tax-deferred and tax-free investments. If you are not convinced yet of the value of tax deferral, then get convinced by using your financial calculator to compare a tax deferred with a tax free and a taxable investment. Project taking the money out of the tax deferred and paying all the taxes on the accumulated earnings at various time periods. That will convince you of the value of the tax deferral. Doing this for the client on a greaseboard in your office can be a powerful presentation.

If you refer to this list of constraints and preferences everytime you prepare a plan, your client will implement your asset allocation suggestions because you believe in it and you know you have covered all the bases.

PORTFOLIOS FOR THE DIFFERENT STAGES OF LIFE

The following sample portfolios are just suggested and are meant as guidelines only. They are a reference or starting point for you to match to your client's stated goals and risk tolerance.

Portfolio #1—Just Starting Out

You can really make a hit with young couples if you will take the time to explain the investment process to them. They are largely ignored by other investment advisors, so you can usually have them to yourself. If you take the time to educate them early on, you will have loyal clients for life.

Category of Investment	Percentage
Income and stability (cash reserves)	10%
Growth and income (current income with capital appreciation potential)	25%
Growth (capital appreciation)	30%
Global growth (long-term global growth using global diversification)	35%

Typical Objectives:

1. Improving lifestyle.
2. Saving for a home or other major purchase.
3. Starting a family; educating children.
4. Beginning a sound retirement program.

Portfolio #2—Mid-Career

Category of Investment	Percentage
Income and stability (cash for liquidity stability, and current income)	10%
Income (current income—possibly using global bonds as well as U.S.)	15%
Growth (capital appreciation)	20%
Global growth (long-term capital growth; using global diversification)	25%
Growth and income (current income; capital appreciation potential)	30%

Typical Objectives:

1. Increasing current income to pay tuition costs.
2. Enhancing income to fund the care of an elderly parent.
3. Financing more recreational activities or longer vacations.
4. Purchasing a major discretionary item such as a second home.
5. Concentrating more on retirement savings.

Portfolio 3—Peak-Earning Years

Category of Investment	Percentage
Income and stability (cash) liquidity; stability; tax-free and taxable current income	10%
Growth (capital appreciation)	10%
High income (current income possibly with global diversification)	10%
Global growth (long-term capital growth with global diversification)	15%
Tax-free income	25%
Growth and income (current income; capital appreciation	30%

Typical Objectives:

1. Minimizing taxes.
2. Accelerating savings for early retirement.
3. Increasing leisure activities and travel time.
4. Building a second home.
5. Helping out elderly parents, children, and grandchildren.
6. Increasing wealth.

Portfolio #4—Retirement

Income and stability (cash liquidity; stability; current income)	10%
High income (current income possibly with global diversification)	10%
Income (income with principal stability)	20%
Tax-free income	30%
Growth and income (current income with growth potential)	30%

Typical Objectives:

1. Maximizing income to meet living expenses.
2. Keeping pace with inflation and protecting purchasing power.
3. Paying for special trips and leisure activities.
4. Saving money for unexpected medical expenses.
5. Helping out children; funding college for grandchildren.
6. Increasing estate value to pass on to heirs.

Figures 18-1 through 18-3 offer some suggestions for portfolio mixes for conservative, moderate, and aggressive investors based on age groups.

Figure 18-1   Asset Allocation Strategies for Various Age Groups—Average Portfolio Mix—Conservative

AGE	GRW FUND	G/I AND/OR BLNCD	HI GRD CORP BD	HI YLD CORP BOND	S/T US GOVT BD	INT BD FD	US GOV BD	TX* EX BD FD	INTNL FUND	CASH/ FXD TX DFRD ANN
20–30s	40%	20%	20%						10%	10%
40–50s	20%	30%	30%						10%	10%
60+***	10%	15%	25%	10%						40%
60+**	10%	15%	25%	10%		10%	20%		10%	

*Use when appropriate.
**Needs current income.
***Does not need current income.

Figure 18-2   Asset Allocation Strategies for Various Age Groups—Average Portfolio Mix—Moderate

AGE	GRW FUND	G/I AND/OR BLNCD	HI GRD CORP BD	HI YLD CORP BOND	S/T US GOVT BD	INT BD FD	US GOV BD	TX* EX BD FD	INTNL FUND	CASH/ FXD TX DFRD ANN
20–30s	60%	20%	10%						10%	
40–50s	30%	35%	20%						15%	
60+***	10%	15%	25%	10%						40%
60+**	10%	15%	25%	10%		10%	20%		10%	

*Use when appropriate.
**Needs current income.
***Does not need current income.

Figure 18-3   Asset Allocation Strategies for Various Age Groups—Average Portfolio Mix—Aggressive

AGE	GRW FUND	G/I AND/OR BLNCD	HI GRD CORP BD	HI YLD CORP BOND	S/T US GOVT BD	INT BD FD	US GOV BD	TX* EX BD FD	INTNL FUND	CASH/ FXD TX DFRD ANN
20–30s	60%	20%							20%	
40–50s	40%	30%	15%						15%	
60+***	20%	30%	25%	10%						15%
60+**	10%	40%	25%	15%					10%	

*Use when appropriate.
**Needs current income.
***Does not need current income.

WHAT ARE THE FIVE BASIC CATEGORIES OF INVESTMENT?

Some say that there are only two classes of investment—debt and equity. In reality, there are five:

1. Equity.
2. Debt.
3. Cash (which is usually debt).
4. Deferred annuities.
5. Life insurance.

So which has the best performance? That depends on the investor's outlook (conservative or aggressive) and numerous other factors. Figure 18-4 provides a list of some of these factors. Make sure that your clients are aware of all these factors for the particular investment vehicles they may be considering. You cannot make up their minds for them, but you can guide them in the right direction.

WHAT INVESTMENT HAS THE BEST PAST PERFORMANCE?

Stocks are the winners hands down! Figures 18-5 through 18-9 show how an investor would have profited by investing in stocks as far back as 1926. The data does not lie. But remember, investing in the stock market requires an aggressive outlook for investing. Not all of your clients will be willing to carry that much risk. For those clients who do not, do your homework and find them the right investment vehicle for their attitude and lifestyle.

Figure 18-4   Where Should You Put Your Money?

What % of assets per category is right for you?	%	%	%	%	%
Five Major Categories of Assets	**Equity Ownership**	**Debt Instrument**	**$$$ Money**	**Deferred Annuities**	**Life Insurance**
Asset Sub-Categories:	Stocks Real Estate Oil & Gas Livestock Collectibles Gems/ Metals Own-Business Mutal Funds	Bonds Treasury Corporate Zero-Coupon Municipal GNMA/ FNMA Mortgages Mutual-Funds	Cash Checking CD's Passbook Money-Market	SPDA FPDA	Universal Whole Life
Is investment free of front end sales charges?	NO/YES	NO/YES	YES	YES	NO
Is there a high degree of liquidity?	NO/YES	NO/YES	YES	NO	YES
Is value known at all times?	NO	NO	YES	YES	YES
Is asset free of investment risk?	NO	NO	YES	YES	YES
Is asset free of interest rate risk?	N/A	NO	YES	NO	YES
Is asset protected by State or Federal laws?	NO	NO	YES	YES	YES
Is asset protected from personal bankruptcy?	NO	NO	NO	NO/YES	NO/YES
Is early surrender penalty known?	NO	NO	YES	YES	YES
Is penalty waived in event of death?	NO	NO	NO/YES	YES	YES
Is penalty waived if paid out over time?	NO	NO	NO	NO/YES	NO/YES
Is interest free of current income tax?	NO/YES	NO/YES	NO	YES	YES
Is there a tax penalty surcharge?	NO	NO	NO	NO/YES	NO/YES
Is asset convertible to guaranteed life income?	NO	NO	NO	YES	YES
Is tax deferred on Social Security Benefits?	NO/YES	NO	NO	YES	YES

(*Continued*)

Figure 18-4   Where Should You Put Your Money?

What % of assets per category is right for you?	%	%	%	%	%
Five Major Categories of Assets	Equity Ownership	Debt Instrument	$$$ Money	Deferred Annuities	Life Insurance
Is spouse allowed to defer income tax at death?	NO/YES	NO/YES	NO	YES	YES
Is asset value increased tax free at death?	NO	NO	NO	NO	YES
Is privacy of ownership guaranteed?	NO	NO	NO	YES	YES
Is asset passed to beneficiary outside of will?	NO	NO	NO	YES	YES
Is there avoidance of probate expenses?	NO	NO	NO	YES	YES

Figure 18-5   Summary of Annual Returns (1926–1991)

Common stocks	12.4%
Long-term corporate bonds	4.7%
Long-term government bonds	4.6%
U.S. Treasury bills	3.5%
Inflation	3.1%

Source: *Stocks, Bonds, Bills, and Inflation 1992 Yearbook*, Ibbotson Associates, Chicago.

IS TENACITY AS GOOD AS DIVERSIFICATION?

There is overwhelming evidence that market timing does not work—*diversification and tenacity* do. I recently attended and spoke at a seminar where the futility of timing was discussed at length and the virtues of diversification and tenacity were extolled. At the end of the seminar, I was still approached and asked what product I was recommending for today? This type of question is frustrating, but we should learn something from it. We should be able to answer the question with good diversification and tenacity recommendations. These might include, ''I generally recommend that someone of your age have 30 percent of their assets in tax-free and other income funds with 50 percent in equities, including some utility funds for growth and income, 10 percent in cash, and 10 percent in tax deferreds. However, every client is different and I recommend we sit down to see how we can adjust this standard portfolio to suit your particular needs.''

**Figure 18-6   Stocks Beat Bonds and Inflation—One-Year Holding Periods
(1926–1990)**

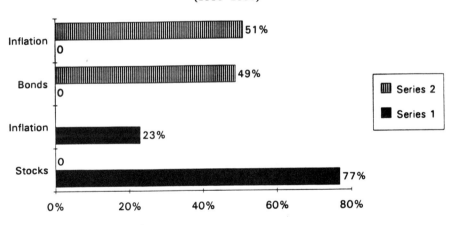

Stocks - S&P 500; Bonds - 20 Yr. US Gov;
Inflation - CPI

**Figure 18-7   Stocks Beat Bonds and Inflation—Five-Year Holding Periods
(1930–1990)**

Stocks - S&P 500; Bonds - 20 Yr. US Gov;
Inflation - CPI

Why does tenacity pay off? Consider this information about holding periods for the stock market as a whole. From the period 1926 to 1990 there were 65 one-year periods, 61 five-year periods, and 56 ten-year periods (see Figure 18-10).

Figure 18-8   Stocks Beat Bonds and Inflation—10-Year Holding Periods
(1935–1990)

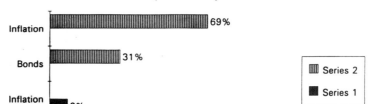

Stocks - S&P 500; Bonds - 20 Yr. US Gov;
Inflation - CPI

Figure 18-9   Stocks Beat Bonds and Inflation—15-Year Holding Periods
(1940–1990)

Stocks - S&P 500; Bonds - 20 Yr. US Gov;
Inflation - CPI

MARKETING FINANCIAL PRODUCTS USING ASSET ALLOCATION

Can you use asset allocation to help you in marketing financial products to your clients? Yes. Although asset allocation is a buzz word right now, many of your competitors still live and breathe to push product. They need new transactions to feed their lifestyle. Asset allocation distinguishes you from the competition.

I use pie charts in my financial plans to graphically illustrate to my clients how their assets are concentrated before my plan and after the plan is implemented. If the client can visually see where that he is over-concentrated in one

Figure 18-10   Holding Period History

	Number of up years	Percentage
One-year periods	45 of 65	69%
Five-year periods	54 of 61	89%
Ten-year periods	54 of 56	96%

area, he will be more likely to listen to your recommendations. I also use pie charts to show liquid versus nonliquid assets. Many small business clients including farmers have most of their investable assets tied up in their business, land, equipment, or other nonliquid assets. A pie chart can show them the need to diversify.

19

Charitable Giving

Some men see things as they are and say "Why?" I dream
things that never were and say "Why not?"

George Bernard Shaw

Learning about charitable giving is one of the most exciting aspects of financial
and estate planning. You get the opportunity to help your client, your client's
family, and a worthy cause. What could be better? How many other professions
give you such opportunities?

The benefits of charitable giving are not just intangible. Giving to charities
has significant and meaningful impact on retirement income, current income
taxes, and estates taxes. In fact, the code sections we will be using here are some
of the few left that offer real opportunity for investment planning.

WHO ARE THE PROSPECTS FOR CHARITABLE
DONATIONS?

Many of my instructors and books on the subject say that a person has to have
charitable or philanthropic inclinations to be a prospect for charitable giving
planning. I have found that not to be entirely true, or at least it is misleading.
As I have said on many prior pages of this book, do not be too quick to judge
your clients as nonprospects. This is also true in evaluating charitable giving
prospects. Just because a client is not active in his church does not mean that
he does not have a charitable inclination. I have found that many clients will
respond readily to the tax savings and the win–win solutions available under
proper planning. Showing them the benefits may bring out an urge to give to
their favorite charity. If it does not, but the client is interested nonetheless, this
is an excellent opportunity for you to mention your favorite charity. Also, many
people will respond to a visit from a dignitary of the local university, hospital,
church, scientific program, and the like. The prospect of having their names
associated with a large contribution or immortalized by an endowed chair at
a university, for example, may appeal to their emotions.

I recommend that you consider the nonprofit organizations in your area as
clients. The larger ones will have staff devoted to helping people make contributions using methods that meet the client's goals. That means that they will
assist you in preparing presentations to clients, usually at no cost or obligation
to you. They recognize the principle that if they help enough people, some of

the contributions will come their way. That makes them an excellent resource. Smaller charities who do not have any fund-raising staff will appreciate the level of expertise you bring to their fund-raising activities. You can make significant contributions to the charity through fund-raising. This can significantly enhance your position within the community overall and especially within the charitable organizations. This will lead to more referrals.

Charitable organizations must be qualified as such by the IRS. Generally, any nonprofit organization providing educational, religious, scientific, medical, or welfare services will qualify. Make sure by having the organization provide certification of its qualification to you or request its status from the IRS. They should be:

- A tax-exempt organization under IRC 501(C).
- A private foundation under IRC 509.
- Some other organization (religious or medical) listed under the percentage limits of IRC 170(b)(1).

WHAT CAN YOUR CLIENTS GIVE?

Cash, of course, is always a viable contribution. Real estate, tangible personal property, antiques and collectibles, securities, life insurance are all acceptable forms of assets for contributions. The particular type of gift that your client will select will depend on many factors including:

1. What does he have to give?
2. Is he giving a pure gift or a deferred gift?
3. Is a current income tax deduction important?
4. Is saving estate taxes a primary goal?
5. Will he need to receive income from the gift and, if so, for how long?
6. Is the property appreciated in value, i.e., is there realized but not recognized capital gain lurking in the gift?

Generally, gifts that do not produce income and cannot easily be converted into assets that do produce income may be less suited overall for charitable giving than gifts that do produce income or can be converted into income producing assets. Appreciated assets that either produce income or can be sold and converted into income producing assets are the best candidates.

WHAT ARE THE TAX BENEFITS?

The Basic Rules on Income Tax Benefits

Gifts and bequests to charity are deductible without limitation for estate tax purposes. You can wipe out your entire estate tax liability by a charitable bequest. Generally, current gifts of unappreciated property are deductible in amounts up to 50 percent of adjusted gross income with the excess carried over for up to five years. Gifts of long-term (one-year) appreciated property are subject to a limit of 30 percent of AGI because the taxpayer is getting the benefit of dodging the tax on the appreciation as well. There may also be alternative minimum tax consequences associated with gifts of appreciated property since the appreciation is considered a tax preference item. In addition, there is a 20 percent limit on gifts to private foundations.

If a client is giving to both public and private charities, it is usually wise to limit the client's contributions to public charities to 30 percent of AGI because any excess will offset the deduction limits to private charities. A corporation's deduction is limited to 10 percent of taxable income computed without regard to operating or capital loss carrybacks.

Estate Tax Benefits

Contributions are generally fully deductible for estate tax purposes. Current gifts are fully deductible. Deferred gifts will be deductible based on IRS tables of their *present value*. These deductions can be calculated from tables published every month by the IRS.

HOW GIFTS ARE MADE FOR MAXIMUM BENEFIT

Current Gifts or Bequests

A current gift or bequest in a will or living trust is the simplest way to make a gift. If the gift is current, then the client will receive a current income tax deduction (subject to limitations mentioned previously) as well as having the asset removed from the estate. If it is a bequest, then the asset will not be subject to estate taxes and there is no limitation.

Charitable Revocable Trusts

Note the term ''revocable.'' This type of trust is rare, but may fit a client's needs. It does not allow a deduction until the property passes to the charity because it is revocable. It does allow the donor to maintain control of his assets during his life. It is primarily used for clients who want control and privacy. Since this type of trust is not subject to probate, assets inside will pass directly to the charity at death and will be deductible for estate tax purposes. You should assist the client in investing the funds for lifetime income or other needs as stipulated. At death, you may get to invest for the charity. This can be part of an estate tax reduction plan when a client does not want to give up control.

Charitable Gift Annuity

With this type of gift, property is transferred to the charity and, in return, the charity agrees to pay the client a fixed amount each year for the rest of his life. The amount of the income as well as the deduction is based on age of the client. Since the payments are in part a return of principal, not all of the payments will be taxable. You should be able to provide the annuity.

Charitable Deferred Payment Gift Annuity

This works like the gift annuity above, except that the payments to the client are deferred until a later date. This works like an IRA with no limits.

Charitable Remainder Trusts

These are probably the most flexible methods of giving to charity and achieving several of the client's goals. They are a five-win solution. They can be set up as CRUTs (*charitable remainder unit trusts*) or CRATs (*charitable remainder annuity trusts*). They work essentially the same way except the annuity trusts pay the client a fixed income each year, while the unit trusts pay a fixed percentage of the annual valuation. They must be administered by a trustee. The trustee may be the donor, the charity, or other independent trustee. The trustee must see that payments are made correctly. In the case of a unitrust, the trustee must see that the assets are revalued each year. When we use mutual funds in the trust, the revaluation is already done by the mutual fund company.

Benefits of CRTs.   The outstanding benefits include:

1. If gifting appreciated property, the client bypasses the capital gains tax.
2. The client gets a current income tax deduction for the future value of the gift that will eventually go to charity. The older your client is and the lower his selected income percentage, the higher his deduction and vice versa.
3. The client gets the asset removed from his estate.
4. The client's income is higher than if he sold the asset, paid capital gains tax, and reinvested the difference.
5. The client can use the savings from income and estate taxes to purchase life insurance to replace the asset for his heirs.

We call this the *five-win solution*. In addition,

6. Your client will get the satisfaction and recognition of making a gift many times larger than would otherwise be possible because he can take lifetime income from the asset he is giving up. He will get recognition for this gift during his lifetime, as contrasted to bequests.
7. There is inflation protection in a unitrust, since the trust is reevaluated every year and income adjusted accordingly.
8. Property in the trust is not subject to probate.
9. With a unitrust, you can elect to receive income in several ways (minimum payout is 5 percent):
   (a) Straight percent of the trust value.
   (b) Income only.
   (c) Income only with a provision that you can make up any income you miss while the trust is paying less than the percentage selected.
   These alternate selections work great with land or other nonincome producing assets.
10. The annuity CRT provides the guarantee of a fixed income each year. You can increase the benefits by funding it with tax-free bonds. Guess who sells the bonds? Amounts must be at least 5 percent of the value.

A Retirement Unitrust

Many professionals fund their retirement using CRTs. Often, CRTs are also used as additions to fully funded retirement plans. As alternates, they compare favorably with many qualified retirement plans and even nonqualified plans. When you consider the cost of administration difference, employee contributions, limits on owner contributions, and the estate tax savings, a retirement unitrust may outperform many small retirement plans. I suggest that you contact a local charity and see if they will run illustrations for a few clients and present the comparisons to them.

An Education Unitrust

A unitrust can be used to fund the education of a child or grandchild. Such a trust is established for a specific period of time (up to 20 years) in order to generate income during the years when the child is going to be in college. The income is taxed to the student as ordinary income and will be at the child's rate since he is over 14 when going to college.

A CRT With a Wealth Replacement Trust

Using the tax savings and after tax income from the CRT, a client can purchase sufficient life insurance to replace the assets placed into the unitrust. By placing the life insurance into an irrevocable life insurance trust, you can make use of your annual gift tax exclusions to pay the premiums and ultimately direct the proceeds to heirs outside of the taxable estate.

Gifts of Life Insurance

Clients can make a gift many times larger than otherwise possible by purchasing a life insurance policy on themselves or another. The premiums are deductible for the client as long as the policy is owned by the charity. Insurance proceeds pass to the charity at death. Payments can be made in lump sums to purchase paid up life insurance or in periodic payments. I usually use interest sensitive whole life policies that will be paid up in 10 years or less. If the client ceases to make payments, the charity has the option of continuing, cashing in for surrender value, or electing reduced paid-up insurance.

An existing policy can also be signed over. The deduction will be the replacement value of the policy less any outstanding loans, as long as that value does not exceed the client's basis in the policy.

This is an excellent way for the financial planner to work with his favorite charity. You can run illustrations of the net cost of the policy after-tax savings and how the total contribution compares to what the client would have given if he had just contributed the premiums.

Gift of a Remainder Interest in a Residence or Ranch

The client gives his home to the charity, while retaining the right to live there for the rest of her life. The charitable deduction is determined by the client's age and the value of the house. At death, the home passes to the charity outside of the estate, saving probate and estate costs.

Charitable Lead Trust

The client transfers asset to charity for a period of time or for the life or lives of certain people. Charity receives income from the trust during this time. When the period is over, the asset reverts to the client or his family—sort of opposite of the CRT. These can be set up during the client's life or at his death. Client may receive an income tax deduction and a gift tax deduction, depending on how the trust is set up.

Pooled Income funds

These are usually for smaller contributors who like the benefits of the CRT. The pooled income fund mingles your client's funds with those of other donors. You receive income based on your share of the pool.

The IRA Receiver CRT

Many clients have large sums invested in IRAs that have not been taxed. At age 70-1/2, they have to start taking taxable distributions. If they die before distributing all the untaxed amounts, heirs can be hit with 55 percent estate taxes and 37 percent income taxes for a total of 92 percent. Since the estate taxes are deductible, the effective rate is around 75 percent in this situation. The heirs wind up with 25 percent. To avoid this, the IRA owner can create a CRT to receive her IRA upon her death with her heirs as the life beneficiary of the CRT. The CRT receives the IRA all at once, free of income tax. The heirs are only taxed on the income distributed from the CRT. The IRAs remainder interest value is left out of the estate; the client gets an income deduction.

MARKETING CHARITABLE GIVING AS A FINANCIAL PRODUCT

Since charitable giving is such a win–win situation, marketing it should be easy. When you approach a charity, you are asking to help them raise money using your expertise and other experts at your disposal. When you approach clients, you can show them how to beat the IRS in different ways while doing something good, something that could even lend them a level of immortality. Here are a few tips to keep in mind when marketing charitable giving:

1. Use a large hospital or other nonprofit organization to assist you in running proposals for your clients.
2. Get on the mailing lists for large nonprofit organizations. They will keep you abreast of the latest developments in the field.
3. Give seminars for clients and the general public on charitable giving or make charitable giving a major part of every estate plan.
4. Learn how to illustrate the five-win solution for CRTs. Showing taxes paid and income earned with and without CRTs is the best way ''to have your cake and eat it too.''
5. Volunteer to help in fund raisers for your local charities. Offer to give seminars on tax-wise ways to give to charity.
6. Write articles for your alumni association newsletter or any publication of a nonprofit organization.
7. Use TOPS.

20

Planning For The Elderly

Genius is the ability to reduce the complicated to the simple.
C. W. Ceran

We cannot attempt to cover all of the many facets of planning for the elderly for two reasons:

1. Some portions are covered in other areas, especially estate planning.
2. The field of planning for the elderly is huge and growing. Some have even dubbed it *financial gerontology*. There are numerous services and books that may be purchased on this single subject.

We will try to give the CPA financial planner enough information in this chapter so that the huge and growing potential for this market is recognized. Also, solutions to some of the needs will be explored and guidelines for further research will be given when complete solutions are not. We will focus on two major aspects:

1. Planning for long-term care costs.
2. Planning for incapacity.

THE OPPORTUNITY

Marketing financial products designed to aid your clients in their ''sunset years'' has taken on more importance than ever before. This is due to a number of facts:

1. People are living longer. The fastest growing age group in America today is 85 and over. The number of people over 65 is expected to double in the next 40 years.
2. Families no longer live as close to each other, creating need for outside assistance.
3. Nursing home care costs are rising with other health care costs, often usurping the life savings of middle-income couples. They consumed 21 percent of America's total health care expenditures in 1990.
4. The quality of life does not necessarily increase with increased years. The problem of incapacity can unravel the best financial plan.

5. The weakness of Social Security, Supplemental Security Income, and Medicaid programs are compounded when you consider the number of workers necessary to support the number of retired in just 20 years, and the national deficit.

6. Retired people have a large share of the discretionary investments and income in America.

7. Approximately one out of 2 people over 65 will spend some time in a nursing home before they die, but only 3 percent are covered by long-term care insurance.

I used to speak to a lot of service clubs. The members would often ask me what the most often asked question in my practice was. I would surprise them when I said, ''How do I protect myself/my parents from the long-term care crisis?'' During my early days of financial planning, almost no information was available and very few solutions. In addition to client requests for help, my mother was diagnosed with Parkinson's disease. This made the problem more urgent and real. I went to the IAFP convention in New York in 1988 specifically to learn more about the long-term care crisis. I came away with some great information, but I was shocked to see how little was available in the way of clear-cut solutions. When I returned to Texas, I began working on my lawyer network and again found few who knew how to practice elder law. During the time since 1988, information and products have come at a fast pace. Apparently, a lot of other people were asking that same question.

PLANNING FOR LONG-TERM CARE—KEY TERMS

Before we begin our discussion of financial products for long-term care, we must define the most common types of care.

Skilled Care. The highest level of nursing home care, where a patient requires constant attendance by a nurse, doctor, or other medical professional. Medicare covers up to 100 days of this type of care *under certain circumstances*—generally after a hospital stay.

Intermediate Care. Nursing home care that requires medical attention or supervision, but not constant attendance.

Custodial Care. This is the care level required by the majority of all nursing home residents. It provides assistance in the *activities of daily living* (ADLs). Although custodial care does not necessarily require a nurse or other trained professional, many LTC policies will only reimburse a facility with a doctor on call, a nurse on staff at all times, and some type of clinical records for all patients. In general, this is what distinguishes a nursing home from a rest home.

Respite Care. This is a service that will temporarily relieve family caregivers from the responsibilities of care to an impaired relative. It may be offered as part of home health care or as a separate service in some LTC policies.

Home Health-Care Benefits. This provision covers the common situation when an elderly person has trouble handling daily activities, but can manage with some assistance at home.

ADLs. An acronym for activities of daily living. This includes taking medication, toileting, walking, eating, dressing, bathing, getting in and out of bed.

Elimination Period. Also called a *waiting period*, this is the time your client will have to pay nursing home costs before the LTC policy will kick in. You can pick your time period usually from 0 to 200 days with 20 days being the norm.

Benefits. In LTC policies, you can pick your benefits and riders, usually based on an amount of coverage per day. These may range from $20 and $200 per day with $60 to 80 the norm, depending on where you live.

Maximum Benefit Period. You also choose how long you want the benefits to last—two years to a lifetime.

Inflation Rider. This provision will increase the benefit amount each year based on a predetermined percentage.

Gatekeepers. These are requirements that must be met before the policy will pay.

These terms are defined here because many of them will be used in subsequent text.

WHO PAYS FOR LONG-TERM CARE NOW?

Medicare. Many people believe that Medicare pays for long-term care costs. In fact, only about 2 percent of such costs are paid for by Medicare. It offers limited coverage for the first 100 days only in a skilled care facility.

Long-Term Care Insurance. Only about 3 percent of people over 65 are even covered by LTC.

Medicaid. Paid 43 percent of the national nursing home bill in 1990.

Personal or Family Resources. Estimated to pay approximately 50 percent of total cost.

HOW DO WE PROTECT OUR CLIENTS?

There are three basic options to protect your clients from a long-term care crisis:

1. Self-funding.
2. Qualifying for medicaid.
3. Long-term care insurance.

A long-term care engagement begins with a few simple questions, such as: "What are you trying to accomplish? Is there enough money to pay for LTC and how long will it last under current costs? Do you want to retain assets for your heirs or for some other reason, or would you make them available to pay for long-term care costs? Can you afford a LTC policy?" These answers will lead you to one of the options stated above.

Self-Funding

If you can catch your clients in their 40s and 50s, and they have substantial income levels, you can possibly prepare adequately by saving for LTC as part of their financial plan. I usually cover it as a part of the final stage of life after retirement and set aside specific assets to fund it. If they get into their 60s and 70s and do not wish to self-fund, then they can still opt for LTC insurance if they qualify medically.

My plans usually show that long-term care funds start being used at about 75. If the client can accumulate adequate funds to pay for nursing home costs through normal life expectancy, then this is my preferred method. However, many clients are adamant about not spending money in a nursing home. Then you point out their other options.

Medicaid

I have given many seminars on the subject of qualifying for Medicaid. "Spending down" as the process is frequently called, was personally distasteful to me in the beginning. It went against my personal and political beliefs. Is seemed to be an effort to "beat the system." However, as I saw more and more rich people qualify for Medicaid, I began to feel that the middle class (most of my clients) should be able to protect their hard-earned assets also. The turning point came when an elderly couple entered a nursing home. They had planned their lives carefully and had been frugal. They had adequate assets to pay for their own care. However, the elderly woman could find no other patients in the nursing home who were paying their own way other than she and her husband. Her question to me was: "Are we being punished for being frugal? I know several people in this nursing home who always made more and lived better than we did, yet the government is paying for them and not for us. I do not understand."

This lady was 92 years old and I did not have an explanation. From that point forward, I helped several people to qualify for Medicaid and preserve their assets for their children. I do not like the system the way it is, but I do not want my clients to be hurt anymore than necessary by it.

How to Qualify for Medicaid.   Your client must be impoverished under the state's definition. To be impoverished, both your assets and income must be below certain levels which vary by state.

Assets.   In Texas, qualifying asset levels are

Individual	$2,000 per month
Couple	$3,000 per month

Qualifying assets include everything except:

1. The personal residence and the land which surrounds it.
2. An auto with a maximum value of $4,500.
3. Insurance policies up to a $1,500 face value.
4. Household and personal goods.
5. Pre-need burial contracts and anything that pertains to the burial site.

In most other states as well, the asset limitation is around $2,000 and the excluded assets are similar.

Income.   In Texas, the total allowable incomes for 1993 were:

Individual	$1,266 per month
Couple	$2,532 per month

These amounts include Social Security! Be very cautious when planning with clients to qualify for Medicaid. Many have incomes that can not be controlled, such as veteran's pension or teacher retirement. After spending down or giving away all of their assets, they may find that they still cannot qualify for assistance because of an income level that they cannot control.

In 31 states, there is no limit to a Medicaid applicant's income so long as that amount is below the cost of the nursing home facility where the patient is living. For example, if a person has an income of $2,000 per month and it costs $3,000 to live in the facility, then that person would qualify. The nursing home would take all of her income, including Social Security, and Medicaid would pay the rest (in this case, $1000). The patient is allowed a living allowance which is usually $30 to $35 per month.

Nineteen states—Alabama, Alaska, Arkansas, Colorado, Delaware, Florida, Georgia, Idaho, Iowa, Louisiana, Nevada, New Jersey, New Mexico, Oklahoma, South Carolina, Tennessee, Texas, and Wyoming—have "income caps" to eligibility. Under Federal law, this cap can be no higher than three times the Federal Social Security income minimum benefit level for the year. In 1993, those levels are three times $422 per month or $1,266 per individual.

Tragic situations often develop when a person cannot qualify for Medicaid because of uncontrollable income, yet does not have the income to pay for nursing home care. This is a case for long-term care insurance and the value of planning ahead.

Now that we know what it takes in income and assets to impoverish your clients, how do you as a financial planner get your client to those levels?

Convert Countable Assets into Exempt Assets

Have your client pay off the mortgage of his home, for example. Some states are more generous than others with this tactic. In Indiana, all income producing property is exempt. Therefore, you could pour a million dollars into an apartment building and still qualify.

Give Away Assets to Children or Other Trusted Family Members

This is the most common practice with my clients because it is simple. Most of the clients who do this type of Medicaid planning do no not have an estate tax problem. They simply give the assets to the children, file a gift tax return, and use their lifetime exclusion.

Anytime a client is contemplating giving up control of assets, he must be counseled thoroughly. As a planner, you may have to make your own judgment as to the ability of the children to handle having large sums of money put in their names that they are supposed to leave alone until the parent dies. If there are several children, then a decision has to be made to split or not split the assets among the children. If they are all given to one responsible child, what assurance is there that the chosen child will share as intended when the parent dies?

Tax Consequences.   When making gifts of this nature, tax consequences must be considered. Assets given away today will not receive the stepped-up basis they would receive if inherited. Also, the assets may generate taxable income to a child who may resent having to pay taxes on income he did not actually receive because he is keeping it for his parent. What about the fair share of taxes that must be paid by his siblings?

Most clients who seek my counseling in this area have approximately $200,000 in liquid assets, a home that is paid for, and $20,000 in annual income. Even though it sounds like I am advising against this method, clients consistently opt for giving away the assets to trusted children. I usually recommend putting the assets into one child's name for simplicity and expense purposes. I generally use a tax-exempt fund to avoid tax consequences. It works very well as long as the client is fully informed.

What About the Home?   Since the home is an exempt asset, most professionals advise against transferring it to others. In Texas, the nursing home patient must state an intent to return to the home to allow the exemption. It is usually granted. However, I recommend transferring the home to children also. If the home is rented, the income could cause disqualification for Medicaid in some states. If it is sold, the proceeds are no longer exempt assets and could disqualify your client. A house must usually be rented or sold to avoid deterioration.

What About a Spouse who is not in Need of Long-Term Care?   This used to be a major problem. Many couples were forced to divorce in order to avoid impoverishing the one *outside* the long-term care facility so that the one *inside* could qualify for Medicaid. A part of the Catastrophic Health Insurance Act did survive that protects healthy spouses from complete impoverishment. The house can be kept, of course, along with approximately $65,000 in other nonexempt assets by a healthy spouse and still have the other spouse qualify for Medicaid. The healthy spouse can also keep all of her/his separate income.

Medicaid Trusts

The idea behind a *Medicaid trust* is to give away your money so that you can keep it. Clients do give up control of their money because the trust has to be irrevocable. The trust can provide some income to the client, but no access to the principal. Be careful that the income does not disqualify your client for Medicaid in your state. I seldom use these trusts in Texas because of that and because of the cost of set up and administration. These trusts work best for clients with assets ranging from $50,000 to around $600,000. They usually have no children to whom assets may be transferred. They also may work for clients who want the income from the trust when they leave the nursing home.

Waiting Period

The waiting period is usually 30 months after transfer of the assets before the client will qualify for Medicaid. This waiting period can be used in conjunction with a LTC policy by electing coverage for only 36 months. When the client enters the nursing home, transfer the assets as described above. When the LTC coverage runs out, the client should qualify for Medicaid. This allows your client to use a combination of long-term care and Medicaid.

Electing to qualify for Medicaid may carry some disadvantages not mentioned above. If a nursing home has both private and Medicaid beds, the Medicaid patient may be the last in line to be admitted. Also, there is some reason to believe that the service for a Medicaid patient is inferior to the private patient. Common sense tells you that would be the case.

Long-Term Care Insurance

Watch for Gatekeepers.   Policies of several years ago formerly had provisions that kept your client from collecting benefits. The most common example was the one that required a three-day hospital stay prior to entering the nursing home. These are not as common today, but still exist in a few policies.

Use Common Sense.   Will the policy pay the full cost of needed care in the local facility?

Consider Inflation Protection.   Inflation protection is usually more important if your clients are younger. Often, as the client is older, choosing a larger daily benefit is cheaper than inflation protection. Just compare the two.

Average Costs.   Costs vary, of course, with age and benefits selected. For a person in the 60 to 65 age group, a policy can be expected to cost from $1,000 to $2,000 per year. At 75 the costs go up to $3,000 to $5,000.

Watch for Home Health Care Riders.   Gatekeepers are still prevalent here. Be sure that your client will be covered if she just needs some assistance at home. Clients want this coverage more than they want nursing home coverage, because most never intend to enter a nursing home.

Selecting Daily Benefits.   Home health care benefits are usually expressed as a percentage of the nursing home care benefits. Be sure to consider what Social Security income the client has when electing coverage. The Social Security income will be used to offset part of the cost of the nursing home. Therefore, the benefits per day would not have to be as high as the actual cost of the nursing home.

Using Other Types of Insurance

Some universal life policies allow a living benefit to be paid to help cover nursing home costs. Second-to-die policies can be purchased on a couple when one may not qualify for long-term care coverage, but will qualify for life coverage in a second to die. This usually requires children affluent enough to cover the costs, with the promise of repayment from the policy. Annuities are often used to generate income to pay for nursing home costs. The income generated can be a regular amount guaranteed for a lifetime.

OTHER SPECIALIZED SERVICES

Nursing Home Inspection

Of course, before anyone places a family member in a nursing home, they want to be sure it will meet the family member's needs. Here are a few tips:

• Walk in unannounced, at least one time.

- Do not let a guided tour be your only impression.
- Visit the patient's rooms as well as the lobby and community areas.
- Observe the staff—Are they friendly to patients? To each other? To management?
- Observe the residents—Are they engaged in any kind of meaningful activity? Do they look clean and cared for?
- Ask around the community—Find families of other patients and ask about their experiences.
- Ask to see the home's inspection reports.
- Watch for call lights that stay on for long periods at nursing stations.

For further education on this subject, contact your attorney network or the network of your broker–dealer. Also check with the National Academy of Elder Law Attorneys in Tucson, Arizona. They have an experience directory that is available to financial planners by calling 602-881-4005. You can also work with your insurance department to contact insurance companies that have much information on the subject. Also contact the Department of Human Services or Welfare Department in your local community for information on Medicaid qualification in your state. The National Association of Insurance Commissioners also has a model long-term care policy.

DEALING WITH INCAPACITY

Since this subject was covered at length in the estate planning chapter, we will cover only summary points here.

As part of planning for either estate or long-term care, the problem of incapacity should be addressed in financial plans. In addition to the long-term care planning issues mentioned previously, your client should consider the following measures to prevent problems in the event of incapacity.

Living Wills/Durable Powers of Attorney for Health Care

Referred to more appropriately as Directives to Physicians in Texas, Living Wills are often called ''Death with Dignity'' documents. They leave instructions to physicians and hospitals as to your client's wishes to be kept alive or not by life-sustaining equipment. They express your client's wishes to have artificial life-support systems discontinued under certain circumstances. Many attorneys prefer the Durable Power of Attorney for Health Care because it gives a person the specific authority to make such decisions. Also, the living will usually only refers to life-support systems, while a durable power of attorney for health care may allow cessation of nutrition and hydration.

Durable Power of Attorney

This authorizes an agent to act on behalf of the client in business transactions. This authority extends into the period when the client is incapacitated.

Living Trusts

These are often used to protect against incapacity, in addition to other estate planning purposes including avoiding probate, etc. The living trust names a successor trustee to act on behalf of the client when incapacitated. If the living trust is funded with the client's assets, the successor trustee has full authority to manage the assets on the client's behalf without going through laborious court proceedings. If the trust is unfunded, then there should be a durable power of attorney allowing the agent to transfer assets into the trust when the client is incapacitated.

MARKETING ELDERLY FINANCIAL PLANNING

Remember the rule, "If you help enough people, money will take care of itself." Elderly planning expertise will bring you lots of referrals from satisfied clients. This market allows you to distinguish yourself from your competition. Adding this element to your financial planning practice changes you from someone who sells investments to someone who cares about his clients.

1. *Conduct seminars on the subject.* We have found long-term care planning to be our most popular topic because most registered representatives are unable to speak on the subject.

2. *Make speeches on the long-term care crisis to service clubs.* Look at the list of books in the curriculum guide for RePP, read one of the books, and make it a topic for a speech.

3. *Include long-term care and elder care in as many financial plans as possible.*

4. *Identify assets.* Just like estate planning, elderly planning helps to identify and locate your client's assets that may need repositioning.

5. *Sell the insurance; invest the assets.* Sell long-term care if that option is the best one for the client. If not, one of the other insurance products could be appropriate. If assets are transferred to the child, an investment in tax-exempt securities might be necessary.

PART IV

Products—The Keys to Successful Financial Plans

21

The Perfect Product

The mind is the limit. As long as the mind can envision the fact that you can do something, you can do it—as long as you really believe 100 percent.

Arnold Schwarzenegger

If you have already read the previous three parts of this book, then you know that I have said repeatedly that talking too much about products to your clients is probably a mistake. You need to talk about solutions to problems and relief from pain. That admonition still stands, but a discussion of product appears as the last part of the book for a reason. Most CPAs see implementation of financial plans as only one thing—product. They want to cut directly to the chase saying. "What products am I going to be pushing at my clients?" But you want to get away from that mentality. Product is certainly an integral and very important part of the process, but not the most important and certainly not the one to get hung up on. Many CPAs develop inertia looking for the perfect product. They look for a product that:

1. Has the highest current yield.
2. Has the highest total return, as stated in the latest edition of *Money* or *Fortune*, for the last 30 days, six months, one year, three years, five years, 10 years, and so on.
3. Has no commission charge but is accompanied by a personal advisor who can be called for advice and consolation at any time.
4. Always listed in the latest "hot list" by *Money* as one of the 10 best places to put $10,000 today—funds that never go down, funds that always go up, all weather funds, funds for all age groups, etc.
5. Never shows up in a newsletter promotional mailing on a cold list of products to get out of (possibly because they were on one of the hot lists above).
6. Is totally liquid.
7. Is tax free or at least tax deferred.
8. Offers accounts to be opened for $25 or less.
9. Allows withdrawals to be made at any time in any amount.
10. Offers investments that can be exchanged for any other investment without tax consequences.

Many CPAs are licensed for over a year without making a single investment for their clients. They actually feel compelled to find the best investment products before making any recommendations to their clients. That is another way of saying they were looking for the perfect product. It is also another form of procrastinating. If they continue that search, it will be a lifetime effort. Their clients will not make investments, at least through the CPA, or they will make them through someone who knows that searching for the perfect investment is foolish. Do not use product search as an excuse for inaction. Your clients need your help.

Do you have to learn about products? Of course you do. Just do not approach products from a fear perspective. We CPAs must overcome our natural inclination to be negative about virtually all products. Most are good. Almost all were designed to fill a perceived need. *Many* products are available to fit almost any need your client may have. Products are tools and most are excellent tools that allow your clients to meet their financial dreams.

Think of the financial planning process as a puzzle. If you find out what your client needs (his goals), what he has, and where he is today, prepare projections as to steps he needs to take to reach his destination. Then you will have a puzzle with only a few pieces missing. Those missing pieces will be the products. The outline of their shapes should be shown in the puzzle. All you have to do is sift through the pieces of products to find the right shape.

What about product sponsors—the mutual fund companies with wholesalers and the insurance companies? They can be your most valuable resource for information, sales assistance, literature, seminars, etc. Use them, but do not abuse them. They will go the extra mile in assisting you to meet your client needs. In return, they expect you to consider their products when implementing your clients' plans.

WHICH PRODUCTS TO USE

I have probably not convinced you that selecting products is fairly easy. I was not easily convinced. With over 10,000 selections to choose from, how can it be easy?

Narrow the Field

Focus on No More than Three Mutual Fund Families.   With the help of the product sponsors, you can become very familiar with three fund families. Within those three, you can probably fill 80 to 90 percent of the product needs of your clients.

This was extremely difficult for me. I enjoy relationships with wholesalers and want to send business to all of them. I thought that I was doing my clients a disservice by not offering every product in the market. I especially did not want to be ''identified'' or ''branded'' by one product. Three fund families will not brand you. At least one or two of the fund families should be fairly well known if you are just starting in the business. All three should probably be known for long-term steady performance. They do not have to be on all the latest ''hot'' lists, but they should have good solid track records.

Pick One or Two Variable Annuity Products.   This should be more than adequate for your needs. Try to pick one that works with one of the three fund families with which you are familiar. Be sure that the insurance company is a strong one. Stability is probably more important than performance in today's market.

Select One Fixed Annuity.   Hopefully, your variable annuity sponsors will also have a fixed annuity. Do not select one based on the highest rate. If you sell by yield, you will die by yield. Select one based on product features and stability of the company.

Select One or Two Insurance Companies for Your Traditional Life Products.   Try to limit it to one. However, your selection may not have a second to die or has a poor term product that may cause you to have to go to a second or third insurance company.

Select No More Than Two Companies for Disability.   One may be for blue-collar workers while a second may be for professionals, for example.

Select One Carrier for Long-Term Care.   We have now narrowed the list of companies you are dealing with to no more than 12. Hopefully, no more than 10. You should still have close to a hundred products from which to choose. That is enough to meet all your client's needs except for individual securities. For those, use the bond department or trading department of your broker–dealer or seek assistance from your RePP center.

PRESENTING PRODUCTS

Use a Plan/Have Only Dependable Horses in Your Stable

If your plan is in place, products will fit in like the missing pieces to a puzzle. You will not have to worry too much about them. If you have done any kind of a reasonable job in selecting your "stable" of products, then you do not have any really bad ones in it. Why take the chance of having a "race horse" in your stable that is also very volatile. Just pick good horses that have good temperaments. They will not bite your clients or kick you. If that is all you have to choose from, you can not make a very large mistake.

If you have used TOPS and have prepared a plan, presenting product should be after the sale is made. If the client is still product sensitive, then use these pointers.

Know the Holdings Inside the Product

If your product has some household names included in it, be sure to open up the prospectus and the annual report and show them to your client. You do not have to memorize every holding, because they change all the time. However, if you open the prospectus and let the client see some products that he can identify with, your sale will be easier.

Tell Stories

Tell success stories of clients who have held this product before. Performance stories are not as effective as stories of individuals like your client who have had positive experiences with the product. For example, you may want to tell about an elderly couple who found that the husband had diabetes and their drug bill was going to go up dramatically. They were concerned about paying for the additional expenses on their current income level. You were able to show them how they could increase their income from this product by a phone call from your office.

You do not have any stories yet? Borrow one or two from the product sponsor. They usually have some typical client situations spelled out in brochures. Do not lie or mislead the client, of course, but you can take combinations of stories that will show the client how certain features of the product can be used in real-life situations.

Stick to the Basics of Investing

When your client becomes overly concerned with product even though you know that you have shown him good quality from your stable because there is nothing but quality in it, return him to the basics of investing. Sir John Templeton stated his basics as follows:

1. Invest for maximum total real return. This is return after taxes and inflation.
2. Invest—Do not trade or speculate.
3. Remain flexible and open-minded about types of investments. There are times to buy stocks, bonds, sit on cash, etc.
4. Buy low—That may be obvious, but most clients will fight tooth and nail to buy high. They want to buy what everyone else likes today. The products on the "hot" lists. Prices are low when demand is low, not when it is high.
5. When buying stocks, search for bargains among quality stocks. If your client is buying a mutual fund, point out what the buying philosophy is of managers of the fund.
6. Buy value, not market trends or the economic outlook.
7. Diversify.
8. Do your homework or hire wise experts to help you.
9. Monitor your investments. Another good service that you will provide for your client.
10. Do not panic. Markets have always and will always change.
11. Learn from mistakes. The only way to avoid mistakes is not to invest—which is the biggest mistake of all. Forgive past errors. If your client has lost his shirt in an investment before, work with him to get past it and not let it freeze him.
12. Begin with a prayer. You can think more clearly and make fewer mistakes.
13. Outperforming the market is a difficult task. In order to do this, you must make *better* decisions than the professionals who manage the big institutions. Unmanaged market indexes are fully invested, while your mutual fund must sit on some cash and pay expenses that the big market does not have.
14. Do not think you have all the answers. Success is a process of continually seeking answers to new questions.

15. There is no free lunch.
16. Do not be fearful or negative too often. For 100 years, optimists have carried the day in U.S. stocks.

Own the Product Yourself

Put your money where your mouth is. You will have trouble convincing your clients to invest if you do not believe it yourself. One of the most powerful presentations of product is to pull out a statement from the product showing you as the owner.

CONCLUSION

Now that we have discussed the need for products, how to choose them, and how to present them, let us take a look at a few outstanding products such as mutual funds, tax-exempt bonds, taxable income instruments, equities, annuities, and insurance products.

22

Mutual Funds

What the mind of man can conceive and believe, the mind of man can achieve.

Napoleon Hill

Let us start with the usual word of caution. This chapter is not intended to be the know-all and end-all of everything you always wanted to know about mutual funds. It is intended to be a very basic explanation—something you can share with a client or at least refer to in explaining mutual funds to your clients.

Do clients know what mutual funds are? Ten years ago, most did not. Today, I think that a slim majority will know of the basic concept of pooling the money of individual investors to increase buying power and the range of investment products available to them. Most do not know much more than that. It is up to us to educate them further.

WHAT ARE MUTUAL FUNDS?

A *mutual fund* is an investment company that pools the shareholders' money and then invests it. The investments are made in accordance with predetermined objectives outlined in the prospectus. The money can be invested in stocks, bonds, money market instruments, or a combination of these investments also called *securities*. Individuals purchasing shares of a mutual fund, in effect, participate in a whole portfolio of securities. Mutual fund share prices are determined at the end of each business day by adding up the value of all the securities in the fund's portfolio after expenses, and dividing the sum by the total number of shares outstanding.

ARE THE FUNDS OPEN OR CLOSED?

Mutual funds are referred to as *open-ended* because they issue a limited number of shares and will repurchase them upon request. *Closed-end* funds issue limited shares and are usually sold on a stock exchange.

MUTUAL FUNDS CAN BE FRONT, BACK, LOW, NO LOADS, OR 12-b-1

Front Load Funds

This type of mutual fund charges an up-front sales fee that ranges from 1 to 8.5 percent (although the 8.5 percent is fast becoming extinct).

Back Load Funds

Back load funds deduct fees from your investment when you cash in your shares. These usually range from 1 to 5 percent depending on how long you have held your shares. They usually disappear after five or six years.

Low Load Funds

These funds charge an up-front sales charge but it is less than normal and usually do not use brokers.

No Load Funds

Sometimes referred to as ''no service'' or ''self service'' funds by the brokerage industry, these funds charge no sales commissions. Funds that pay commissions primarily market and distribute their funds through registered representatives in the brokerage industry. No load funds have to distribute their products through advertising and other channels of distribution. These distribution costs are included in the expenses of the fund and referred to as administrative costs, management costs, or part of the ''expense ratio''. No load funds do have a place in the market and occupy a large share of it. No loads are excellent investment vehicles for individuals who have the knowledge, experience, inclination, and time to select and balance their own portfolios, monitor their investments' performance, and coordinate with their risk tolerance and stated financial goals.

12-b-1 Funds

This type of mutual fund has no initial start-up sales charges. Continuing fees are paid to the fund company by the investor in order to pay our commissions. With most 12-b-1s, there is also a back end surrender charge in case the customer wants to get out before the ongoing charges have been sufficient to recover the cost of the commission. These types of funds have received a lot of negative press because of the ''hidden'' nature of the charges. Whether or not the funds deserve this press is subject to interpretation. I think they are probably just marketed incorrectly. Some funds do have excessive ongoing charges. Comparing them to a front end charge is difficult because the comparison depends on the length of time held and the rate of the fund. However, a few rules of thumb might help.

1. The longer the client stays in the fund, the better the front end fund looks.

2. Anything over 1 percent ongoing charge is probably a little high if the client is going to stay longer than five years.
3. Fund charges of 1 percent or less are fairly competitive with front end loads from up to 10 years.
4. At 20 years or longer, the client is better off with a front end.

A–B–C–D SHARES

In a constant attempt to meet market demands, mutual fund companies are continuing to change the way that shares may be priced in terms of commission. Most of the changes are improvements. In the early days of mutual funds, some funds had to be marketed at loads up to 50 percent. We are still recovering from those early days of overpricing. Today, many mutual fund companies are offering us an alternative for pricing to meet our clients' comfort levels. In other words, we can work with our clients to determine the best way to purchase the shares. In actual practice, this may mean that brokers and planners will price the shares based on what they think will be best received by the client. The press will attack again saying that clients are being misled. I usually try not to make commissions a point of argument with my client. They either need my help or they do not. If they do, they are going to pay for it. I refuse to be pulled into arguments about loads versus no load. However, I do like having the ability to select the type of pricing best suited to my client's tendency to stay long term, risk profile, sales resistance, etc. The key questions are always the same: "Will the client be better off with this investment or not?" and "What counts is how much money the client has left after all fees, not how much he paid in fees."

A-Shares.   These carry a standard front end load.

B-Shares.   These have a sliding contingent deferred sales charge (i.e., they are back end loaded).

C-Shares.   The definition varies according to the mutual fund company you are dealing with, but these usually have a low or no front load, a low or no deferred load if sold before a specified period of time, and pay a trail commission of 1 percent or so to the representative. Some are offered only to institutional accounts. In this case, there is usually not a trail commission paid to the representative, but a small 1 percent fee up front.

D-Shares.   These shares pay an annual fee of 1 percent to representatives, with no front or back load to the client.

I like the concept of D-shares. 100 percent of the client's money will go to work instantly. You will not get as much money up front, but you will get paid to manage the money and to keep it invested. Most of the different types of shares are traced separately by mutual fund companies, but will convert to regular shares after a certain period of time, usually after all contingent deferred sales charges go away.

NAV OR POP

NAV

This acronym stands for *net asset value*. It describes the true value of each share in a mutual fund, determined by adding up the value of all the securities in the fund after expenses, and dividing by the number of shares outstanding.

POP

POP stands for *public offering price*. This price includes the commission. So why do we have NAV and POP? Having both is similar to marketing any type of security. The commission does not jump out and grab the customer by the throat if it is included in the POP. The customer will notice a drop in share price on his next statement when he purchases a load fund at POP. That is preferable to showing shares purchased at NAV, then showing the commission as a separate line item on the statement and deducting it from the value in the account.

With all of these types of share pricing, it is obvious that the press has created a lot of make-believe villains and monsters for the consuming public's awareness. In its desire to create news (I can not really agree that it is a desire to protect the public), the press has made many people wary of seeking the advice they need or making any investment move at all. The securities industry and its salesmen must also take on a large share of the blame for being too product and commission oriented. As a CPA financial planner, you need to personally deal with the issue of getting paid and how you are going to get paid. For assistance on handling client objections, refer to Part 2.

TYPES OF MUTUAL FUNDS

This is not intended to be an academic presentation of all the features, benefits, risks, etc., involved in selecting mutual fund types. It is intended to be a general guide to types.

Equity-Oriented Mutual Funds

Aggressive Growth Funds.   These funds are invested in companies that may have substantial risk in order to have the potential for higher returns. They are often used synonymously with small cap or emerging growth funds which invest in small or startup companies with excellent potential for growth.

Specialized or Sector Funds.   These funds restrict their holdings to the securities of companies in a particular industry, service, or region.

Long-Term Growth Funds.   These invest in companies that have chance for capital appreciation over a long period of time. The dividend income will be nominal. They are often used synonymously with *big cap funds*.

Equity Income Funds.   These invest in stocks that pay dividends so that the investor has a chance for capital appreciation as well as income. They are also called *growth and income funds*.

Balanced Funds

Balanced funds are designed for investors seeking total return from a combination of dividends and capital appreciation. They invest in common stocks that pay dividends, preferred stocks, utility stocks, convertible bonds, and cash equivalents.

Corporate Bond Funds

Corporate bond funds invest in either high or low quality bonds. Some corporate bond funds invest in both, some in only high quality. Funds that invest in low quality usually do so in order to get the yield and are called *high yield funds*.

Government Securities Funds

Government securities funds invest in direct obligations of the U.S. government such as T-Bills, T-Notes, T-Bonds, and pass-through certificates of the Government National Mortgage Association (GNMA). It may also invest in securities backed by an agency of the U.S. government such as the Federal Home Loan Corp. (FHLMC), Fannie Mae (FNMA), and Student Loan Marketing Association (SLMA).

Municipal Bond Funds

These invest in bonds issued by a state, city, or local government. Interest income earned on these investments is exempt from federal taxation. Most other types of funds are some variation of the categories listed here.

MUTUAL FUND ADVANTAGES

Diversification

A mutual fund invests in more securities than most individuals can afford to own. By purchasing shares in a mutual fund, you are spreading your risk over a number of investments rather than just one. This keeps your client from "putting all his eggs in one basket."

Affordability

Most mutual funds have low investment minimums, making them accessible to nearly everyone.

Professional Management

Instead of assuming the time-consuming chore of choosing individual companies whose stocks or bonds are "good investments" for your client's portfolio, fund managers do this for you. Managers handle the investments in accordance with guidelines set out in the fund's prospectus. These professionals have up to the minute information on trends in the financial markets as well as in-depth data on potential investments.

Convenience

This is my favorite reason for recommending mutual funds. Clients invariably have needs that were different than they had when they originally invested. They may need to slightly change monthly income, withdraw a small amount of principal, add a few dollars to their account, and so forth. I like to be able to accommodate their needs.

Mutual funds provide monthly, quarterly, and annual reports. Many now provide your clients with their tax basis in the shares purchased, total returns, dividends paid, transactions made, and the like.

Flexibility

Keep it in the Family.   Most mutual funds are part of a family, allowing your client to transfer portions of his investment into any of the other funds without incurring another commission charge.

Automatics.   You can automatically reinvest dividends, withdraw dividends or portions of principal, take portions of your distributions and have it sent to another mutual fund or other source, and you can automatically do dollar cost averaging from one fund in the family to another one.

Getting Your Money Out

Many funds have checkwriting privileges; most have wire redemption privileges, direct redemption by mail, or redemption by phone.

Putting Money In

You can assist your client with direct purchases by mail or wire. Additional investments can usually be made by the client using ''deposits slips'' provided by the mutual fund company.

Break-Points.   Commissions decrease when investments exceed certain break-points which usually start with $25,000.

Letters of Intent.   If a client signs a LOI (usually part of the application) committing to purchase a specified amount within a specified time period (usually one year), the client can qualify for immediate discount.

Rights of Accumulation.   A client may qualify for the reduced sales charges by referencing existing accounts within the fund family. The current purchase is linked with prior purchases to qualify for the breakpoint discounts.

Buying at NAV

Most mutual funds allow purchases at NAV (without sales charges) if the amount purchased is $1 million or more. Also, most allow registered representatives to invest at NAV.

23

Tax Exempts

Order—Let all your things have their places; let each part
of your business have its time.

Benjamin Franklin

One of the factors almost always listed in any client's definition of the perfect
investment is tax benefit. Clients love beating the IRS. Municipals allow them
to do that most of the time. I say most of the time because there are certain
municipals that are subject to the AMT (alternative minimum tax) and a rare
few are even taxable.

HOW TO BUY TAX EXEMPTS

Individual Bonds

Individual bonds may be purchased for your clients by calling your broker's
bond department and advising them of your client's needs and risk tolerance.
The broker will provide you with a list of current offerings that come closest
to your targeted objectives. You generally need to act quickly, because bonds
do not usually last long after being put on the market.

Advantages:

1. Known maturity date.
2. Known principal and interest payment dates.
3. Only one issuer to investigate.
4. Usually readily marketable.
5. Tax basis easily tracked.
6. Easily compared to CDs.

Disadvantages:

1. Cannot add to your investment or partially liquidate easily.
2. Can have some principal "trickling" back to the client during the holding
   period. Client may not realize that his principal is being returned.

3. Risk is 100 percent on one issuer.

4. Events relating to the bond may not reach you as advisor until too late to take needed action (call announcements, downgrading of rating, etc.).

5. Cannot adjust income to meet client's changing needs.

Unit Investment Trusts

Unit investment trusts (UITs) are like a closed box of bonds with nice ribbon around it. Contrast this with mutual funds which are in an open box where bonds are bought and sold regularly. These UITs are "packages" of several bonds that are bought by an investment management company which markets "units" of the trust (usually in denominations of $1,000 to $5,000).

Advantages:

1. Fixed payments of principal and interest.

2. Call provisions available from packaging company.

3. Information on status of municipalities available.

4. Known maturity dates, although there may be several.

5. Most allow automatic reinvestment of principal or interest or both into a mutual fund family.

6. Risk is spread over several issues.

Disadvantages:

1. May involve yield to maturity, yield to call, and estimates of total return based on unknown factors.

2. Not as easy to liquidate as a mutual fund.

3. May have to explain different initial payments to the client because of accrued interest in the purchase price, buying between payment dates, etc.

4. Principal "trickles" in and may not be understood by client and he may fail to reinvest.

5. Cannot adjust income to meet client's changing needs.

6. Tracking tax basis can be difficult if principal distributions are erratic.

Mutual Funds

Advantages:

1. Risk is spread over many issuers.

2. Allows flexibility in investing, income distribution, and withdrawals. Can adjust to meet client's changing needs. Allows for minimal investments and withdrawals, changes in income distributions, etc.

3. Tax basis may be provided by mutual fund company.

4. Professional management.

5. Affordability.

Disadvantages:

1. No known maturity date (client cannot say for sure when he is going to get his money back) because there are so many issues in the fund and they may be actively traded.
2. Client may not identify with a mutual fund share as readily as he does with a bond certificate.
3. Client may pay taxes on gains taken in the fund and distributed to him.
4. Funds look less like a CD to a client who understands only CDs.

MUNIS AND TAXES

One of the most overlooked and best sales tools around is learning how to use taxable equivalent yield and its cousin *after-tax net*. Most financial advisors use taxable equivalent yield to wow their clients and the client's may not have the foggiest notion of what they are talking about. They often buy only because the investment is tax free. In today's environment, taxable equivalent yield is not as meaningful as it usually is because tax-exempt yields are already as much or more than taxable yields on CDs. It does not take a "rocket scientist" client to figure out that this may be a good deal. However, this situation, like all others, is temporary and we must learn how to use all the tools at our disposal while explaining that munis are not without risk.

Taxable Equivalent Yield

It is what you keep that counts, correct? Show your clients the current tax-exempt yield on bonds. Convert that rate to a taxable equivalent rate as follows:

Tax-exempt rate   5%
Tax rate   28%
Taxable equivalent yield
    1.00 less tex rate .28 = .72
    5% divided by .72 = 6.944%
    Test your work as follows:
      6.944% less 28% = 5.00%

Explain to your client that he would have to have a 6.944 percent CD to keep as much money as he will with a 5 percent tax exempt. Then convert the illustration into at least a $100,000 CD, even if you are talking about $10,000. The importance of the difference will be more apparent to the client using $100,000 than using $10,000.

After-Tax Net

Just as effective as the taxable equivalent yield and easier to quickly comprehend by most clients is the after-tax net. Calculate by subtracting taxes from the current CD rate.

CD or equivalent investment rate   5%
Tax rate   31%
Net rate on CD   3.45%

Figure 23-1   It's What You Keep That Counts!

	Taxable Investment	Tax-Exempt Investment	
Amount	$100,000	$100,000	
Yield	6%	5%	
Income annually	$6,000	$5,000	
Taxes at 31%	(1,860)	(0)	
Net	$4,140	$5,000	
Value in 10 Years*	$150,029	$162,889	
Difference			$12,860

*Assumes no fluctuation in principal and all income reinvested.

Clients can readily identify that they are only keeping 3.45 percent. Subtract inflation of 3 percent from 3.45 percent and the client is getting a *real rate of return* of .45 percent. If the client is still not convinced, show him the illustration in Figure 23-1. Do not use a preprinted table to show your client these numbers! Calculate them right in front of him on a greaseboard or a yellow pad. In today's economy, these numbers will be even more dramatic because tax-exempt yields often exceed taxable yields on CDs.

The three methods of calculating of munis created by the Tax Reform Act of 1986 include:

1. *The true tax exempt.* Less than 10 percent of the proceeds are for private use and security and less than 5 percent used for loans to nongovernmental people, i.e., the proceeds are predominantly used for public purposes or they are in a 501(c)(3) qualified security.
2. *Private activity.* Exempt facility such as multifamily housing, airports, wharves, mass transit, sewage, solid waste, electricity, gas, water, hydro, heating and cooling, hazardous waste. Other exemption qualifications include small issue industrial development bonds, student loans, mortgage revenue, and redevelopment. These will be tax exempt but will be considered preference items for the AMT.
3. If none of the exemptions are met, then the bond is considered for private purposes and will be taxable.

In addition to these qualifications, a distinction must be made between those whose carrying costs can be deducted by banks and thrifts (at an 80 percent rate) and those whose carrying costs cannot be deducted. The determining factor is whether or not the issuer expects to issue less than $10 million in tax-exempt debt during the current calendar year. If the issuer is issuing more than $10 million in a year and bank carrying costs are 80 percent deductible, then they are not tax exempt. If the bank carrying costs are not deductible, then tax exempt status still applies.

Does the above sound complicated? This information is relatively easy to determine when investing in munis by either of the three methods. Do not decide to avoid bonds subject to AMT altogether. They usually pay a quarter to a half percentage point more than the other bonds, and less than 1/20th of 1 percent of the population pay the AMT.

TAX EXEMPTS VERSUS NONDEDUCTIBLE IRAs

When doing calculations comparing tax-free investments with tax-deferred investments (such as IRAs and annuities), add some sizzle for clients who have always primarily invested in CDs. Many will argue about the need to "pay as they go." Since you are going to have to pay taxes on the money sometime, why put it off? Again, do not use a table to show the client; make a customized presentation for the client using your greaseboard and your financial calculator.

Let us assume our client is now 39 and plans to take his IRA at 59. Set up something like Figure 23.2 for illustration purposes.

Now, most clients will not remove their IRAs all at once; interest rates can change. This type of illustration done before the client's eyes (based on his age) will contribute a lot to his education and can assist him in making an educated decision about whether he wants to do a nondeductible IRA.

THE SAFETY OF TAX EXEMPTS

The default rate on munis is about .3 percent over the last 50 years. However, that does not mean that there is not a risk. If your client's bond happens to fall in that .3 percent, then the pain is just as great.

Get Insurance or Not?

I usually do not buy insured bonds if I am buying through a UIT or mutual fund. However, I do have several clients who like the insurance. It comes with a cost ranging around 10 to 50 basis points, but if it makes your client comfortable, I recommend it. Also, the muni market is very fragmented now and rating services may not be current for an issuer. Brokerage houses have very limited inventories for munis. When supply dries up, there is usually a lot of demand for insured issues.

Figure 23.2   Nondeductible IRAs versus Tax Exemptions

	Nondeductible IRA	Tax Exempt	
Annual investment	$2,000	$2,000	
Rate of return	6%	5%	
Annual tax	none	none	
Value in 20 years	$77,985	$69,438	
Tax rate	33%	33%	
Tax if withdrawn	$25,735	$0	
Net remaining	$52,250	$69,438	
Difference			$17,188

Rating Services

A typical rating services is Moody's. Another is Standard and Poor's. Moody's has a little different system than S&P, but both are considered excellent. A typical Moody's rating looks like this:

Description of Rating	Grade
Loans are of the best quality, enjoying strong protection from established cash flows of funds for their servicing or from established and broad based access to the market or refinancing, or both.	MIG 1
Loans are of high quality, with margins of protection ample, although not as large as in the top-rated group.	MIG 2
Loans are of favorable quality, with all security elements accounted for but lacking the undeniable strength of the preceding grades. Market access for refinancing, in particular, is likely to be less established.	MIG 3
Loans are of adequate quality, carrying specific risk but having protection commonly regarded as required as an investment security and not distinctly or predominantly speculative.	MIG 4

Nonrated bonds can be good buys, though. Many fairly strong issuers may just not want to pay for a rating. However, unless you know something about the nonrated issuer, it is probably best to keep your risk-averse clients away from those issues. If bought, they should probably be part of a portfolio in a mutual fund that also holds some rated bonds.

How about interest-rate risk? Long-term munis fluctuate with changes in interest rates in similar fashion to other bonds.

24

Taxable Income Instruments, Zero Coupon Bonds, and CMOs

What this power is I cannot say, all I know is that it exists and it becomes available only when a man is in that state of mind in which he knows exactly what he wants and is fully determined not to quit until he finds it.

Alexander Graham Bell

CORPORATE BONDS

Corporate bonds are issued by corporations as a way for them to borrow money from investors, rather than banks. They are sold in denominations of $1,000 each. They usually pay a fixed amount of interest and have a fixed maturity date. Bondholders are creditors whose claims must be satisfied before stockholders upon liquidation of the company.

The major types of corporate bonds are:

1. *Mortgage bonds*—secured by real estate.
2. *Equipment trust certificates*—secured by specific equipment.
3. *Debentures*—unsecured, supported by the creditworthiness of the issuing corporation.

They can be purchased individually (usually in units of at least $10,000), as part of unit investment trusts, or in mutual funds. All three methods were discussed in the last chapter on tax exempts. Advantages and disadvantages are the same.

Moody's and Standard and Poor's rate all corporate bonds. They have their own letter codes for quality (e.g., AAA, BB, or C, with AAA being the highest for both). Check to see how senior the bond is to other bonds issued by the company. Is the bond callable? Be sure that your bond offers at least five years of payments before the issuing company can call it in.

GOVERNMENT BONDS

These are very similar to corporate bonds, except they are issued by the U.S. government. Treasury bonds are backed by the full faith and credit of the U.S.

government. They are also free from state income tax. Treasury bills, notes, and bonds are direct debts of the U.S. Treasury, but maturities are under five years and over five years, respectively.

The Government National Mortgage Association (GNMA or Ginnie Mae) is also part of the federal government. Its securities are backed by the full faith and credit of the U.S. Treasury. Essentially, you are investing in a pool of mortgages put together by the agency. The mortgages are mostly for single-family homeowners.

When mortgages are prepaid or refinanced, the payment is apportioned to the certificate holders on a pro rata basis and may cause your client's principal to ''trickle in'' and go unnoticed by the client.

Risk

How can there be risk in something backed by the full faith and credit of the good old U.S. of A? Putting aside the matter of the burgeoning national deficit, the risk involved is one of interest rates. Purchasing a long-term U.S. government security has the same interest-rate risk as purchasing a long-term municipal or a long-term corporate bond.

ZERO COUPON BONDS

What Are They?

Zeros became available in 1981 when U.S. Treasury bonds were split into their principal and interest components and sold separately. When you buy a zero, you actually own a bond's interest coupon, reissued as a new security, that will be paid out in a lump sum at maturity. That means that there are no semiannual interest payments as there are with other bonds. Maturity dates could be in a few months or as long as 30 years. There are zero versions of Treasury, government agency, corporate, and municipal bonds.

Who is Your Target Market for Zeros?

1. Investors saving for retirement.
2. Parents putting money away for their children's or grandchildren's college education.
3. Speculators betting on interest rate shifts.

Note this widely divergent market. Zero coupon Treasuries, for example, have appeal to the very conservative investor who wants the assurance that a certain, predetermined amount will be paid to him at a predetermined time. Because long-term zeros fluctuate at roughly twice the rate of a conventional bond, they also appeal to speculators betting on interest rate swings. The wider swing in value is due to interest not being paid out until maturity. It is reinvested at the same rate. With conventional bonds, interest is paid out semiannually and can be reinvested at the new rates. Investors, on the other hand, do not have reinvestment risk.

What is Their Appeal?

1. High, guaranteed return if held until maturity. Particularly with treasuries, investors are guaranteed to get their investment back if held until maturity.
2. A low price that is a fraction of the typical bond's $1,000 face value. Investors like owning a zero with a face of $100,000 and possibly only paying $20,000 for it. It makes them feel secure and richer than they are.

What Are the Risks?

The principal fluctuations are worse than other bonds, but that can also mean great opportunity for gains. For municipals or other corporate bonds, check the ratings and use the same precautions you would with any other bond investment. Be sure to ask whether the zero is callable and determine both the yield to maturity and the yield to call. Try to buy only noncallable for your conservative clients.

CMOs

Collateralized mortgage obligations (CMOs) were introduced in the early 1980s to help minimize the reinvestment and interest rate risks of standard mortgage-backed securities such as Ginnie Mae's. Collateralized mortgage obligations take the cash flows from a lot of mortgage-backed securities and splits them into a group of bonds with different maturates. Most of these bond classes receive interest from the mortgages—the collateral. But principal repayment go first to the class with the shortest maturity. When these bonds are retired, the principal gets channeled to the bonds with the next shortest maturity. The process continues until all the classes are paid off.

A dozen maturity classes, called *tranches* (French world for slice), is the norm today. Instead of one security with a stated final maturity of 15 to 30 years, there may be classes with final maturities estimated at three years, five years, ten years, and so on. But the prepayment risk is not entirely eliminated, so CMOs command higher yields relative to gilt-edged bonds, such as Treasury issues.

The appeal of CMOs was expanded by the introduction of the Real Estate Mortgage Investment Conduit (REMIC) security in 1987. REMICs offer preferred tax treatment of both issuers and investors. REMICs are structured into classes with different interest rates, average lives, prepayment sensitivities, and maturities. Investors can select the class that best fits their needs.

REMIC interests, both regular and residual, are treated as qualifying real estate assets for thrifts and real estate investment trusts (REITs) seeking to meet applicable tax qualification requirements. CMOs make monthly interest and principal payments. The interest is subject to both state and federal income taxes.

25

Equities and Annuities

Resolution—Resolve to perform what you ought; perform
without fail what you resolve.

Benjamin Franklin

EQUITIES

The case for equities is so overwhelming that I will not attempt to improve on
what has already been done. Some of the best marketing material for any profession is available from product sponsors, etc., stating the history of the market
since inception. Use it. Put up displays in your office.

In an equity investment, you take an ownership position in an asset or business. The return is based on the demand for that asset of business, so there are
various degrees of risk involved. Over time, they have generally proven to be
rewarding investments and excellent inflation hedges.

Dealing with Fear

Many registered representatives deal with fear by avoiding it. If clients are uneducated about the stock market, they will put them into ''guaranteed'' government funds. In the 1980s, many clients were disturbed to discover that government securities also fluctuate.

When you ask the average client what he thinks of when you mention risk
in investments, he will usually answer ''stocks.'' When I first began educating
myself and my clients about investing and presenting a few products, they would
always ask, this is not ''stocks'' is it? This is insured, is it not? I admit to a great
deal of frustration in those early days. However, I kept right on telling the story
to anyone who would listen. The change occurred when I started believing myself. That is when my presentations changed from wooden and tentative to enthusiastic and confident.

So how do you overcome the phobia about stocks to your less sophisticated
clients? Educate, educate, educate! Have patience when you have to repeat the
same story. The evidence in favor of equities is overwhelming if you can get
your clients to listen. Use the same principles outlined in previous portions of
this book of concentrating on the client's problems, pain, and solution. State
your investment philosophy. Save for the short term; invest for the long term.
Keep an emergency fund. Invest regularly. Diversify. Keep a long-term perspective.

What are the Long-Term Results?

From 1926 to 1992, these results were obtained from the following investment categories.

Common stocks	10.3%
Long-term government bonds	4.8%
U.S. Treasury bills	3.7%
Inflation	3.1%

Investing for Real Returns

Clients should be educated to invest for total return after taxes and inflation. It is vital to protect purchasing power. One of the biggest mistakes that people make is putting too much money into fixed income securities. If inflation averages 4 percent, it will reduce the buying power of $100,000 to $68,000 in just 10 years. Show your clients how prices have increased over time.

	1982	1992	Percentage Increase
Average home	$69,000	$122,000	77%
McDonald's milkshake	.80	1.39	74%
Paperback book	3.30	6.45	95%
Man's haircut	8.00	14.00	75%
1st class stamp	.20	.29	45%
Ice cream cone	.85	1.79	110%

When to Invest

Clients have been giving me excuses about timing from the beginning. They ask, "Do you think that now is a good time to invest?" It is revealing to look back over history at the so-called wrong times to invest. There have always been and will continue to be problems with investing. There are very few, if any, times when all signals are right for investing. During those times, most people will not invest because it is not popular to do so. The answer for clients when they ask when is a good time is "now" or "anytime." History has shown that despite short-term fluctuations that include high and low periods, the financial markets have provided investors with outstanding long-term growth. History also tells us to be in the market during upturns.

Use Dollar Cost Averaging

With dollar cost averaging, your client invests a fixed amount of money at regular intervals. If share prices go up, this fixed amount will purchase less shares. If prices go down, the fixed amount will buy more shares. Using this method, more shares will be accumulated at a lower average cost.

Timing Does Not Work

Teach your clients that trying to outguess the market is futile. Relax and let your investments work for you.

Be Contrarians

Buy when demand is low. Buy when all your friends and colleagues are selling.

Tax Benefits in Stocks

Stocks enjoy some tax benefits. Growth is not taxed until you sell the stock or investment in the mutual fund. Capital gains still enjoy a maximum rate that is lower than the maximum tax rate.

ANNUITIES

During the early years of my CPA practice, I was a big deal killer on annuity sales. Whenever clients asked my advice about an annuity purchase, I usually took the easy way out and advised against it. Why? Because annuities were not as good in those days as they are today. However, the primary reason was that I had read most of the information made available to me and it was largely negative. The primary complaint? You give up control when you annuitize. Today, annuities are a large part of my practice because they fit certain needs that clients have and they have many benefits. Also, they are probably one of the easiest products on the market to sell. Consider some of these advantages:

1. Tax-deferred earnings.
2. Very similar to a CD.
3. Interest and principal payments are guaranteed by the insurance company for the fixed portion of the contract (and by a state guaranty fund in some states up to certain limits).
4. Various options for taking your money out. Some products offer up to fifteen ways to take distributions.
5. Guaranteed lifetime income option available.
6. With variable annuities, you have a choice of a guaranteed investment or a variable investment with a chance for growth.
7. Guaranteed death benefit in almost all contracts for variable annuities. If the annuitant dies before payments have begun and his variable account is lower than his cost, his beneficiary is guaranteed to receive no less than 100 percent of the purchase payments.
8. No dollar limits as with IRAs.
9. No mandatory distribution at age 70-1/2 unless the annuity is in a qualified plan.
10. Enjoys protection from creditors.
11. Telephone switching in variable annuities available on most products.
12. Automatic dollar cost averaging available in some products if you want to increase potential return while minimizing risks.
13. No maturity date hassle and interest rate negotiation as with CDs.
14. Rates are competitive with CDs and usually exceed them by 25 to 150 basis points.
15. Privacy. Annuities do not even show up on your tax return.
16. Annuity earnings do not count in determining if Social Security benefits will be taxed.

17. Most annuities have 10 percent withdrawal privileges each year without any deferred sales charge.

18. Affordable. Most flexible premium annuities will accept $25. Other annuities will require from $1,000 to $10,000 as an initial investment.

19. Many investment options are available with variable annuities.

20. Withdrawals may be made without penalty for death, disability, hardship.

21. Statements for fixed annuities are in dollars, not shares, which is less confusing for some clients.

22. In a variable contract, the client can switch between accounts without tax consequences.

23. There is usually not a front-end commission.

24. Variable accounts are not assets of the insurance company and thus not subject to credit risk.

How do annuities compare with other investments? See Figures 25-1 through 25-3 for a comparison with IRAs, life insurance, and CDs.

Here are the disadvantages:

1. Subject to surrender charges that usually last from five to 10 years.

2. Early withdrawal penalties apply before age 59-1/2 unless there is a scheduled withdrawal based on life expectancy.

3. If the contract is annuitized, the owner loses control of his principal.

4. Contract charges for administration in variable contracts are usually higher than with most mutual funds.

Figure 25-1   How Annuities Compare to Other Investments—Nondeductible IRAs versus Annuities

Nondeductible IRAs	*Nonqualified Annuities*
Nondeductible and deductible IRAs are pooled together for tax purposes. Upon withdrawal, nontaxed portion is considered to have been withdrawn first even if kept in separate accounts.	Annuities are treated separately. Most of the payments will be tax free since it was originally funded with after-tax dollars.
Distribution must begin at age 70-1/2 or penalties are incurred.	No age limit on nonqualified plans.
$2,000 a year maximum contribution.	No maximum contribution.
10% early withdrawal penalty from IRS.	Same as IRAs.
Cannot purchase beyond age 70-1/2.	Some contracts have no age limit.
Flexibility in rolling over into other investments. Choices are wide.	Can only be exchanged for another annuity.
Most investment options available.	Can purchase fixed or variable. Options are limited based on accounts provided by insurance company.
Nontax surrender penalties—depends on type of investment made.	Surrender penalties usually disappear in 5 to 10 years depending on product.

Figure 25-2   Annuities versus Investment Life Insurance

Annuities	*Investment Life Insurance*
Functions as retirement fund accumulator.	Functions as retirement fund accumulator *with a death benefit.*
Provides for capital growth without taxation (inside buildup).	Provides for capital growth without taxation (inside buildup).
Mortality charge deducted only in variable separate accounts where death benefit is offered.	Mortality charge deducted (usually larger).
Avoids probate.	Avoids probate.
At death—growth in excess of premiums paid is taxed as ordinary income.	Death benefits pass tax free to heirs.
Borrowing—treated as taxable distribution to the extent of the policy appreciation borrowed (unless a qualified plan).	Borrowing is considered a tax-free loan.
Surrender charges—IRS 10% penalty if surrendered before age 59-1/2 plus ordinary income tax *on appreciation.*	If surrendered, capital appreciation in excess of premiums paid is taxed regardless of age.
Premium is paid for various settlement options including lifetime income.	Premium is paid for a lump sum death benefit.

Figure 25-3   Nonqualified Annuities versus CDs

Annuities	*Non-IRA CDs*
Tax-deferred growth.	All income currently taxable.
$4,000 per year at 8% tax deferred for 30 years = $489,383.	$4,000 per year at 30 yrs, at 8% taxable = $320,652. Your contribution to Uncle Sam = $168,731.
Withdrawals before age 59-1/2 incur a 10% IRS penalty; withdrawals are taxed on a LIFO basis (earnings come out first).	Premature withdrawal penalty that is perpetual. Taxes are paid each year on earnings.
Surrender charges range from 0 to 10% usually on *principal only.*	Premature withdrawal penalty on *earnings and principal.*
Fixed or variable investments options.	Fixed only
Annual maintenance fees possible.	None.
Frontloads or commissions are possible on some products; most have none.	None.
Not subject to probate.	Subject to probate unless with joint tenants with right of survivorship.
Lifetime income options available.	Lifetime income options not available.
Several pay-out options available.	Lump sum or interest only pay-outs.

5. Mortality charges apply in variable accounts where death benefit is offered.
6. At death, growth (or earnings) in excess of premiums paid is taxed as ordinary income.
7. Annuitant may be at an interest rate disadvantage at withdrawal time if interest rates are down and the annuitant wishes to annuitize.

TYPES OF ANNUITIES—FIXED VERSUS VARIABLE

Fixed

Fixed annuities are very similar to certificates of deposit. In explaining to clients, I compare them to a CD with an insurance company. The fixed annuity is simply a contract with an insurance company to pay a certain rate of interest for a specified period of time. You can assist your clients in selecting the time period that best suits their needs. You can usually tell which way the insurance company feels interest rates are headed by looking at their offerings of interest rates for varying periods of time. If their rate for a five-year guarantee is less than their one-year contract, then they think rates are coming down. They want to encourage the client to take the one-year deal so that they can renew at lower rates. If they encourage clients to lock in rates for longer periods of time, that may mean that they feel interest rates are going up. Do they know something that we do not? Probably not, but it is an interesting sales point for a client.

What happens at the end of the guarantee period? Most contracts allow the client to select another guarantee period. Some just renew at the current rate.

Is there danger of the insurance company "hooking" the client with a high rate until they get them trapped inside the contract and then dropping the rates? That used to be more of a factor than it is today. Insurance companies know that they cannot get away with such tactics today. They know that competitors will chew them up if they try such tactics. Some contracts offer "bail-out" provisions if the interest rate is dropped more than a certain amount such as 2 percent. Those bail-out clauses have become less important in today's interest rate environment. What is more important is the guaranteed rate. Some contracts still carry a 4.5 percent minimum. Many of my clients thought this insignificant only a few years ago. Today, they see it as a nice safety net.

What happens when the guaranteed periods are used up and the surrender charge period is all gone? Then the client has the option of renewing or looking at one of the withdrawal options if she is over age 59-1/2. If under age 59-1/2, she can also consider a 1035 exchange.

Variable

Variable annuities could be one of the most flexible and multi-purpose products on the market today. They are probably not going to be the highest performer for a specific purpose (although performance can certainly be outstanding), but they do meet many investor goals.

Variable contracts combine the features of the fixed annuity with the flexibility of a group of mutual funds. The client can allocate his money to a fixed account and to a group of mutual funds (choices usually range from five to nine). He can switch from one account to another without tax implications.

Variable accounts are not assets of the insurance company and thus not subject to creditors' claims. Since a mutual fund company has never failed, this can give some comfort to your clients who are worried about insurance companies.

Some variable accounts are managed by a mutual fund company separate from the insurance company; other are managed by a company that is owned by the insurance company.

Flexible versus Single Premium

Some contracts will accept only single premiums of a certain minimum. Most minimums are $5,000. Others will accept periodic regular payments. A bank draft plan or a retirement plan contract may be required.

Immediate versus Deferred

Immediate annuities start paying income immediately. You should be sure that your client has other assets before committing to an immediate annuity. Also, check with two or three companies to determine who has the best distribution based on the option selected by your client. Just because your client is invested in an immediate annuity and is drawing income, does not necessarily mean that the contract is "annuitized" in the usual definition of that term. Annuitization usually means that a portion of the client's principal is being distributed to him with each payment and that the distribution option is fixed and unchangeable. Most immediate annuities however, are "annuitized." Once the client selects an option, it is permanent.

ANNUITY FEATURES AND OPTIONS

Surrender Charges

Surrender charges are sometimes called *contingent deferred sales charges* (CDSC). The specter of "tying your money up" is in a close race with insurance company safety as the number one deterrent for annuity sales. Surrender charges are usually plain vanilla percentages paid by the client who takes his money out before the surrender period is up. However, there are certain misconceptions in clients' minds that should be addressed.

1. Most contracts guarantee that you will never get less than your original investment back. Clients usually think of losing their principal.
2. Even in contracts that will take part of your principal, they usually have a clause that says that you can withdraw in the first year without losing any of your original investment. If you get past the first year, most interest earnings are going to be adequate to keep you from getting back anything less than the amount of your original investment. Also, the surrender penalties begin declining with the second year.
3. Check to see if the sales charge applies to both principal and accumulated interest. Most apply to principal only.
4. Check to see if the contract begins a new surrender period every time new money is deposited. In a lot of 403(b) accounts, for example, many in-

surance companies start a new period every month (i.e., the client never gets totally past the surrender period). Your contract should start a surrender period with the first deposit and protect all future deposits within this same time period.

5. Most surrender charges are waived in event of disability or death.

Withdrawal Rights

Most contracts allow your client to withdraw 10 percent of the contract once each year without incurring any surrender charges. This will not protect him from the IRS however.

Loan Provisions

Many contracts have loan provisions that allows the contract owner to borrow at 2 percent net interest. In other words, the company will charge 2 percent more on the borrowed funds than it pays for the money on deposit. Loan provisions are usually found in 403(b) and 401(k) contracts.

Commissions

Most annuities have no front-end commission, so that all of the clients money goes to work from the time of the investment. The insurance rep is paid a previously specified rate depending on the contract.

Death Benefit

Most variable annuities have a mortality feature often referred to as the ''die in a down market'' clause. If your client dies before annuity payments begin, the beneficiary will receive no less than the original purchase payments made plus any earnings realized.

Withdrawal Options

Withdrawal options require your close scrutiny with the client and represent one of the major sales points we make to our clients to get them to select our products. They will need consultation at time of withdrawal. These are summary descriptions of a few common withdrawal options. Many contracts have up to fifteen options, but most are some variation of these.

Interest Only.   Allows the client to withdraw interest only.

Straight Life or Lifetime Only.   Pays the client until he dies, no matter how short or how long that is. If you die too soon, the insurance company will get to keep some of your investment. Since there is that risk, they come with highest monthly payment.

A Life and Period Certain.   Pays the client and his beneficiary for at least a specified number of years, (period certain) typically 10, 15, or 20 years. This guarantees that either the client or his beneficiary will receive payments for the certain period of time selected. Benefits are usually 5 to 8 percent less than under the straight life option.

Installment Refund.   Pays back your original investment to your beneficiary if you die. Usually pays 4 to 5 percent less than the straight life.

Cash-Refund Annuity.   Works like the installment refund, except that the survivor receives the balance of the original investment in a *lump sum*.

Joint and Survivor.   Pays until the client and spouse are dead. The amount of the benefit is based on both ages. Survivor benefits can also be reduced by 25, 33, or 50 percent if the client selects. This can also be combined with the period certain options.

Lump Sum.   Pays a lump sum value in the contract; seldom used because of the tax consequences. The remainder after taxes will rarely produce the same income as one of the other options.

SELECTING ANNUITY PROVIDERS

Selection of annuity products is very similar to selecting any investment product, especially one offered through an insurance company. You should have products that are competitive, and that are flexible to meet your client's changing needs. Features to look for when selecting an annuity product might include:

1. Strength of the insurance company.
2. Severity of surrender charges and length of the surrender period.
3. Whether surrender charges apply to the entire contract value or just to the principal invested.
4. Options on retirement. This is probably one of the most important. Are there an adequate number of options available for withdrawal of the client's money?
5. Transfer privileges within the variable accounts should be liberal and usually without cost.
6. Annual maintenance fee should be low or should have a guarantee never to increase.
7. No initial sales charge.
8. How commissions are paid to you and whether or not there is a trail.
9. Is automatic dollar cost averaging available?
10. What is the minimum investment and are subsequent premiums flexible?
11. Are loan provisions available?
12. Frequency of account statements. Some are only annual. Ask for quarterly.
13. Automatic asset allocation—some clients will automatically rebalance your accounts in the variable side.
14. Annual withdrawal privileges.
15. Past performance in the variable accounts.
16. Wide range of investment options.
17. Interest rate history in fixed accounts as compared to T-Bill or CD rates.

DOES TAX DEFERRAL REALLY PAY OFF?

Many clients would prefer to pay as they go rather than run the risk of tax rates heading up and paying higher rates at retirement. It is hard to argue against the possibility that tax rates might go up. Also, many annuity buyers intend to make just as much money if not more in retirement than they did in their working years.

Does tax deferral then pay off? I have often compared tax deferred investments with tax-free and taxable investments in client meetings. This works very effectively. Start with an open mind as to which will win in various situations. You should tell the client that you do not know what the outcome will be. Let the client pick the interest rates and do the comparison right in front of him. After doing this several times over the years, I concluded that tax deferral is much more powerful than I originally thought. If the client stays in an in-

Figure 25-4   Testing the Value of Tax Deferral With a Single Investment

	Taxable CD	*Tax Free*	*Tax Deferred*
Original investment	100,000	100,000	100,000
Rate of return	5%	4%	5%
Tax rate	31%	31%	31%
After-tax rate	3.45	4	5
Tax rates at W/D:			
Assumed rate 1	31%	31%	31%
Assumed rate 2	35%	35%	35%
Assumed rate 3	40%	40%	40%
Assumed rate 4	50%	50%	50%
Value in 5 Years	**118,482**	**121,665**	**127,628**
Tax at rate 1 if W/D	0	0	8,564
Tax at rate 2 if W/D	0	0	9,670
Tax at rate 3 if W/D	0	0	11,051
Tax at rate 4 if W/D	0	0	13,814
Value After Taxes:			
Rate 1	118,482	121,665	119,064
Rate 2	118,482	121,665	117,968
Value in 10 Years	**−140,380**	**148,024**	**162,889**
Tax at rate 1 if W/D	0	0	19,496
Tax at rate 2 if W/D	0	0	22,011
Tax at rate 3 if W/D	0	0	25,156
Tax at rate 4 if W/D	0	0	31,445
Value After Taxes:			
Rate 1	140,380	148,024	143,393
Rate 2	140,380	148,024	140,878
Value in 20 Years	**197,065**	**219,112**	**265,330**
Tax at rate 1 if W/D	0	0	51,252
Tax at rate 2 if W/D	0	0	57,866
Tax at rate 3 if W/D	0	0	66,132
Tax at rate 4 if W/D	0	0	82,665
Value After Taxes:			
Rate 1	197,065	219,112	214,078
Rate 2	197,065	219,112	207,464
Rate 3	197,065	219,112	199,198
Rate 4	197,065	219,112	182,665

vestment for five years or longer, deferral usually pays off. The results, of course, depend on the variance in the rate of return and the tax rates used. However, clients almost always wind up with more money under tax deferral if the holding period is 10 years or more. Learn to do these calculations well enough so that you can do them right in front of the client. They are much more powerful prepared in front of their eyes. Figure 25-4 is a format that you might consider.

Value in 20 Years	**197,065**	**219,112**	**265,330**
Tax at rate 1 if W/D	0	0	51,252
Tax at rate 2 if W/D	0	0	57,866
Tax at rate 3 if W/D	0	0	66,132
Tax at rate 4 if W/D	0	0	82,665
Value After Taxes:			
Rate 1	197,065	219,112	214,078
Rate 2	197,065	219,112	207,464
Rate 3	197,065	219,112	199,198
Rate 4	197,065	219,112	182,665

So what does this chart tell us? If you surmised that tax exempts are the best deal given these rates, you are correct. What else does it tell us?

If tax rates remain the same, staying in the investment for five years will still yield more in tax deferred than taxable, even considering that an investor would take all of his money out of the annuity and pay taxes all at once (something that almost never happens).

Tax rates can go up to 35 percent and tax deferral still pays off after 10 years. Tax rates can go up as high as 40 percent and tax deferral pays off at the end of 20 years.

What is wrong with these calculations? I gave the annuity the same rate as the CD. Annuities usually pay from 25 to 150 basis points more. I assumed in all cases that the annuity would be withdrawn in a lump sum with all taxes being paid in one year. Something that seldom happens.

Now take a look at Figure 25-5.

MARKETING ANNUITIES

Annuities are one of the easiest investment products to market. They are easy for clients to understand because they are similar to CDs. They also have some excellent benefits, as stated earlier, that the client will understand.

The Liquidity Objection

Overcoming the liquidity objection is usually fairly easy once you get over it yourself. The most effective way to get over it is to use the illustrations on the previous pages. Taking the money out is not as bad as it seems. Also, point out the differences between CDs and annuities. Relate the surrender penalties to early withdrawal penalties. Show the client that most products never allow the client to lose principal. Show the various ways to take money out.

The Treasure Chest

I explained my treasure chest presentation in an earlier chapter of this book. I use a similar approach to sell annuities. Most annuity prospects have funds

Figure 25-5   Testing the Value of Tax Deferral with Periodic Investments

If You Invest $4,000 Per Year For:	5 Years	10 Years	20 Years	30 Years	40 Years
and your investment grows at an annual rate of **6%**. Your money will grow to this amount if you pay taxes annually at 28%	22,746	50,849	128,466	246,942	427,788
With tax deferral it grows to	23,901	55,887	155,971	335,207	656,191
The Difference	**1,155**	**5,038**	**27,505**	**88,265**	**228,403**
At 8%—with current taxation	23,733	55,135	151,662	320,652	616,604
At 8%—with tax deferral	25,344	62,582	197,692	489,383	1,119,124
The Difference	**1,611**	**7,447**	**46,030**	**168,731**	**502,620**
At 10%—with current taxation	24,757	59,808	179,676	419,919	901,423
At 10%—with tax deferral	26,862	70,125	252,010	723,774	1,947,407
The Difference	**2,105**	**10,317**	**72,334**	**303,855**	**1,045,984**

that are not being used and are not needed for liquidity. Draw treasure chests for your client. One or more chests may contain funds that meet other needs such as income. Show that chest with the top open. Illustrate money coming out for living expenses, etc. Also show the IRS dipping its black hand into the chest annually for its share of the money. Then draw a chest with a lock on it. That is the annuity. The client can slap the IRS's hand away until the client is ready to withdraw money. It may be sort of hokey, but it works.

The Umbrella

My wife Jan will testify that I am not an artist. I can barely draw stick men. I do use my grease board and try to draw illustrations, however, because I believe that most people are visual learners.

One of the most effective ways I have found to educate clients about variable annuities is with the umbrella. I draw the umbrella on the grease board and show some rain falling. The rain represents taxes and the umbrella represents the variable annuity. On the left side of the umbrella, I draw a single box which represents the fixed portion of the variable annuity. I explain how this is like a guaranteed investment contract with the insurance company or a CD with an insurance company. On the right side, I draw several boxes representing the mutual fund options for the variable side. I may put amounts in the boxes, but usually I just show the client's ability to switch around between the boxes without incurring any tax liability.

Who are the Prospects for Annuities?

- Clients who have substantial funds for liquidity purposes invested in taxable instruments.

- Clients who already own an annuity.
- 403(b) prospects such as school teachers, and all employees of 501(c)(3) organizations.
- Clients who own taxable mutual funds.
- Anyone who has a tax problem.
- Clients who have nondeductible IRAs.
- Clients who own any taxable bond or taxable bond mutual fund, especially government funds.
- Clients past age 50 who are accumulating funds for retirement.
- Retired clients with tax problems.
- Clients who are having their Social Security benefits taxed.
- Clients who like to actively manage their mutual funds but hate the tax consequences of trading.
- Clients can use annuities to fund the premium on long-term care contracts by using the 10 percent penalty free withdrawal available every year. The client is protected against the single largest threat to his assets while those assets continue to grow without taxation.

26

Insurance Products

The greatest discovery of the 19th century was not in the realm of physical science. It was the power of the subconscious touched by faith.

William James, Father of American Psychology

The definitions, marketing ideas, and client applications of insurance were included in Part 3 of this book. I include insurance products again in this part to allow more discussion about the products themselves. Insurance products are in abundance just like mutual funds. For accountants, they are more difficult to understand because the terms used vary from one product to another. Also, the insurance industry has grown up under a facade of marketing terms that fail to describe the way things really are. Today, for example, the American Society of CLU and ChFC have developed an insurance illustration questionnaire described as being ''on the cutting edge of a major industry concern.'' The IQ is said to be ''leading a quiet revolution dealing with a major industry concern—responsible use of life insurance illustrations in the sales process.''

The IQ is a series of questions designed to help life insurance agents gather specific information from their companies regarding assumptions used in generating life insurance sales illustrations. The premise is to learn from insurance companies what assumptions are used in illustrations regarding:

- Mortality.
- Interest or crediting rates.
- Expenses.
- Persistency.

If the agent knows these things, he should be better able to help clients make informed decisions about how the policy being proposed helps meet their objectives. The IQ is new, so do not expect immediate and positive industry reaction. However, the IQ questions can help you to evaluate illustrations for your clients.

SOME BASIC QUESTIONS TO ASK ANY INSURANCE COMPANY

These are some questions you should probably ask of the insurance company or the person who is assisting you in making a client presentation.

1. Is the policy participating or nonparticipating?
2. Describe any nonguaranteed elements in the proposal.
3. Describe what is guaranteed in the proposal.
4. Do the underlying experience factors for any nonguaranteed elements differ from current experience? If they do, please describe.
5. Is there a substantial probability that the current illustrated values will change if current experience continues unchanged?
6. Are new and existing policyholders treated the same with regard to pricing?

Mortality

1. Are mortality rates used lower than recent company experience (five years)?
2. Are improvements in mortality rates assumed?
3. Do mortality rates vary by product?

Interest or Crediting Rates

1. How is the interest rate determined (i.e., is it gross or net of expenses, etc.)?
2. Does the rate exceed the current earning rate on the company's investments that back this group of policies?
3. Does the interest rate vary by policy duration? By product?
4. Do the interest rates include capital gains?

Expenses

1. Do expenses used reflect recent company experience? For what period? If not, how did you arrive at the expense charges?
2. Are expense determinations consistently determined for new as well as existing policies?
3. Do the expenses vary by product?

Persistency

1. If actual persistency is better than assumed would illustrated values be less?
2. Persistency bonuses are paid or credited to all policyholders who pay premiums for a minimum for a specified number of years. Are bonuses included in the illustrations?

Do you have to ask these types of questions of your insurance company on each illustration you prepare or have prepared for your client? If so, I submit that most of us would not do much insurance business. So what does the CPA-planner do in the meantime? Do we wash our hands of the whole thing because the industry has problems with illustrations or give up and leave it to insurance agents? We must continue to meet our client needs in this area. Insurance planning is part of the financial planning process just as estate planning is. *You cannot do an effective job for your clients without knowing about this area.* This does not mean that you cannot make an investment for a client without doing insurance or an estate plan; it just means that you must be able to deal with these issues because clients do have needs in this area.

So how do you effectively deal with them?

1. *Limit the number of companies that you deal with.* Stick with companies that have long histories of customer service, high ratings, and meeting projections.

2. *Limit your products.* It is not necessary to know every last detail about every product, but you should know how illustrations are prepared, what needs the product is supposed to fill, etc.

3. *Learn by doing.* Inertia is still your greatest enemy. You must start using illustrations in your analysis of insurance products in real-life client situations. You will never learn unless you begin.

4. *Use the competition.* Look at competitors' illustrations and compare theirs with yours, item by item. Look at illustrations for other products within the same company. Get your insurance department to explain why one product is better than another. Look also at other companies with whom you do business. Ask for their solutions to the same customer need. Then you can show the client that you investigated more than one product to fit their needs, and more important, why you selected the one you did.

5. *Ask dumb questions.* We CPA types are use to being on the receiving end of questions. We do not ask them, we answer them. Swallow your pride, make a commitment to learn for the sake of your clients, and do not be afraid to say I do not know. Then find out by asking all the people and resources you can find. From each of these fact-finding missions, you will become a little more astute in this area. *Client situations are always the best way to learn.*

6. *Use plain language cover sheets for presentations.* Most insurance illustrations will not help you to sell the product. That is doubly true if you do not completely understand the illustration. Focus on the key points you want to achieve for your client. Find where these are shown in the illustration and highlight for the client. We try to prepare cover sheets explaining in simple language the various components of the illustration.

7. *Use a caution cover sheet.* Use the cover sheet shown in Figure 26-1 to explain how the insurance illustration process is often abused.

Figure 26-1 Caution

It is often said that an insurance professional had better be the "first and only" or the last person to prepare an insurance illustration. Unfortunately, this is true. If given the opportunity, we can also beat any competitive quote. This is true not only because we have a variety of insurance companies and products to choose from, but an infinite variety of "assumptions" that we can make regarding future interests rates, etc.

What does this mean to you, the consumer? It means that you must ask each professional you are dealing with what assumptions were made to arrive at the numbers in your illustration. The cheapest policy is not always the best policy! Be sure that your insurance professional has made realistic assumptions that are in your best interest. Always deal with professionals that you know and trust.

We have prepared the attached illustrations using the best information available to meet your financial goals.

8. *Use "outside" services.* Services such as INSMARK have developed a great business by capitalizing on the insurance industry's inability to speak English. Such programs prepare better illustrations using the insurance company products than the insurance company can produce on its own. Lawyers again?

9. *Make your insurance illustrations goal oriented.* Develop narrative and numbers that tie into the illustration but also focus on what has to be done to reach the client's goals. Remember, people do not buy life insurance; they buy what it does.

WHOLE LIFE

Whole life is also known as *straight life* and *ordinary life.* It usually provides insurance protection at a level premium for the lifetime of the insured. Thus the term "whole" life. Premiums pay for the client's insurance and administrative costs as well as funding a cash value account.

Many whole life policies also earn insurance company dividends (if they are participating) that add to the cash value. Such dividends often exceed the premium in later years and the client can use the dividends to pay his premiums. This product is primarily insurance, not an investment, and that is how it should be sold.

Whole life policies are enjoying a resurgence because of concern about economic uncertainty and the unrealistic interest rate assumptions used in various other policy types. Consumers like the guarantees present in whole life. Also, whole life now has many riders that make it a lot more attractive. Such riders include survivorship life, paid up additions, and enhanced term riders.

Limited Pay Whole Life

A form of whole life where premium payments are adjusted to pay for lifetime protection but premiums stop after a specified period of time.

Interest Sensitive Whole Life

Interest sensitive whole life is also called *current assumption whole life.* In one type of ISWL, the level premium is subject to period change. In another, the premium remains level but may vanish. These were introduced in the 80s to reflect that decade's higher interest rates and lower mortality costs. They are nonparticipating, in that they do not pay dividends in the traditional sense. They guarantee that a fairly high rate of interest will be credited on the cash values, but they credit a *current* rate of interest to the policy. The money which builds up at the current interest rate is referred to as the "cash accumulation account" to distinguish it from the guaranteed cash values.

In the first type of policy, the idea is to provide a person with a whole life policy for a premium rate that is below that of traditional whole life. That will work when current interest rates are higher than the guaranteed rates. Again, the premium may fluctuate after certain periods based on how good or bad the assumptions were when the original premium was set. If the premium goes up, the policy holder can:

1. Pay it to keep the death benefit the same.
2. Pay the old lower premium and take a reduced death benefit.

3. Pay the old lower premium, keep the same death benefit, and take money out of the cash accumulation fund to make up the difference (if there is enough money in it).

If the premium goes down:

1. Keep the death benefit and pay a lower premium.
2. Keep paying the old premium and get more death benefit.
3. Keep the old death benefit, pay the old premium, and put the difference in the cash accumulation account.

Those options relate to the type of policy that was issued to keep premiums below standard whole life rates. In the type that is designed to vanish premium, current rates of interest are credited on every dollar of policy value, so the policy owner can participate in the company's earnings from its investments.

UNIVERSAL LIFE PRODUCTS

Regular Universal Life

Universal life is right for the client who wants permanent coverage but wants the flexibility to manage the policy in terms of premiums paid, death benefits, and cash value buildup. I usually tell my clients that universal life policies place your premium dollars into three buckets. One goes to pay for mortality (the death benefit), one goes for expenses, and the other goes into an interest bearing account. The best thing about universal life is that the client has the flexibility to control his premium in order to control death benefit and cash value buildup.

When the client purchases the policy, assumptions have to be made about interest rates. These assumptions affect the level of premiums to be paid and the cash value to be built up. If interest rates fall below those used in the assumptions, not only may a client find that his cash value is not growing, he may find it used up to pay expenses and mortality costs. The only way to keep the policy in force is to increase the premiums or reduce the death benefit. Both options are available. Does this mean that universal life policies are bad? Of course not. It just means that you must be careful of your assumptions and be sure that your client does not wind up without coverage or cash value.

Variable Universal Life

This has the same features as a regular universal life policy, but allows the client to invest his cash value (the investment portion of the account) into variable accounts. These are usually managed mutual funds that invest in stocks, bonds, money market instruments, and the like. The potential for greater return is more available than with the traditional universal life that is dependent on interest rates for performance.

TERM INSURANCE

Term insurance is "pure" insurance for short-term needs. It provides protection against financial loss resulting from death during a specified period of time. Premiums may be level or increasing during the specified period of time.

The death benefit may also decrease during the time period in decreasing term policies. *Increasing term* is often sold as a rider to a standard term policy.

Most *level-term policies* contain an option to allow the policyowner to renew the contract within certain limitations. The policy is renewable at the insured's new age with evidence of insurability. Companies usually put some limits on age, number of years, number of renewals, etc.

Level-term policies and riders usually stipulate that the owner can convert all or part of the policy or rider to any form of permanent insurance without evidence of insurability. Conversion is almost always at the new age of the policyholder.

SURVIVORSHIP LIFE

Survivorship life is a traditional whole life policy that insures two lives, but the death proceeds are paid after both insureds have died. The policy has guaranteed cash values, but they are lower than similar single life policy cash values. It has fixed level premiums, and rates are lower than individual life rates because they are based on a joint life expectancy. This can minimize the impact if one of the insured has impaired health. Riders may be available to convert to two individual policies.

This type of policy is used for:

1. Insuring key employees if a company's continued success depends on two employees (i.e., if the company could survive one death, but not both).
2. Funding a buy-sell for a business where the husband and wife are co-owners. At the death of the first spouse, the business is transferred to the surviving spouse. At the death of the second, the death benefit is used by the remaining employees to purchase the business from the estate.
3. Increasing the value of a couple's estate that they wish to pass to heirs.
4. To provide liquidity to pay estate taxes and administration costs.

DISABILITY INSURANCE

Disability insurance pays you a monthly income if you are unable to work because of injury or illness. Disability protects your most valuable asset, your ability to earn a living. When a person is disabled, his family's needs continue as well as his own. In fact, disability increases the need for income. At age 42, you are four times more likely to become disabled for at least three months before retirement than you are to die.

What to Look for in Policies

Definition of Disability.   You should look for *own occ* coverage. This means that you will receive benefits if you cannot work in your *own occupation*, even if you work in another closely related occupation. The least desirable definition is "any occ." This means that if you can get a job (any job) you will not receive benefits. Most policies compromise between the two definitions by two methods:

1. They pay benefits under *own occ* rules for a limited period of time such as one to five years, when *any occ* rules take over.

2. They pay benefits if you cannot work in a "related occupation." For example, a practicing attorney might be able to teach law. If he could he would lose benefits. If he could only get work as a ditch-digger, he would not lose benefits. Own occ features cost 5 to 15 percent more. Do not discard a policy just because it does not contain the most favorable definition of own occ. Sometimes, it makes more sense to buy higher monthly benefits than get protection from *own occ*.

Elimination Period.   This is the time you have to wait for benefits to begin after you become disabled. Maybe it should be called the waiting period. Selecting the elimination period is usually up to the policyowner. If the client can afford a 90-day wait, then that is probably what should be bought. Thirty-day elimination periods will cost about 40 percent more than 90 days. Going to 180 would only save about 15 percent from the 90-day wait.

Benefit Period.   Most benefits stop at age 65 when Social Security steps in. For younger clients, you may want to recommend lifetime benefits since they may not be able to build up retirement benefits if disabled while young. This will cost about 20 percent more.

Residual Benefits/Partial Disability.   With this provision, you can return to work part time and still receive a portion of the total disability payment. These are called *residual benefits* and they continue as long as you need them. Generally, the loss of income after you return part time must be at least 20 to 25%. *Partial benefits* (usually 50 percent of your total benefits) are paid if you are only partially disabled. These partial benefits usually stop after three to six months.

Earned income is all that is covered. Check to see if the policy covers bonuses and commissions also. See how the income level is calculated. Many contracts use the higher of the prior 12 months or two consecutive years in the past five. Check to see if the insured has to be under a physician's care. Good residual benefits will boost the premium by 20 to 25 percent.

COLA.   The cost of living adjustment will increase your monthly benefits automatically to counter inflation usually based on the consumer price index or at a specified rate up to a specified annual maximum. This costs about 25 percent more.

Renewability.   Insist on a policy that is at least guaranteed renewable, which means that the insurer cannot cancel your coverage as long as you pay your premiums or raise your premium unless it boosts premiums in general. The best one is a *noncancelable policy*, which guarantees that your policy cannot be revoked and that your premium cannot be increased. This feature may cost a lot more, however.

Waiver of Premium.   Why buy disability if you are going to use the proceeds to pay for disability coverage? After the insured has been totally or partially disabled (usually for 90 days), the insurer "waives" additional premium payments until the policyholder's disability terminates.

Maximum Benefits.   Some policies replace about 85 percent of your gross income. You can buy policies for lower percentages. The most common is about 65 to 70 percent. The maximum benefits obtainable may depend on whether you client will take a physical before the policy is issued. If he does, he can increase the maximum from $3,000 to $4,000 per month to about $15,000 to $20,000 if that much coverage is needed.

Definition of Illness and Exclusions/Limitations.   The key factor relates to when the illness/injury occurs versus when the policy begins. Generally, the illness must occur or become known *after* the policy is in force. ''First manifest'' means ''first becomes known.'' Watch for the term ''first contracted'' or ''begins.'' Coverage could be denied under these definitions if the illness was in existence before the policy begins *even though its existence was not known.*

Marketing Disability Insurance

Use these definitions to explain in simple terms what a policy does and what it covers. Use statistics in Figure 26-2 to identify the need.

Of every 1,000 Americans the number who will be disabled for at least 90 days before 65 is shown in Figure 26-3. Three percent of all mortgage foreclosures are caused by death, but 48 percent are caused by disability.

Clients insure their lives, homes, cars, and possessions, but fail to insure their most valuable asset, their ability to earn a living. In any given year, however:

1 in 106	People die
1 in 88	Homes catch fire
1 in 70	Autos are involved in an accident resulting in disability, injury, or death
1 in 8 people	Are disabled for at least 8 days.

Use these figures to sell your client on the need for disability insurance.

Figure 26-2   Disability Insurance Needs

Current Age	Chance of Disability	Years
30	50%	4.7
40	45%	5.5
45	40%	5.8
50	34%	6.2

Figure 26-3   Number of Americans Disabled Before Age 65

Age	Number Disabled
25	522; 1 of 2 or 52%
35	480; 4 of 9 or 48%
45	401; 2 of 5 or 40%
55	266; 1 of 4 of 26%

27

Long-Term Care Products

For the unprepared, old age can truly be the Winter of Life;
for those who prepare, it is the Season of Harvest.

Many CPA–financial planners have a very negative view when it comes to long-term care products; they see it as health insurance. It think of it as a cross between disability and health, with more emphasis on disability. When long-term care products were first introduced, they were pretty bad. The insurance companies simply had no history on how to write the product nor any statistics on which to base claims experience or premiums. To protect themselves, they installed ''gatekeepers'' in most of the early products which kept the policies from offering good coverage.

Today's policies are much better. They offer protection for what is one of the biggest threats to savings for elderly people. The long-term care problem is a national crisis. As a financial planner, you need to include a recommendation for protection from this crisis in almost every plan you prepare.

In Part 3 of this book, I covered the need for long-term care. Having had my mother enter a nursing home almost two years ago, and dealing with home health care for several years prior to that, I have had first-hand experience with this major problem. I have also helped many clients to deal with it.

Unfortunately, there is no one simple answer for dealing with the problem. At least I have found none to be perfect. No solution that fits every situation. There is no way to tell you which benefits to choose if long-term care insurance is chosen as the best solution for a client. However, using the information in this section and Part 3 should give you enough information to help your client to make the best decision.

FEATURES TO LOOK FOR IN LTC

Nursing Home Daily Benefits

Take the average daily cost of nursing homes that your client is likely to use and convert to a monthly cost. Subtract the client's Social Security income. That will give you the amount that the client will have to spend out of his own pocket per month. Convert this to a daily rate and add about 5 percent because the client will be able to keep a small portion of Social Security benefits. That should give you a daily rate to shoot for in selecting the daily benefit in the policy. Find out if there is a maximum amount of benefits that will be paid.

Level of Care

Be sure that all levels of care are covered. Most care is at the custodial level. Your policy should cover skilled nursing care, intermediate care, and custodial/personal care.

Home Health Care

Your policy should cover home health care. Staying at home as long as possible with visiting nurses is preferable to most people. Do not be in a position of having to tell your client that they will have to enter a nursing home to be covered.

How Long Will Benefits Last?

Get answers for each level of care mentioned above—home health care, custodian, skilled nursing, and intermediate. In most policies, you and your client can select these time periods from two years to lifetime. There is no answer for every client. You have issues of age, affordability of premiums, other assets available, and the like.

Forty percent of patients stay in a nursing home two and a half years. Only 10 percent stay over five years. My mother has been a patient for one and a half years, but had home health care for three years prior to that. Many of my clients use three years as the period of coverage. This gives them an opportunity to give away their assets when they start needing care, and get past the 30-month waiting period for Medicaid. During the 30 months, the insurance is paying. After the waiting period is over, the client may be able to qualify for Medicaid. However, watch out for income that cannot be controlled when using this option because it may disqualify your client for medicaid coverage.

Inflation Adjustment

For younger clients, I usually recommend this protection. For older ones, I usually opt for a larger daily benefit. Look at the difference in cost and make your selection accordingly. Pay attention to how much the benefits go up and what the increase is based on.

Elimination Period

This is the waiting period before a policy starts paying benefits. Most recommend a short waiting period of 30 days or less. Most policies have elimination periods that start with 0, 20, and go up to 100 days. Fifty percent of people who enter nursing homes stay 90 days or less. I usually differ from most experts on this point. I usually sell long-term care to prevent a person's entire estate from being consumed in the last years of his life by illness. Therefore, I am very comfortable with 100-day elimination periods even with the statistics. However, this goes to the issue of affordability and client resistance to paying premiums. If he is reluctant to pay premiums, but can pay for 100 days of nursing home care, I think the 100-day elimination may be preferable.

Preexisting Conditions

Find out if you will be covered for a preexisting condition. If so, how long before coverage begins?

Excluded Impairments

Ask about excluded illnesses or impairments such as Alzheimer's Disease, senility, or dementia. These should be covered.

Gatekeepers

Watch for special conditions that must be met before coverage beings. Older policies required a three-day hospital stay before entering a nursing home. Most patients go directly from home to a nursing home. Be sure that the policy pays if the owner cannot perform the activities of daily living without assistance (eating, taking medicine, bathing, etc.).

Waiver of Premium

The premium should be waived when benefits begin. Find out what this costs. Figure 27-1 is a reproduction of the NAIC (National Association of Insurance Commissioners) policy comparison checklist from their brochure ''A Shopper's Guide to Long-Term Care Insurance.'' You can obtain this brochure by writing them at 120 W. 12th Street, Suite 1100, Kansas City, MO 64105.

Figure 27-1   Policy Comparison Checklist
(Use This Checklist to Help Select a Policy)

	Policy A		Policy B		Policy C	
	Yes	No	Yes	No	Yes	No

What Are The Benefits?

1. Does the policy provide benefits for the following expenses?

	Policy A		Policy B		Policy C	
–skilled nursing care	□	□	□	□	□	□
–intermediate care	□	□	□	□	□	□
–custodial/personal care	□	□	□	□	□	□
–home health care	□	□	□	□	□	□

2. Does it pay for any nursing home stay regardless of the kind of care you receive?

	□	□	□	□	□	□

3. How long will benefits last?

	Days	Days	Days
–skilled nursing care	_____	_____	_____
–intermediate nursing care	_____	_____	_____
–custodial/personal care	_____	_____	_____
–home health care	_____	_____	_____

	Days/Years	Days/Years	Days/Years
–maximum benefits	_____	_____	_____

4. Are benefits adjusted for inflation?

	□	□	□	□	□	□

How and by how much? _____ _____ _____

When do automatic increases stop?

How Much Does The Policy Pay?

	Per Day	Per Day	Per Day

5. What is the maximum amount the policy will pay for:

	Policy A	Policy B	Policy C
–skilled nursing care?	$_____	$_____	$_____
–intermediate nursing care?	$_____	$_____	$_____
–custodial/personal care?	$_____	$_____	$_____
–home health care?	$_____	$_____	$_____
–any nursing home stay?	$_____	$_____	$_____

	Yes	No	Yes	No	Yes	No

6. Is there a limit on the total amount the policy will pay?

	□	□	□	□	□	□

7. If so, what are the limits?

	Policy A	Policy B	Policy C
–skilled nursing care	$_____	$_____	$_____
–intermediate nursing care	$_____	$_____	$_____
–custodial/personal care	$_____	$_____	$_____
–home health care	$_____	$_____	$_____
–overall limit	$_____	$_____	$_____

How Many Years Will The Policy Pay And How Much Each Year?

	Policy A	Policy B	Policy C
1 year	$_____	$_____	$_____
2 years	$_____	$_____	$_____
3 years	$_____	$_____	$_____
4 years	$_____	$_____	$_____
Lifetime	$_____	$_____	$_____

Figure 27-1   (Continued)

	Policy A	Policy B	Policy C
What Are The Limits And Exclusions?			
8. How long is the elimination or waiting period before benefits begin?	Days	Days	Days
–nursing home care	_____	_____	_____
–home health care	_____	_____	_____
9. How long will it take before you are covered for a pre-existing condition?	Days _____	Days _____	Days _____
10. Does the policy cover Alzheimer's disease if you develop the disease after you purchase the policy?	Yes ☐ No ☐	Yes ☐ No ☐	Yes ☐ No ☐

	Policy A	**Policy B**	**Policy C**
11. Is a prior hospital stay required for:	Yes No	Yes No	Yes No
–skilled nursing care	☐ ☐	☐ ☐	☐ ☐
–intermediate nursing care	☐ ☐	☐ ☐	☐ ☐
–custodial/personal care	☐ ☐	☐ ☐	☐ ☐
–home health care	☐ ☐	☐ ☐	☐ ☐
12. Is a prior skilled nursing home stay required before the policy will pay for:	Yes No	Yes No	Yes No
–intermediate care	☐ ☐	☐ ☐	☐ ☐
–custodial/personal care	☐ ☐	☐ ☐	☐ ☐
–how many days?	_____	_____	_____
13. What is the monthly premium excluding riders?	$_____	$_____	$_____
Yearly premium?	$_____	$_____	$_____
14. What is the cost of the inflation rider?	$_____	$_____	$_____
15. Is there a waiver of premium clause?	Yes ☐ No ☐	Yes ☐ No ☐	Yes ☐ No ☐
If so, what does it cost and when does it begin?	$_____	$_____	$_____
16. Is there any discount if both you and your spouse buy a policy?	Yes ☐ No ☐	Yes ☐ No ☐	Yes ☐ No ☐

	Nursing Home A	Nursing Home B
17. How much do nursing homes charge for:		
–skilled care?	$_____/mo	$_____/mo
–intermediate care?	$_____/mo	$_____/mo
–custodial/personal care?	$_____/mo	$_____/mo

	Home Health Agency A	Home Health Agency B
18. What do home-health care agencies in your area charge?		
–skilled care	$_____/visit	$_____/visit
–unskilled care	$_____/visit	$_____/visit

(Continued)

Figure 27-1 (Continued)

	Policy A	Policy B	Policy C

19. Is there a local agent for the company who will answer questions about each policy you are considering?

Name _____
Phone _____
Company _____
Address _____

Name _____
Phone _____
Company _____
Address _____

Name _____
Phone _____
Company _____
Address _____

Toll Free Number

Company A	Company B	Company C
_____	_____	_____

Long Term Care Proposal

CLIENT: _____

AGE: _____

COMPANY: _____

____ PREFERRED   ____ STANDARD
____ MONTHLY PREMIUM ____ QUARTERLY ____ ANNUAL
____ DAILY BENEFIT (20–120) $____
____ HOME HEALTH CARE ____ % OF DAILY BENEFIT

____ COVERAGE WITH INFLATION PROTECTION ____/YEAR
        TILL AGE ____

	15 DAY ELIMINATION	90 DAY ELIMINATION
____ One Year	N/A	N/A
____ Two Year	$	$
____ Three Year		
____ Four Year	$	$
____ Six Year	$	$
____ Lifetime	$	$

____ COVERAGE WITHOUT INFLATION PROTECTION

	15 DAY ELIMINATION	90 DAY ELIMINATION
____ One Year	N/A	N/A
____ Two Year	$	$
____ Three Year		
____ Four Year	$	$
____ Six Year	$	$
____ Lifetime	$	$

Appendixes

Appendix A

Data Gathering Packages

	PACKAGE #
Personal and Family Data	1
Goals and Investment Philosophy	2
Personal Financial Data	3
Income and Expense Planning (Budgeting)	4
Policy Listing	5
Estate Planning Data	6
Advisor and Document Listing	7

PACKAGE #1—PERSONAL AND FAMILY DATA

This package is self-explanatory. If the client is a tax client or existing investment client, most of it should be completed before the client comes in for a data gathering session. The inheritances section is important in planning for retirement, insurance needs, etc. It can be a "downer" to prepare a plan that says the client is in deep trouble in several areas, only to find out that he stands to inherit a trust fund worth mega-bucks in two years.

Figure A-1

DATA GATHERING

(1)

PERSONAL & CONFIDENTIAL DATA

Client _____

Date _____

Comments _____

_____

_____

_____

_____

_____

_____

Figure A-2

PERSONAL AND CONFIDENTIAL DATA

NAME OF CLIENT _____

PRESENTED BY

NAME _____

ADDRESS _____

TELEPHONE _____

DATE _____

Figure A-3

CLIENT AND SPOUSE DATA

CLIENT NAME _____

ADDRESS _____

BIRTHDATE _____
RETIREMENT AGE _____
SOCIAL SECURITY AGE _____
MORTALITY AGE _____

MARRIED _____
SINGLE _____
SINGLE PARENT _____

SPOUSE NAME _____

BIRTHDATE _____
RETIREMENT AGE _____
SOCIAL SECURITY AGE _____
MORTALITY AGE _____

Figure A-4

CHILDREN'S DATA

NAME	AGE	COLLEGE START DATE	COLLEGE YEARS TO FUND	YEARLY COLLEGE COST	IMPAIRMENTS IF ANY

GRANDCHILDREN'S DATA

NAME	AGE	COLLEGE START DATE	COLLEGE YEARS TO FUND	YEARLY COLLEGE COST	IMPAIRMENTS IF ANY

INHERITANCES

DOES CLIENT EXPECT TO INHERIT?   YES____   NO____

NATURE OF ASSETS_____

VALUE $_____IN TRUST___YES____NO_____

OUTRIGHT__YES____NO_____

FROM WHOM?_____AGE_____

DOES SPOUSE EXPECT TO INHERIT?   YES_____   NO_____

NATURE OF ASSETS?_____

VALUE $_____IN TRUST___YES____NO_____

OUTRIGHT__YES____NO_____

FROM WHOM?_____AGE_____

PACKAGE #2—GOALS AND INVESTMENT PHILOSOPHY

Goals

These are absolutely necessary for any plan. Even if you do find out all of the client's goals, you need to know his goal for the particular problem or investment you are working on. For example, if you are just changing a CD into a mutual fund, you need to know if his goal with the investment is growth, income, etc. I highly recommend getting the client to complete this one on his own. It will hook him into the financial planning process. We frequently mail this form to the client before the data gathering interview to allow time for completion. *This is one of the few forms that a client will complete.*

Investment Philosophy

This is necessary for any plan that involves investments of any kind. Let us hope that all of yours do. The form is broken into philosophy and temperament just to see if the client will answer the same way. Many are confused about the level of risk they are willing to assume. If they are, then a more comprehensive risk profile may be needed. In that case, I usually ask a few more questions such as:

1. "If your investments were to go down in value steadily over a period of twelve consecutive months, would you lose sleep?"
2. "Have you ever had a sick feeling in the pit of your stomach from a fear of losing value in an investment you made?"
3. "Do you consider yourself a short-term or a long-term investor?"
4. "Do you understand the risk–reward principle?"

Textbooks say that most clients will overstate their willingness to take risks. I have found the opposite. Most say no risk until they are educated about purchasing power risk and the effects of inflation. A few more words about dollar–cost averaging, and the reduced risk of asset allocation, and most clients will be prepared to accept a little more risk than they thought originally.

A Tale of Two Investors

I usually attach this to the risk profile as a beginning of the education process about risk. Some may say that I am exercising undue influence on my client's risk profile. I do not think so. I believe that clients must be educated about all types of risk, especially purchasing power and interest rate risk. If, after that education, they still cannot withstand any principal fluctuation, I advise accordingly and get them to sign a waiver.

As a final test of risk, I usually ask the "crybaby" question. "John, are we in agreement that these are long-term investments? Do you understand that I have told you about principal fluctuation? In other words, do you know that your investment could be worth less two or more years from now than it is worth today? If that happens, are you going to be a crybaby or a prudent investor who sticks it out for the long term? If you're going to be a crybaby, let's undo this thing today."

Figure A-5

DATA GATHERING
(2)
GOALS/INVESTMENT PHILOSOPHY

Client _____

Date _____

Comments_____

_____

_____

_____

_____

_____

_____

Figure A-6

<u>GOAL</u>

BELOW IS A LIST OF MY/OUR FINANCIAL GOALS IN THE ORDER OF
IMPORTANCE.

1. _____

2. _____

3. _____

4. _____

5. _____

6. _____

7. _____

8. _____

Figure A-7

FINANCIAL GOALS WORKSHEET

CHECK YOUR GOALS - THEN RANK THEM BY PRIORITY	IMPORTANT (CHECK)	YOUR RANKINGS (1-10)
FINANCE CHILDREN'S EDUCATION	( )	( )
BUY A NEW HOME (PRIMARY OR VACATION)	( )	( )
BUY A NEW CAR/BOAT/FURNITURE/OTHER PERSONAL PROPERTY_____	( )	( )
TRAVEL EXTENSIVELY	( )	( )
REACH THE PROPER LEVEL OF INSURANCE PROTECTION FOR MYSELF AND MY FAMILY	( )	( )
SAVE FOR RETIREMENT	( )	( )
REDUCE/ELIMINATE DEBT	( )	( )
SET-UP A RESERVE/EMERGENCY FUND	( )	( )
BE FINANCIALLY INDEPENDENT AT AGE____	( )	( )
SUBSTANTIALLY CONTRIBUTE TO FAVORITE CHARITY/INSTITUTION	( )	( )
INVEST IN THE STOCK MARKET	( )	( )
HELP SUPPORT ELDERLY PARENT(S)	( )	( )
INVEST IN REAL ESTATE (LAND, RENTAL PROPERTY)	( )	( )
START/BUY/EXPAND OWN BUSINESS	( )	( )
START A FORMAL RETIREMENT PLAN FOR MY BUSINESS	( )	( )
LEAVE LARGE ESTATE FOR CHILDREN	( )	( )
OTHER_____	( )	( )
OTHER_____	( )	( )
OTHER_____	( )	( )

Figure A-8

MY/OUR INVESTMENT POLICY

	YOU	SPOUSE
I. INVESTMENT PHILOSOPHY:		
A. ATTITUDE TOWARD RISK		
1. VERY CONSERVATIVE (COMFORTABLE ONLY WITH LOWEST RISK)	( )	( )
2. CONSERVATIVE (WILLING TO ASSUME ONLY LIMITED RISK)	( )	( )
3. AVERAGE (WILL ASSUME MODERATE LEVEL OF RISK)	( )	( )
4. MODERATELY AGGRESSIVE (ACCEPTS HIGHER-THAN-AVERAGE RISK)	( )	( )
5. AGGRESSIVE (RISK TOLERANCE IS VERY HIGH)	( )	( )

OVERALL, I RATE MY TOLERANCE TOWARD RISK AS

(1-10 WITH 1 = RISK AVOIDER AND 10 = RISK TAKER)   ( )   ( )

	YOU	SPOUSE
II. INVESTMENT TEMPERAMENT (CHECK ONLY ONE)		
1. VERY CONSERVATIVE AND MORE INTERESTED IN CONSERVING CAPITAL THAN IN MAKING IT GROW. WILLING TO ACCEPT MODERATE INCOME AND NOMINAL CAPITAL GAINS POTENTIAL IN EXCHANGE FOR MINIMUM RISK.	( )	( )
2. INTERESTED ONLY IN HIGH QUALITY INVESTMENTS AND WILL BE QUITE SATISFIED WITH A REASONABLE CURRENT RETURN AND SOME GROWTH POTENTIAL.	( )	( )
3. LIBERAL CASH RETURN WITH A CHANCE FOR CAPITAL APPRECIATION	( )	( )
4. CAN ACCEPT A LOWER LEVEL OF INCOME NOW IN ORDER TO AIM FOR CAPITAL APPRECIATION AND GROWTH OF INCOME IN THE FUTURE.	( )	( )
5. WILLING TO ACCEPT RELATIVELY HIGH RISKS IN EXCHANGE FOR THE POSSIBILITY OF ABOVE AVERAGE CAPITAL GAINS AND APPRECIATION.	( )	( )

A TALE OF TWO INVESTORS

Playing and winning the investment game is not easy. Lack of market knowledge and errors in judgment haunt many novice (and some experienced) investors in their quest for higher returns. Moreover, investors often make mistakes that actually leave them poorer.

Although there are no guarantees in investing, your performance should improve if you avoid mistakes common to naive investors.

WHERE DO YOU STAND?

THE NAIVE INVESTOR

1 SETS NO GOALS.

2 FAILS TO RECOGNIZE INVESTMENT RISKS.

3 INVESTS IN "HOT TIPS."

4 FOLLOWS THE CROWD IN CHASING YESTERDAY'S OPPORTUNITIES.

5 PLACES TAX ADVANTAGES INHERENT TO SOME INVESTMENTS AHEAD OF INVESTMENT MERIT.

6 LACKS DISCIPLINE AND INVESTS SPORADICALLY.

7 CANNOT RESIST PUTTING EVERY EGG INTO ONE INVESTMENT BASKET.

8 CLINGS TO INVESTMENT LOSERS WHILE WAITING FOR A TURNAROUND (HOPING TO BREAK-EVEN)

THE PRUDENT INVESTOR

1 DEFINES SPECIFIC FINANCIAL GOALS AND THE TIMING/COSTS OF THESE GOALS.

2 KNOWS THE PERFECT INVESTMENT DOES NOT EXIST. STOCKS ARE CYCLICAL, MONEY MARKET RATES FLUCTUATE, REAL ESTATE IS ILLIQUID, AND SO ON.

3 BELIEVES RUMORS AND TIPS ARE WORTH EVERY PENNY PAID TO HEAR THEM.

4 AVOIDS CROWD FAVORITE AND SEEKS OUT UNRECOGNIZED VALUES THAT SHOW PROMISE FOR TOMORROW.

5 MAKES PROFIT THE PRIMARY MOTIVE AND PREFERS TO AVOID EXPENSIVE AUDITS.

6 INVESTS CONSISTENTLY TO SMOOTH THE UPS AND DOWN OF MARKET CYCLES.

7 DIVERSIFIES AND CORRELATES INVESTMENTS TO MINIMIZE RISK AND MAXIMIZE OPPORTUNITY FOR REWARD.

8 SETS REASONABLE SELL TARGETS AND CONTINUALLY INVESTIGATES NEW INVESTMENT OPPORTUNITIES.

A TALE OF TWO INVESTORS (CONTINUED)

THE NAIVE INVESTOR

9. FAILS TO TAKE PROFITS BEFORE PROFIT-TAKERS MOVE IN AND SEND PRICES TUMBLING.

10. FAILS TO TRACK HIS INVESTMENTS.

11. HAS UNREALISTIC PERFORMANCE EXPECTATIONS FOR HIS PORTFOLIO.

12. FAILS TO ADEQUATELY PROTECT IMPORTANT ASSETS.

13. PROCRASTINATES AND DOES NOTHING - AND LOSES VALUABLE TIME.

14. MEANDERS THROUGH LIFE WITHOUT ANY FINANCIAL STRATEGIES - LEAVING ALL TO CHANCE.

THE PRUDENT INVESTOR

9. SELLS BEFORE THE EXCITEMENT SUBSIDES, OCCASIONALLY TAKING PARTIAL PROFITS.

10. MONITORS HIS PORTFOLIO CONSTANTLY FOR ECONOMIC, MARKET, AND REGULATORY CHANGES - AS WELL AS CHANGES IN PERSONAL CIRCUMSTANCES.

11. UNDERSTANDS AND RESPECTS THE EFFICIENCY AND UNCERTAINTY OF THE FINANCIAL MARKETS.

12. MANAGES RISK OF LOSS TO LIFE, INCOME, HOME, AUTO, ETC.

13. UNDERSTANDS THE VALE OF TIME AND THE "MIRACLE OF COMPOUND INTEREST" IN INVESTING.

14. OBTAINS PROFESSIONAL ADVICE TO DEVELOP STRATEGIES FOR MANAGING ASSETS AND INCOME CONSISTENT WITH HIS GOALS AND PHILOSOPHIES.

SUCCESSFUL INVESTMENT MANAGEMENT REQUIRES STRICT ADHERENCE TO SOUND PRINCIPLES. IF YOU'RE GOING TO PLAY THE INVESTMENT GAME - PLAY IT SMART!

Package #3—PERSONAL FINANCIAL DATA

This should be the easiest part of the financial plan for CPAs. It is essentially a statement of personal financial condition for the client. When I am encouraging the client to give me the information to complete it, I call it the "Get out of town" statement. "What size check would I have to write to take everything you own and tell you to get out of town?" Preparing a statement of personal financial condition is something that the majority of your clients have never done. For shame; most CPAs have never done it either.

You will be surprised at the interest your client will show in their "get out of town" number. It gives them a benchmark to measure their past performance and future progress. It involves them in the process. You are the one who provided them with the benchmark. Presto—a relationship has been strengthened.

Completing the Forms

The two summary sheets show what the client *owns* and what he *owes*. We are speaking about assets and liabilities, of course. Assets are broken into productive (or earnings) and personal. This distinction is made because personal assets can sometimes cloud your thinking and that of your client. The client could be a millionaire on paper yet have no income if his assets are all personal. Productive assets can usually be counted on for income in retirement. Personal assets often cannot. I also like to segregate productive assets into liquid and nonliquid. Liquidity is an important feature for yourself and your client. A client may be rich in assets, yet virtually have no liquidity. This is a call for diversification. The opposite liquidity situation may also call for diversification.

Supplemental Schedules

When gathering data from clients, I like to have lots of room to put in numbers. I get all tied up when there is no room to write. That is why I made a schedule to go with each line on the asset section and the liability section. Asset schedules are in numerical sequence and liabilities are in alphabetic sequence. You may want to take off these references when presenting the plan to the client. I leave them on, because they help me to find detail if my client has a question. They are also invaluable for completing prospect forms and assigning projects to follow up on maturing CDs, for example.

Figure A-10

DATA GATHERING

(3)

PERSONAL FINANCIAL DATA

Client _____

Date _____

Comments _____

_____

_____

_____

_____

_____

_____

Figure A-11

Name _____

Date _____

WHAT I/WE OWN

PRODUCTIVE ASSETS:
LIQUID ASSETS
CASH (1) $_____

CERTIFICATES OF DEPOSIT (2)   _____

STOCKS (3)   _____

BONDS (4)   _____

MUTUAL FUNDS (5)   _____

US GOV'T SECURITIES (6)   _____

LIFE INSURANCE CASH VALUES (7)_____

TOTAL LIQUID ASSETS $_____ [A]

NON-LIQUID ASSETS
LOANS RECEIVABLE (8) $_____

RENTAL PROPERTY (9)   _____

OTHER REAL ESTATE (10)   _____

I.R.A.'S (11)   _____

OTHER RETIREMENT ACCOUNTS(12) _____

PRACTICE/BUSINESS VALUE (13) _____ _____

TOTAL NON-LIQUID
PRODUCTIVE ASSETS   _____ [B]

TOTAL PRODUCTIVE ASSETS [A+B] $_____ [C]

PERSONAL ASSETS:
HOME (15A) $_____

VACATION HOME (15B)   _____

HOME FURNISHINGS (15C)   _____

AUTOMOBILES (15D)   _____

OTHER PERSONAL ASSETS (15E) _____

TOTAL PERSONAL ASSETS   _____ [D]

TOTAL NON-LIQUID ASSETS [B+D]   _____ [E]

TOTAL ASSETS
$_____ [F]

Figure A-12

Name _____
Date _____

WHAT I/WE OWE

HOME MORTGAGE: (A-1) $_____ [G]

OTHER REAL ESTATE:
      VACATION HOME (A-2)   _____
      RENTAL PROPERTY (A-3)   _____
      OTHER (A-4)   _____

      TOTAL OTHER REAL ESTATE   _____ [H]

AUTO LOANS: (B)   _____ [I]
CREDIT CARDS/INSTALLMENT LOANS:(C)   _____ [J]
OTHER DEBT:
      OTHER SECURED DEBT (D)   _____
      BUSINESS AND
       INVESTMENT OBLIGATIONS (E)   _____
      OTHER LIFE INSURANCE
       CASH VALUE LOANS (F)   _____
      OTHER (G)   _____

      TOTAL OTHER DEBT   _____ [K]

TOTAL LIABILITIES: [G THRU K] $_____ [L]

NET WORTH CALCULATION:

      TOTAL ASSETS $_____ [F]

      TOTAL LIABILITIES   (-)   _____ [L]

      NET WORTH [F-L] $_____ [M]

Figure A-13

Name_____

Date_____

FINANCIAL STATEMENT WORKSHEETS
ASSETS

SCHEDULE #1:   CASH (CHECKING, SAVINGS, MONEY MARKET)

BANK OR MUTUAL FUND	TYPE OF ACCOUNT	INTEREST RATE	CURRENT BALANCE
		%	$
		%	$
		%	$
		%	$
		%	$
		%	$

SCHEDULE #2:   CERTIFICATES OF DEPOSIT

BANK NAME	TERM	MATURITY DATE	INTEREST RATE	AMOUNT
			%	$
			%	4
			%	$
			%	$
			%	$
			%	$
			%	$

Name _____
Date _____

ASSETS

SCHEDULE #3: MARKETABLE SECURITIES - STOCKS

DESCRIPTION	DATE BOUGHT	ORIGINAL COST	INCOME	CURRENT MARKET VALUE
		$	$	$
		$	$	$
		$	$	$
		$	$	$
		$	$	$
		$	$	$
		$	$	$
		$	$	$
		$	$	$
		$	$	$

SCHEDULE #4: MARKETABLE SECURITIES - BONDS, COMMODITIES, INCLUDE FARM CROPS AND CATTLE

DESCRIPTION	DATE BOUGHT	ORIGINAL COST	INCOME	CURRENT MARKET VALUE
		$	$	$
		$	$	$
		$	$	$
		$	$	$
		$	$	$
		$	$	$
		$	$	$

Name _____

Date _____

ASSETS

SCHEDULE #5: MUTUAL FUNDS

DESCRIPTION	DATE BOUGHT	TYPE OF FUND	# OF SHARES	CURRENT MARKET VALUE
				$
				$
				$
				$
				$
				$
				$
				$
				$
				$

SCHEDULE #6: U.S. GOV'T SECURITIES

DESCRIPTION	DATE BOUGHT	ORIGINAL COST	MATURITY DATE	CURRENT MARKET VALUE
		$		$
		$		$
		$		$
		$		$
		$		$
		$		$
		$		$
		$		$
		$		$

Figure A-16

ASSETS

SCHEDULE 7A CASH SURRENDER VALUE & 7B LIFE INSURANCE LOANS

<u>LIFE INSURANCE</u>

GROUP:

<u>CLIENT</u>

COMPANY	BENEFICIARY		FACE AMOUNT
$			$
$			$
$			$

SPOUSE

$			
$			
$			

TERM: PERSONALLY OWNED

CLIENT

COMPANY	ISSUE DATE	LOAN AMOUNT	BENEFICIARY	CASH VALUE	FACE AMOUNT	PREMIUM
		$		$	$	$
		$		$	$	$
		$		$	$	$
		$		$	$	$
		$		$	$	$

325

Figure A-17

TERM: PERSONALLY OWNED
SPOUSE

COMPANY	ISSUE DATE	LOAN AMOUNT	BENEFICIARY	CASH VALUE	FACE AMOUNT	PREMIUM
		$		$	$	$
		$		$	$	$
		$		$	$	$
		$		$	$	$
		$		$	$	$

PERMANENT: PERSONALLY OWNED
CLIENT

COMPANY	ISSUE DATE	LOAN AMOUNT	BENEFICIARY	CASH VALUE	FACE AMOUNT	PREMIUM
		$		$	$	$
		$		$	$	$
		$		$	$	$
		$		$	$	$
		$		$	$	$

SPOUSE

COMPANY	ISSUE DATE	LOAN AMOUNT	BENEFICIARY	CASH VALUE	FACE AMOUNT	PREMIUM
		$		$	$	$
		$		$	$	$
		$		$	$	$
		$		$	$	$
		$		$	$	$

326

Figure A-18

OWNED BY OTHERS ON CLIENT AND SPOUSE:

COMPANY	ISSUE DATE	LOAN AMOUNT	BENEFICIARY	CASH VALUE	FACE AMOUNT	PREMIUM
		$		$	$	$
		$		$	$	$
		$		$	$	$
		$		$	$	$
		$		$	$	$
		$		$	$	$

OWNED ON LIVES OF OTHERS:

COMPANY	ISSUE DATE	LOAN AMOUNT	BENEFICIARY	CASH VALUE	FACE AMOUNT	PREMIUM
		$		$	$	$
		$		$	$	$
		$		$	$	$
		$		$	$	$
		$		$	$	$
		$		$	$	$

NAME _____

DATE _____

Figure A-19

ASSETS

SCHEDULE #8: NOTES, MORTGAGES & ACCOUNTS RECEIVABLE

DEBTOR	SECURITY	STATUS	INTEREST RATE	ORIGINAL DATE	MATURITY DATE	MONTHLY PAYMENTS	UNPAID BALANCE
			%			$	$
			%			$	$
			%			$	$
			%			$	$
			%		$	$	$
			%		$	$	$

SCHEDULE #9A: RENTAL PROPERTY

DESCRIPTION	DATE BOUGHT	COST	INCOME	MORTGAGE BALANCE	CURRENT VALUE
		$	$	$	$
		$	$	$	$
		$	$	$	$
		$	$	$	$
		$	$	$	$
		$	$	$	$

SCHEDULE #10: FARM COMMERCIAL & OTHER REAL ESTATE (EXCL. PERSONAL RESIDENCE OR VACATION HOME)

DESCRIPTION	DATE BOUGHT	COST	INCOME	MORTGAGE BALANCE	CURRENT VALUE
		$	$	$	$
		$	$	$	$
		$	$	$	$
		$	$	$	$

Figure A-20

NAME _____

DATE _____

ASSETS
SCHEDULE #11: IRA'S

WHERE INVESTED	RATE	MATURITY	CURRENT VALUE
			$
			$
			$
			$
			$
			$

TOTAL $ _____

SCHEDULE #12: OTHER RETIREMENT ACCOUNTS

WHERE INVESTED	TYPE OF ACCOUNT (SEP-ETC.)	ESTIMATED INCOME AT RETIREMENT	CURRENT VALUE
		$	$
		$	$
		$	$
		$	$
		$	$
		$	$

TOTAL $ _____

Figure A-21

NAME _____

DATE _____

ASSETS

SCHEDULE #13: INVESTMENTS IN BUSINESS, PARTNERSHIPS JOINT VENTURES & CLOSELY HELD CORPORATIONS (ACTIVE ONLY)

*TYPE OF BUSINESS	BUSINESS NAME	% OWNED	NUMBER OF SHARES	BUSINESS **FORM	ESTIMATED ANNUAL EARNINGS	NET WORTH	*** PERSONAL LIABILITY	ESTIMATED CURRENT VALUE
					$	$	$	$
					$	$	$	$
					$	$	$	$
					$	$	$	$
					$	$	$	$
					$	$	$	$
					$	$	$	$
					$	$	$	$
					$	$	$	$
					$	$	$	$
					$	$	$	$
TOTALS					$	$	$	$

*   Indicate retail, wholesale, mfg. product, etc.

**   Indicate proprietorship, partnership, corporation, etc.

***   Indicate personal borrowing against business assets. DO NOT include corporate loans that you only guarantee personally.

Figure A-22

NAME _____

DATE _____

ASSETS
SCHEDULE #14: OTHER NON-LIQUID ASSETS

DESCRIPTION	ORIGINAL COST	LOANS	ESTIMATED MARKET VALUE
FARM OR OTHER EQUIPMENT			
	$	$	$
	$	$	$
	$	$	$
	$	$	$
	$	$	$
	$	$	$
	$	$	$
	$	$	$
	$	$	$
		TOTAL	$

LIMITED PARTNERSHIPS			
	$	$	$
	$	$	$
		TOTAL	$

OTHER			
	$	$	$
	$	$	$
	$	$	$
	$	$	$
	$	$	$
	$	$	$
	$	$	$
		TOTAL	$

Figure A-23

NAME_____

DATE_____

ASSETS

SCHEDULE #15:   PERSONAL ASSETS

	DATE BOUGHT	COSTS & IMPROVEMENTS	CURRENT VALUE
15 A PERSONAL RESIDENCE DESCRIPTION/ADDRESS		$	$
		$	$
15 B VACATION HOME DESCRIPTION/ADDRESS		$	$
		$	$
15 C HOME FURNISHINGS		$	$
		$	$

15 D AUTOS & OTHER VEHICLES DESCRIPTIONS	CURRENT VALUE
	$
	$
	$
	$
TOTAL	$

15 E OTHER PERSONAL ASSETS	CURRENT VALUE
JEWELRY	$
COLLECTIBLES (NOT HELD FOR INVESTMENT)	$
OTHER	$
	$
	$
TOTAL	$

Figure A-24

NAME_____

DATE_____

<u>LIABILITIES</u>

SCHEDULE A: REAL ESTATE MORTGAGES

(A-1) PERSONAL RESIDENCE (HOME) (SEE SCHEDULE 15 FOR ASSET)

MORTGAGE/CREDITOR	INTEREST RATE	MATURITY DATE	PAYMENT	UNPAID BALANCE
			$	$

(A-2) VACATION HOME MORTGAGE

			$	$
			$	$

(A-3) RENTAL PROPERTY MORTGAGES (SEE ASSET SCHEDULE 9)

DESCRIPTION OF PROPERTY	INTEREST RATE	MATURITY DATE	PAYMENT	UNPAID BALANCE
			$	$
			$	$
			$	$

(A-4) OTHER REAL ESTATE MORTGAGES (SEE ASSET SCHEDULE 10)

DESCRIPTION OF PROPERTY	INTEREST RATE	MATURITY DATE	PAYMENT	UNPAID BALANCE
			$	$
			$	$
			$	$

SCHEDULE B - AUTO/VEHICLE LOANS

DESCRIPTION OF VEHICLE	CREDITOR	INTEREST RATE	MATURITY DATE	PAYMENT	UNPAID BALANCE
				$	$
				$	$
				$	$

SCHEDULE C CREDIT CARDS AND INSTALLMENT LOANS

CREDITOR	INTEREST RATE	PAYMENT	DUE DATE	UNPAID BALANCE
			$	$
			$	$
			$	$
			$	$
			$	$
			$	$

SCHEDULE D - OTHER DEBT

CREDITOR	SECURITY	INTEREST RATE	PAYMENT	DUE DATE	UNPAID BALANCE
			$		$
			$		$
			$		$
			$		$

Figure A-24   (Continued)

SCHEDULE E -   BUSINESS & INVESTMENT OBLIGATIONS
           SEE ASSET   SCHEDULES 13 & 14

CREDITOR	SECURITY	INTEREST RATE	PAYMENT	DUE DATE	UNPAID BALANCE
			$		$
			$		$
			$		$
			$		$
			$		$
			$		$
			$		$
			$		$
			$		$
			$		$

SCHEDULE F -   LIFE INSURANCE CASH VALUE LOANS
           SEE ASSET SCHEDULE 7

INSURANCE COMPANY	POLICY #	INTEREST RATE	PAYMENT	DUE DATE	UNPAID BALANCE
			$		$
			$		$
			$		$
			$		$

SCHEDULE G - OTHER DEBT NOT LISTED

CREDITOR	SECURITY	INTEREST RATE	PAYMENT	DUE DATE	UNPAID BALANCE
			$		$
			$		$
			$		$

PACKAGE #4—INCOME AND EXPENSE PLANNING

Planning for income and expenses is an important part of any financial plan but especially for retirement planning. I have found it extremely difficult to obtain adequate information from the client on income and expenses. Most have no idea of what their current living expenses are, much less what they will need in retirement. Most clients will provide you with a goal for income, however, and that is usually the starting point I use rather than doing an in-depth analysis of today's living expenses with projections for retirement. If the goal is unrealistic in terms of their current income or assets or fails to consider inflation, then I will counsel with the client about more realistic expectations. If my client is highly motivated and willing to go through the process, I will assist in doing an in-depth analysis of living expenses. That is very time intensive, however, and often yields information that is not decisive.

That is a long way of saying that I usually use a realistic retirement income expectation based on the client's current income and income goal for retirement. If a client wants to travel extensively, for example, I may use a retirement income goal that is larger than today's income. If a client expects to have a lot of debts paid off at retirement, then a reduction in income may be appropriate. If a client has a limited amount of assets and is only a short time away from retirement, then you adjust expectations accordingly.

For those situations where a more thorough analysis is needed and the client will not cooperate in gathering actual income and expense numbers, I use the "Determining Living Expense Needs from the Tax Return" form. Using this form, I can gather estimated amounts from the tax return or its supporting data to arrive at an educated estimate of living expenses. It is not perfect, but it is useful. Most of the items can be taken directly from the tax return; others have to be estimated. For example, some CPAs may freeze on the expense item "commuting expense." That is easy. You know where your client works and where he lives. Just estimate the round-trip mileage for 50 weeks out of the year and multiply by the IRS standard mileage rate. This item can be eliminated or reduced in retirement. Medical expenses, however, can be expected to increase dramatically. Are you getting the drift of the form? It is to compare major expenses today versus retirement. Try preparing one for yourself. It is more accurate than you might think.

If you still want more detail, try the Income/Expense Inventory. I have seldom used this form except in workshops.

Figure A-25

DATA GATHERING

(4)

<u>INCOME & EXPENSE PLANNING</u>
<u>(BUDGETING)</u>

Client _____

Date _____

Comments _____

_____

_____

_____

_____

_____

_____

Figure A-26

DETERMINING LIVING EXPENSE NEEDS
(FROM THE TAX RETURN)

TODAY'S DOLLARS

	TODAY	AT RETIREMENT
RECEIPTS		
WAGES & SALARY	_____	TO BE DETERMINED
INTEREST	_____	" "
DIVIDENDS	_____	" "
TAX-FREE INCOME	_____	" "
BUSINESS INCOME	_____	" "
CASH FLOW FROM RENTALS PENSIONS, ETC.	_____	" "
SOCIAL SECURITY BENEFITS	_____	" "
TOTAL RECEIPTS	==========	" "
EXPENDITURES		
TAXES - FEDERAL INCOME FICA	_____	_____
MORTGAGE PAYMENTS	_____	_____
PROPERTY INSURANCE TAXES	_____	_____
OTHER LIABILITY	_____	_____
MEDICAL EXPENSE (INCLUDING INSURANCE)	_____	_____
CONTRIBUTIONS	_____	_____
EMPLOYEE BUSINESS EXP.	_____	_____
*CONTRIBUTIONS TO RETIREMENT PLANS	_____	_____
COMMUTING EXPENSE	_____	_____
JOB RELATED EXPENSE	_____	_____
TOTAL EXPENDITURES	==========	==========
BALANCE FOR SAVINGS & NORMAL LIVING EXP.	_____	_____
LESS SAVINGS	_____	_____
NORMAL LIVING EXPENSE	_____	_____
TOTAL FUNDS REQUIRED	==========	==========

*Do not include Tax Sheltered ORP/403(b), etc., since they have already been excluded from salary number.

Figure A-27

INCOME/EXPENSE INVENTORY

A.   INCOME:

1.   Use your most recent pay stub to estimate your total income for the next 12 months. If your income is irregular (overtime/self-employment), use an estimate you feel is reasonably conservative.
Husband_____ + Wife_____ /12=_____(1)
(estimated annual income)

2.   Enter monthly withholding (enter husband & wife separately)
_____ + _____ + _____ = _____(2a)
_____ + _____ + _____ = _____(2b)
(federal tax)   (FICA/Soc.Sec)
(other payroll deductions will be entered in appropriate budget categories)

3.   Determine Net Spendable Income   =   _____(3)
(line 1 minus lines 2a and 2b)

B.   EXPENSES:

1.   use your check register and all other available records to determine your average monthly <u>fixed</u> expenses for the past 12 months:

    a.   GIVING   _____/12= _____(1a)

    b.   SAVINGS (include payroll deductions that go into savings)
        Emergency Fund _____/12= _____(4)
        Retirement Fund _____/12= _____(5)
        Education Fund   _____/12= _____(6)
        _____ _____/12= _____(7)
        _____ _____/12= _____(8)
        _____ _____/12= _____(9)
        TOTAL SAVINGS   _____(1b)
        (add lines 4 thru 9)
        HOUSEHOLD EXPENSES

    c.   Mortgage/Rent   _____/12= _____(1a)
        Property Taxes   _____/12= _____(10)
        Insurance Premium _____/12= _____(11)
        Electric/Gas   _____/12= _____(12)
        Water/Sewer   _____/12= _____(13)
        Sanitation   _____/12= _____(14)
        Telephone   _____/12= _____(15)
        Cable TV   _____/12= _____(16)
        Maint/Repairs   _____/12= _____(17)
        Other   _____/12= _____(18)

        TOTAL HOUSEHOLD EXPENSES   _____(1c)

Figure A-27   (Continued)

d.   AUTO EXPENSES
Loan Payments _____/12= _____(20)
Insurance Premium _____/12=
License _____/12= _____(22)
Gas/Oil _____/12= _____(23)
Maint/Repairs _____/12= _____(24)
Other _____/12= _____(25)

TOTAL AUTO EXPENSE _____(1d)

e.   DEBTS (include all debts except home mortgage and auto loans)
Other Real Estate _____/12= _____(26)
Credit Cards _____/12= _____(27)
Other _____/12= _____(28)

TOTAL DEBTS _____(1e)
(add lines 26 thru 28)

f.   MEDICAL EXPENSES (do not include reimbursed expenses)
Insurance Premium _____/12= _____(29)
Doctor _____/12= _____(30)
Dentist _____/12= _____(31)
Prescriptions _____/12= _____(32)
Other _____/12= _____(33)

TOTAL MEDICAL EXPENSES _____(1f)
(add lines 29 thru 33)

g.   INSURANCE * (do not include homeowner's, auto, and medical
insurance)
Life Insurance _____/12= _____(34)
Disability Ins. _____/12= _____(35)
Liability Ins. _____/12= _____(36)
Other _____/12= _____(37)

TOTAL INSURANCE PAYMENTS _____(1g)
(add lines 34 thru 37)

TOTAL FIXED EXPENSES _____(1h)
(add lines 1a,b,c,d,f and g)

*(include payroll deductions)

Figure A-27   (Continued)

2.   Determine your average monthly <u>variable</u> expenses for the past 12 months:

    a.   FOOD/GROCERIES _____ /12= _____ (2a)
        (do not include eating out)

    b.   CLOTHING
        Purchases   _____ /12= _____ (38)
        Cleaners   _____ /12= _____ (39)
        TOTAL CLOTHING   _____ (2b)
        (add lines 38 and 39)

    c.   ENTERTAINMENT/RECREATION
        Eating Out   _____ /12= _____ (40)
        Baby-sitting   _____ /12= _____ (41)
        Vacation   _____ /12= _____ (42)
        Lessons   _____ /12= _____ (43)
        Club Dues   _____ /12= _____ (44)
        _____   _____ /12= _____ (45)
        _____   _____ /12= _____ (46)
        TOTAL ENTERTAINMENT   _____ (2c)
        (add lines 40 thru 46)

    d.   MISCELLANEOUS EXPENSES
        Personal Care   _____ /12= _____ (47)
        Allowances   _____ /12= _____ (48)
        Gifts(birthdays,
        etc)   _____ /12= _____ (49)
        Christmas   _____ /12= _____ (50)
        _____   _____ /12= _____ (51)
        _____   _____ /12= _____ (52)

        TOTAL MISCELLANEOUS   _____ (2d)
        (add lines 47 thru 52)
    TOTAL VARIABLE EXPENSES   _____ (2c)
    (add lines 2a,b,c, and d)

C.   SUMMARY

NET SPENDABLE INCOME (LINE 3)   _____ [53]
TOTAL FIXED AN VARIABLE EXPENSE   (-)_____ [54]
(add lines 1h and 2e)

SURPLUS/DEFICIT   =_____ [55]

PACKAGE #5—INSURANCE

The problem with insurance data gathering for CPA–financial planners is that insurance is usually not part of the tax return. Clients do not associate their CPA with insurance. Most CPAs like it that way. However, if you are going to be a full-service financial planner, insurance is an integral part of the process. Although about one third of the plans we prepare have not had this information, our goal is to put it into 90 percent.

Gathering the data is actually quite easy. Just explain to the client that the amount and type of insurance that they have is integral to planning for college education, retirement, investment allocation, estate planning, etc. I often explain that insurance rates have changed dramatically during the last 20 years. Most of the rate changes have been decreases because of longer life expectancies. They could be paying too much for insurance or have the wrong type to fit their goals today. In any event, we need to know how much they have and what type it is.

Be sure to ask the client to bring in health and disability policies as well as life. Once you have the policies, you can usually find all the information you need about the policy type, cash surrender value, premium, etc. Very often, an old policy is a poor investment of premium dollars because of the high mortality rates under the old policy that were never adjusted. They can often exchange the old policy for a new one (assuming no health problems) and get more insurance, a higher rate of return, or pay less premiums for the same amount of insurance.

Pay close attention to the ownership of policies. This may determine whether or not their face value will be included in the taxable estate. I have seen many cases where insurance policies alone cause a client to have a taxable estate. Clients are surprised to learn that one of the primary beneficiaries of their life insurance is going to be the IRS.

Figure A-28

DATA GATHERING

(5)

<u>INSURANCE LISTING</u>

Client _____

Date _____

Comments_____

_____

_____

_____

_____

_____

_____

_____

Figure A-29

LIFE INSURANCE

GROUP:

<u>CLIENT</u>

FACE AMOUNT	COMPANY	BENEFICIARY	MONTHLY PREMIUM
$			$
$			$
$			$
$			$
$			$

<u>SPOUSE</u>

FACE AMOUNT	COMPANY	BENEFICIARY	MONTHLY PREMIUM
$			$
$			$
$			$
$			$
$			$

PERSONALLY OWNED:

<u>CLIENT</u>

CASH VALUE	FACE AMOUNT	COMPANY	TYPE	ISSUE DATE	LOAN AMOUNT	BENEFICIARY	PREMIUM

<u>SPOUSE</u>

CASH VALUE	FACE AMOUNT	COMPANY	TYPE	ISSUE DATE	LOAN AMOUNT	BENEFICIARY	PREMIUM

TOTAL CLIENT CASH VALUE _____ PREMIUM _____ FACE VALUE_____

TOTAL SPOUSE VALUE _____ PREMIUM _____ FACE VALUE_____

GRAND TOTAL $======== $======= $=======

Figure A-30

OWNED BY OTHERS ON CLIENT AND SPOUSE:

CASH VALUE	FACE AMOUNT	COMPANY	TYPE	ISSUE DATE	LOAN AMOUNT	BENEFICIARY	PREMIUM

OWNED ON LIVES OF OTHERS

CASH VALUE	FACE AMOUNT	COMPANY	TYPE	ISSUE DATE	LOAN AMOUNT	BENEFICIARY	PREMIUM

Figure A-31

HEALTH AND DISABILITY

INCOME REPLACEMENT

INSD	TYPE POLICY	DATE ISD.	PRM	MO. INC.	WAITING PERIOD	BENEFIT PERIOD	MO. INC.	WAITING PERIOD	BENEFIT PERIOD

DEFINITION OF DISABILITY,
EACH
PLAN_____

MEDICAL REIMBURSEMENT

TYPE POLICY	DATE ISSUED	PRM	ROOM & BOARD	SURGICAL SCHED.	INIT. DED.	CORRIDOR DED.	CO-INS.	MAX. BENEFIT

*G=GROUP   C=COMMERCIAL   GR=GUARANTEED RENEWABLE
NC=NONCANCELLABLE

PACKAGE #6—ESTATE PLANNING

If you are like myself and a lot of CPAs, I hated estate planning for many years. I hated it because I did not know enough about it. I chose to believe that most of my clients would not be affected by it. The more estate tax returns I did, however, the more I realized that a lot of my clients were being robbed unnecessarily by the IRS. Asking a client's heir to write checks in the hundreds of thousands to pay estate taxes was a wake-up call for me.

Estate planning, like income tax planning, is complicated. However, like income taxes, the rules can be reduced to a few basics. Once you have the basics, you can branch out into the more complicated items. If an estate is complex, then recognize that help is needed and get it. Your client will expect you to do that. Your primary responsibility is to *recognize* estate-tax problems, *communicate* them to the client, and assist him in solving them. You do not have to be an attorney or estate-tax specialist to do that.

The data gathering forms in our package are designed to get the basic information required to recognize problems or needs if some exist. When you can recognize the problem and communicate the problem to the client then the solutions can be developed.

Figure A-32

DATA GATHERING

(6)

<u>ESTATE PLANNING</u>

Client _____

Date _____

Comments _____
_____
_____
_____
_____
_____
_____

Figure A-33

ESTATE PLANS

Does client
have a will?   ___Yes   ___No   Date_____   Date last
reviewed_____

Does spouse
have a will?   ___Yes   ___No   Date_____   Date last
reviewed_____

ASSETS	PLANS FOR DISPOSITION	ASSETS	PLANS FOR DISPOSITION

Who will need asset management advice as a survivor?
___ Client   ___ Spouse   ___ Children   ____ Other Heirs

GIFTS

TO WHOM MADE	NATURE OF ASSETS	DATE MADE	VALUE	JOINT WITH SPOUSE (YES/NO)

TRUSTS FOR BENEFIT OF OTHERS

DESCRIPTION	MARKET CURRENT VALUE	ORIGINAL VALUE	BENEFICIARY	TRUSTEE	IRREVOCABLE (YES/NO)

Who established trust: client and/or spouse? _____

What is purpose of trust? _____

Should the survivor retain or liquidate assets after the first death?_____

Figure A-33   (Continued)

Is there a need for a living trust? i.e.:

       Asset management in event of disability.

       Probate will be expensive and time consuming.

       Need for privacy. If so, see separate trust package.

Should your assets be passed to your heirs without erosion upon the second death?

_____

If you wish to have part of your assets retained and part liquidated, specify amount or percentage you wish to retain: _____

Do you want to pass some of your assets to a charity, a church or an educational institution: Describe: _____

_____

_____

Do you plan to make any gifts or establish a trust within the next five years? If so, describe: _____

_____

Figure A-34

FAMILY SURVIVORSHIP INFORMATION

Date of marriage _____   Client divorced   ____Yes   ____No

Spouse divorced   ____Yes   ____No

Children born of previous marriages: names _____

_____

Adopted by spouse   ____Yes   ____No

Describe financial obligations from previous marriages: _____

_____

Describe special needs or impairment of all dependents: _____

_____

Amount of emergency fund family should have in event of death of client $ _____
spouse $_____

Should mortgage be paid off in event of death of client?
            ____YES   ____NO

Should non-working spouse work in event of client's death?
            ____YES   ____NO

How much can spouse earn: $_____

Survivor's Monthly Income Objective (spendable)
Dependence period $_____   Blackout period $_____   Retirement $_____

Family Monthly Income Objective (spendable)
Percent of final salary _____% or Specified amount $_____

PACKAGE #7—ADVISOR AND DOCUMENT LISTING

We usually know most of this information about our clients and can complete the forms with very little assistance. When we do not know the information in advance, it is important to obtain it. It could be embarrassing to go through a long presentation to the client on the benefits of buy–sell agreements only to find out later that they already have a very nice one in place. This information is easy to obtain but also easy to ignore. Why take a chance? At least ask the client if he has it. Even if he never brings you a copy, you will at least know that he has it.

Figure A-35

DATA GATHERING

(7)

ADVISOR & DOCUMENT LISTING

Client _____

Date _____

Comments_____

_____

_____

_____

_____

_____

_____

Figure A-36

ADVISORS

NAME _____

ADDRESS _____

PHONE _____ PERSONAL _____ BUSINESS

ATTORNEY _____

_____

ACCOUNTANT _____

_____

BANKER _____

_____

FINANCIAL PLANNER _____

_____

INSURANCE AGENTS _____ _____

_____

OTHER _____

_____

TO WHOM DO YOU TURN WITH SERIOUS FINANCIAL DECISIONS? _____

_____

ARE YOU CONSIDERING ANY FINANCIAL PROPOSALS? _____

_____

DOCUMENT CHECKLIST

OBTAIN A COPY OF THE FOLLOWING DOCUMENTS:

	DATE OBTAINED	COMMENT
BUY-SELL AGREEMENT		
DEFERRED COMPENSATION AGREEMENT		
FINANCIAL STATEMENT		
QUALIFIED PLAN CENSUS		
RETIREMENT PLAN DESCRIPTION		
EMPLOYMENT BENEFITS DESCRIPTION		
TRUST DOCUMENTS		
OTHER (LIST)		

Appendix B

How To Prepare Financial Plans—Sample Plans

You now know what data has to be gathered and how to gather it. You can use the forms provided in this book or develop your own. You can also use software. I have had many CPAs say that the data gathering process seems very old-fashioned after preparing tax returns completely by computer. That may be true. However, most of these CPAs never take another alternative. They are looking for the "quick and easy" way to do plans. That is perfectly natural. However, if the search for the quick and easy is keeping you from doing plans at all, I suggest you try this alternative. I have found it to be less time consuming than any financial planning software on the market. The key ingredient to the entire recipe is understanding. If you understand the calculations and methods used in preparing the plan and can communicate them to the client, then I do not care how you prepare the plans. Just do not use automation as an excuse for not preparing them.

MODULES AND "THE BASICS"

We had "packages" in our data gathering forms. We call them "modules" in our financial planning forms. Just as we have basic required data gathering forms, we also have basic required modules for financial plans. These modules are numbered 1 through 11, but the basics are in modules 1 through 4, 8, and 11.

Our modules are both tangible forms and intangible parts to the financial plan. It is not necessary to use forms as we do to do the parts of a financial plan. I know the parts so well now that I seldom use the forms. They were invaluable during the first couple of years, however. The forms kept me *focused*. Whenever I drew a blank, or could not come up with a solution, or felt that there might be something I was overlooking, the forms brought me back on track. Think of them as checklists. I still keep a set of the basics close by whenever I am working on a plan.

Figure B-1

CLIENT _____

DATE _____

FINANCIAL/INVESTMENT PLAN
MODULE DIRECTORY

MODULE #			CHECK MODULES REQUIRED	
			BASIC	ADVANCED
1.	INTRODUCTION		X	
	A	COVER LETTER		
	B.	COVER SHEET		
	C.	TABLE OF CONTENTS		
2.	YOUR GOALS		X	
3.	PLAN SUMMARY		X	
4.	ASSETS AVAILABLE TO MEET YOUR GOALS		X	
	A.	FINANCIAL DATA SHEETS (FROM DATA GATHERING)		
	B.	FUNDS AVAILABLE LISTING		
5.	ASSETS REQUIRED TO MEET YOUR GOALS			
	A.	FUNDS REQUIRED SHEET		
	B.	DETERMINING LIVING EXPENSE NEEDS		
	C.	FINANCIAL PLANNING WORKSHEET		
	D.	COLLEGE EDUCATION PLANNING WORKSHEET		
6.	ESTATE PLANNING			
	A.	PROJECTING ESTATE VALUES & TAXES		
	B.	LIQUIDITY TEST		
7.	INSURANCE NEEDS			
	A.	LIFE INSURANCE NEEDS WORKSHEETS		
	B.	DISABILITY NEEDS WORKSHEET		

Figure B-1   (Continued)

8.   OUR RECOMMENDATIONS   ___X___   _____

    A.   HOW WE RECOMMEND YOU REACH   _____   _____
        YOUR GOALS (STEPS)
    B.   OTHER RECOMMENDATIONS   _____   _____

9.   ASSET ALLOCATION   _____   _____

    A.   ASSET ALLOCATION/INCOME ANALYSIS _____   _____
    B.   DIVERSIFICATION PLAN/INVESTMENT   _____   _____
        PYRAMID
    C.   PRODUCT ANALYSIS   _____   _____
        1.   HISTORIC PERFORMANCE DATA   _____   _____
        2.   CDA ILLUSTRATIONS   _____   _____
    D.   HYPOTHETICAL ILLUSTRATIONS   _____   _____

10.   PROSPECTUSES, APPLICATIONS, BROCHURES   _____   _____

11.   IMPLEMENTATION INSTRUCTIONS   ___X___   _____

MODULE #1—INTRODUCTION FORMS

These are so easy, they hardly seem worth mentioning. However, they are important to the plan. They help the client to see that the plan was custom designed for her, and help her to find the appropriate sections.

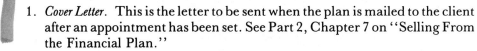 1. *Cover Letter*. This is the letter to be sent when the plan is mailed to the client after an appointment has been set. See Part 2, Chapter 7 on ''Selling From the Financial Plan.''

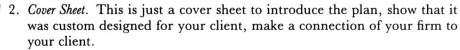 2. *Cover Sheet*. This is just a cover sheet to introduce the plan, show that it was custom designed for your client, make a connection of your firm to your client.

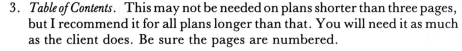 3. *Table of Contents*. This may not be needed on plans shorter than three pages, but I recommend it for all plans longer than that. You will need it as much as the client does. Be sure the pages are numbered.

Figure B-2

INTRODUCTION

Figure B-2   (Continued)

Date _____

Name _____
Address _____
City_____

Dear _____ :

I have enclosed an Investment/Financial Plan based on a review of your current financial conditions and financial goals you wish to attain. I hope you will have time to review the plan prior to our scheduled meeting on_____ at _____.

I think this plan will put you on the "right path". Look it over, make your notes and bring it with you to our meeting. I look forward to discussing it with you.

Sincerely,

Registered Representative

Figure B-2   (Continued)

A PERSONAL

FINANCIAL/INVESTMENT PLAN

PREPARED ESPECIALLY FOR

_____

_____

Name of Your Company

& First Global

Figure B-2   (Continued)

TABLE OF CONTENTS

<u>PAGE</u>

1.   YOUR GOALS

2.   PLAN SUMMARY

3.   ASSETS AVAILABLE TO MEET YOUR GOALS

4.   ASSETS REQUIRED TO MEET YOUR GOALS

5.   ESTATE PROJECTIONS

6.   INSURANCE NEEDS

7.   OUR RECOMMENDATIONS

8.   ASSET ALLOCATION ANALYSIS

      A.   PAST AND FUTURE PERFORMANCE

      B.   DIVERSIFICATION PLAN

      C.   MUTUAL FUND DATE

      D.   ANNUITY DATA

9.   PROSPECTUSES, APPLICATIONS, BROCHURES

MODULE #2—GOALS

This is only a restatement of the goals the client provided to you in the data gathering process. Obviously, you do not show any other goals on the form. Just show your client's stated goals. If you are only working on an education fund, then that will be the only goal shown. Remember, this is a customized plan.

When you set up the client goal sheet, print it and put it in plain sight all of the time you are working on the plan. When presenting the plan to the client, reread the goals and ask: ''Are we in agreement that these are the goals you are trying to reach?''

Figure B-3

YOUR FINANCIAL GOALS

Figure B-3   (Continued)

NAME _____

DATE _____

YOUR GOALS

\#   SHORT TERM (1 TO 3 YEARS)

____   SAVE FOR_____TO BE PURCHASED IN_____YEARS.
ESTIMATED AMOUNT REQUIRED $_____.

____   SAVE FOR_____ ___TO BE PURCHASED IN_____YEARS.
ESTIMATED AMOUNT REQUIRED $_____.

____   OTHER_____
AMOUNT $_____TIME_____

____   ESTABLISH AN EMERGENCY FUND.

____   ESTABLISH A FUND FOR RECURRING "LARGE" EXPENSES.

INTERMEDIATE GOALS (4 TO 10 YEARS)

____   GOAL _____
TIME _____
AMOUNT $_____

____   GOAL _____
TIME _____
AMOUNT $_____

SPECIFIC TIME GOALS & LONG RANGE

____   CHILDREN'S EDUCATION
       CHILD 1 -YEARS TILL COLLEGE _____AMOUNT REQUIRED
       IN TODAY'S DOLLARS $_____.
       CHILD 2 -YEARS TILL COLLEGE _____AMOUNT REQUIRED
       IN TODAY'S DOLLARS $_____.
       CHILD 3 -YEARS TILL COLLEGE _____AMOUNT REQUIRED
       IN TODAY'S DOLLARS $_____.

____   RETIRE OR ACHIEVE FINANCIAL INDEPENDENCE AT
AGE_____IN_____YEARS. I DEFINE FINANCIAL INDEPENDENCE AS AN
ANNUAL INCOME OF $_____WITHOUT WORKING.

____   REDUCE TAX LIABILITY AND ACHIEVE HIGHER "AFTER TAX" RETURN.

____   OTHER

       GOAL _____
TIME TO REACH_____
AMOUNT $_____

       COMMENTS_____
_____
_____

MODULE #3—PLAN SUMMARY

I like to do a plan summary up front. It goes with my belief in:

1. Telling your clients what you are going to tell them.
2. Tell them.
3. Tell them what you told them.

It is easy to confuse this summary with the recommendations at the end of the plan. The summary is more of a sequential step process for all of the things that the client needs to do in order to reach his goals. The recommendations are usually arranged in order of the goals stated and are more detailed than the summary. The summary may summarize several steps included in the recommendations. Again, if possible, I like to have the summary steps stated in *sequential order*.

Depending on the type of client you are dealing with, the summary sheet or the recommendation sheet or both may be the only sheets necessary to discuss with the client. If your client is a ''get to the point'' type of person, then go with the summary. If the client is more analytical, then you may need to go over the plan page by page. I recommend starting with the summary. Watch the client's reactions, then proceed accordingly.

Figure B-4

PLAN SUMMARY

Figure B-4   (Continued)

CLIENT_____

DATE _____

PLAN SUMMARY

These are the steps you should take in order to achieve your goals.

<u>Dates</u>

1.   _____   _____

      _____   _____

2.   _____   _____

      _____   _____

3.   _____   _____

      _____   _____

4.   _____   _____

      _____   _____

5.   _____   _____

      _____   _____

6.   _____   _____

      _____   _____

7.   _____   _____

      _____   _____

8.   _____   _____

      _____   _____

MODULE #4—ASSETS AVAILABLE TO MEET YOUR GOALS

This module can be a nicely printed version of the Statement of Financial Condition completed as part of data gathering. I do not usually include the detail schedules as part of the plan but keep the list available for reference. For analytical types I may include the detailed lists. Often, it is supplemented with assets *separately listed* that are applicable to this plan only. For example, if the client's only stated goal for this plan is to retire at age 60 with an annual income of $50,000, you would only include assets available for this purpose. Education funds, personal residence, autos, and so on, would not be included because they will not be available to meet this goal.

This is the starting point. It brings both you and your client to a focus point from where you are starting. It helps both of you understand the distance that must be traveled to reach your goals.

Figure B-5

ASSETS AVAILABLE TO MEET YOUR GOALS

Figure B-5   (Continued)

Name _____

Date _____

WHAT I/WE OWN

PRODUCTIVE ASSETS:
 LIQUID ASSETS
  CASH (1) _____
  CERTIFICATES OF DEPOSIT (2) _____
  STOCKS (3) _____
  BONDS (4) _____
  MUTUAL FUNDS (5) _____
  US GOV'T SECURITIES (6) _____
  LIFE INSURANCE CASH VALUES (7) _____

  TOTAL LIQUID ASSETS _____ [A]

 NON-LIQUID ASSETS
  LOANS RECEIVABLE (8) _____
  RENTAL PROPERTY (9) _____
  OTHER REAL ESTATE (10) _____
  I.R.A.'S (11) _____
  OTHER RETIREMENT ACCOUNTS(12) _____
  PRACTICE/BUSINESS VALUE (13) _____ _____

  TOTAL NON-LIQUID
  PRODUCTIVE ASSETS _____ [B]
  TOTAL PRODUCTIVE ASSETS [A+B] _____ [C]

PERSONAL ASSETS:
  HOME (15A) _____
  VACATION HOME (15B) _____
  HOME FURNISHINGS (15C) _____
  AUTOMOBILES (15D) _____
  OTHER PERSONAL ASSETS (15E) _____

  TOTAL PERSONAL ASSETS _____ [D]
  TOTAL NON-LIQUID ASSETS [B+D] _____ [E]

TOTAL ASSETS _____ [F]

Figure B-5   (Continued)

Name _____

Date _____

WHAT I/WE OWE

HOME MORTGAGE: (A-1)   _____[G]

OTHER REAL ESTATE:
      VACATION HOME (A-)   _____
      RENTAL PROPERTY (A-3)   _____
      OTHER (A-4)   _____

      TOTAL OTHER REAL ESTATE   _____[H]

AUTO LOANS: (B)   _____[I]
CREDIT CARDS/INSTALLMENT LOANS:(C)   _____[J]
OTHER DEBT:
      OTHER SECURED DEBT (D)   _____
      BUSINESS AND
      INVESTMENT OBLIGATIONS (E)   _____
      OTHER LIFE INSURANCE
      CASH VALUE LOANS (F)   _____
      OTHER (G)   _____

      TOTAL OTHER DEBT   _____[K]

TOTAL LIABILITIES: [G THRU K]   _____[L]

NET WORTH CALCULATION:

      TOTAL ASSETS   _____[F]

      TOTAL LIABILITIES   (-)   _____[L]

      NET WORTH [F-L]   _____[M]

MODULE #5—ASSETS REQUIRED TO MEET YOUR GOALS

This section is a critical part of almost any plan prepared, from the smallest to the largest. It tells the client and you the funds necessary to gather before the client's goal can be obtained.

Funds Required

For each goal stated by the client, you must be able to quantify as much as possible the assets that must be accumulated in order to reach the goal. For example, if a client's goal is to educate an 11-year-old daughter, then you must be able to determine the approximate amount of college costs in seven years. If the client has a good idea of where the daughter will go to school, then you can obtain the information easily. Several of the mutual fund sponsors provide specific college cost information; often the parents will know the cost or you can make a call to the university. Once you know today's cost, you can easily project the cost in seven years using an assumed inflation rate and your financial calculator. You can determine the monthly savings required the same way.

The funds required sheet is just a reminder of what you are trying to accomplish. You can use it like it is or design your own. We usually take the basic information on the form and customize it for the client presentation.

Determining Living Expense Needs

This is the same form referred to in the data gathering section supplemented with an income statement for the current year. *Again, we seldom use the income statement form,* unless we need to convince the client of living expense needs, or if retirement is imminent and income will be limited. We will include this as part of the plan only if it is critical to the client's goals.

Financial Security Planning Worksheet

I use this form in almost every financial plan that involves any type of investment toward retirement. Even if the client is not retirement minded, I believe it is prudent to point out the funds that may be required to have a secure retirement. The amounts are very surprising to most people.

This form is important enough to warrant line-by-line instructions.

1. *Current Annual Living Expense Needs.* If you completed the Determining Living Expense Needs form or the Income Statement for the year form, then fill in the amounts determined. If not, just use the tax return to estimate what the clients are spending. If you are working with long range goals, it is permissible to just use adjusted gross income from the tax return for this number.

2. *Projected Annual Living Expenses at Financial Security or Retirement.* If my clients are enjoying their current standard of living and want to maintain it into retirement, I will usually leave the number here the same as number 1. If they are young and have not reached a desired standard of living yet, then I may increase it. If they are only a few years away from retirement and expect to reduce debt, move, etc., to reduce living expenses, then I may reduce. *Do not get hung up here!* Just pick a number that you

think is appropriate for the client's education, location, etc., one that represents a good standard of living and go with it. *Another point: This figure is in today's dollars!*

3. *Number of Years to Financial Security or Retirement.* This is self-explanatory. Remember to ask the client when he wants to be financially secure. Financial security and retirement are often two separate goals.

4. *Forecasted Inflation Rate.* Do not be hung up on today's inflation rate. Inflation has been with us for over 50 years and has averaged about 4 percent. Do not be afraid to use historical averages or to adjust for location. Some will argue that they are not affected as heavily by inflation because they are not buying houses. All true, but who knows whether they may be affected more in some areas of their living expense and less in others. Do not argue about it. Just ask the client what he thinks his personal rate will be.

5. *Annual Living Expenses in Future Dollars.* Using your financial calculator (see Appendix C), convert line 2 to future dollars using the years and inflation rate.

6. *Retirement Benefits.* Remember what the end result is that we are looking for: *How much money is the client going to have to accumulate to support his desired lifestyle in retirement?* If he already has a retirement plan that you have nothing to do with, then you are dealing with a segregated portion of his other assets. If you are also assisting with the retirement plan as to how much to contribute, then you may not want to include it here but include it in the bottom number and segregate the earning assets needed *inside* retirement plans and *outside*.

   This was a major hang-up for me if neither the client nor I knew much about the client's retirement plan. How could I forecast this number? I found some rules of thumb that showed the average plan provided about 30 percent of salary at retirement, with the low being 15 percent and a high of 60 percent. If the plan is good, the employee will generally know what he can count on. If it is not, then he will not. A phone call to the company may tell you. In order to avoid being hung up on this number, I estimate at about 20 to 40 percent depending on what I know about the company. As for Social Security, I estimate the maximum benefit based on today's maximum benefit of just under $1,200 per month. If the client is under 30, I do not consider Social Security.

7. *Net Annual Income Required From Investment.* This is line 5 less line 6. This is the amount the client himself must generate for retirement from investments.

8. *Expected After-Tax Rate of Return.* Use a conservative rate based on a portfolio of diversified investments. I usually use a rate ranging from 2 to 8 points above inflation, depending on the client's risk profile. The higher the risk profile, then the higher the rate you can project.

9. *Capital Needed for Retirement.* This is line 7 divided by line 8. This will tell you the amount of money you will need to have invested in order to produce the income needed on line 7.

10. *Liquidation Proceeds of Investments Not Needed After Retirement.* List all the assets that the client plans to liquidate in order to fund his retirement. This can have a major impact on the earnings required. For example, if a client intends to sell a highly valued personal residence at retirement

and live in an apartment, then the after-tax proceeds would be available to invest in an earning asset.

11. *Net Investment (Earning Assets) Needed.* This is line 9 less line 10. This is what the client will need to accumulate. Now you have a target for which to aim. The plan should start to have meaning for you.

College Education Planning Worksheet

If your client has stated a goal of educating his children, he probably has no idea of the costs he may incur. If he has not stated it as a goal and has minor children, then you need to ask about college funding. This form allows you to highlight for the client the need to plan ahead.

1. *Current Four-Year Cost of College.* If you do not know this cost:
   (a) Ask the client if he does.
   (b) Call the college.
   (c) Call your favorite product sponsor.
   (d) Call your regional training center.
2. *Number of Years to College Enrollment.* This is self-explanatory.
3. *Forecasted Inflation Rate.* College cost inflation has been running well ahead of the national rate. You may want to use a higher percentage here.
4. *College Costs in Future Dollars.* This is the inflation rate applied in the current costs for number of years.
5. *Less Other Funds Available.* If the client has funds set aside already, they should be included here.
6. *Net Amount Required for College Funding.* You can get more exact here showing how much is required for year one, year two, three, four, etc. I think it is a waste of time unless the client requests you to do this. Remember, these are estimates anyway.
7. *Monthly Investment Required.* Use your financial calculator to calculate the monthly investment required. The rate of return will depend on the client's time horizon and risk tolerance. Most clients will usually tolerate a little bit more risk in a college education fund than in other investments.

Figure B-6

ASSETS REQUIRED

Figure B-6   (Continued)

FUNDS REQUIRED TO MEET YOUR GOALS

GOAL	DESCRIPTION	TODAY'S DOLLARS	FUTURE DOLLARS

_____   _____ $_____   _____

                    _____

                    _____

To reach your goal, you'll need to invest _____today, or _____ per _____ for_____years.

_____   _____ $_____   _____

                    _____

                    _____

To reach your goal, you'll need to invest _____today, or _____ per _____ for_____years.

_____   _____ $_____   _____

                    _____

                    _____

To reach your goal, you'll need to invest _____today, or _____ per _____ for_____years.

_____   _____ $_____   _____

                    _____

                    _____

To reach your goal, you'll need to invest _____today, or _____ per _____ for_____years.

Total investment required today $_____ or _____ per month for _____ years.

Figure B-6   (Continued)

DETERMINING LIVING EXPENSE NEEDS
(FROM THE TAX RETURN)

	TODAY'S DOLLARS	
	TODAY	**AT RETIREMENT**
RECEIPTS		
WAGES & SALARY	_____	TO BE DETERMINED
INTEREST	_____	" "
DIVIDENDS	_____	" "
TAX-FREE INCOME	_____	" "
BUSINESS INCOME	_____	" "
CASH FLOW FROM RENTALS		
PENSIONS, ETC.	_____	" "
SOCIAL SECURITY BENEFITS	_____	" "
TOTAL RECEIPTS	===============	" "
EXPENDITURES		
TAXES - FEDERAL INCOME		
FICA	_____	_____
MORTGAGE PAYMENTS	_____	_____
PROPERTY INSURANCE		
TAXES	_____	_____
OTHER LIABILITY	_____	_____
MEDICAL EXPENSE		
(INCLUDING INSURANCE)	_____	_____
CONTRIBUTIONS	_____	_____
EMPLOYEE BUSINESS EXP.	_____	_____
*CONTRIBUTIONS TO		
RETIREMENT PLANS	_____	_____
COMMUTING EXPENSE	_____	_____
JOB RELATED EXPENSE	_____	_____
TOTAL EXPENDITURES	==============	===============
BALANCE FOR SAVINGS & NORMAL		
LIVING EXP.	_____	_____
LESS SAVINGS	_____	_____
NORMAL LIVING EXPENSE	_____	_____
TOTAL FUNDS REQUIRED	==============	===============

*Do not include Tax Sheltered ORP/403(b), etc., since they have already been excluded from salary number.

Figure B-6   (Continued)

INCOME STATEMENT

For the Year Beginning January 1, _____ and ending December 31, _____.

1. Income
    Wages or salary
        Husband   _____
        Wife   _____
    Dividends and interest   _____
    Capital gains and losses (e.g., sale of stock)   _____
    Rents, annuities, pensions, and such   _____
    Other_____
    TOTAL INCOME   _____
2. Taxes
    Personal income taxes   _____
    Social Security and disability taxes   _____
    TOTAL TAXES   _____
3. Amount remaining for living expenses
    and investments (Subtract taxes from income)   _____

4. Living expenses	Fixed	Variable
Housing		
Utilities	_____	_____
Repairs	_____	_____
Insurance	_____	_____
Taxes	_____	_____
Rent or mortgage payments	_____	_____
Other_____	_____	_____
Food		
Clothing (including laundry, dry cleaning, repairs and personal effects)	_____	_____
Transportation		
Gas	_____	_____
Repairs	_____	_____
Licenses	_____	_____
Insurance	_____	_____
Auto payment or purchase	_____	_____
Recreation, entertainment and vacations		
Medical		
Doctor	_____	_____
Dentist	_____	_____
Medicines	_____	_____
Insurance	_____	_____
Personal	_____	_____
Life Insurance	_____	_____
Other expenses_____	_____	_____
Subtotal	_____	_____

    TOTAL ANNUAL LIVING EXPENSES   _____

5. Amount remaining for savings and investment   _____

6. TOTAL OF 2,4 and 5   _____

Figure B-6   (Continued)

How Much Will You Need?

FINANCIAL SECURITY PLANNING WORKSHEET

Date _____

Client _____

Prepared by _____

1. Current annual living expense needs   _____

2. Projected annual living expense at financial security or retirement   _____

3. Number of years to financial security or retirement   _____

4. Forecasted inflation rate   _____

5. Annual living expense in future dollars   _____

6. Less Retirement benefits, Social Security, Corp. retirement   _____

7. Net annual income required from investment   _____

8. Expected <u>after</u> <u>tax</u> rate of return   _____

9. Capital needed for retirement   _____

10. Less liquidation (after tax) proceeds of investments not needed after retirement

      1.   Personal real estate   _____
      2.   Business real estate   _____
      3.   Business equipment, Goodwill, etc.   _____
      4.   Other _____   _____

                    _____   _____

                    _____   _____

      Subtotal

11. Net Investment (earning assets) needed   ==============

Figure B-6   (Continued)

HOW MUCH WILL I NEED?

COLLEGE EDUCATION PLANNING WORKSHEET

CHILD'S NAME _____

DATE _____

1. Current 4 year cost of college (Room, Board, Tuition)   _____

2. Number of years to college enrollment   _____

3. Forecasted inflation rate   _____

4. College costs for 4 years in future dollars   _____

5. Less other funds available   _____

6. Net amount needed for college funding   _____

7. Monthly investment required at _____%   _____

CHILD'S NAME _____

DATE _____

1. Current 4 year cost of college (Room, Board, Tuition)   _____

2. Number of years to college enrollment   _____

3. Forecasted inflation rate   _____

4. College costs for 4 years in future dollars   _____

5. Less other funds available   _____

6. Net amount needed for college funding   _____

7. Monthly investment required at _____%   _____

TOTAL MONTHLY INVESTMENT REQUIRED AT %   ============

TOTAL MONTHLY INVESTMENT REQUIRED AT %   ============

MODULE #6—ESTATE PLANNING

Projected Estate Values and Taxes

Sounds like a lot of work, right? *Wrong*! Column one on this form is a virtual duplication of the personal financial data sheet included in module 4. It just adds life insurance that will be included in the total estate. Columns two, three, four, and five are used to calculate values for the estate at various times in the future. I seldom use these columns anymore, unless more exact numbers are needed or requested. I simply forecast a growth rate for the estate based on inflation and other factors of which I am aware. Again, *the purpose of this form is to alert the client to a problem and help him understand why it exists.* There will be plenty of time to get more exact later.

After you arrive at the total estate value, you can go to any tax guide and use the tables there to calculate the estate tax due. Also, there is a lot of software available to assist in calculating estate taxes if more detail is required.

Note that the form refers to the estate tax due at the second death. Your client may know that the marital exclusion will protect assets passed to the spouse at the first death from estate tax, but may not have considered the tax that will be due when the surviving spouse dies. Also, most of my clients had wills that kept them from using their own $600,000 exclusion because they "buried" it in the marital exclusion. More about this in the estate planning section.

Estate Liquidity Test

After the approximate estate and taxes are calculated, the next question is "How are the taxes going to be paid?" The estate liquidity form will alert both you and your client to any liquidity problems. Subtracting nonliquid assets from the total estate will arrive at net liquid assets (line 3). Because the total estate number includes insurance that is owned by the client and thus taxable to the estate, the liquid assets will include this insurance, also. Subtracting liquidity needs (line 4) from liquid assets will arrive at the net liquidity shortage or a liquidity surplus (line 5). If there is a liquidity surplus, then no further calculations are required. If a shortage, then subtract all insurance available to meet liquidity needs, but not taxable to the estate. This is insurance on the client's life but not taxable in the estate because the client has no control or ownership of the policy. The net result (line 8) should be the approximate amount of additional insurance required.

Figure B-7

ESTATE VALUES/CURRENT AND PROJECTED

	CURRENT VALUE	ADDITIONS/ WITHDRAWAL RATE	GROWTH RATE	VALUE IN 10 YEARS	VALUE IN ___ YRS (YOUR AGE ___)
PRODUCTIVE ASSETS					
LIQUID ASSETS:					
CASH					
CD'S					
STOCKS					
BONDS					
MUTUAL FUNDS					
US GOV'T SEC.					
LIFE INS. CASH					
TOTAL LIQUID ASSETS					
NON-LIQUID ASSETS					
LOANS REC					
RENTAL PROPERTY					
OTHER REAL ESTATE					
IRA'S					
OTHER RETIREMENT ACCTS					
PRACTICE/BUSINESS VALUE					
OTHER NON-LIQUID ASSETS					
TOTAL NON-LIQUID ASSETS					
PRODUCTIVE ASSETS					
TOTAL PRODUCTIVE ASSETS					

Figure B-7 (Continued)

ESTATE VALUES/CURRENT AND PROJECTED

	CURRENT VALUE	ADDITIONS/ WITHDRAWAL RATE	GROWTH RATE	VALUE IN 10 YEARS	VALUE IN ___ YRS (YOUR AGE ___)
PERSONAL ASSETS:					
HOME					
VACATION HOME					
HOME FURNISHINGS					
AUTOMOBILES					
OTHER PERSONAL ASSETS					
TOTAL PERSONAL ASSETS:					
TOTAL NON-LIQUID ASSETS					
TOTAL ASSETS					

384

Figure B-7   (Continued)

ESTATE VALUES/CURRENT AND PROJECTED

	CURRENT VALUE	ADDITIONS/ WITHDRAWAL RATE	GROWTH RATE	VALUE IN 10 YEARS	VALUE IN ___ YRS (YOUR AGE ___)
LIABILITIES					
HOME MORTGAGE					
OTHER REAL ESTATE					
VACATION HOME					
RENTAL PROPERTY					
OTHER					
TOTAL OTHER REAL ESTATE					
AUTO LOANS					
CREDIT CARDS & INSTALLMENT LOANS					
OTHER DEBT:					
OTHER SECURED DEBT					
BUSINESS & INVESTMENT OBLIGATIONS					
OTHER LIFE INSURANCE CASH VALUE LOANS					

385

Figure B-7 (Continued)

ESTATE VALUES/CURRENT AND PROJECTED

	CURRENT VALUE	ADDITIONS/ WITHDRAWAL RATE	GROWTH RATE	VALUE IN 10 YEARS	VALUE IN ____ YRS (YOUR AGE ____)
OTHER:					
TOTAL OTHER DEBT					
TOTAL LIABILITIES					
NET WORTH CALCULATION:					
TOTAL ASSETS					
TOTAL LIABILITIES					
TOTAL NET WORTH					
ADD LIFE INSURANCE/FACE VALUE OWNED BY CLIENT & INCLUDED IN TAXABLE ESTATE					
TOTAL ESTATE VALUE					
ESTIMATED ESTATE TAX 2ND DEATH					

MODULE #7—INSURANCE NEEDS

Life Insurance Needs Worksheet

This form is excellent for arriving at a desired level of insurance coverage for your client. It should be understandable to the client.

1. *Line 1—Annual Income Required to Support Family.* At this time in the financial plan, you should know what your client's annual living expense needs are. When one spouse dies, that living expense need may increase or decrease. For example, if a wife who is a homemaker dies, the additional costs for sitters for the children may more than offset her normal expenses for clothing, food, etc. As a rule of thumb, I use a 15 percent reduction in living expenses when one spouse dies which may be adjusted for various circumstances.

2. *Line 2—Income Available.* This is a total of other income sources available when one spouse dies. Social Security benefits may be available for minor children, the surviving spouse may be able to continue to work or go back to work, and there may be income from other investments. However, do not include income from investments set aside for college or retirement.

3. *Line 4—Capital Base Required to Produce Additional Income.* This is line 3 divided by a reasonable rate of expected return. This rate should be conservative.

4. *Line 5—Lump Sum Requirements.* These are the payments that may be required at death. Judgment and client consultation is required here, but you can make some reasonable predictions as to which debts would need to be paid because of the loss of one spouse's income. Funeral and settlement costs vary from state to state, but I use a rate of 8 percent of the estate for probate costs, administrative costs, funerals, etc.

5. *Line 6—Total Capital Required.* This is a total of lump sum requirements (bills that must be paid within one year of death) and income requirements.

6. *Line 8—Sale of Other Assets and Assets Available to Meet Liquidity Needs.* The client may have assets that will not be retained if one spouse dies. The proceeds from their sale can be used to reduce insurance requirements. Similarly, the client may have assets that can be used to meet lump-sum requirements. For example, education funds can reduce the lump-sum requirements.

Disability or Income Continuation

The disability worksheet is purposefully kept simple and should be self-explanatory.

1. *Line 1—Total Income Needs.* Monthly living expenses should be available from other sections of the plan. Business overhead expenses are applicable if the client has a business that would need to be continued in the event of his short- or long-term disability.

2. *Line 2—Income Available if Disabled.* Be sure to determine if the current coverage is long term or short term. Most corporate benefits policies are short term. Social Security usually has a long-term waiting period in order to qualify and usually requires total and permanent disability. Be sure that investment income does not include funds set aside for retirement or other specific purposes such as education funds.

Figure B-8

LIFE INSURANCE NEEDS WORKSHEET

NAME_____

DATE_____

HUSBAND_____ WIFE_____

ANNUAL INCOME REQUIRED TO SUPPORT FAMILY   _____
(1)

INCOME AVAILABLE
    SOCIAL SECURITY   _____
    SPOUSE'S INCOME   _____
    INCOME FROM OTHER INV.   _____

                    _____

    TOTAL INCOME AVAILABLE   _____
(2)

ADDITIONAL INCOME REQUIRED (LINE 1 MINUS LINE 2)   _____
(3)

CAPITAL BASE REQUIRED TO PRODUCE ADDITIONAL
INCOME @ ____% (LINE 3___%)   _____
(4)

LUMP SUM REQUIREMENTS:
    DEBT PAYMENTS   _____
    FUNERAL & ESTATE COSTS   _____
    ESTATE TAXES   _____
    EDUCATION COSTS   _____
    OTHER   _____

    TOTAL LUMP-SUM REQUIREMENTS   _____
(5)

TOTAL CAPITAL REQUIRED   _____
(6)

TOTAL LIFE INSURANCE IN FORCE   _____
(7)

LESS: SALE OF NON EARNING ASSETS   _____
      ASSETS AVAILABLE TO MEET
        LIQUIDITY NEEDS   _____   _____
(8)

TOTAL ADDITIONAL INSURANCE NEEDED   _____
(9)

Figure B-8   (Continued)

DISABILITY NEEDS WORKSHEET

YOU

TOTAL MONTHLY LIVING EXPENSES   _____

BUSINESS OVERHEAD NEEDS (IF APPLICABLE)   _____

TOTAL INCOME NEEDS   _____ $ (1)

INCOME AVAILABLE (IF DISABLED)

      Current disability Coverage   _____ $
      Social Security (If permanently &
         totally disabled)   _____ $
      Spouse's Income   _____ $
      Investment Income   _____ $
      _____   _____ $
      _____   _____ $

      TOTAL INCOME AVAILABLE   _____ $ (2)

ADDITIONAL DISABILITY INSURANCE NEEDED   _____ $ (3)
    (Line 1 minus line 2)

===

YOUR SPOUSE

TOTAL MONTHLY LIVING EXPENSES   _____

BUSINESS OVERHEAD NEEDS (IF APPLICABLE)   _____

TOTAL INCOME NEEDS   _____ $ (1)

INCOME AVAILABLE (IF DISABLED)

      Current disability Coverage   _____ $
      Social Security (If permanently &
         totally disabled)   _____ $
      Spouse's Income   _____ $
      Investment Income   _____ $
      _____   _____ $
      _____   _____ $

      TOTAL INCOME AVAILABLE   _____ $ (2)

ADDITIONAL DISABILITY INSURANCE NEEDED   _____ $ (3)
    (Line 1 minus line)

MODULE #8—OUR RECOMMENDATIONS

How We Recommend You Reach Your Goals

This is the "tell them what you told them" part of the plan. I usually try to cover each goal again with specific recommendations to reach each of them. Emphasize advantages of taking the recommended steps. This is the solution part of the sale when you are presenting the plan. I also often repeat the funds required for each goal to remind the client where he is trying to go.

Other Recommendations

This is my reminder sheet to see if I have covered everything that might apply to this client. If I find something on this list that properly belongs in another part of the plan, I go back and add it in the appropriate place.

Figure B-9

HOW WE RECOMMEND YOU REACH YOUR GOALS

GOAL	DESCRIPTION	FUNDS REQUIRED

<u>GOAL</u>   <u>DESCRIPTION</u>   FUNDS
                                                         <u>REQUIRED</u>

____   _____ $_____

          _____

          Steps to Reach:
             (1)_____

             (2)_____

          Advantages:_____

                     _____

____   _____ $_____

          _____

          Steps to Reach:
             (1)_____

             (2)_____

          Advantages:_____

                     _____

____   _____ $_____

          _____

          Steps to Reach:
             (1)_____

             (2)_____

          Advantages:_____

                     _____

Figure B-9   (Continued)

HOW WE RECOMMEND YOU REACH YOUR GOALS
(Cont'd)

GOAL	DESCRIPTION	FUNDS REQUIRED

GOAL   DESCRIPTION

FUNDS
REQUIRED

_____   _____ $_____

_____

Steps to Reach:
    (1)_____

    (2)_____

Advantages:_____

_____

_____   _____ $_____

_____

Steps to Reach:
    (1)_____

    (2)_____

Advantages:_____

_____

_____   _____ $_____

_____

Steps to Reach:
    (1)_____

    (2)_____

Advantages:_____

_____

Figure B-9   (Continued)

OTHER RECOMMENDATIONS

___LIVING TRUST

___LIVING WILLS

___POWERS OF ATTORNEY

___INSURANCE - LIFE

___INSURANCE DISABILITY

___BUY-SELL AGREEMENTS

___ESTATE TAX REDUCTIONS

    ___GIFTS

    ___CHARITABLE BEQUESTS

    ___CHARITABLE TRUSTS

___RETIREMENT PLANS

___OTHER _____

              _____

              _____

MODULE #9—ASSET ALLOCATION

This section of the plan is optional depending on the client's goals. If you are recommending a reallocation of the client's assets to achieve higher income, better diversification, or just to reach a goal faster, I believe it is important to illustrate visually what you are trying to achieve.

Asset Allocation/Income Analysis

When one of the client's primary goals is to increase income, I often use this form to illustrate how reallocation can increase income. It also serves the dual purpose of showing what percentage of the client's assets are invested in the various categories. It also shows percentages of liquidity or nonliquidity. I do not recommend including the form itself in the plan, but use it as the base for preparing *pie charts* showing how the client's assets are currently distributed versus how they would be distributed under your plan. You can also show total income under current allocation and income expected under your recommendations. If you do include the chart as part of the plan, I recommend subtotals and summarization as much as possible.

Diversification Plan/Investment Pyramid

I use these forms to show clients where their investments will be positioned on the investment pyramid and how liquid or marketable they are. This form is usually used for my own purposes only in preparing to meet client objections and for the highly analytical client. I usually supplement this with comparative pie charts which are prepared using Harvard Graphics.

Historic Performance and Hypothetical Illustrations

For the product-oriented client, I may include a hypothetical illustration for the products I am recommending as part of the plan. These hypotheticals will show historic performance if investments had been made in the past similar to the investments I am recommending today. The software for such illustrations is available from CDA, Morningstar, and most investment companies. If you mention product, enclose prospectuses.

Figure B-10

_____

_____
_____
_____

During the last _____ years, an investment in _____ produced an annual rate of return of _____%. Based on these prior results, your investment of _____% could grow to $_____ in _____ years.

Using a more conservative projected return of _____, your investment plan could grow to $_____ in _____ years.

These projections are for illustration purposes only and do not guarantee future results. There is risk associated with this investment. If you do not fully understand that risk after reviewing this plan, please ask us for details.

_____

Registered Representative

ASSET ALLOCATION INCOME ANALYSIS

NAME:

DATE:

	CURRENT			OUR PLAN		
PRODUCTIVE ASSETS	AMOUNT	% OF TOTAL	INCOME	AMOUNT	%OF TOTAL	INCOME
LIQUID ASSETS:						
CASH						
CERTIFICATES OF DEPOSIT						
TOTAL CASH	$	$	$	$	$	$
STOCKS -						
INDIVIDUAL						
MUTUAL FUNDS						
TAX FREES -						
INDIVIDUAL						
UIT'S						
MUTUAL FUND						
BONDS -						
INDIVIDUAL						
MUTUAL FUNDS						
OTHER MUTUAL FUNDS:						
INTERNATIONAL						
PRECIOUS METALS						

Figure B-10 (Continued)

ASSET ALLOCATION INCOME ANALYSIS CONTINUED

PRODUCTIVE ASSETS	CURRENT				OUR PLAN		
	AMOUNT	% OF TOTAL	INCOME		AMOUNT	% OF TOTAL	INCOME
U.S. GOV'T SEC.							
LIFE INS. CASH VALUE							
CD/ANNUITY. TAX DEF.							
OTHER LIQUID ASSETS:							
CROPS (IN STORAGE)							
CATTLE							
OTHER							
TOTAL LIQUID ASSETS	$	$	$		$	$	$
NON-LIQUID ASSETS:							
LOANS & NOTES							
REAL ESTATE							
IRA'S							
OTHER RET. ACCTS.							
BUSINESS VALUES							
TAX DEF. ANNUITIES							
OTHER							
TOTAL NON-LIQUID	$	$	$		$	$	$
TOTAL PRODUCTIVE ASSETS	$	$	$		$	$	$

DIVERSIFICATION PLAN

NAME _____

DATE _____

INVESTMENT DESCRIPTION	RISK SPREAD				LIQUIDITY/MARKETABILITY		
	RISK LEVEL	AMOUNT	%		LIQUIDITY/ MARKETABILITY	AMOUNT	%
HIGHEST LEVEL RISK							
LOWEST LEVEL LIQUIDITY/ MARKETABILITY							
SUBTOTAL							
SIXTH LEVEL:							
SUBTOTAL							
FIFTH LEVEL:							
SUBTOTAL							
FOURTH LEVEL:							
SUBTOTAL							
THIRD LEVEL							
SUBTOTAL							
SECOND LEVEL							

Figure B-10 (Continued)

DIVERSIFICATION PLAN CONTINUED

INVESTMENT DESCRIPTION	RISK SPREAD			LIQUIDITY/MARKETABILITY		
	RISK LEVEL	AMOUNT	%	LIQUIDITY/ MARKETABILITY	AMOUNT	%
SUBTOTAL						
FIRST LEVEL:						
SUBTOTAL						
LOWER LEVEL:						
SUBTOTAL						
TOTAL						

NOTE: Risk levels may not match liquidity levels; therefore, some investments may be listed twice in description column but only once for risk and liquidity/marketability.

Figure B-10   (Continued)

Diversification Plan
Explanation of Categories
for Risk and Marketability/Liquidity

Highest Risk
Lowest Liquidity/
Lowest Marketability

1. Real Estate Investment Properties
2. Collectibles

Level Six
Low Marketability
Low Liquidity

1. Precious Metals in Bulk
2. Limited Partnerships
3. Closely Held Stock

Level Five
Medium Marketability
Some Liquidity

1. Speculative Individual Stocks & Bonds
2. Puts & Calls
3. Futures Contracts

Level Four
High Marketability
Some Liquidity

1. Aggressive Growth Mutual Funds
2. International Mutual Funds
3. Sector Mutual Funds
4. Option Trading Mutual Funds
5. Precious Metals & Mining Mutual Funds
6. Savings Bonds
7. Long-Term CD's

Level Three
High Marketability
Medium Liquidity

1. Balanced Growth & Income Funds
2 High Grade Convertible Securities
3. High Grade Preferred Stock
4. High Yield Corporate Bonds
5. High Yield Tax-Exempts

Level Two
High Marketability
Medium to High Liquidity

1. High Grade Tax Exempts-Long Term
2. High Grade Corporate Bonds-Long Term
3. Government Securities-Long Term

Level One
High Marketability
Medium to High Liquidity

1. High Grade Tax Exempts-Short Term
2. High Grade Corporate Bonds
3. Life Insurance Cash Values

Lower Risk
Highest Liquidity
Highest Marketability

1. Money Market Accounts
2. Checking and Savings

High Liquidity   Can sell the investment with minimal or no risk of loss at any time
    after purchase.
High Marketability   Can sell the investment at anytime buy may have some risk of
    loss.

Figure B-10   (Continued)

THE INVESTMENT PYRAMID

		AMOUNT OF INVESTMENT	%

		AMOUNT OF INVESTMENT	%
Highest Risk	Futures Contracts	_____	_____
Sixth Level	1. Speculative Individual Common stocks & bonds	_____	_____
	2. Collectibles	_____	_____
	3. Precious Metals (In Bulk)	_____	_____
Fifth Level	1. Limited Partnerships	_____	_____
	2. Real Estate Investment Properties	_____	_____
	3. Puts & Calls	_____	_____
Fourth Level	1. Aggressive growth Mutual Funds	_____	_____
	2. International Mutual Funds	_____	_____
	3. Sector Mutual Funds	_____	_____
	4. Option Trading Mutual Funds	_____	_____
	5. Precious Metals & Mining Mutual Funds	_____	_____
Third Level	1. Balanced Growth & Income Funds	_____	_____
	2. High Grade Convertible Securities	_____	_____
	3. High Grade Preferred Stock	_____	_____
	4. High Yield Corporate Bonds	_____	_____
	5. High Yield Tax Exempts	_____	_____
Second Level	1. High Grade Tax Exempts-Long Term	_____	_____
	2. High Grade Corporate Bonds Long-Term	_____	_____
	3. Government Securities-Long-Term	_____	_____
First Level	1. High Grade Tax Exempt-Short-Term	_____	_____
	2. High Grade Corporate Bond-Short-Term	_____	_____
	3. Life Insurance Cash Values	_____	_____
Lowest Risk	1. Money Market Accounts	_____	_____
	2. Government Securities-Short-Term	_____	_____
	3. Insured Checking & CD's	_____	_____
	4. Savings Bonds	_____	_____

Figure B-10   (Continued)

THE INVESTMENT PYRAMID

NAME _____

DATE _____

YOUR
INVESTMENT
<u>AMOUNT</u>

HIGHEST RISK	$	HIGHEST $_____
	$$	
SIXTH LEVEL	$$$	SIXTH $_____
	$$$$	
FIFTH LEVEL	$$$$$	FIFTH $_____
	$$$$$$	
FOURTH LEVEL	$$$$$$$	FOURTH $_____
	$$$$$$$$	
THIRD LEVEL	$$$$$$$$$	THIRD $_____
	$$$$$$$$$$	
SECOND LEVEL	$$$$$$$$$$$	SECOND $_____
	$$$$$$$$$$$$	
FIRST LEVEL	$$$$$$$$$$$$$	FIRST $_____
	$$$$$$$$$$$$$$	
LOWEST RISK	$$$$$$$$$$$$$$$$$	LOWEST $_____

$ Increasing risk of loss of principal (toward top of pyramid)
   Increasing potential for capital appreciation (toward top of pyramid)

$$$$$$$$$ Increasing risk of purchasing power (toward bottom of pyramid)
   Increasing safety of principal (toward bottom of pyramid)

MODULE #10—PROSPECTUSES, APPLICATIONS, AND BROCHURES

In my early planning days, I loaded my plans up with as much information as possible. Prospectuses were required because I mentioned product in my early plans. This caused the plans to be bulky and intimidating to my clients, myself, and staff.

This module is not given to the client now. Products are almost never mentioned in the plans and applications are prepared but held at our office until the client meeting.

MODULE #11—IMPLEMENTATION INSTRUCTIONS

It is embarrassing when your client gives you instructions to go ahead with the plan and you have to fumble with what to do next or cannot give your assistant instructions. It is extremely important that all paperwork be completed while the client is ready to act. It is unprofessional to have to ask the client to come back for additional paperwork.

To avoid this embarrassment, write detailed instructions on an implementation instruction sheet that is not forwarded to the client. This sheet provides information as to all investments to be made including the products to be used and from where the funds are coming. This sheet is extremely useful for yourself and your staff. A lot of plans create complicated trails of funds that need to be documented properly.

This form is provided to your assistant when the plan is completed so that ample time will be available to complete applications before the client arrives. When the client is ready to make a decision to act, the paperwork should be ready.

The implementation sheet may also include some actions that must be delayed until some time in the future. This may involve insurance policies that should be issued after underwriting is complete, CDs that have not matured yet, etc. When this is the case, be sure that tasks are assigned in your time management system so that follow up is made.

Figure B-11

PERSONAL INVESTMENT PLAN

CLIENT _____
DATE_____

PLAN IMPLEMENTATION STEPS
(Internal Use Only)

Client authorization Date _____

	Due Date	Comp. (X)
Project		
_____	____	____
_____	____	____
_____	____	____
_____	____	____
_____	____	____
_____	____	____
_____	____	____
_____	____	____
_____	____	____
_____	____	____
_____	____	____
_____	____	____
_____	____	____
_____	____	____
_____	____	____
_____	____	____
_____	____	____
_____	____	____
_____	____	____
_____	____	____
_____	____	____
_____	____	____
_____	____	____
_____	____	____
_____	____	____
_____	____	____
_____	____	____

Figure B-12

REGISTERED REPRESENTATIVES
INVESTMENT TRACKER

DATE: _____
CLIENT: _____
ADDRESS: _____
PHONE _____

Current Investments

NAME	TYPE	AMOUNT	% OF TOTAL	YIELD/ RETURN

Planned Investments

NAME	TYPE	AMOUNT	% OF TOTAL	YIELD/ RETURN

Appendix C

Using the Financial Calculator to Solve Financial Planning Problems

There are basically two financial calculators on the market that meet the needs of financial planners. The Texas Instruments BA55 (TI) and the Hewlett Packard 12c (HP). The information that follows is designed to help financial planners take advantage of these calculators when dealing with the most common financial planning applications.

I had an FC (financial calculator) for over ten years before I ever learned how to properly use it. I just assumed it was going to take a lot more time to learn than it actually did. I still do not know how to use all of the functions, but I know the basics and I know how to look up the others. I was forced to learn how to use it when studying for CFP exams. You can learn the basics by just following the formulas on the following pages. The most common formulas are in the front.

Why learn how to use a ''calculator'' when computers are getting smaller and smaller? I get lots of smirks when I mention how valuable my HPc is to my sales production. ''Sophisticated planners use portable computers. I carry my notebook everywhere,'' I am consistently told. However, I have never been beaten in a challenge for speed of a financial calculator with a notebook. By the time my computer friend has unfolded his notebook, turned it on, and booted up the software, I have the answer flashing on the HP. That is because of the necessity to boot the software and because computers are meant to do lots more than just financial calculations. Financial calculations are all that financial calculators do. I think we should call them financial computers.

Why is an FC so important?

- It answers great sales questions that you should be asking your clients.
- It helps you hit your clients' hot buttons with actual projected numbers.
- It rescues you instantly when your client starts playing ''what if'' games with your carefully prepared plan. Sure, a computer will do the same thing if you have it handy. However, if you use your FC to run different answers for your client, you can leave your computer with the original proposal. Changing a computer plan several times can distract you from making the sale.
- It is more believable than you. Flashing that tiny screen in front of the client is very powerful.
- It makes you able to sell with believable projections no matter where you are. You literally can carry your FC everywhere.
- It settles arguments and shuts up nay-sayers.

This chapter will discuss how to make the most common calculations in financial planning. Let us start with some easy ones.

FINDING THE FUTURE VALUE OF A SINGLE SUM

The future value of a single sum is usually the easiest time value concept to understand and compute. The term "single sum" refers to a lump-sum payment or receipt at one point in time. The future value of a single sum is the future amount of an initial deposit when it is compounded for a given number of periods and at a given interest rate. When a deposit is made, interest is earned on the deposit in the first period. In subsequent periods, interest is earned not only on the original deposit, but also on the interest earned in each of the previous compounding periods. Thus, interest is earned on increasing amounts over time.

Formula—Future Value of a Single Sum

	Texas Instruments	Hewlett Packard
1. Enter present value	Amount PV	CHS Amount PV
2. Enter interest rate for the compounding period (monthly, quarterly, annually)	%i	%i
3. Enter number of compounding periods	#n	#n
4. Calculate future value	2nd FV	FV

On a bank draft plan, to arrive at the future value of periodic investments, calculate the initial deposit plus regular monthly payments at the beginning of each month.

On the Hewlett Packard 12c financial calculator, you would:

1. Enter payment—(chs pmt)
2. Enter initial deposit—(chs pv)
3. Enter interest rate (for monthly compounding divide by 12)—i
4. Enter number of compounding periods—N
5. Find FV

FINDING THE PRESENT VALUE OF A SINGLE SUM

The present value of a single sum is the present worth of a sum to be received in the future when discounted for a given number of periods and at a given interest rate. Present value is determined by reversing the compounding process, a process known as discounting. The three known variables used to compute a present value of a single sum are the future value, the discount rate, and the number of discounting periods. Present value concepts are important in comparing the value of a dollar to be received at different points in time. Rather than measuring the sum of a present amount at some future date, present value is concerned with determining the current value of a future sum. The interest rate used when determining present value is commonly called the opportunity cost. It represents the annual rate of return that could be earned currently on an investment. For example, if an investor can earn 8 percent compounded annually on an investment vehicle, the investor's opportunity cost of not receiving (investing) dollars today is 8 percent.

Formula—Present Value of a Single Sum

	Texas Instruments	Hewlett Packard
1. Enter future value	Amount FV	Amount FV
2. Enter interest rate for the compounding period (monthly, quarterly, annually)	%i	%i
3. Enter number of compounding periods	#n	#n
4. Calculate present value	2nd PV	PV

Formula—Number of Compounding Periods
(How Long to Accumulate a Future Value)

Knowns: Present value
Future value
Interest rate

	Texas Instruments	Hewlett Packard
1. Enter present value	Amount PV	Amount PV
2. Enter future value	Amount FV	Amount FV
3. Enter interest rate (per compound period)	%i	%i
4. Solve for # of periods	2nd n	n

Formula—Solve for Interest Rate

What interest rate will you have to earn in order to reach known future dollars when you start with known present dollars and known periods of time?

Knowns: Present value
Future value
Time period

	Texas Instruments	Hewlett Packard
		CHS
1. Enter present value	Amount PV	Amount PV
2. Enter future value	Amount FV	Amount FV
3. Enter number of periods	#n	#n
4. Solve for interest	Due i	i

Formula—To Clear Calculator, Set Decimal and Function

	Texas Instruments	Hewlett Packard
1. On/c 2nd	CMR mode	Clear
2 = 2 Decimal places	or	1. On f Fin.
	Due fix	Clear
		F Reg. F
2. 2nd mode untic "fin" shows		2 = 2 Decimal places

Formula—Rule of 72

How long to double you money

Knowns: PV (made up)
FV (twice the present value)
Interest rate

	Texas Instruments	*Hewlett Packard*
1. Enter present value	Amount PV	Amount CHS PV
2. Enter future value	Amount FV	Amount FV
3. Enter interest rate	%i	%i
4. Solve for time	Due n	n

OR

Divide interest rate into 72

PRESENT VALUE OF AN ANNUITY (PVOA)

In the preceding sections, the techniques for determining present value and future value of a single sum were presented. However, many financial planning applications involve payments or receipts at periodic intervals instead of a lump-sum payment or receipt. An annuity is a stream of equal periodic payments or receipts occurring at uniform intervals.

Annuities can be classified by the timing of the payments or receipts. There are two different types of annuities: an ordinary annuity and an annuity due. For an ordinary annuity, the payments or receipts are made at the end of the period. Mortgage note payments, auto note payments, quarterly dividends, and semiannual interest payments are examples of an ordinary annuity. Insurance policy premiums and lease payments are examples of an annuity due where the payments or receipts are made in advance or at the beginning of the period.

Formula—Present Value of an Ordinary Annuity

What is today's value of a stream of future receipts or payments received or invested at the end of each period. Examples of ordinary annuities are mortgage or auto note payments, quarterly dividends, semiannual interest payments.

Knowns: Payment
Interest rate
Number of payments

	Texas Instruments	*Hewlett Packard*
1. Enter payment	Amount PMT	Amount CHS PMT
2. Enter interest rate	%i	%i
3. Enter number of payments	#n	#n
4. Solve for PVOA	2nd PV	PV

Formula—Present Value of an Annuity Due (PVAD)

What is today's value of a stream of future receipts or payments received or invested at the beginning of each period? Examples of annuities due are insurance policy premiums and lease payments.

Knowns: Payment
Interest rate
Number of payments

	Texas Instruments	*Hewlett Packard*
1. Enter payment	Amount PMT	Amount CHS PMT
2. Enter interest rate	%i	%i
3. Enter number of payments	#n	#n
4. Solve for PVAD	DUE PV	G Beg. PV

Formula—Future Value of an Ordinary Annuity (FVOA)

To what does a series of equal payments at the end of each period accumulate?

Knowns: Payments
Interest rate
Number of payments

	Texas Instruments	*Hewlett Packard*
1. Enter payments	Amount PMT	Amount CHS PMT
2. Enter interest rate	%i	%i
3. Enter number of periods	#n	#n
4. Solve for FVOA	2nd FV	G End FV

Note: For more frequent payments than annual, divide interest rate by 4 if quarterly, 12 if monthly, etc., and increase # of periods accordingly.

Formula—Future Value of an Annuity Due

To what does a series of equal payments at the beginning of each period accumulate?

Knowns: Payments
Interest rate
Number of payments

	Texas Instruments	*Hewlett Packard*
1. Enter payments	Amount PMT	Amount CHS PMT
2. Enter interest rate	%i	%i
3. Enter number of periods	#n	#n
4. Solve for FVOA	Due FV	g Beg. FV

Note: For more frequent payments than annual, divide interest rate by 4 if quarterly, 12 if monthly, etc., and increase # of periods accordingly.

Formula—Payment on Future Value of Ordinary Annuity (FVOA) or Annuity Due (FVAD)

How much does client have to invest during each period to attain a specific goal (amount)?

Knowns: Future value or goal
Interest rate
Time number of periods

	Texas Instruments	Hewlett Packard
1. Enter FV	Amount FV	Amount FV
2. Enter interest rate	%i	%i
3. Enter number of periods	#n	#n
4. Solve for payment FVOA/FVAD	2nd PMT	G End PMT
	Due PMT	G Beg. PMT

Formula—Present Value of a Serial Payment (Payment Adjusted for Inflation)

How much does a client have to invest today to receive a certain periodic income expressed in today's dollars adjusted for inflation in future years?

Knowns: Assumed rate of inflation
Assumed rate of interest
Payment (income) desired in today's dollars
Number of years income is to be received

	Texas Instruments	Hewlett Packard
1. Calculate interest factor (discounted for inflation)	(1 + interest rate ÷ 1 + inflation rate) (−1) × 100 e.g., 1.08 ÷ 1.05 = 1.02857 − 1 × 100 = 2.85714	Same
2. Enter discounted interest rate (adjusted for inflation)	Amount i	Amount i
3. Enter payments in today's dollars	AMT PMT	AMT PMT
4. Enter number of payments	#n	#n
5. Solve for PVAD (beginning of period)	Due PV	G Beg. PV
PVOA (end of period)	2nd PV	G End PV

Formula—Serial Payment for a Future Sum

What must a client save for each period in order to attain a financial goal adjusted for inflation?

Knowns: Assumed rate of inflation
Assumed rate of interest
Number of periods to reach goal
Goal in today's dollars

	Texas Instruments	Hewlett Packard
1. Calculate interest factor (discounted for inflation)	(1 + interest rate ÷ 1 + inflation rate) (−1) × 100 e.g., 1.08 ÷ 1.05 = 1.02857 − 1 × 100 = 2.85714	Same
2. Enter future value (goal in today's dollars)	Amount FV	Amount FV
3. Enter interest factor (Step 1)	Amount i	Amount i
4. Solve for payments OA (end)	2nd PMT	G End PMT
AD (beginning)	Due PMT	G Beg. PMT

Formula—Policy Cost per $1,000

$$\frac{(\text{Annual Premium} + \text{CSV End of Prior Year}) \times (1 + \text{Rate of Interest}) - (\text{CSV End of Current Year} + \text{Dividend})}{(\text{Face Value} - \text{CSV}) \times (.001)}$$

Formula—Yield to Maturity or Annual Internal Rate of Return on a Bond (Equal Periodic Cash Flow)

Knowns: Purchase price
Coupon rate and payment
Maturity date
Maturity value

Hewlett Packard

1. Enter cost — Amount CHS G PV
2. Enter periodic payment — Amount G PMT
3. Enter number of payments remaining — # G FV (exclude last pmt.)
4. Enter maturity value — Face value + last interest payment
   G PMT f IRR # of payments per year, X

OR — OR

1. Enter cost as percent of par — Amount PV
2. Enter interest rate as payment — % PMT
3. Enter date of purchase — e.g., 1-19-80 = 1.011980 ENTER
4. Enter date of maturity — e.g., 1-19-84 = 1.011984 f YTM

Formula—Yield to Call or Internal Rate of Return

Hewlett Packard

1. Enter purchase price — AMT CHS PV
2. Enter callable price — AMT FV
3. Enter coupon amount — AMT PMT (periodic payment amt.)
4. Enter # of payments to call — #n
5. Solve for yield — i

Formula—Current Yield

Bonds:

Current Interest Payment ÷ Price of Bond

Mutual Funds:

Current Interest Payment ÷ Offering Price

ANNUAL RATE OF RETURN FOR INVESTMENT VEHICLES WITH NO PERIODIC CASH FLOWS

Types of investment vehicles include zero coupon bonds, collectibles, precious metals, Treasury bills, options, futures contracts, raw land, warrants, and mutual funds.[1] *Note:* The following steps are to be used before each calculation or results will be inaccurate.

Texas Instruments		*Hewlett Packard*	
On/c, 2nd, CL mode, 2nd, CL mem		On, f, clear REG, f, clear FIN	
TI BA55 (FIN mode)		*HP 12C*	
$800 = PV	800 = CHS, g, CFo	800 = CHS, g,	800 = CHS, PV
4 = n	0 = g, CFj	CFo	4 = n
$1000 = FV	0 = g, CFj *or*	0 = g, CFj, *or*	1000 = FV, i
CPT, %i	0 = g, CFj	3, g, Nj	
	1000 = g, CFj	1000 = g, CFj	5.74% = i
5.74% = i	f, IRR	f, IRR	
	i = 5.74%		

i = annual rate of return (IRR) earned on the investment

[1] Mutual funds (when all dividends and capital gains are reinvested) are treated like an investment vehicle with no periodic cash flow because the periodic dividends as well as their compounding is already reflected in the total value of the fund. The problem is to determine what the total value of the fund today represents as a rate of return on the initial investment. If the periodic dividend payments are included in the calculation, they would be counted when received and in the total value of the fund today.

Formula—Yield to Maturity Zero Coupon Bond (No Periodic Cash Flows) A-4 (Clear F Reg F Fin)

	Hewlett Packard	*Texas Instruments*
1. Enter cost	Cost CHS PV	PV
2. Number of years to maturity	#n	#n
3. Maturity value	Amount FV	FV
4. Solve for interest	i	2nd %i

CURRENT PRICE OF A BOND

The current price of a bond is determined by computing the present value of the bond's interest income stream plus the present value of the bond's value at maturity. The bond's coupon rate will determine the dollar amount of interest income per year. The yield to maturity on bonds of comparable quality and maturity is used as the discount rate in the calculations. Since most bonds pay interest semiannually, the number of compounding periods (n) is doubled, the discount rate (i) is divided by two, and the interest payment (pmt) is the total annual interest income divided by two.

For example, assume AAA-rated bond with a face value of $1,000 and a coupon rate of 9 percent, payable semiannually. The bond matures in 15 years. Comparable bonds with the same maturity are yielding 10 percent. Based on the preceding information, what is the current price of the bond? Solving for present value:

Texas Instruments	Hewlett Packard
FV = 1000	10 = i
Pmt = 90 ÷ 2 = 45	9 = Pmt
i = 10% ÷ 2 = 5	1.011980 = Enter
n = 15 × 2 = 30	1.011995 = f, Price
PV = $923.14	Data entered, and answers are in percent of par value for HP. See back of calculator.

Formula—Current Price or Value of a Bond

What's a bond worth in current market?

1. Enter yields of comparable bonds being issued today	%i
2. Enter coupon rate of this bond	% PMT
3. Enter date of purchase (i.e., Jan. 19, 1986 = 1.011986)	Date ENTER
4. Enter date of maturity	Date f
5. Solve for price	*Price

*Note price will be stated as % of par. Move decimal 1 place to right.

Formula for Zero Coupon Bond

1. Enter maturity value	AMT FV
2. Enter interest rate on comparable bonds as P	%i
3. Enter years to maturity	#n
4. Solve for current value	PV

ANNUAL RATE OF RETURN FOR INVESTMENT VEHICLES WITH UNEQUAL PERIODIC CASH FLOWS

Types of investment vehicles include common stock, GNMAs, limited partnerships, REITs, income-producing property.

The objective of this problem is to solve for the interest rate (IRR) which will equate the future values (annual income and capital appreciation) to the present value (initial investment) of the stock. The known factors are: $4,000 initial investment, $7,000 appreciated value of stock, $200 dividend year 1, $250 dividend year 2, and $300 dividend year 3.

Texas Instruments	Hewlett Packard
$4,000 = ±, PV	4,000 = CHS, g CFo
$200 = Sto 1	,200 = g, CFj
$250 = Sto 2	,250 = g, CFj
$7,300 = Sto 3	7,300 = g, CFj
= CPT, 2nd, IRR	f, IRR
i = 25.62%	i = 25.62%

i = annual rate of return (IRR) earned on the investment

Formula—Rate of Return on Stock, Mutual Funds, GNMAs, Limited Partnerships, REITs, Income-Producing Property (Unequal Periodic Cash Flows)

Single Investment	*Hewlett Packard*
1. Enter cost of security	AMT CHS G PV
2. Enter 1st year's dividends and capital gains***	AMT G PMT
Enter 2nd year's dividends and capital gains	AMT G PMT
Enter 3rd year's dividends and capital gains	AMT G PMT
3. Enter sale price or market value including last dividend and capital gain amount	G PMT*
4. Solve for IRR	f IRR**

*This example assumes stock held for four years. Step #3 counts as another year. Always include last dividend in sale price.

**IRR will be slightly understated if dividends are paid quarterly or monthly.

***If calculating for periods of less than one year, annualize dividends (i.e., if one month's dividends paid—multiply by 12 and add to current market value).

Formula—Rate of Return on Stock, Mutual Funds, GNMAs, Limited Partnerships, REITs, Income-Producing Property (Periodic Investments).

Periodic Investments

If periodic investments are made, calculating IRR with financial calculator will be inefficient. Each investment return would have to be annualized. If over one year, go to MF-Hypo (CDA) option for systematic constant dollar investments or systematic increasing dollar investments.

1. Enter original investment	AMT CHS G PV
2. Enter 1st year's subtractions, investments	AMT CHS G PMT
2a. Enter 1st year's dividends and capital gains	AMT G PMT
3. Enter 2nd year's subtractions, investments	AMT CHS G PMT
3a. Enter 2nd year's dividends and capital gains	AMT G PMT
4. Enter sales price or market value including last dividend and capital gain amount	AMT G PMT
5. Solve for IRR	f IRR

Formula—Intrinsic Value of Stock (Value Based on Dividends or Rate of Return Desired by Client)

1. Dividend × expected growth rate (i.e., 4% + 1 = 1.04) 1.04 × dividend
2. Subtract × expected growth rate from required rate of client
3. Divide #2 into #1

Example: Annual dividend 2.45 × 1.04% = 2.548
         12% client expected rate −4% = 8%
         2.548 ÷ 8% = 31.85 value

Formula—Expected Rate of Return on Stock

1. Dividend × expected growth rate (e.g., 4% + 1 = 1.04) 1.04 × dividend
2. Dividend #1 by market price
3. Add #2 to dividend expected growth rate

Formula—Internal Rate of Return on Options

1. Enter purchase price of option	CHS G PV
2. Enter sales price of option	G PMT
3. F, IRR*	

*If held for six months, multiply by 2.

Formula—Intrinsic Value of a Convertible Bond

In Terms of Its Stock

1. Divide conversion value of stock into $1,000 to get number of shares
2. Multiply # of shares by current market price

In Terms of Its Debt

1. Enter yields of comparable bonds being issued today	%i
2. Enter coupon rate of this bond	% PMT
3. Enter date of purchase (i.e., Jan. 19, 1986 = 1.011986)	Date ENTER
4. Enter date of maturity	Date f
5. Solve for price	Price*

*Price will be stated as % of par. Move decimal 1 place to right.

Formula—Weighted Average Expected Return for a Portfolio

1. Determine % of portfolio for each investment type
2. Multiply #1 percentage by expected return for that investment
3. Add results of #2 together for all investments in portfolio

PORTFOLIO BETA COEFFICIENT

The beta coefficient for a portfolio is the summation of the betas for the individual securities weighted by the proportion of each security to the overall portfolio.

For example:

	Amount Invested	Weight in Portfolio*	Beta	Weighted Beta Coefficient**
Stock A	$5,000	.25	1.2	.3
Stock B	15,000	.75	.8	.6
	$20,000			.9

*5,000/20,000 = .25, 15,000/20,000 = .75.
**.25 × 1.2 = .3, .75 × .8 = .6.

The weighted beta coefficient for the portfolio is .9, which indicates that the riskiness of the portfolio is slightly less than the overall market, which has a beta of 1. Weighting a portfolio allows investors to choose risky investments (high betas) to get a high return yet have a low overall level of risk by combining the risky investments with investments that have a low level of risk (low betas). Calculating the weighted beta enables investors to identify the effect of risk on a portfolio when evaluating investment vehicles.

Formula—Beta Coefficient

---

1. Determine % of portfolio for each stock
2. Multiply beta of stock × #1 to get weighted beta coefficient
3. Add results in #2 for each stock together to determine for total portfolios
   1.0 = overall market

THE P/E RATIO

One term often used by investors is the P/E ratio, which is the ratio of a *stock's price to the firm's per share earnings*. By expressing each firm's stock price relative to its earnings, this ratio facilitates the comparison of firms. The P/E ratio indicates the amount that the market is willing to pay for each dollar of earnings. A P/E of 12 means that the stock is selling for 12 times the firm's earnings and that the market believes that $1 of earnings is currently worth $12. There is also the implication that if earnings increase by $1, the price of the stock will rise by $12.

Firms in the same industry tend to have similar P/E ratios. The average P/E ratio for the industry may be indicative of the appropriate P/E ratio for an individual firm's stock. If the company's ratio is higher than the industry's average, it may indicate that the stock is overvalued.

Unfortunately, security analysis and selection are not that simple. If a firm has an excellent record of earnings growth and the security market anticipates that this growth will continue, the P/E ratio tends to be higher than the industries average. This higher growth has value. These earnings may achieve a higher price, in which case the stock sells for a higher P/E ratio. If a firm is considered to be riskier than is typical of firms in its industry, the P/E ratio tends to be lower. The earnings of a firm involving greater risk are worth less. Thus, the stock's price and the P/E ratio are lower than industry's average.

While the P/E ratio is frequently used, it does not tell the investor much about the firm. Of course, it does permit easy comparison of firms but it considers only the earnings and the price of the stock. It tells nothing of how the earnings were achieved or why the market may view one firm's earnings as inferior or superior to the earnings of another firm.

Formula—Yield Over Period of Time for Income-Type Investments

Use Regular Calculator	Investments	New Balance	# of Days
1. Enter original investment × days held	1,000	1,000	36 = 36,000
2. Enter subsequent investments × days held	100	1100	25 = 27,500
Enter subsequent investments × days held	200	1300 ×	90 = 117,500
3. Total	N/A	N/A 151	18,000
4. Determine average daily investment	181,000 ÷ 151 = $1,199		
5. Add total dividends and capital gain distribution (income)			$100
6. Determine average daily earnings	100 ÷ 151 days = $.66225		
7. Annualize earnings	.66225 = $242		
8. Divide by average daily balance	242 ÷ 1,199 = 20.18%		

Formula—Total Return for Mutual Funds

Per Share

$$\frac{(\text{Ending NAV}-\text{Beginning NAV}) + (\text{Dividends and Capital Gains}) \text{ for Period for Each Share}}{\text{Original NAV}}$$

Total Investment

$$\frac{(\text{Ending NAV} \times \text{\# of Shares Originally Purchased Less Beginning NAV} \times \text{\# of Shares Originally Purchased}) \text{ Plus Dividends and Capital Gains}}{\text{Original NAV} \times \text{\# of Shares Originally Purchased}}$$

*Result must be annualized (i.e., divide by # of days then multiply by 365, or other method based on period used).

**Use public offering price if you want the negative effect of commissions on return. Use net asset value if you want to measure management performance only.

***POP—Public Offering Price includes commissions.

NAV—Net Asset Value.

Index